Presidential Campaigns and American Self Images

Presidential Campaigns and American Self Images

EDITED BY
Arthur H. Miller
and
Bruce E. Gronbeck

Westview Press
BOULDER • SAN FRANCISCO • OXFORD

Copyright © 1994 by Westview Press, Inc.

Published in 1994 in the United States of America by Westview Press, Inc., 5500 Central Avenue, Boulder, Colorado 80301-2877, and in the United Kingdom by Westview Press, 36 Lonsdale Road, Summertown, Oxford OX2 7EW

Library of Congress Cataloging-in-Publication Data
Presidential campaigns and American self images / edited by Arthur H.
    Miller and Bruce E. Gronbeck.
        p.   cm.
    Includes bibliographical references and index.
    ISBN 0-8133-1885-8. — 0-8133-8899-6 (PB)
    1. Presidents—United States—Election.   2. Political culture—
United States.   3. Electioneering—United States.   4. Communication
in politics—United States.   I. Miller, Arthur H., 1942–   .
II. Gronbeck, Bruce E.
JK528.P74   1994
324.63'0973—dc20   94-27733
                                                                                             CIP

Printed and bound in the United States of America

The paper used in this publication meets the requirements
of the American National Standard for Permanence of Paper
for Printed Library Materials Z39.48-1984.

10   9   8   7   6   5   4   3   2   1

Contents

Preface

University House at the University of Iowa's Oakdale Research Campus was founded in 1977 by then-President Willard R. Boyd and Vice President for Educational Development and Research D. C. Spriestersbach. Situated in Oakdale Hall, originally the state's primary tuberculosis sanitarium, University House was thought of as a retreat for University faculty, a place where they could get away from their daily chores while on leave. With no office phones, a library service, and other academic support, University House was a site for interesting, cross-disciplinary conversation, coffee, contemplation, and personal reinvigoration.

External funding by The Andrew Mellon Foundation and the Exxon Foundation brought in faculty from regional liberal arts colleges, often teaming with University of Iowa faculty on projects expected to have both instructional and scholarly payoffs. Nearby Kirkwood Community College used it as a site for faculty development and seminars, often directed by University of Iowa scholars. A major grant from National Endowment for the Humanities in 1984 made University House the home of The Renaissance Connection Consortium, which presented nine regional conferences and ten books and art exhibits in cities and towns across the state of Iowa. And, too, more and more faculty took advantage of Director Jay Semel's experience in obtaining federal and foundation grants and in administration, and so used University House as the location for executing the projects thus funded.

Next, University House began running its own internally funded program—a summer competitive, collaborative research grant program to bring University faculty out on cross-disciplinary research projects. The program was of special interest to an Iowa alumnus and loyal supporter of both sporting and academic activities, Dr. C. Esco Obermann, who was a member of University House's Advisory Committee. He argued that such research should be a central mission for University House, bringing together a full range of teacher-scholars from varied backgrounds and institutions, engaging in free-flowing dialogue on matters of theoretical and practical importance, and then circulating the results of deliberations widely. He saw its purpose as:

to: (1) facilitate the quality of research at the University of Iowa by
giving support and expression to the reality that knowledge and its
applications are basically multidisciplinary; (2) encourage the discov-
ery of new knowledge through research performed within the context
of that axiom; (3) attract to the University of Iowa scholars who have
the capabilities necessary to conduct that type of research; (4) encourage contribution of funds to University House, matching and supple-
menting funds in support of scholars receiving Obermann Fellow-
ships; (5) enhance the status and reputation of the University of Iowa
as a leader in multidisciplinary research and publication (Obermann
1990).

Dr. Obermann not only advocated such an expansion of University
House programming, but also backed up his advice with funds for an
annual summer seminar for scholars from inside and outside the University of Iowa.

In the summer of 1991, President Hunter Rawlings III along with
Vice Presidents Peter Nathan and James Morrison obtained approval
from the Board of Regents to name University House the University of
Iowa Center for Advanced Studies. The Center was inaugurated with its
first summer seminar, "Presidential Campaigning and American Self
Images," codirected by a political scientist, Professor Arthur H. Miller,
and a rhetorical critic, Professor Bruce E. Gronbeck. Thanks to Dr. and
Mrs. Obermann's grant and the University's matching monies, eleven
scholars gathered at the Center for four weeks of writing, presentation,
critique, and revision.

Selected competitively from off-campus were Obermann Fellows
Monica Bauer, Western New England College; Ronald Lee, Indiana
University; Milton Lodge, SUNY at Stony Brook; Joanne Morreale,
Northeastern University; David Woodard, Clemson University; and
Harold Zullow, Rutgers University. In addition to Professors Miller and
Gronbeck, Iowa-based Obermann Fellows included G. R. Boynton, Cary
Covington, and Dianne Rucinski. Fellows were elected for their schol-
arly strengths and range of specialties. The codirectors wanted as many
topics covered as possible, both to open up the full range of questions
inhering in the topic and to provide essays for this volume.

The strengths and range of the Fellows are illustrated in the following essays. Still, some important topics were not especially well represented in the seminar. So, two additional papers were recruited to
broaden this volume: Daniel Merkle and Peter Miller were asked to
write about the role of public opinion polls in presidential elections, and
David Birdsell was asked to extend some of the thinking found in his
book on presidential debates in a new essay.

The Obermann Summer Seminars continue annually at Iowa's Center for Advanced Studies, thanks to the generosity and vision of C. Esco Obermann, support from Vice President for Research David Skorton, the developmental talents of Center Director Jay Semel, the efficiency of the Center's staff, Lorna Olson and Lynette Wright, the work of the directors, and the willingness of solid scholars to put themselves in a no-holds-barred, month-long critique and revision session. This and future volumes will be testaments to the creative force and rigor of the seminars.

As we send this volume to press, therefore, we wish to thank C. Esco and Avalon L. Obermann for their generosity; the University support provided by President Rawlings, Vice President Skorton, and University of Iowa Foundation Director Darrell Wyrick and his staff; Peggy Dozark, Glenn Richardson, Kent Kroeger, and Warren Sandmann, who served as research assistants for the Fellows while at the Center; advertising support given by various professional organizations; Jennifer Knerr of the Acquisitions department of Westview Press as well as numerous others in production who helped the codirectors put out their first camera-ready typescript for publication; University of Iowa students Andrew Peebler, Sarah DeBower, and Monda Maines, who devoted countless hours to preparing the camera-ready copy; Vanessa Shelton of the University's Office for Public Information, who secured us multiple radio interviews and newspaper stories; and to the Ely, Iowa, Fire Department, whose Fourth of July breakfast showed the visiting Fellows a marvelous set of American self images.

We hope the book raises some new questions about some old topics and forwards the great dialogue over how this country should conduct its presidential electoral processes.

Arthur H. Miller
Bruce E. Gronbeck

Reference

Obermann, C.E. (1990). Memorandum 11 May 1990. Iowa Center for Advanced Studies Archives, Iowa City, IA.

PART ONE

Presidential Campaigning
in America

The Study of Presidential Campaigning: Yesterday's Campaigns and Today's Issues

Bruce E. Gronbeck and Arthur H. Miller

[W]e have entered a political era in which electoral choices are of little consequence because an electoral system in disarray can generate neither the party unity nor the levels of public agreement necessary to forge a winning and effective political coalition. The underlying explanation is that the political and economic forces driving our national politics have created a system in which the worst tendencies of the political culture—the hype, hoopla, and negativity—have been elevated to the norm in elections, gaining a systematic dominance in campaign content as never before (p. 14).

With these words political scientist Lance Bennett launched a book *The Governing Crisis: Media, Money, and Marketing in American Elections* (1992) that captured much of the disgust and frustration that affected even scholars of political campaigning during the early 1990s. Not only did 19 percent of the American voters in 1992 cast their ballots for the independent candidate H. Ross Perot, but we suspect an even larger percentage of the academy's professional election junkies talked of presidential campaigning in harsh, even condemnatory terms.

Consider the scene as Campaign '92 was opening:

- America witnessed a steady decline in voter turnout over the previous thirty years, coming dangerously close to a minority election in 1988, when only 50.1 percent of the eligible voters cast ballots.

- Incumbents were being returned to the U.S. House of Representatives at a 98 percent clip.

- The 1988 elections, from local to presidential contests, cost the country $2,727,500,000—an amount more than double what had been spent in 1980 (Alexander & Bauer 1991).

- One presidential candidate was facing possible federal charges for Iran-Gate, another was having his marital problems spread across even respectable newspapers, senators were facing questions of undue influence in the wake of the Keating Five's humiliation, and an alarmingly high percentage of House members were found to have bounced checks on Capitol Hill.

- During the fall of 1991 a Supreme Court nominee was despoiled by charges of sexual harassment and obscene conversation.

- By 1990, 77 percent of those polled thought the U.S. government was run for the benefit of a few big interests—triple the percentage who expressed that belief in 1960 (Miller & Borrelli 1991; Bennett 1992).

There is little wonder that Wilson Carey McWilliams ended an electoral post mortem with these sentiments: "For both Republicans and Democrats, the election of 1988 indicates the need for a new civility, and for the kinds of word and deed necessary to affirm, for the coming century, the dignity of self-government" (Pomper et al. 1989, p. 200).

To help us understand how America's vision of its own political system can be so stained, what elements of that system seem responsible for our current self image, and yet why most voters think an election will bring a better tomorrow, this introduction will touch on the history of American presidential campaigning, offer what we think is a constructive understanding of the idea of "political image," and then preview the themes of the rest of the book.

Electoral Booming with "The Voice of Grog"

In 1888 the Scottish scholar James Bryce observed that "an American election is held to be, truly or falsely, largely a matter of booming" (quoted in Jamieson 1984, p. 3). He was impressed with the steady stream of "booms"—processions, bands, flags, badges, and enthusiastic spectators—that marked the three-month contest. Tocqueville was equally impressed with American campaigning:

The political activity that pervades the United States must be seen in order to be understood. No sooner do you set foot upon American ground than you are stunned by a kind of tumult ... To take in hand the regulation of society, and to discuss it, is his biggest concern, and so to speak, the only pleasure an American knows (quoted in Bennett 1992, p. 69).

The free-wheeling, display-oriented political campaign has always been a part of the American experience. Our practices of "electing time" (Black 1973) are not a product of the electronic age. A visit to the Smithsonian Institution's Division of Political History and its presidential campaign collection will demonstrate that "politics had been a spectator sport before television" (Melder 1992, p. vii). Madison may have decried the "spiritual liquor and other treats" that appeared during electing time (quoted in Bennett 1992, p. 67), but he could not stem the flow.

American politics has always turned on more than the great issues of controlling resources. Even during the first complete election year, 1792, a newspaper editor opined *"That the Voice of the People, was the Voice of Grog"*— a reference to the "Treats" Madison abhorred (quoted in Boller 1985, p. 6). Political labels bloomed that year as well, with vice-presidential candidate John Adams called "His Rotundity" and "His Superfluous Excellency"; the Republican paper, the *Massachusetts Centinel*, was bothered by his "lawless lust of POW'R in embryo," describing him as "the first spawn of hell" (Shields-West 1992, pp. 5-6).

Public display, various methods for securing voter allegiances, and scurrilous campaigning are deeply embedded characteristics of American electoral culture. The Adams-Jefferson election of 1796 was a free-for-all, as hired horsemen carried *ad hominem* attacks on handbills around New England. By 1828, the electors favoring Andrew Jackson or John Quincy Adams were tallied in newspapers, and the electorate tripled that year, excited by the legend of "Old Hickory"; Jackson enthusiasts marched through town squares carrying tall hickory poles, wearing hats adorned with twigs from that tree. In 1852, Gen. Winfield Scott, Whig opponent of Franklin Pierce, was the "Hero of Vera Cruz" or "Old Fuss and Feathers" to his supporters, but a "military chieftain" who believed only in "Gunpowder Glory" to the Democrats.

Lincoln's second campaign was racially coded, as the Democrats wanted "The Constitution as It Is, The Union as It Was, and the Negroes Where They Are"; Lincoln was taunted with the song "Fight for the Nigger," even as his supporters sang "Battle Hymn of the Republic," "We Are Coming Father Abraham, 600,000 More," and "Rally Round the Cause, Boys." In 1872, after Horace Greeley lost the early (September) elections, he took the unprecedented step of campaigning on his own behalf, giving more than 200 speeches about Grant's scandals and the bloody Civil War. *The New York Sun* said the race was "a shower of mud."

McKinley's front porch campaign of 1896 featured altered ambulations. As he sat on his front porch, delegations would parade by him; by election day some 750,000 people representing thirty states had passed by. His only real problem was souvenir hunters, who all but destroyed his grass, frontyard fence, and famous porch. In 1900, Theodore Roosevelt, a more animated campaigner, joined his ticket, putting on 21,000 miles at a speed that led Mr. Dooley to comment, "'Tis Tiddy alone that's runnin', an' he ain't a-runnin', he gallopin'." John Hay said Roosevelt was "more fun than a goat." In his turn in 1912, Woodrow Wilson was an even more aggressive campaigner, establishing once and for all the party representative's right and even obligation to move among the people with pomp and promises.

But it was 1924 that brought probably the biggest change to American presidential campaigning. That year saw the entry of both the campaign film, a biographical construction of Calvin Coolidge's life, and radio into elections. Coolidge's silent film was exhibited across the country in movie houses (Morreale, Chapter 2). Radio was important for the presentation of the political conventions, especially the seventeen-day, politically charged marathon the Democrats mounted (Becker & Lower 1962).

The step to televisual politics in the 1950s was shorter than many assume: it united the immediacy and livingroom penetration of radio with the visuality (at least once the technology improved in the 1960s) of film, offering the complete multi- and mass-mediated discourse that characterizes electoral politics today. Visual ads came in earnest in 1952, as did televised convention coverage; computerization was approached seriously by the Kennedy's in the 1960s, and Boorstin's pseudo-events (1961) became the stock in trade of electioneering aimed at getting candidates on the evening news (see Jamieson 1984; Boller 1985; Melder 1992; Shields-West 1992).

A complete history of presidential campaigning would present endless parades, songfests, sloganeering, salooning, sun-drenched and torch light rallies, promises and preachments, big lies and little truths, and enough words to disturb even the Valley of Tranquillity. The campaign practices of particular years are symptoms of the American political culture—signs of what we value, what we seek to reform, who we are, what we fear in the world around us, and whom candidates hope we become. For all of the "treats" Madison snorted about, for all the silliness many associate with cheesehead hats from Wisconsin and with the Republicans' vaunted balloon drops during conventions, and for all of the cynicism that creeps into news stories and op-ed commentaries on the quadrennial rite, we can learn much about the American political culture by studying its campaign practices carefully.

The Centrality and Complexity of "Political Image"

Presidential campaigns have been subjected to multiple and divergent modes of study and commentary. Campaign managers and media consultants have been writing books about the making, packaging, and selling of presidential candidates at least since Joe McGinnis (1969) demonstrated that there is a sizable audience for such work. Political scientists in recent years have focused on the mechanisms of campaign operations (e.g., Orren & Polsby 1987), predictions of voter behavior (e.g., Patterson 1980), and the effects of campaigning on electoral outcomes (Bennett 1992). Since Theodore White's successful *The Making of the President* series (1961, 1965, 1969, 1973), some journalists and many professors of journalism have stepped back from mere reporting to write about campaign processes, particularly the role of media and reportage in shaping and framing the stories featured in various campaigns, as well as the roles of debates, endorsements, ads, and news content on elections (e.g., Davis 1992). Students of history have generally featured particular candidates (e.g., McGinnis 1969) or aspects of campaigns (e.g., Duncan, 1991). Communication specialists have studied audience responses to various sorts of campaign messages (e.g., Nimmo & Combs 1990) and rhetorical critics, especially, recently have examined the sociodrama acted every four years (e.g., Trent & Friedenberg 1991).

While each of these approaches has taught us much about presidential campaigning, most disciplinary vantages have failed to integrate the pieces into an overarching conception of campaigns or to sketch the big picture: a broad, cross-disciplinary, theoretically rich understanding of presidential campaigning as an important arena within which American culture is constructed, as well as something relevant to the operations and general well being of American society. That is the burden of this book.

The key to comprehending relationships between campaign activities and both American culture and American political practices, we believe, is to make sense of and take seriously the idea of the "political image." We must grasp the processes of what Parenti calls "inventing reality" (1986/1993) as they occur through campaign activities. And, we must understand that invented political realities are precisely that—realities. What is real in political society is that which is paid attention to, defined, valued, disputed, and ultimately seized powerfully by some segment or another of political society. Furthermore, by noting what is talked about as important or significant in any given election, we can index the state of the political culture—of what we call American self images—at the time.

The word "image" is a rich one, not only in English but also well back into its Latin roots. *Imago* was a dense term, having associated with it not only the notion of likeness or imitation, but also phantom or fantasy in one direction and idea or conception in the other (*OED*). Central to this range of uses for the word is the vantage of the human spectator, the act of looking, the data of vision. A political image at bottom is that which is seen in political contexts and what is made of that which is seen. It is no accident that Murray Edelman introduced his groundbreaking *The Symbolic Uses of Politics* (1964) with the argument that

> For most men most of the time politics is a series of pictures in the mind, placed there by television news, newspapers, magazines, and discussions. The pictures creates a moving panorama taking place in a world the mass public never quite touches, yet one its members come to fear or cheer, often with passion and sometimes with action ... Politics is for most of us a passing parade of abstract symbols, yet a parade which our experience teaches us to be a benevolent or malevolent force that can be close to omnipotent (p. 5).

What must be made absolutely clear in all this is that politics is not somehow *unreal* or *false* because it is freighted with symbols and visualized in images. We cannot somehow dismiss showmanship, political ritual, speeches, and televised debates as "mere politics." Politics, after all, is a human or social activity. A coal field is but compressed and solidified petroleum until political-nationalist values are attached to it in a dispute between France and Germany and it has no political significance until people contend for its energy-producing capabilities. A coal field is but a natural phenomenon until converted symbolically into a political value, i.e., until it is assigned human significance and made an object of collective worth. The political is symbolic to its core.

The consequences of politics, of course, are very, very real. The whimsy possible in poetry, wherein symbols can be wholly liberated from the *dasein*, the out-there, usually is not present in political discourse, for, as Kertzer (1988, p. 4) notes, "There is a continuous interaction [in politics] between the ways people have of dealing with the physical and social universe and the actual contours of that universe." Kertzer takes "interaction" as his key metaphor. We can go further than that in suggesting that, in politics, the symbolic and the real are *amalgamated*. Politics amalgamates symbolic meaning—of signification, of attitudes, of values—with the structures and resources of the social and physical worlds. Political images are the lenses with which we look at those amalgamations.

Presidential Campaigning and American Self Images

What is different about this book, then, is that we treat the political campaign and election as an enlarged process of social construction. Through the various chapters, we elaborate on three centers of activity by which Americans construct political images and discursive rationales for the way we go about campaigning and for what the outcomes of campaigns "ought" to be. (1) One important center for symbolic activity is the *candidates, their organized staffs*, and *agents*. On the bases of previous experience, polling information, the behest of organized interest groups, and the advice of various consultants, candidates construct campaign events and messages that sculpt images of themselves and their opponents, the citizenry and its role in a free society, and American society itself. (2) The *mass media* take up aspects of these messages as well as others they themselves build. Some parts of candidates' messages are transmitted passively, as though the media were mere conduits; more frequently, the media are actively framing messages in unexpected ways, as they select what to cover, interject conflict and drama through juxtapositions and narration, and tell us what to expect as they interpret and evaluate what we have seen. The print and electronic media thus are both reconstructing candidates' messages and constructing a set of their own. (3) The *public*, in turn, ignores, adjusts, responds to, and evaluates all of these messages.

This sorting is not a passive act. The voter-citizen is an active participant in the process of social construction. Considerable writing on voter behavior (e.g., Campbell et al. 1960; Abramson et al. 1990) treats election outcomes as the sum of individual-level reactions to the candidates, issues, and parties encountered in the campaign. Our approach is different in that we treat the citizen-voter as actively engaged in constructing political meanings and reality out of the myriad messages and symbols that they encounter in a campaign. This includes not only images of the various candidates—the tax and spend liberal image of Dukakis in 1988, the caring, young populist version of Clinton in 1992—but also constructed self-perceptions of the voters themselves and a collective public itself (see Merkle & Miller, Chapter 9).

The public's responses generally are drawn between positive and negative poles: at times, they react with hope to portrayals of a new world, and at other times, with fear and pessimism to negative portrayals of opponents and the state of the Republic at large. Individuals do all this privately in small gatherings and—more intriguingly today—publicly in the form of opinion polls.

Across the now-almost two years that comprise an American presidential campaign—from the preannouncement visits to Iowa to the mythic celebrations at conventions and on to the election eve visits in candidates' livingrooms—the candidates, the press, and the public construct verbal-visual images of each other. Somehow, amidst all of the thousands upon thousands of messages that come at us via print, radio, television, bumper stickers, cartop signs, billboards, buttons, ribbons, and airplane trailers over the football stadiums of autumn, we hold an election. We do more than merely elect someone president. We create and experience self images of those candidates, the press's place in society, and ourselves as citizens. Those self images are affirmed in the process of campaigning, and finally reaffirmed by the people of this country when they enter a local public hall to cast their votes.

The totality of these constructed images conveys a portrait of American political culture. The portrait is as real, and yet as abstracted, as Monet's beloved lilypond paintings. Moreover, just as the movement of the sun across the skies, a change in the season, or a shift in Monet's mood produced a different reflection on the lilypond surface, so also do the unique circumstances of each campaign produce variation in the portrait of American self images. Each successive portrait reflects the constructed reality of the time, while a comparison across portraits provides clues to the process of interaction between the enduring and ephemeral elements in the environment that combine to produce each amalgamation—a completed portrait.

Parts II, III, and IV of the book deal respectively with the three centers of symbolic activity—candidate-generated images, mass-mediated images, and images of the voter-citizen. In reality, of course, the world of politics is not separated into compartments, but evolves via the dynamic interactions among these centers of social construction. Nevertheless, examining each center individually allows us to look at peculiar features of political symbols or images: for example, the special and evolving roles of campaign films during this century, candidates' tools for attempting to control press coverage, and ways Americans have thought about the relationship between money and politics. The use of a tripartite structure for the heart of this book permits concrete analysis. At the end, however, in Part V we will assemble the parts in an enlarged statement about relationships between presidential campaigning and American self images. Only then will we be able to explain why this society is willing to invest two years and nearly three billion dollars (an amount that rises with each passing election) to elect its public officials. We also will conclude with a methodological meditation and critical thought in forging research strategies when approaching a project as gargantuan as understanding a presidential election.

This book went to press shortly after the 1992 campaign, after a campaign won by a man who said repeatedly "I still believe in a place called Hope." As Harold Zullow (Chapter 12) demonstrates later in this book, Americans seemingly always believe in a place called Hope during election time. Even when we are wracked with discord, driven to distraction by our economic plight, or frozen in a potentially mortal conflict as in the Cold War of the 1950s, America finds grounds for hope and optimism. Even when our self images are at their darkest, we find glints that shine through that darkness—lights bright enough to guide the country through the night.

It is difficult to say why there is always a light in the darkness that America so often experiences. For all of its cumbersomeness and expense, we believe, the processes by which America selects its leaders are some of the sources of that light. We grumble about unkept promises, yet we listen to them. We are aghast at the expense, yet we bear it. We berate our politicians as a class, yet return our local representatives to office almost all of the time. Such paradoxes will be addressed in *Presidential Campaigning and American Self Images.*

PART TWO

Candidate-Generated Images in Presidential Campaigns

Introduction

Candidate-Generated Images in Presidential Campaigns

Bruce E. Gronbeck

Certainly the most visible and even ordinary activities that comprise a presidential campaign are those generated by candidates and their staffs. As we noted in Part I, this was not always so. For most of America's history, campaigning was a party activity. The cultural assumption was that groups of like-minded *citizens* should articulate sets of ideas and policies (platforms) and then ferret out *representatives* who would further those ideas and seek to enact those policies when victorious at the polls. Such campaigns were viewed as "the largest folk festival in the world" by the nineteenth century (Melder 1992, p. 8)— testament to the centrality of the citizen role in electoral politics.

But, as we noted in Part I, by the early twentieth century we acknowledged that the center of the process had moved; platforms were built as much for particular candidates as for the parties, and soon candidates took responsibilities for constructing many of the major planks in those ideological structures. Franklin Roosevelt, in particular, took over party and campaign structures for his party in 1936 and perhaps was determinatively responsible for the emergence of candidate-centered campaigns. And with the growth of the so-called imperial presidency in the electronic age, the *president* clearly controls the presidency and runs campaigns in most ways independent of party (Bennett 1992, esp. Morreale Chapter 2).

Today, most candidate-generated images form the featured messages of a presidential campaign. Given the influx of big money and armies of communication consultants into presidential election campaign organizations, it is clear that candidate-generated messages contain more political information than other-generated (e.g., news) messages (Kern 1989). That is a profoundly important fact as we contemplate the present electoral system in the United States; its implications are enormous.

Consider: the good-government view of leadership and elections in a western democracy suggests that independent voters, with the help of the watchdog Fourth Estate, the press, survey the sociopolitical scene, identify problems, evaluate solutions proposed to those problems by would-be leaders, and then cast their votes for the candidates most representative of their views. In contrast to that good-government vision are the pictures of American politics that emerged through a series of regional focus groups run by The Harwood Group for the Kettering Foundation and reported in the pamphlet, *Citizens and Politics: A View from Main Street America* (1991). A fundamental conclusion reached in that study was:

> Those citizens interviewed for this study now believe that individual Americans simply do not count in politics—they can no longer play a meaningful role. As previous chapters have illustrated, citizens say they are denied access to the political debate of policy issues. Their ability to affect politics is overshadowed—rather, overwhelmed—by a larger force they call the 'political system,' a leviathan made up of media that seem to promote controversy over substance, expensive and negative campaigns, all-too-powerful special interests, and influence-peddling lobbyists. Even public officials, they argue, all too often disregard the interests of citizens. The combination of these factors ... has rendered individual citizens unnecessary in politics (p. 34).

The clash of the good-government and corrupt-system views of presidential campaigning features, primarily, the communication activities of candidates and their staffs: do candidates mean what they say or say what they are told to? Is what you see really what you get? How are you to understand issues: are the central issues candidate's motivations and acts or, rather, the status of various aspects of American society and economy?

What Americans see as they watch their candidates do battle for high office is a raging battle between the "oughts" of good government, oughts they have been taught since grade school days, and the "is's" of electric rhetoric—the high-profile, high-priced, shiny-picture messages of a campaigning system designed for a quarter-billion people, ninety-nine percent of whom own and regularly watch television. In the fight between ideals and reality, voters often feel hurt and discouraged, many convinced that campaigns toy underhandedly with voters' emotions, filling the air with smoke and mirrors capable of showing nothing of political importance to the citizenry.

Certainly, the most discussed sources of candidate-generated images have come from political advertisements. Between the Bush and Dukakis campaigns in 1988, $55 million was devoted to buying media time, with $34 million of that spent on the short spot—the ten-, twenty-, thirty-, and sixty-second ad (Alexander & Bauer 1991). Those ads have come to dominate the processes of campaign message-making and have great power in creating and evoking images of America: the appeal to collective fear in Reagan's "bear in the woods" ads of 1984; the racially coded ads about criminals (Willie Horton, the "revolving doors" in prisons) launched by Bush in 1988; the appeal to patriotism and pride in Americanism found in Perot's "purple heart" ad of 1992. Such ads drive between our favorite sitcoms, hammering over and over on voters with inescapable force.

Let it not be forgotten, however, that candidates spend their millions on other sorts of messages as well. They flit from state to state, and then county to county, making five, six, or ten speeches a day in hopes of convincing far-flung voters that they love and need them. They purchase buttons, billboards, and all of the other mini-media they can assemble to distribute precinct by precinct. They even engage in particular behaviors that they hope will be interpreted in symbolically positive ways. So, 1992 Democratic contender Tom Harken periodically spent days doing manual labor—working on a construction site, a mine, an assembly line—so as to demonstrate his connectedness with ordinary folk. Bill Clinton started his post-convention campaigning with a bus tour to symbolize his closeness to the middle-class in contrast to Bush, whom he portrayed as distant and aloof. As well, both Clinton and H. Ross Perot performed in electronic "town halls," not so much to be in touch with mere citizens as to make material their commitments to grass-roots influence upon political outcomes (Nimmo 1992).

In Part II, we investigate three sources of candidate-generated images. Joanne Morreale examines the longest-lived visual medium, the campaign film depicting candidates' biographies or political résumés, especially over the last quarter century, when it was incorporated into party conventions as well as exhibited independently. She demonstrates film's power to articulate particular kinds of candidate- and party-centered images that capture party ideology and that thematically ground candidates. The expanse of a candidate's film is useful as backgrounding device. Ronald Lee examines political speeches for their verbal images: as vehicles for the construction of thoughts and visions of civic virtue, again over the last quarter century. Through the analysis of speeches, he reveals candidate-generated political images at their most uplifting, as a force in civic education and responsibility.

Previous research has suggested that campaign ads, as we have said, are important sources of electoral information. Since the 1972 election it has been clear that voters acquire more political information from candidates' commercials than from television news reports of campaigns (Patterson & McClure 1976; Kern 1989). Bruce Gronbeck looks at the underbelly of candidate-controlled ads, the attack ads so prevalent at the end of this century. He argues that candidates' ads can be forces for positive political judgment when done well, but that they degenerated into narrational weapons capable of injuring the social order especially in the 1988 campaign; character assassination in turn can damage the political system itself if we do not demand its control.

Other candidate-generated messages, certainly, should be studied: news conferences, candidates' nights, talk show appearances, billboards and bumper stickers, computerized letters, fund-raising appeals, radio and television specials, dirty tricks, announcements, concessions, and everything in-between. We offer these three studies as but samples of themes we believe must be explored in today's political environment by today's scholars if we are to understand and evaluate the relationships between candidate's discourses and American self images.

2

American Self Images and the Presidential Campaign Film, 1964-1992

Joanne Morreale

Since presidents were first elected by popular vote in 1824, campaigns have deliberately crafted the candidates' images. At a time when tradition discouraged presidential aspirants from openly seeking office, personal characteristics were the most efficacious means to promote a candidacy. By the 1830s, published accounts of candidates' lives and careers were essential campaign tools, and they have remained important during their transformation from print to film to televisual forms.

The age of television personalized presidential politics (Merelman 1976). As traditional party identifications have declined and television's popularity has risen, campaigns spend millions of dollars inventing images that will appeal to otherwise uncommitted voters. Although presidential scholars often overlook campaign films, they provide a comprehensive structured storehouse of political images. The films comprise a rhetorical genre that is both a set of rules for discursive production and particular instantiations of those rules (Mattelart 1990, p. 142). As formulaic presentations, the films have their roots in the print biographies of presidential candidates. Jackson supporter John Henry Eaton penned one of the first biographies for Andrew Jackson, and it documented the personal history and professional accomplishments of the man who would be president. To some extent, Jackson's image as the "Cinncinnatus of the West," also applicable to George Washington (Brown 1960, p. 87), remains the model for later books, newsreel-type films, and current televised political programs.

Like the print biographies, the presidential campaign films establish a candidate's character by relating how his background, personal life, and early career have equipped him for the presidency. Personal biographies, most often used for relatively unknown challengers, primarily identify the candidates and the people whom they represent. Resumé films, more often the tools of incumbents, remind viewers of candidates' accomplishments in public life. Both sub-genres articulate the candidates and their vision of the country by portraying familiar characters and stock dramas from the corpus of American mythology.

Presidential campaign films also encapsulate campaign themes and issues, and they provide a shorthand account of the historical context in which a campaign is conducted. In recent years, they have become representative anecdotes of campaigns. The Reagan (1984), Bush (1988), and Dukakis (1988) campaigns showed their films as a prelude to the candidate's nomination acceptance address, a defining moment for candidates and their vision. Beginning with McGovern (1972) and Nixon (1972), filmmakers commonly recut the primary or convention films, added convention and other campaign highlights, and then rebroadcast the entirety as a paid political program. The Reagan (1984) campaign expanded their 19-minute convention film by adding clips from the candidate's acceptance speech and the convention, intercut with symbolic images of America and Americans. This film initiated his 1984 general election campaign, airing simultaneously during prime-time on all three major networks. The Bush (1988) filmmakers structured their expanded version of the convention film as a campaign chronology, providing a final election-eve punctuation mark. Further, candidates often use pieces of their films as spot advertisements. The Nixon (1972) campaign initiated general election advertising with a five-minute spot cut from the convention film; the Bush (1988) campaign strategists designed the convention film so that the last sixty seconds comprised an intact commercial that they used to kick off his general election campaign (Rossen, Interview).

Although it is beyond the scope of this chapter to determine the criteria for "successful" films or to determine such films' effects on voters' decisions, considering presidential campaign films as a rhetorical genre of political discourse helps to articulate both continuities and shifts in presidential image-making practices. As representative anecdotes, these films inform us about the ways presidential candidates use television to project images of self, country, and the people; they illustrate the ways that viewers' self images and the wider matrix of a society's image of itself are created through discourse. Moreover, their visual form enables the analyst to better understand the construction of political messages by exploring texts that combine verbal, audiovisual, and production codes. Despite the voluminous study of politics and television, few scholars have explored the specifically visual nature of campaign narrative.

This essay will address the continuities in presidential campaign films through a discussion of candidates' evocations of myth to construct images of self and others. The term myth has several definitions, I concur with Lévi Strauss's account of myths as narrative forms that arise from the desire to resolve a contradiction; myths provide a resolution that helps people to alleviate tension. Two myths are central in presidential campaign films: One concerns the presidential character, where candidates face the conflicting requirements of being both leaders and men of the people. A second myth concerns the nature of the country and its people. Candidates typically construct a country either in a state of crisis or its dialectical opposite, resolution.

The candidate's image, marked by consistencies and digressions across the films, reveals the mythic construction of presidents at different sociohistorical junctures. Candidates typically embody the myths of the American Dream that reflect their ideology; they may be leaders above the people, populist men of the people, or in some cases, they appear to synthesize both qualities. To some extent, leaders need to show empathy with the common citizen, while populist candidates must demonstrate their capacity to lead. The emphasis depends on the situational exigencies and to some degree party. Democrats, as the majority party, are more often men of the people, while Republicans are leaders. As the Republican base widens in the seventies and eighties, candidates attempt to synthesize both images, as does Bill Clinton in 1992.

Evocations of mythic images provide stable points of identification amidst shifting conditions of production and reception. Thus I also assess the ways presidential campaign films have evolved to accord with changes in technology, politics, and the audience. As campaign films become representative anecdotes, they shift from the traditional documentary form to the more innovative hybrid documentary-advertisement. The films generally fall into two production categories that coincide with the candidates' mythic visions: high-technology production techniques characteristic of the hybrid documentary-advertisement typically affirm a regressive, idealized vision of "traditional" America, while conventional, less highly produced documentary films are apt to envision crisis and the need for change. The former, most evident in the films produced for Republican candidates, reflects an audience-centered approach to political communication that relies upon televisual marketing principles to construct images of candidate, country, and "The People" (McGee 1975). The latter, characteristic of most Democratic candidates' films, remain candidate-centered; they do not fully exploit marketing techniques or take advantage of television's communicative strengths and capabilities.

Images of the Candidate: Leader vs. Man of the People

The biographical campaign films, like the books, trace the trajectories of candidates' lives and careers. Whether emphasizing populism or leadership, candidate backgrounds appear remarkably similar (see Brown 1960). They commonly learn the value of hard work and love of country from their fathers, while their mothers instill religious and moral principles. They always have a happy childhood. Candidates are self-made men who rise from humble beginnings. They appear as good students, virile athletes, and devoted husbands and fathers.

The McGovern Story (1972) is a classic example of this presidential narrative. The film places the candidate securely within American mythology. Producer Charles Guggenheim asserts that he selected key elements of McGovern's background to make him attractive to voters: "He was a man who came out of the heartland in a difficult time and place, a man with fortitude, energy, and individualism, a man from modest means who showed great bravery during the war" (Guggenheim Interview). The film begins with McGovern's early history, illustrated by still-photographs of his parents, his childhood homes, and the churches built by his father, a Methodist minister. He grows up on a farm on the prairie; he acquires a gentle spirit from his mother, and the value of Christian principles, hard work, and a love of history from his father. His father's immigrant experience establishes McGovern's roots in the heartland. In an on-screen interview, his friend historian Leonard Chenoweth mentions that McGovern is close to the soil. His comment implies that McGovern identifies with a hardworking, virtuous American people.

Typically, the films illustrate the candidates' ability to rise above the ordinary with an account of a hardship that has been endured. Often they use heroism during war to simultaneously instill patriotic feelings. McGovern enters World War II as a pilot, illustrated by requisite battle footage and on-camera testimony from one of his men. Gunner Bill McEvoy recounts McGovern's heroism that earned him the Distinguished Flying Cross. (Yet, the narrator closes this scene by remarking that McGovern was "haunted" by the war, thus undercutting the image of the hero.) Archival World War II battle footage, complete with sound effects of exploding bombs, makes vivid the heroic World War II exploits of Kennedy, Ford, McGovern, and Bush. In the other films a crew member also recalls an epic event, illustrated with grainy, black-and-white battle footage unrelated to the actual incident. The only actual Navy file footage of a candidate documents the heroism of young George Bush on a World War II rescue mission, where graphics overlaid on the grainy images declare their authenticity. On some occasions, filmmakers construct heroism. Producer Phil Dusenberry presents Ronald Reagan's survival of an assassination attempt as a heroic exploit in his 1984 campaign film. In a departure from tradition, Reagan provides his own testimony about the shooting and his recovery as footage taken by news cameras replays the incident.

The candidates' image, marked by consistencies and digressions across the films, reveals the mythic construction of presidents at different sociohistorical junctures. Candidates embody different versions of American ideology; they may be leaders above the people, populist men of the people, or in some cases, they appear to synthesize both qualities. Obviously, populist candidates need to show that they have leadership qualities, while leaders need to show that they are in touch with the common citizen. The emphasis depends on the situational exigencies and to some degree party.

Films that stress the candidate's populist characteristics closely follow the model of Andrew Jackson. An outspoken military hero with little political experience, Jackson was neither humble nor qualified enough to fit common conceptions of the president (Heale 1982). To counter this negative, W.H. Eatons' biography portrayed him as a moral, virtuous outsider, a common man of the people who stood in contrast to the corrupt, power-hungry Washington establishment. This myth is at the root of the American experience.

In terms of modern day campaigns, Gerald Rafshoon's *Jimmy Who?* (1976) closely resembles Jackson's narrative. In a clip from a Carter speech, the candidate avows, "This has been a long and a personal campaign, a kind of humbling experience, reminding us that the ultimate political influence rests not with the power brokers, but with the people." The narrator also describes Carter as "the dark horse candidate from Georgia." The film stresses that the media at first did not take Carter's candidacy seriously, but the hard work of the common people who believed in him made it possible. Carter's volunteer "peanut brigade" canvasses in New Hampshire. Ordinary citizens' voices and images, rather than testimony from colleagues alone, populate the film. In a political arena defined by widespread post-Watergate distrust of politicians, Carter was a challenger who positioned himself as a virtuous outsider, a man of the people who wore blue jeans and farmed peanuts for a living (the film did not mention that he was a millionaire).

There is an alternative image that appears throughout American history: the heroic, uniquely talented leader who rises above the ordinary. He is patterned after George Washington, often reluctant but duty-bound to serve. This image was evoked by the avuncular Eisenhower, closely emulated in John Kennedy's *The New Frontier* (1960), and all of the Nixon films: *Ambassador of Friendship* (1960), *Nixon: A Self-Portrait* (1968), *Change without Chaos* (1972), and *Richard Nixon: Portrait of a President* (1972). Because Kennedy was widely perceived as too young and inexperienced, *The New Frontier* emphasized his leadership qualities. The narrator repeatedly refers to him as a leader, and the film emphasizes his training and experience. The film eludes mention of his privileged background, but concentrates upon accomplishments such as authoring the book *Profiles in Courage*, his World War II heroism, and his Senate career.

Richard Nixon consistently presented himself as a leader in his films.

Ambassador of Friendship (1960) dealt only with his foreign policy expertise. Nixon identifies himself with the nation; the two are symbolically equivalent. He maintains this image as an experienced leader in *Change Without Chaos* (1972). The film's masculine language constructs him as a dynamic man of action: he attacks, insists, marshalls, assaults, launches, explores, probes, and penetrates. The active tense structures sentences so that he alone initiates events. Single-handedly, "he reverses the basic priorities of the United States government." President who stress leadership qualities often act alone; as in Nixon's films, they are photographed working in solitude or walking by themselves.

Nixon's "personal" film, *Portrait of a President* (1972), attempted to counter public perceptions that he was cold and distant. The film portrayed him as humorous, spontaneous, and shy. He plays the piano to celebrate Duke Ellington's birthday at a White House reception, and he jokes with his interpreter at a public gathering in Communist China. His daughters Julie and Trischa give on-camera interviews; Trischa fortuitously recalls that he was too shy to tell her his feelings on her wedding night, so he slipped a note under her door. He places a wreath on a small child's grave in Leningrad, a gesture that demonstrates his compassion. But *Portrait of a President* also repeats many of the scenes from *Change Without Chaos* that connote leadership, and the film concludes as Nixon walks along the shore with his pant legs rolled up, a man alone with his responsibilities. He is humanized, but still not a man of the people.

Despite Nixon's constancy, candidates' images often shift as they move from challenger to incumbent. Though Gerald Rafshoon produced both films, Carter's *Jimmy Who?* (1976) portrays him as a man of the people, while *This Man, This Office* (1980) presents him as an experienced leader. Carter is aligned with past Democratic and Republican presidential heroes in the latter film. Friends and colleagues endorse his candidacy, and ordinary Americans disappear. In contrast, challenger Ronald Reagan is unquestionably a leader in his (untitled) 1980 biographical film. Reagan needed to combat perceptions that he was not qualified to be president. Visual techniques accented his leadership qualities; in more than one instance, his blue-tinted figure stood out from the crowd in black-and-white group photographs. In 1984, with his re-election virtually assured, he synthesized the two images and became a man of the people as well as a leader.

Humphrey's *What Manner of Man* (1968) provides an early example of an attempt to portray the candidate as simultaneously a leader and man of the people. According to advertising director Joe Napolitan, the film's purpose was twofold: to depict Humphrey as a gentle, benevolent, "ordinary" fellow and a firm, decisive leader with a proven track record (Interview). The film was deliberately unslick, and showed the human side of the candidate as well as the aggressive man of action; he was a man of peace and a man willing to fight for his principles, a man of sentiment and a man of substance. The film attempted to integrate these opposing sides of Hubert Humphrey, who symbolized the tensions that defined the people of the United States.

The film softens Humphrey's image while maintaining his credibility as a leader. But in order to construct him as a man of the people, the opening scenes cast him in a less-than-heroic mold. Jimmy Durante almost mispronounces his name. Humphrey prepares for a television appearance and is obviously uncomfortable. The narrator reminds viewers that the campaign had virtually no money in September. Enactments performed for the film emphasize his fallibility. The rest of the film presents Humphrey as a man of strength through a reiteration of his accomplishments: rare footage recounts his 1948 convention speech for civil rights; hecklers interrupt his presidential nomination acceptance speech and he feistily fights back, and the film visualizes his experience as Senator and Vice-President with still photographs and stock footage. A clip where Humphrey appears with John Kennedy at the ceremonial signing of the nuclear test ban treaty lends him credibility by linking him with a martyred Democratic hero. Similarly, Bill Clinton's *The Man from Hope* (1992) links him with Kennedy in early symbolic footage where the young representative of Boy's Nation shakes hands with the then-President in 1962.

What Manner of Man, like many other Democratic candidates' films, makes Humphrey a man of the people by portraying flaws and fallibility. The Republican films, in contrast, more positively project their candidates as both men of the people and leaders, and they do so through visual and narrative means. For Republicans, candidates embracing both opposing images coincide with an increasingly optimistic vision of an American where crises have been resolved. The American Dream is under siege in Goldwater's *Choice*; Nixon and Ford suggest that they have overcome the threat and are working toward achievement of the Dream; Reagan articulates its fulfillment and synthesizes opposing myths of the president. George Bush perpetuates the Reagan vision in 1988, though he injects it with negative reminders of the America represented by liberal democracy. But in 1992, with the Bush campaign in disarray, the vision collapses. The Bush campaign film is structured as a reiteration of the qualities of great former presidents that George Bush ostensibly shares. It attempts to establish Bush as a leader primarily by linking him with leaders of the past. There is no effort to link him with the people—a miscalculation in a campaign where he was routinely accused of being out of touch with his constituencies. The film is obsessed with America's past glory of the Republican party rather than the present.

In contrast to the Republicans, Democratic candidates after Kennedy and Johnson are prone to represent the pessimistic side of the American

Dream; they are flawed representatives of a country in crisis. But Bill Clinton diverges from this pattern in 1992. He mimics the successes of the Republican past presidential candidates and defines himself as leader and man of the people. His campaign film, *The Man from Hope*, identifies him with the prototypical candidate. He was portrayed as "a man with a modest, small town background, no stranger to adversity, who matured into a man who believed deeply in family and country" (Grimes 1992, A-11). More than any other Democratic candidates' films, *The Man from Hope* synthesizes the image of the candidate as leader and man of the people.

Images of the Country: Crisis vs. Resolution

The presidential campaign films derive their dramatic images of the country from the Jackson narrative, which is itself a secular version of the American Edenic monomyth (Nimmo & Combs 1980). The nostalgic image of a lost paradise that can be restored by a heroic yet humble savior, and its antithesis, the fall from grace, permeates Western philosophy and religion, and has a particular incarntation in American ideology. Presidential candidates typically invoke one or the other aspects of this vision. The constructed context of the Jackson candidacy played on fundamental fears and anxieties that corruption, decay, and loss of moral virtue threatened the republic, as well as an optimistic belief in America's ability to fulfill its promise of liberty, justice, and equality. Jackson's biography "invoked a republic that had once been virtuous, happy, and free, but had degenerated so its *raison d'être* was in jeopardy. The vision was of a once proud people reduced to servility by the corrupt machinations of voracious officeholders" (Heale 1982). In the 1960s, the Republicans appropriated the positive vision of hope and marketed it, while the Democrats, bereft of symbols after the "failure" of the Great Society, increasingly lapsed into the vision of despair.

Barry Goldwater's *Choice* (1964), one of the more important films to emerge, articulates the Republican vision that eventually came to dominate American politics. *Choice* responds to the schizophrenia of a culture split between the ordered familiarity of tradition and the novelty of change and innovation. It juxtaposes two opposing visions of America: the good, moral bastion of traditional values and the evil wellspring of liberal decadence. *Choice* simplifies the complex as it contrasts images of a corrupt, morally bankrupt America with images of an innocent, virtuous land and people (though the former are far more prevalent than the latter). Blacks rioting in city streets are juxtaposed with well-scrubbed white children reciting the pledge of allegiance in a classroom. Images of strip-tease joints and teenagers dancing the twist cut to Main Street America, picnics, and children saluting the flag. Rapid cuts and montages from more than one camera angle create a feeling of confusion, and these techniques only depict the morally corrupt America. The virtuous America is represented with shots that are slower paced and from a single point of view. The pulsating, sexually suggestive rhythms of Afro-Cuban jazz accompany images of the morally decadent America, while orchestral arrangements of hymns or marches accompany images of the "good" America. As the film progresses, the "good" images disappear and the film takes on a darker tone. Narrator Raymond Massey warns that both Americas are possible, but people must choose one.

Choice constructs viewers who are not committed to the culture of consumption, whose values are rooted in tradition rather than belief in progress. It addresses white middle class voters who yearn for the mythic America; blacks are not part of this myth, although they are part of the evil city. Liberal permissiveness and the ethic of consumption are openly attacked as the sources of current crisis. The film defines the current state of affairs as a moral crisis, thus disassociating it from its economic and political contexts. The film articulates the otherwise inchoate, if in a simplistic fashion, and it provides a position from which those addressed by the film can understand profound cultural transformation. The images in *Choice* appear in later Republican films; the film set the terms for subsequent Republican discourse, and it presaged the marketing appeals to those who would become the New Right.

After *Choice*, both Democratic and Republican presidential campaign films address a disruption of the social order. Humphrey's *What Manner of Man?* (1968) depicts crisis, particularly in its presentation of the candidate as a flawed representative of the American people. *Nixon: A Self-Portrait* (1968) offers an idealized portrait of America as a strong country with a responsibility to lead the rest of the world. Nixon embodies positive American values, and the film disavows the strife sundering the nation.

The 1972 presidential campaign films further polarized their images of America and Americans. *The McGovern Story*, aired during the primaries and general election campaign, wallowed in despair as the candidate recited a litany of problems without resolutions. *The Nixon Years: Change without Chaos* rejuvenated Goldwater's theme of a choice between two Americas. *Change without Chaos* opens with a montage of images similar to those that appeared throughout *Choice*: news footage of blacks rioting and looting, students burning draft cards, a group of white demonstrators for national welfare rights, a school bus with its windows smashed, an eviction, and riot police subduing a crowd. At the end of the stream of images, a horrified woman screams, "This is America?" In the thirty-minute version of the film, the camera cuts to a static, serene image of the White House, and then to the 1968 Republican National Convention and Richard Nixon's acceptance speech, beginning the narrative of Richard Nixon as a heroic leader, alone responsible for transforming chaos to order. The narrator proclaims: "He will meet each issue with deliberation, weigh all the evidence, think through his decision, and then act." Whereas *Choice* presents chaos as dominant, the Nixon film uses the same images to emphasize the restoration of order.

The McGovern Story dwells on the past and its problems; no solutions are offered. Even the narration is entirely in the past tense. Its structure is regressive rather than forward-moving, its message nostalgic rather than celebratory. Shadows and silhouettes predominate, and shots are linked primarily through dissolves that give the film a soft feel. But the visual technique works against the candidate. McGovern is accorded none of the distance that signals a leader, nor is he associated with symbols of leadership. He rides buses rather than airplanes; he solicits donations a dollar at a time; he talks with disgruntled groups of Americans in stark, dimly lit factories and auditoriums. The cinema verite technique was deliberately unsophisticated. These scenes were accurate depictions of his presidential campaign, but they were not "presidential."

After the Watergate debacle, and in the midst of an economic recession, in 1976 both *Jimmy Who?* and the (untitled) Ford film envisioned not crisis but movement toward resolution. *Jimmy Who?* was a lighthearted denial of social discord and a celebration of Jimmy Carter. The Ford film attempted to carry Nixon's message further by relegating social disorder to the past and emphasizing the candidate's humanity and accomplishments in office. The film stressed that America was better off than it had been, and ended with an upbeat song played by a marching band, "I'm feeling good about America, I'm feeling good about me."

But in 1980, Carter stopped smiling and Ronald Reagan's "new beginning" began in earnest. Carter's *This Man, This Office* returns to the themes of incompetence and fallibility characteristic of Humphrey and McGovern's images. The opening shot depicts Carter sitting alone at his desk. His head is down, and a closed fist supports his forehead in a gesture of resignation. The narrator reiterates a list of derogatory terms used to describe other presidential candidates, followed by a shot of Carter that implicitly connects him with these figures. The film acknowledges his unpopularity, and serves as an apology for the first four years of the Carter presidency. It provides little to vote for; even the Carter campaign does not seem convinced by the candidate.

Reagan's eight-minute 1980 convention biography, however, celebrates America's renewal in the sketches of a picture that took full shape in 1984. The film details Reagan's life and career, emphasizing the self-made man from America's heartland. It concludes with a montage of Americans smiling, cheering, waving flags, lining the streets of their community. These people become the ordinary citizens in his 1984 *A New Beginning*, a film that establishes that the good, traditional America of *Choice* is Ronald Reagan's America. *A New Beginning* indicates the resolution of crisis that had plagued the country. Negative images are at a minimum in this film; instead, the sun rises, Americans raise the flag, marry, build houses, work, and prosper. The Statue of Liberty is shot as it undergoes reconstruction; people are happy and content.

George Bush continues the theme of American resurgence in 1988, even using images identical to those that appeared in the Reagan 1984 film. More so than Reagan, his film evokes the memory of a dark past, of the potential Fall. Images of rioting and demonstrations from the 1960s and 1970s serve as reminders of what has been overcome, as Bush's invocation of his commitment to the pledge of allegiance and his opposition to furlough programs implicitly warns of the perils of President Dukakis. But overall, the Bush film celebrates traditional American values and the virtuous community established by Ronald Reagan; Bush is of this community, as indicated by the closing scene where Bush, the nurturing father, steams corn in the kitchen and picnics with his extended family.

In contrast to the Republicans' idealized vision, the Mondale (1984) and Dukakis (1988) films mirror crisis. The short Mondale convention film continues the Democratic tradition of candidates' self-deprecation. "What was your nickname in high school?" the narrator asks Mondale. "Crazy legs," the presidential aspirant replies. While Reagan's America is sun-filled and pristine-clean, Mondale's America is polluted and trash-laden. In one scene, a woman drives a car past a toxic waste dump and talks about deaths from leukemia in her community. The Dukakis convention film also fails to positively symbolize the candidate or his vision. Dukakis does not appear in the film at all, nor does his wife or children; rather his cousin, actress Olympia Dukakis, is on-screen narrator who walks viewers through the pedestrian film. Whereas viewers are invited into Bush's kitchen, they see only Dukakis' garage and backyard. Olympia drags out an antique snowblower and marvels that he has used the same machine for twenty years. Her comment intends to indicate that he is frugal, but it also implies that he is cheap. In another sense, her comment venerates a conservative impulse, a resistance to change that undercuts the very premise upon which Dukakis' candidacy rests.

The 1992 campaign films reverse this pattern. As the economy worsened and the public mood plunged into pessimism, the Republican story seemed to come to an end. The Bush film implicitly acknowledges malaise. Narrator Robert Mitchum obliquely refers to Reagan's "new beginning" as something less than the realization of the American Dream, setting the tone of the entire film by stating, "Today as a new dawn breaks over America, we face *tough challenges* and new opportunities." There are few symbols or narrative statements in the film that recall the hope and optimism of Reagan's America. More common are quotations from past presidents such as Dwight D. Eisenhower, "No easy problems have ever come to the presidents of the United States. If they are easy to solve, someone else has already solved them."

Clinton, on the other hand, learned from the performances of past candidates, Democrat and Republican. His campaign appropriates the Republican vision of resurgence, as indicated by his film's title, *The Man from Hope*. The film uses the family as a metaphor for the country, and asserts that crises can be overcome. By presenting Clinton as a leader within the family who protected his mother and brother from his abusive stepfather, the film implies that Clinton would also protect the American people. Clinton even uses the language of domestic violence in an excerpt from a campaign speech "what I want you to know is that the hits I took during the election are nothing compared to the hits the people in this state and this country are taking every day of their lives under this administration." In particular, the expanded election-eve version of the campaign film borrows images characteristic of Reagan's America to convey a positive, upbeat, optimistic feeling: smiling, flag-waving, celebrating Americans line up along rural farmlands and on main street America, as the candidate greets farmers, businesspersons, babies, elderly, blacks, whites, men and women in the heartland of America.

From 1964 to 1992, the Republicans' films consistently developed a coherent theme by appropriating the positive face of the American Dream. But every story comes to an end, and the Democrats were able to pick up the loose narrative threads and weave a tale of their own. At this juncture, it appears that the Democrats have re-appropriated the optimistic side of American mythology. In doing so, they have also managed to use televisual techniques that had been the domain of Republican candidates.

Evolution of the Televisual Campaign Film: From Documentary to Hybrid

While presidential candidates' images of self, country, and people remain relatively constant over time, the form of the presidential campaign film has changed radically. Throughout the twentieth century, Republican candidates have embraced innovative media forms, in part because they have more money with which to do so, and in part because they have connections to business and industry where new technologies are developed and utilized. In 1923, William Fox produced a 16-minute silent "newsreel" for Republican Calvin Coolidge. Herbert Hoover also had two campaign films in 1928: *Upbuilding with Prosperity*, a silent biographical film produced by H. S. Kimberly, and *Master of Emergencies*, an hour long résumé film produced by the Brown Brothers.

The Republicans first televised a presidential campaign film. In 1948,

Universal Pictures produced a short theatrical newsreel to promote Thomas Dewey's candidacy. *The Dewey Story*, sponsored by the Republican National Committee, aired locally on one station, WNBT, in New York on October 31. The Truman campaign protested the *The Dewey Story* when it was distributed to Republican theater owners across the country. Truman's campaign manager warned the newsreel companies that the Democratic Congress would investigate how distribution arrangements were made for the film (Redding 1958). In response, the newsreel companies grudgingly pooled their resources and made a film for Truman. Unlike the Dewey film that used paid actors to dramatize the candidate's life, *The Truman Story*, spliced together at the last minute, used newsreel footage of President Truman. The film played in movie theaters throughout the final week of the campaign. Later films took their cue from *The Truman Story* and made extensive use of actuality footage rather than dramatizations.

From 1952 to 1964 the newsreel companies produced biographical portraits of the two major party candidates, and broadcast them in theaters as "public service announcements." They structured these like newsreels, consisting of still photographs, actuality footage of the candidate and the important people and places in his life, and some enacted scenes. The anonymous, but authoritative voice of a male narrator in the tradition of the March of Time newsreel made these images coherent.

Television first played a significant role in American politics in 1952. The medium both responded to and helped to initiate transformations in political discourse. Both Stevenson and Eisenhower hired advertising agencies to help them construct television appeals, but in Stevenson's case, the Joseph Katz advertising personnel were considered technicians rather than strategists. Stevenson had a thirty-minute televised documentary, *Campaigning with Stevenson*, that intercut biographical material with footage of speeches on the campaign trail. Eisenhower used the Madison Avenue firm of Batten, Barton, Durstin, and Osborne, and set up an organization independent of BBD&O, headed by Rosser Reeves of the Ted Bates Agency, that produced the first spot commercials and planned television strategy. An election-eve celebration of the new television technology, called *Report to Ike*, aired simultaneously coast-to-coast on all three networks. It combined biographical material and staged film footage with the "live" transmission of groups of supporters assembled across the country to participate in the giant electronic rally. Eisenhower sat in front of a television set in a studio designed to look like a living room, accompanied by vice-presidential candidate Nixon and their wives. He watched himself watching himself on television, seemingly at one with the viewers at home.

The Eisenhower campaign's extensive financial resources made *Report to Ike* possible, and other candidates could not afford such an elaborate production. One Kennedy documentary, *The New Frontier* (1960), was not even shown on television. Filmmakers designed the early films for small gatherings of supporters; the early films functioned to inform local party leaders of the candidate's program, to reinforce support, and perhaps to motivate volunteers (Wolper 1991). The Nixon campaign televised *Ambassador of Friendship* (1960) only during the California primary. They scheduled it on national television the Sunday before the election, but Nixon canceled at the last minute because he wanted one last chance to speak directly to the American people (Wyckoff 1968).

After 1964, campaign films always aired on television, while televised speeches and rallies declined. In 1964 Barry Goldwater broadcast several half hour speeches on Tuesday evenings, but they did poorly compared to entertainment on the other networks; this was the last time any candidate invested heavily in half-hour speeches. Spot advertisements and entertainment-oriented programs became the alternatives. Although many pundits predicted the demise of thirty-minute political programs with the rise of advertising, campaign strategists recognized that lengthy films could accomplish more than advertisements: they could help people feel that they knew candidates and give extensive accounts of their accomplishments. The films, increasingly produced for general television audiences rather than partisan supporters, continued to define candidates and their visions.

The Citizens for Goldwater-Miller Committee produced *Choice* in 1964, partly due to their dissatisfaction with Goldwater's old style political advisers' bland use of television. *Choice* makes use of innovative visual techniques in order to repudiate innovation; sound and image predominate over the word. Arguments are often implicit, relying on previous cultural knowledge. In the film's only admittedly staged scene, a Lincoln Continental intermittently speeds across the screen; its brakes screech and an unidentified driver tosses beer cans out the window. This alludes to a widely reported incident where Lyndon Johnson took four reporters on a tour of his ranch. He reputedly drove ninety miles per hour in his Lincoln Continental, drinking beer and discarding the empty cans out the window.

By 1968, television's increasingly dominance, combined with the continuing decline in party affiliations, facilitated the establishment of professional media specialists as central players in political campaigns. These consultants supplanted advertising agencies and the cadre of lawyers who advised candidates in the past. The consultants were more than mere advertising experts. They had the skills to plan strategy as well as produce commercials; they knew how to get their candidate free media exposure by staging "newsworthy" events that would play well on television. Polls were taken to check the public pulse as often as time and money allowed, and candidates were fashioned in response to poll data. The Nixon campaign relied on television to modify the public's negative perceptions of the candidate, as opposed to the candidate himself. Rather than source oriented persuasion, Nixon's marketing strategy sought to cajole viewers by investigating what people wanted, and fashioning the candidate's image in response.

Nixon's effort was a significant moment in the development of the modern telemarketing campaign. His November Group, a predecessor of Reagan's 1984 Tuesday Team, consisted of an ad hoc group of Madison Avenue advertising experts, all of whom pooled their talents. Ex-television producer Roger Ailes, subsequently involved as a consultant in most Republican campaigns, came on board during the 1968 election. Informed by the media theories of Marshall McLuhan, they took advantage of television as a medium that could convey impressions of intimacy and immediacy; television was a medium of impressions, where "viewers were invited in without making an intellectual demand"(McGinnis 1970, p. 23). *Nixon: A~ Self Portrait* departs from generic conventions and illustrates the "effeminate" style of political discourse—self-disclosure, narrative, and personal—characteristic of television (Jamieson 1988, p. 89). The biographical film did not stringently adhere to the documentary form; reporter Warren Wallace interviewed Nixon on-camera, in a seemingly spontaneous conversation. Although Wallace remained off-camera, Nixon sat facing him and thus the viewer, as he candidly related his personal life history. Still photographs that connoted authenticity and diverse settings animated the otherwise visually dull talking head interview. The interview frame had several advantages: Nixon could appear relaxed and casual, speaking off the cuff; close-ups of his face enabled viewers to scrutinize him, to feel that they were getting to know him; the interview, which simulated a conversation, created a feeling of intimacy that would have been hard to capture in a conventional documentary format. The marketing technique allowed Nixon to showcase his strengths while also reflecting the image most people wanted to see.

The Nixon campaign transformed all later campaigns. By 1972, increasingly powerful political consultants and media specialists were inextricably involved in both party's campaign strategies. The 1972 campaign marked the apogee of the documentary campaign film. Award-winning documentarians produced both the Nixon and McGovern campaign films: Charles Guggenheim for McGovern, and David Wolper for Nixon. Guggenheim, an old friend of McGovern, also took on the advertising for the campaign. The Republicans hired Wolper only to make documentary films. He produced a biography, *Portrait of a President*, and a résumé film, *The Nixon Years: Change Without Chaos*. While Guggeheim had a great deal of latitude, Erlichman gave Wolper specific instructions about what to include in the films (Interview).

Change Without Chaos, a film designed for a television audience, includes appeals to demographic groups who represent generic Americans rather than special interests. The film offers a range of positions that allows it to be read favorably by a wide variety of viewers from different, even oppositional, social formations. For example, *Change Without Chaos* nods to minorities in a segment that describes Nixon's entrepreneurship program for small businesses. African American, Mexican American, and Native American businessmen appear on camera to acknowledge the benefits they received from the program. While these figures could be positive figures of identification for minority viewers, they more likely reassure the predominantly white Nixon supporters.

In another scene, Nixon's voice announces that welfare was a "disastrous mess," as he shakes hands with a black woman. The shot implies that blacks are the primary recipients of welfare. Yet, when Nixon asserts that his welfare reform plan would make sure that every American had basic needs met, two poor white children in a rural slum are photographed. In this way, voters who resent welfare as a "handout" to minorities are not alienated. In addition, Nixon's averred opposition to busing, repeated in both films, reassures the conservative white constituency that while his programs may get blacks off welfare, they don't require racial integration. *Change Without Chaos* reinforces stereotypes and preconceptions as it plays to those from white, rural, small towns who eventually became galvanized as the New Right. Race, associated with welfare, urban values, and centralized government, was a potent unifying force for this traditional American constituency.

The 1976 campaign, crafted entirely for television marketing, signaled the political campaign film's transformation from a documentary to a hybrid documentary-advertisement. Adman Malcolm MacDougall made Ford's campaign film under the auspices of consultants Doug Bailey and John Deardourff. The troubled campaign, under constraints of time and organization, had no advertisements until the last three weeks of the general campaign, and the Ford election-eve film simply compiled these ads, along with a five-minute convention biography, into one presentation.

Gerald Rafshoon's *Jimmy Who?* also eschewed the conventional documentary format, using special effects, animation, song, and graphics to grab viewers' attention. These new films aimed to entertain as much as inform; they were less substantive than earlier films and more concerned with creating a mood that surrounded the candidate. They were less realistic and more symbolic. In the conventional documentaries, illustrative "proofs" such as still-photographs, archival footage, or film footage of the candidate supported the narrator's verbal assertions. In the hybrid films, complex visual images unrelated to the "actuality" accompany or supplant narration. The Ford film concluded with an upbeat song, intercut with patriotic symbols. *Jimmy Who?* used devices such as cartoons, song, and a superimposition of a picture of the candidate against a moving background to move the film out of the realm of actuality. Both films aimed primarily to secure the attention, then affection of the elusive viewer by adopting television's entertainment values. They also illustrated the television candidate's reluctance to alienate any particular voting bloc by making specific claims. Their films associated the candidates with general, noncontroversial values such as honesty, family, patriotism.

When both candidates' polls showed that target groups most wanted leadership in 1980, they reverted to sober, unslick documentary forms. Carter stopped smiling, while Reagan's short convention biography, on the surface obeying traditional generic conventions, used visual manipulations to imply leadership. But 1984 marked a new landmark in political filmmaking, when Reagan's *A New Beginning* seamlessly intermeshed documentary and advertising forms. Reagan's Tuesday Team, an ad hoc group of Madison Avenue creative advertising experts, had ample time to do market research and testing. They used pre-testing strategies to a greater extent than ever before to develop their campaign themes. *A New Beginning* constructed a unified American community of adherents to mythic Main Street America and the positive values of hope and optimism. Ronald Reagan reflected desirable images of America and Americans back at them; according to pollster Richard Wirthlin, Ronald Reagan represented "America's idealized image of itself." Producer Phil Dusenberry, an advertising man with no previous campaign experience, created a high production value film that reproduced advertising images whose positive associations were already familiar to viewers; *A New Beginning*'s images referred to other images rather than reality. The Republicans intermeshed the fantasy of advertising with the perceived reality of documentary; both were embodied in the figure of Ronald Reagan.

George Bush repeated the Reagan formula in his 1988 campaign film, while the Democrats repeated theirs. Dukakis initially reported that he would use the Republican model of an ad hoc group of Madison Avenue advertising experts. But the Democrats, who have not gone to Madison Avenue since Joe Napolitan fired Doyle, Dane and Bernbach from the 1968 Humphrey campaign, have no experience with Madison Avenue. As noted by political consultant Dan Payne, Democratic candidates do not know how to use such structures (Interview). The Republicans have had an organization in place for years, and they know who to hire for what tasks. The confused and disorganized Dukakis campaign did not succeed at organizing an ad hoc group. Dan Payne produced the convention film, but there was no lengthy film that carried on its themes during the general campaign. Bush's film, in contrast, introduced his themes at the convention, replayed them as advertisements during the campaign, and then recapped the campaign with an expanded version of the film on election-eve.

In 1992, Bill Clinton was the first Democratic candidate in years to learn from the mistakes of his predecessors. Clinton had a well-organized staff made up of young political operatives, seasoned Democratic consultants, and Madison Avenue advertisers. His Communication Director George Stephanopoulos had worked on Dukakis's 1988 presidential campaign. The advertising team was headed by Frank Greer, who had worked for Walter Mondale in 1984, although his associate, Mandy Grunwald, became chief advertising strategist. Roy Spence, also on Mondale's team, came out of retirement from politics to serve as creative advertising adviser. In addition, Squier, Eskew, Knapp, and Ochs, the top Pennsylvania Avenue Democratic consulting firm, came on board. Bob Squier was a veteran of past presidential campaigns, first working as television producer for Hubert Humphrey in 1968. Squier also produced Jimmy Carter's 1980 *This Man, This Office.* The campaign hired a Madison Avenue advertising agency, Deutsch, Inc., known for producing controversial, innovative advertisements. Clinton's long time friends, producers Harry Thomason and Linda Bloodworth-Thomason (creators of the television series *Designing Women*), were responsible for creating televisual campaign materials, in particular the biological campaign film, *The Man from Hope.* The film took the form of a documentary while retaining the purpose of an advertisement; it demonstrated a keen awareness of the requirements of emotional televisual communication that appeared "authentic." The visual techniques—soft lighting, dissolves, integrated on-camera interviews, slow, sentimental music—supported the film's message that Bill Clinton was an earnest, sincere candidate who aimed to "re-unify" the country under his leadership.

But the Republicans' tight organization fell apart in 1992. The incumbent candidate George Bush suffered from the loss of the key political operatives who had been active in Republican presidential politics in the past. Bush's former campaign manager, James Baker, was serving as Secretary of State and had no desire to rejoin a political campaign, media consultant Roger Ailes declined to formally participate although he served as informal adviser, and master strategist Lee Atwater died the year before from a brain tumor. Moreover, many veterans of the Reagan and Bush campaigns served in new and unfamiliar capacities in the Bush 1992 campaign. Pollster Robert Teeter, involved in Republican campaigns since Richard Nixon's 1972 campaign, became campaign chairman for the first time, while Fred Steeper took over as pollster. Up until the Republican Convention in August, Teeter shared control of the campaign with Chief of Staff Sam Skinner, but the resulting sharing of responsibilities meant that no one figure could make decisions. Until James Baker's reluctant return as campaign Chief of Staff in August, there was no decisive leadership.

The campaign followed the previous Republican models and recruited an *ad hoc* team of creative advertising experts from Madison Avenue that became known as the November Company. The November Company was headed by Martin Puris, who had no previous experience producing political advertisements, and only two creative members of the November Company had worked on political campaigns before. Unlike the past three Republican presidential elections, the inexperienced media team received little direction and their campaign materials, including the campaign film, were not widely heralded. Republican political consultant and presidential campaign veteran Ed Rollins referred to the 1992 Bush effort as "the worst campaign ever seen."

The Bush campaign film, shown only at the Republican National Convention, was a hybrid form that made use of innovative televisual techniques, but to no avail. Its style borrowed from new trends in television documentary filmmaking that began with Ken Burns's extremely successful *Civil War* series. As in *The Civil War*, the Bush film consisted entirely of still-photographs, lithographs, paintings, and archival film footage as different voices animated quotations from former great presidents. Only the once-maligned Richard Nixon, resuscitated in the film and heralded for his determination, and Ronald Reagan, hailed for his leadership, spoke for themselves.

Despite the use of documentary rather than slick advertising techniques, the film was not a throwback to earlier modes of presidential campaign communication. It was made for a video generation inured to a visual bombardment. The music was almost a character in this film. Harsh, edgy, and forceful, it was uncharacteristic of the soft music that usually appears in campaign films. There were no cuts—all of the shots in the entire film were linked by dissolves. Images overwhelmed the minimal narration and appeared on screen at record-breaking speed, so much so that it was impossible to assimilate them all at one viewing. In contrast to the conventional documentary films where narration explicated the flow of images, the visuals that appeared here received no explication. In this way, the film appeared to "speak" without actually saying anything. But it reflected the lack of cohesion and control in the upper echelons of the campaign. Though the film was stylistically innovative, it lacked a message or forward-moving vision. Its regressive fixation on the past and dead icons was most similar to Jimmy Carter's *This Man, This Office*, also a defensive attempt to excuse an incumbent's record. The campaign film did not reappear during the campaign.

Conclusions

Ever since 1968, the Republicans have benefited from a steady organization of political consultants. They have been able to refine and develop their marketing techniques, as demonstrated by their consistency of themes throughout the years and by the evolving form and functions of their campaign films. As the films evolve into hybrid documentary advertisements, they become representative anecdotes of their campaigns. Democratic candidates benefit from no such organization or strategic unity. Since television's inception, Democratic presidents have been the exception. New candidates rarely ask advice of losing campaigns, and thus they tend to repeat the same mistakes. Their marketing and televisual communication techniques lag behind the Republicans. The Republicans have become fluent in the language of television; their visual and verbal messages support one another, while the Democrats often undercut verbal messages with incongruent visual forms and images. The party of progress uses regressive communication tools, while the party of traditional values uses every technological means at their disposal to make their vision palatable.

To some extent, the Republican party is more ideologically narrow, and thus it is easier to construct a vision that appeals to the generic Republican. The Democrats, a coalition party that has increasingly been losing its coalitions, do not seem able to construct a positive vision of what they represent. In both 1984 and 1988, their candidacies were defined by what they stood against. The Republican vision moves from apocalypse to redemption as it evokes myths and values rooted deep in the American psyche; it provides Americans with the figures of hope and reassurance they crave, defined against the background of the other—black, urban, liberal, progressive Americans.

While both Democrats and Republicans drew from American mythology, until recently the audience-oriented Republicans projected images and evoked myths that addressed deep-seated yearnings, while the candidate-centered Democrats reflected images of the candidates with little regard for the hopes and desires that fueled the American psyche. The Republicans, fluent in the language of television, provided visual and verbal messages that supported one another and bound their constituencies, while the Democrats often undercut verbal messages with incongruent visual forms and images. The party of progress often sold its candidate with regressive communication strategies, while the party of traditional values marketed their vision with advanced technological tools.

Yet, by 1992 it was apparent that George Bush was not a savior who could redeem the country, which was falling deeper and deeper into recession. The Republicans had not delivered on their promise of "a new beginning" and George Bush seemed to forget what he represented or why he even came. Democratic candidate Bill Clinton was able to construct and market a positive vision of what he represented; his promise of renewed hope for redemption through change more closely resonated with the lived experience of most Americans. Whether the 1992 election campaign marked a genuine shift in the televised approach of the Democrats remains to be seen.

Lamenting television marketing techniques as subversions of democratic principles, as Democrats are wont to do, serves no purpose in the modern media-centered political environment. The marketing of politicians continues, with or without Democratic participation. This analysis of one genre of political discourse, the presidential campaign film, indicates the vast differences that divide the two parties' approaches. The Republicans have had years of practice, but the Democrats need to equalize the playing field. The tortoise may be virtuous, but in the world outside of fable, its the hare who wins the race.

3

Images of Civic Virtue in the New Political Rhetoric

Ronald Lee

"Image" could not innocently become prominent in the contemporary vocabulary, because it was the progeny of virtue and desire. The child of virtue models character to elevate the ethical over the expedient. The child of desire seduces reason with passion. Yet, these functions are hardly distinct, for the virtuous can appear desirable and the desirable can appear virtuous. This conflation has led to all the trouble: the pleasant appearing as the good, the worse appearing as the better, the false appearing as the true.

This dialectical tension existed in the earliest theorizing on image. Aristotle (1932, 1356a) defined *ethos* as a means of persuasion that resides in the character of the speaker. In other words, *ethos* creates a desirable impression of the rhetor's virtues among members of the audience. Aristotle well understood the political implications of managing impressions of virtue. He commented not only on the ethical appeals of speakers but on the character of governmental arrangements. He wrote, "We should have a command of the character of each form of government; since for each form its own character will be most persuasive; and these political characters must be ascertained by the same means as the character of individuals" (1366a).

This essay concerns the match between political arrangements and images of civic virtue. In the last twenty-five years, Americans have changed the means by which they select their leaders and, as a consequence, the projected character of candidates, citizens, and the state also changed. Others have analyzed the changes in political infrastructure—rise of media campaigns, demographic changes in the electorate, party reform, the use of political consultants, the decline in partisanship, and the rest—but, by and large, the New Politics as rhetoric remains unexamined. Of course, there are rhetorical analyses of particular new politicians, particular new ideologies, and particular new strategies of campaigning, but these studies do not offer a general account. In fact, in only a few cases did the analysts recognize that they were describing a phenomenon that transcended the individual case and altered rhetorical practice.[1]

In what follows, I chart the changes in and speculate on the consequences of these new images of civic virtue. I argue four claims: (1) The institutional changes associated with the so-called New Politics have altered the function of the electoral system. (2) The resulting new political rhetoric is profitably conceptualized as a new populism. (3) This populist discourse encompasses new images of civic virtue. (4) These new images have serious political consequences.

Before I begin, I need to add a word about the discourse I have chosen to analyze. I have drawn examples from the discourse of Democratic Party candidates entered in the presidential primaries, 1968-1988. Much of what I have to say also applies to the Republican Party and many would argue with considerable justification that the GOP has adapted more successfully to the New Politics. I suspect the Republican Party with its narrower and more conservative ideological base finds the new political appeals quite compatible with its traditional vision. Moreover, the expression of populist conservatism (New Right or social conservatism), especially in Reagan's discourse, has been the object of considerable analysis (Dallek 1984; Denton 1988; Erickson 1985; Gronbeck 1986). The contrary traditions of electoral discourse in the Democratic Party make the peculiar stresses of the New Politics all the more interesting; Democrats have been forced to shape an unnatural message. Consequently, liberals have redefined in dramatic ways the meaning of civic virtue. I understand that asserting characterizations of discourse as "compatible" or "unnatural" are themselves claims to be proven. In this sense I am proceeding abductively; the essay's conclusions will provide evidence for its premises. In the essay's final sections I will return to the rhetorical relationship between recent incarnations of liberal and conservative discourse.

Institutional Change and Altered Electoral Function

Immediately prior to the upheavals of the system in 1968, discontented political factions had no point of entry into two-party politics. As Nelson Polsby (1983) phrased it, the nominating process employed "elite" rather than "mass" selection criteria (pp. 3-4). Candidates were chosen from among a small group of experienced office holders who had spent many years serving the party. Primaries, in the words of Harry Truman, were mere "eye wash." For example, the bid of Estes Kefauver for the Democratic presidential nomination in 1952, strengthened by his performance in the televised hearings on organized crime and his triumph in most of the primaries, was frustrated by the nomination of Adlai Stevenson.

Under this closed process, candidates representing non-establishment interests found little choice but to launch third-party efforts. For instance, dismayed by what he saw as Truman's abandonment of the principles of the New Deal and unable to challenge the President's nomination, Henry Wallace launched a futile third-party effort. These efforts were futile because they were so easily coopted; Truman moved to the left to attract disaffected Democrats and then attacked Wallace for his communist support.[2]

With changes in nomination rules and the rise of media campaigns, opportunities for an increasingly populist politics emerged. These new political candidates, ordinarily legitimate party figures, openly identify themselves with oppositional interests in a struggle against established leadership. The efforts of Eugene McCarthy, Robert Kennedy, and George McGovern exemplify this form of campaigning (McCarthy 1969; Newfield 1969; Simons, Chesebro, & Orr 1973).

Now, threats to political stability are defused in new ways. First, "participation" serves as a symbol of system legitimacy. "Political participation symbolizes influence for the powerless," Edelman (1977) wrote, "but it is also a key device for social control. In consequence, liberals, radicals, and authoritarians all favor participation, a tribute to the term's symbolic potency and semantic hollowness" (p. 120). By offering a channel for participation, established party figures refute the opposition's claim that the system is closed and unsympathetic to its grievances. Second, once enticed into the electoral arena, opposition ideology gives way to the instrumental demands of a winning campaign. Strategies of polarization that serve radical interests are replaced by strategies of identification to persuade farmers in Iowa, factory workers in Chicago, and small business operators in Los Angeles. As a result, rhetorical imperatives change the angry denunciations of agitators into the measured oratory of serious political candidates.[3]

As a variation of the New Politics, disaffected factions have engaged directly in electoral politics. With the conscious realization that backing surrogate candidates fails to bring consequential change, opposition groups have run their own candidates in party primaries. In its fullest expression this is not merely a symbolic candidacy (e.g., Shirley Chisolm) but a serious attempt to gain power through electoral campaigns (Boyte 1978; Boyte 1980; Lee 1986). The candidacy of Jesse Jackson, especially in 1984, exemplifies this form of political action.

The difficulty with the "long march through the institutions" is that the process transforms radical ideology into respectable reformist opposition (Schelsky 1974). The demands of electioneering and the requirements for institutional effectiveness preclude major challenges to dominant interests.

Carl Boggs (1983) posed this dilemma in the language of the left: "At what point does adaptation to the 'American Heritage' become a synonym for adaptation to bourgeois hegemony?" (pp. 356-357). After all, participation "stresses votes and influence rather than autonomous popular struggles" (p. 349). For example, the conventional wisdom that characterized Reverend Jackson as a more responsible campaigner in 1988 than in 1984 might be understood as the observation that he sacrificed the discourse of opposition for the rhetoric of electoral success.

The new political changes alter the function of the selection process. Previously, elite-dominated selection procedures screened out opposition demands. Now, mass-dominated selection procedures transform opposition demands. This shift in function dramatically alters campaign messages.

The New Populist Discourse

A sketch of the conditions that promote the new political rhetoric would suggest that the New Politics features themes of opposition and participation, excuses coalition-building appeals, emphasizes the candidate as individual rather than as a representative of party interests, and constructs the candidate's persona as outsider not insider. To get beyond such a general characterization, I now outline the concrete manifestations of these new appeals. Loosely categorized, the discourse of Democratic presidential contenders, 1968-1988, falls into three categories: factional populism, stylistic populism, and coalitional traditionalism. The first two categories represent the "new" and the last a remaining strain of the "old."

Factional Populism

This populist manifestation characteristized the candidacies of George McGovern, Alan Cranston, and the early Jesse Jackson. Each candidate's campaign promoted particular anti-establishment interests. McGovern (1972) closely tied his campaign to movement issues. The Senator pledged to "halt the senseless bombing of Indochina on Inauguration Day." He promised "within 90 days of my inauguration, every American soldier and every American prisoner will be out of the jungle and out of their cells and back home in America where they belong" (p. 611).

Alan Cranston championed the nuclear freeze movement (Solo, 1988, pp. 145-170). On the front of his campaign brochure the following words appeared: "to date, the only Presidential candidate who has a life long record of working to end the threat of nuclear war ... the only candidate who has made a verifiable *nuclear freeze the central focus* of his campaign ... the only candidate with the courage to state that fundamental change in our attitudes and the style of our leaders is essential for our survival is ... ALAN

CRANSTON" ("Our Generation" n.d, 1).

Similarly, Jesse Jackson's candidacy represented black interests. "My constituency," Reverend Jackson (1987) told the 1984 convention, "is the damned, the disinherited, the disrespected, and the despised. They are restless and seek relief. They've voted in record numbers. They have invested faith, hope, and trust in us. The Democratic party must send them a signal that we care. I pledge my best not to let them down" (p. 3).

This sense of populism is close to the term's familiar historical referent. Agrarian populists represented an aggrieved constituency motivated to political action by the unsavory economic behavior of Eastern bankers and industrialists. The same exigencies, which once created third-party candidacies, now result in factional populist campaigns. With the comparative ease of entry, we would expect more such efforts under party reform.

Stylistic Populism

In the absence of a galvanizing national issue candidates continue to use populist discourse. As a result, the "new" is transformed from program to adjective. It is no longer the "new what"—as in the "new foreign policy" or the "new civil rights agenda"—but just the "new." Here the "new" is not a political interest, but a moral *ethos*. New political leadership promises to heal the American spirit. Jimmy Carter's 1976 announcement address diagnosed the country's ills in just these terms: "Our commitment to these dreams [promises of decency, equality, and freedom, of an honest and responsible government] has been sapped by debilitating compromise, acceptance of mediocrity, subservience to special interests, and an absence of executive vision and direction" (Carter 1977, p. 430).

Jerry Brown ran a much similar campaign, yet one uniquely marked by the Governor's California-Zen rhetoric. During the 1976 primary campaign, Brown parodied the old instrumental politics: "'In massive assault on urban decay he today proposed a six-point program, including a blue-ribbon commission ... '" He added, "I mean I can write these things in my sleep. All it is, it's an illusion. It's the two-page program. I'm turned off by that stuff, and I think the American people are turned off by it, and I'm not going to do it." As an alternative, he offered "maybe a reconcilement to the basic uncertainty of life, and that provides a certain form of certainty" (A. Lewis, 1976, p. 29). As Anthony Lewis (1976) commented, Brown was "a symbolic opposite to the old Humphrey politics of promise and spending" (p. 29).

In both populist manifestations, factionalist and stylistic, candidates contrast the "new" with the "old." The "new" may represent the agenda of an anti-establishment faction or the prophet's call for moral betterment in the presence of a debased old politics. Put differently, factionalist populism finds justification in acts while stylistic populism finds justification in agent and agency.

Coalitional Traditionalism

Coalitional traditionalism describes the campaign discourse of Edmund Muskie and Walter Mondale. George McGovern defeated the pre-primary favorite Edmund Muskie in 1972, but Mondale succeeded with the traditional appeals that had served Democratic politicians since Roosevelt. Mondale (1984) filled his convention address with appeals to the various factions that made up the New Deal coalition: the elderly—"You did not vote to savage Social Security and Medicare"; Jews—"America condemns [the Soviet] repression of dissidents and Jews"; union members—"To big companies that send our best jobs overseas, my message is: We need those jobs at home. And our country won't help your business—unless your business helps our country"; farmers—"You did not vote to destroy family farming" (pp. 642-644).

I am not contending that the new political incentives are so powerful that they screen out all vestiges of the old political rhetoric. I am arguing, however, that what was once the rhetorical norm is now merely an aberration. Remember Mondale nearly lost to a much less well organized new politician. "Gary Hart," Alan Ehrenhart (1987) observed, "did as much as anyone to discredit [interest groups], taunting Walter Mondale from New Hampshire to California ... as the candidate beholden to grasping labor unions who hoped to place a tool in the White House" (p. 955). As a result, Mondale looked "uncomfortably like yesterday's man" ("Hart's Run" 1984, p. 11).

New Images of Civic Virtue

Speaking of "new" versus "old" in politics always invites skepticism. After all, the New Land, the New Deal, and the New Frontier pre-dated party reform. Generational appeals—the claim that a new generation of leaders is needed to face a new set of more complex problems—have constituted campaign boilerplate from the beginning of electoral politics. In Gary Hart's rhetoric of "new ideas," for instance, he purposely reiterates the generational appeals of John F. Kennedy. Yet, despite the "new's" long political history, the upheaval of 1968 fundamentally changed the term's use. A comparison of the "new" and the "old" provides the data necessary to support this claim. In doing this, I consider what constitutes an "image of civic virtue" and examine campaign discourse 1932-1968, the "old," and 1968-1988, the "new," to substantiate the alteration of images.

In recent years moral philosophers have spilled a great deal of ink discussing the nuances of "virtue." Simply put, a moral evaluation of virtue depends on the requisite relationship between behavior and intention

(MacIntyre 1981, ch. 14), the ratio between act and purpose (Burke 1969, pp. 3-20, 42).⁴ To pronounce an individual's action patriotic, for example, requires the knowledge that the behavior was done for the good of the country. Consequently, the revelations of profiteering from the Contra diversion severely undercut Oliver North's patriotic image. Virtue always inquires about both what was done and why it was done. When virtue enters the arena of electoral politics, additional questions get asked. Who is virtuous? Where are the virtuous to be found? How can politics be virtuous?⁵ These last three questions dominate the new political discourse and by implication redefine civic virtue.

Who. The new political turn in electoral campaigning identifies the virtuous as common citizens. This veneration of the ordinary person finds expression in all definitions of populism. For example, "Populism proclaims the will of the people as such is supreme over every other standard" (Shils 1956, p. 98) or "Any creed or movement based on the following premise: *virtue resides in the simple people, who are the overwhelming majority, and in their collective traditions*" (Wiles 1969, p. 166).

Surprisingly, the differing visions of John and Robert Kennedy capture the redefinition of "The People." In his Yale commencement address on June 11, 1962, John Kennedy (1962) gave the fullest expression of the elitism inherent in the New Frontier.⁶ He began with the premise that politics had changed since the early days of the republic. "Today," he told his audience, "these old sweeping issues have largely disappeared. The central domestic problems of our time are more subtle and less simple." These new problems did not relate to "basic clashes of philosophy or ideology, but to ways and means of reaching common goals—to research for sophisticated solutions to complex and obstinate issues" (p. 578). The President said, "[T]he unfortunate fact of the matter is that our rhetoric has not kept pace with the speed of social and economic change. Our political debate, our public discourse on current domestic and economic issues, too often bears little or no relation to the actual problems the United States faces." This was because "what we need are not labels and clichés but more basic discussion of the *sophisticated and technical* [my emphasis] questions involved" and this was "basically an *administrative or executive problem* [my emphasis] in which political labels or clichés do not give us a solution" (p. 580). As an example, the President discussed budgetary and banking policy: "I am suggesting that the problems of fiscal and monetary policy in the sixties as opposed to the kinds of problems we faced in the thirties demand subtle challenges for which *technical answers—not political answers* [my emphasis]—must be provided" (p. 581).

The so-called heir apparent to Camelot, a scant five-and-a-half years later, created in the name of the New Politics a counter-vision that supplanted the New Frontier in Democratic Party discourse. Moreover, Robert

Kennedy's rhetoric justified the new vision by directly critiquing the New Frontier (obviously not by name). The very title of the Senator's book, *To Seek a Newer World*, captured the tension between the technical and the ideological. In almost direct counterpoint to his brother's Yale address, Kennedy (1967) wrote, "Every generation has its central concern, whether to end war, erase racial injustice, or improve the condition of the working man. Today's young people have chosen for their concern the dignity of the individual human being." He continued, "They demand a limitation upon excessive power. They demand a political system that preserves the sense of community among men" (p. 16).

For Robert Kennedy the ordinary citizen, especially as part of a local community, was the actor capable of formulating virtuous political action. Most pronounced in his civil rights discourse but present in his discussions of all domestic issues, Kennedy contrasted the futile designs of Washington planners with the meaningful efforts of individual communities. He wrote, "Everything that is done must be in direct response to the needs and wishes of the people themselves. To do this, it will be necessary to create new community institutions that local residents control, and through which they can express their wishes" (Kennedy 1967, p. 42). Later, Kennedy approvingly quoted Lewis Mumford, "Democracy, in any active sense, begins and ends in communities small enough for their members to meet face to face" (p. 53). This vision that political wisdom springs spontaneously from ordinary Americans in concrete communities defined Robert Kennedy's populism.

A second part of Robert Kennedy's critique of the New Frontier aimed at his brother's discussion of political discourse. John Kennedy complained that ideological talk frustrates the sophisticated thinking required to solve the difficult technical problems of the new age. By contrast, Robert Kennedy argued that the technical jargon of the Washington bureaucrats frustrates the expression of the community's will. This frustration precluded the meaningful citizen participation necessary to the solutions of our most difficult social problems.

John and Robert Kennedy represent rhetorically what came before and after. President Kennedy fit comfortably in a Democratic Party tradition. Franklin Roosevelt, a frequent reference in John Kennedy discourse, celebrated visionary leadership's ability to lead an often wayward people. In his 1932 Democratic Party acceptance address, he identified progress with the virtues of Woodrow Wilson. "Our indomitable leader," Roosevelt insisted, "in that interrupted march [of progress] is no longer with us, but there still survives today his spirit ... Let us feel that in everything we do there still lives with us, if not the body, the great indomitable, unquenchable, progressive soul of our Command-in-Chief, Woodrow Wilson" (Rauch 1957, p. 70). Later in the address, Roosevelt chastised the public for its lack of virtue: "Let us be frank in acknowledgment of the truth that many amongst us have made obeisance to Mammon, that the profits of specula-tions, the easy road without toil, have lured us from the old barricades. To return to higher standards we must abandon the false prophets and seek new leaders of our own choosing" (p. 73).

Interestingly, John Kennedy picked up Roosevelt's theme in his discus-sion of the Presidency before the National Press Club. He asserted, "Despite the increasing evidence of a lost national purpose and a soft national will, F.D.R.'s words in his first inaugural still ring true: 'In every dark hour of our national life, a leadership of frankness and vigor has met with that under-standing and support of the people themselves which is essential to vic-tory'" ("Text" 1960, p. 14). Later in the speech, Kennedy provided an even clearer expression of a virtuous president creating rather than reflecting the public will. The president "must act," Kennedy said, "in the image of Abraham Lincoln summoning his war time cabinet to a meeting on the Emancipation Proclamation. That Cabinet had been carefully chosen to please and reflect many elements in the country. But 'I have gathered you together,' Lincoln said, 'to hear what I have written down. I do not wish your advice about the main matter—that I have determined for myself'" (p. 14).

In the same spirit, Adlai Stevenson's discourse resonated with the theme of virtuous leadership calling out the best in an often straying public. In his 1952 acceptance address, Stevenson (1952) said, "That is the test of a political party—the acid, final test. When the tumult and the shouting die, when the bands are gone and the lights dimmed, there is the stark reality of responsibility in an hour of history haunted with those gaunt, grim spectres of strife, dissension and materialism at home, and ruthless, inscrutable and hostile power abroad" (p. 646). A few sentences later, he added, "Let's tell them the truth, that there are no gains without pains, that this is the eve of great decisions, not easy decisions ... long, patient, costly struggle which alone can assure triumph" (p. 646).

Finally, Lyndon Johnson's 1960 pre-convention campaign emphasized the importance of the virtuous insider. The country needed, he said, a leader of tested experience and not merely a popular conduit of public sentiment. He emphasized, "Since 1937, in F.D.R.'s time, I have known the Presi-dency—and the men in it—intimately." He warned, "All the forces of evil in this world will stand ready to strike at freedom through whatever weaknesses America shows. Those forces will have no mercy for innocence, no gallantry toward inexperience, no patience toward errors" ("Transcript" 1960, p. 18).

Robert Kennedy's rhetoric represented a new generation of discourse. In this new portrayal, leaders are neither containers nor progenitors of virtue, but, rather, corrupt agents whose moral salvation depends on deposing political interests for identification with the people's innate goodness. Jimmy Carter's 1976 campaign theme, "A Government as Good as Its People," struck perfectly this shift in virtue from leader to follower. He played this rhetorical chord in his announcement speech: "The root of the problem is not so much that our people have lost confidence in government but that government has demonstrated time and again its lack of confidence in the people." The way out of our moral crisis is to bridge "this chasm between people and government" and "for American citizens to join in shaping our nation's future" (Carter 1977, p. 44). In 1988, Bruce Babbitt (1988) wove this vision of ordinary citizen virtue into his economic program. "Somehow," he explained, "we got the idea that innovation and company performance depend on a tiny, elite corps of highly paid executives, and that their workers are interchangeable units of labor." In his vision, "We must turn away from a concept of employees as mere costs, and toward an understanding that they are among a company's most important assets" (p. 8). Jesse Jackson, politically schooled in the civil rights movement, sees virtue among the least fortunate. It is from their effort, their empowerment, that America may become virtuous. In the conclusion of his 1984 convention speech, Reverend Jackson (1987) constructed this theme: "Jesus was rejected from the inn and born in the slum. But just because you were born in a slum does not mean that the slum was born in you. With a made-up mind, which is the most powerful instrument in the world, you can rise above your circumstances" (p. 18).

The old politics located virtue in the qualities of leadership that called "The People" to aspire to be better than they are. The New Politics transforms this calculus and finds virtuous leadership only among those who aspire to be as good as the people. In answer to "Who is and is not virtuous?" the new politicians respond that elites are cut off from the source of virtue and only a representative of the ordinary people may possess political morality.

Where. Answering the question "Where are the virtuous to be found?" requires clarification of its terms. Only extremists, racists, and fanatic nationalists answer this question literally, but all political visions address the question symbolically.[7] Put in the form of American electoral politics, the question reads, "In what form of community do the virtuous reside?"

The "old" and the "new" correspond to two different visions of community. The old community of the New Deal and the Great Society was a national community. The new community of electoral populism is a local community. "The idea of national community," William Schambra (1985) observed, "[has], in fact, been in decline for over a decade and a half" (pp. 31-32). Lyndon Johnson's oratory of the Great Society described a national community. Johnson appealed to the conception of America as a single community in which the federal government provides sustenance for its inhabitants. "I see a day ahead with a united nation," Johnson said, "divided neither by class nor by section nor by color, knowing no South or North, no East or West, but just one great America, free of malice and free of hate, and loving thy neighbor as thyself." "I see a family" that "takes care of all of its members in time of adversity ... I see our nation as a free and generous land with its people bound together by common ties of confidence and affection, and common aspirations toward duty and purpose." America, he argued, must "turn unity of interest into unity of purpose, and unity of goals into unity in the Great Society." Johnson understood his civil rights program as "often painful but always successful reconciliation of different people into our national community" (quoted in Schambra 1985).

Johnson's predecessor, John Kennedy, constantly spoke of a citizenry that should throw off its traditions in favor of a new national vision. He told the delegates in Los Angeles, "All over the world ... young men are coming to power—men who are not bound by the traditions of the past—men who are not blinded by the old fears and hates and rivalries—young men who can cast off the old slogans and delusions and suspicions" (Kennedy 1960, p. 611). In the context of his acceptance address this is not an attack on the coalitional interests of the party but a progressive call for a rupture with provincialism. For Kennedy this new community depended on national leadership: "The Presidency is the most powerful office in the free world. Though its leadership can come a more vital life for our people ... For it is the Executive Branch that the most crucial decisions of this century must be made in the next four years" ("Kennedy Statement" p. 44).

This old liberal vision sees regional and ethnic differences as hidebound provincialism, efforts of states and localities as the futility of the unsophisticated, and societal problems giving way to the rational thought of science (Schambra 1982, pp. 42-46). Such a vision necessarily celebrates the president and his administrative apparatus as the leader and structure of this new world of enlightenment. This form of liberal politics must appeal to the expertise of an elite.

In striking contrast, Jimmy Carter captured the virtue of a politics rooted in local community. In his campaign speeches, he was fond of telling a story about reading *War and Peace* when he was twelve years old. After explaining the circumstances under which he tackled the thick volume, he interpreted the book's meaning for an American audience during the election season. He started, "But the book is not about Napolean or the Czar of Russia. It is about the common ordinary people—barbers, housewives, privates in the army, farmers, and others—and the point Tolstoy makes is that the course of human events, even the greatest historical events, are controlled and shaped not by the leaders of nations but by the combined hopes and dreams and aspirations and courage and conviction of the common ordinary people" (Carter 1977, p. 75).

In a speech less than a week before the election, Carter (1977) provided a vision of America that stands in stark contrast to Lyndon Johnson's national community. At the Kennedy-Lawrence Dinner in Pittsburgh, Carter crafted this image:

> Our country is made up of pluralism, diversity. A lot of different kinds of people. But that's not a sign of weakness, it's a sign of strength. Some people have said that our nation is a melting pot. It's not. Whether we came to this country two years, twenty years, two hundred years ago—it doesn't matter. The point is why we came to this country. But when we come here, we haven't given up our individuality, our pride in our history or background or commitments or habits. We become not a melting pot but a beautiful mosaic. Different people, different beliefs, different yearnings, different hopes, different dreams (p. 243).

In the same vein, Jesse Jackson (1987) described his "rainbow coalition" in much the same words as Carter described America. He said, "America is not like a blanket, one piece of unbroken cloth—the same color, the same texture, the same size. It is more like a quilt—many patches, many pieces, many colors, many sizes, all woven and held together by a common thread" (p. xvii). Whether Jackson's "quilt" or Bush's "thousand points of light," the new political rhetoric rejects the unity of national community. As Jimmy Carter rightly observed, the melting pot is a spent image.

The New Politics provides a new answer to the question, "Where are the virtuous to be found?" They are found in far-flung, diverse local communities that are held together by ethnic heritage, regional traditions, and other forces of permanence. What were once thought of as the roadblocks to progress are here portrayed as the fertile soil that raises a moral citizenry.

How. The question "By what means can politics be virtuous?" focuses on issues of agency. In the old political vision, political party, as it represented organized interests, was the means to good government. In the new political vision, the agency of political virtue is participation. The source of political vice is nearly always some institutional impediment to the full force of the public will. Most often, new politicians characterize this impediment as the old interests of the party.

Estes Kefauver's case against President Eisenhower in a 1955 speech to the Democratic leadership in Chicago testified to "party's" virtuous status in the old politics. "I certainly would not feel," he said, "that I have anything like the personal attractiveness that President Eisenhower does, but I do sincerely believe that the party is awfully hard for him to pull alone, and that—there is broader and wider and greater strength in the Democratic party than in the Republican one, that this greater strength would more than make up for the great influence and the tremendous charm of President Eisenhower" ("Texts" 1955, p. 66). In stronger language, the same case was made by the nominee at the 1956 convention. "The truth is," Governor Stevenson (1956) said, "that the Republican party is a house divided. The truth is that President Eisenhower, cynically coveted as a leader, is largely indebted to the Democrats in Congress for what accomplishments he can claim" (p. 680).

John Kennedy echoed this theme at the National Press Club in 1960: "The facts of the matter are that legislative leadership is not possible without party leadership, in the political sense—and Mr. Eisenhower prefers to stay above politics." He continued, "But no President, it seems to me, can escape politics ... [I]f he blurs the issues and differences between parties—if he neglects the party machinery and avoids his party's leadership—then he has not only weakened the political party as an instrument of democratic process—he has dealt a blow to the democratic process itself" ("Text" 1960, p. 14). All of these Democratic candidates unashamedly championed the working class and spoke of agenda consistent with the interests of the coalition of groups that represented labor, agriculture, the elderly, and the poor.

By contrast, post-1968 candidates run around, and often against, the party. These candidates distance themselves from "special interests" and run as an individual above politics. They tell voters that virtue will triumph when a president has a deep and abiding empathy for the concerns of the ordinary citizen. In this sense, candidates' most important qualifications for office are not matters of administrative experience, legislative proposals, or foreign policy initiatives, but their ability to mirror the feeling of the electorate.

The new political candidates expend considerable rhetorical energy on reiterating the match between their dispositions and the dispositions of the electorate. It is not merely an issue of understanding the people's interests, but, more importantly, actually feeling these interests in a visceral way. The candidate, as a feeling conduit, must come from a different place than traditional politicians. "This year," Jimmy Carter (1977) told a Town Hall Forum audience, "voters were looking for new leaders, leaders who were not associated with the mistakes of the past. This is suggested not only by my own campaign but by the success that Governor Jerry Brown achieved in several Democratic primaries, and that Governor Reagan achieved in the Republican campaign. For however else we may differ, Governors Brown and Reagan and I have in common that fact that we are all outsiders as far as Washington is concerned, and committed to major changes in our nation's government if elected President" (p. 140). Only from this place among the people can the voters find the person to channel their feelings to government.

The New Politics provides a new answer to the question "By what means can politics be virtuous?" The answer is not an ideological program, not a set of policies, but a state of emotional being. The president's capacity to radiate the moral fervor of "The People" assures a virtuous state. The candidate promises to translate such fervor into progress. This form of action defies philosophical labels because its ultimate end is realized in an emotional sense of well being.

The New Ideology of Civic Virtue

The virtues establish normative criteria by which individuals can judge citizen performance of social roles. In ancient Greece, Homer captured the meaning of *arete* in his epic portrayal of the warrior-king Achilles. Likewise, contemporary political discourse, by identifying heroes and villians, instructs "The People" in what counts as virtuous civic behavior. Once understood, these virtues and vices form the basic building blocks of ideology.

I have described the old political vision and the new political critique of that vision. The "new" characterizes the "old" as "a politics of interest group bargaining, normally conducted by professionals; or a politics of the nation, expressing generalized visions of common purpose uniting disparate groups" (Evans & Boyte 1986, p. 5n). In an effort to contain conflict between interest groups, legislators wrote bills creating independent regulatory agencies to arbitrate clashes between labor and business, developer and environmentalist, investor and market. The important decisions that should succumb to the public will were relegated to bureaucratic decision making. The resultant bureaucratic rationality usurped moral leadership with a utilitarian calculus that pushes aside cultural standards and tradition. Modern liberal government severed political justification from notions of human purpose.

In reaction, the new political rhetoric collapses the distinction between agency and purpose. Citizen empowerment is both the means and ends of politics. "All our 'new politicians,'" Garry Wills (1979) argued, "share the assumption that modern man's trouble comes from the fact that he is not participating in affairs, either because he was never given the chance (he is *un*politicized, like the blacks in the South) or because new conditions prevent him from continuing his participation (he is *de*politicized, like the discontented middle class)" (pp. 462-463). In this vision, participation gives rise to a democratic consciousness, which leads to the formation of genuine political community, and, ultimately, to the creation of a virtuous political state.

In the New Politics, citizens are victims. The new political discourse suggests that old political arrangements are corrupted or enfeebled. Robert Kennedy and Eugene McCarthy claimed that the selection process was undemocratic (party bashing); Jimmy Carter argued that government was morally dishonest (politician bashing); Gary Hart contended that present ideas sapped the nation's sense of purpose (liberal bashing); and Richard Gephardt maintained that old arrangements sacrificed national economic interests (Japan bashing). Such appeals define vast segments of the public as abandoned victims of elite interests. Thus, each candidacy becomes a crusade to sweep out the corrupt, the unresponsive, and the incompetent.

Thus, virtue motivates resentment against the old arrangements. Virtuous citizens play out their role as a moral people by participating in a new political narrative and identifying with the candidate-hero. Candidate identification becomes a substitute for genuine action. By acting as supporter, the viewer becomes a meaningful participant in the community. Given the collapse of agency and purpose, civic virtue requires only this form of pseudo-participation.

Traditionally, partisan commitments defined public philosophy. The party standard bearers identified with a coalition of interests that placed them along a liberal-conservative continuum. This form of political rhetoric identified a candidate's ideology by the purposes it articulated, the policies it sought to enact. But the collapse of agency and purpose, the decline of party, and the repudiation of organized interests do not permit the ideological portrayal of an ideal society. After all, the place where left and right meet is in a belief in the righteousness of an unfettered public will. Sociologists Schweitzer and Elden (1971) recognized that "on several issues proponents of both the New Left and the conventional Right often attack the system together." "It is a response," they argued, "essentially to the growing structural complexity of a larger, mass, post-industrial society characterized by an increasing bureaucratization of personal lives in most organizational spheres of social life and a concomitant removal of power sources from the everyday world of the individual" (p. 161).

Yet, given this general ideological construction of the new populism, there still remains liberal-conservative, Democratic-Republican differences. The two visions are *structurally* consonant—each focuses on the force of the people's virtue—but they are *ideologically* disconsonant in that each differs in describing the nature of virtue. If one accepts this distinction, the axes progressive-traditional and local-national form an interesting ideological matrix. The four quadrants in Figure 3.1 represent the parties' four electoral visions; the top two are the old politics and the bottom two are the New Politics.[8] The local-national axis captures the structural similarity because in each vision virtue springs from "The People" living in local communities. The progressive-traditional axis captures the ideological dissimilarity because the resultant impulse of "The People" differ.

Conservative populists trace the origins of their vision (often called "small republicanism") back to the Antifederalists. Consequently, conservatives follow a line of development from Patrick Henry's arguments

Figure 3.1 Matrix of Liberal and Conservative Visions

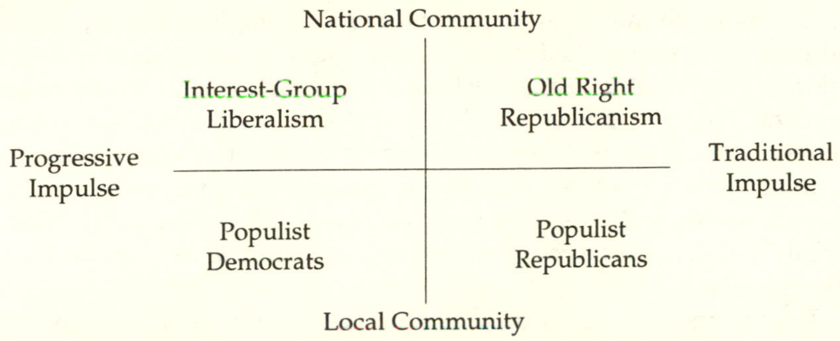

National Community

Interest-Group Liberalism	Old Right Republicanism

Progressive Impulse   Traditional Impulse

Populist Democrats	Populist Republicans

Local Community

against strong national government to Goldwater's states rights rhetoric to Reaganism. The Federalists, accordingly, argued for a strong central government to promote commerce. Hence, "there would be a sort of civic virtue to be had from the everyday and ordinary activities of a people engaged in commerce and pursuit of self-interest" (McDowell 1987, pp. 125-126). Antifederalist opposition rested on the conviction that civic virtue must be nurtured in local community. "The underlying (and largely unifying) sentiment that characterized Antifederalism," Gary McDowell (1987) wrote, "was the belief that a 'community of mere interest' was insufficient to secure safe republican government and political liberty. The Antifederalists believed that 'the American polity had to be a moral community if it was to be anything, and they saw the seat of that community must be in the hearts of the people'" (p. 126). This continuous ideological strain in conservative thought permits the Republicans to employ a cohesive populist message. Since the purging of the moderate (so-called Rockefeller) wing of the GOP, appeals to traditional values in local community draw together Republican voters (Polsby 1983, pp. 85-88).

Liberal populists find inspiration in agrarian revolts, labor uprisings, suffrage struggles, and the civil rights movement. In this story, these struggles created true democratic consciousness that led "The People" to see the inconsistency between principle and performance. These historical antecedents provide evidence for populism's progressive impulse (Boyte 1986). As a consequence, progressives may serve their political ends with the language of populism and avoid discourse associated with European socialism. "The [language of the] left in the modern world has been able to name the problems," Boyte (1986) argued. "But its solutions have been trapped by the very terms of the system that it challenges" (p. 5). In the wake of the welfare state's perceived failure and Nixon's silent and new majorities, populist terminology permits the simultaneous affirmation of progressivism and denunciation of interest-group liberalism. Unfortunately this heritage—labor movements, civil rights, etc.—was built on political visions of national community. Martin Luther King, Jr. championed integration and defined a people unmarked by race. Labor unions gained power by forming national unions that cut across the traditions of individual craft and particular plant. Electoral power was built on these different groups finding common ground to create a progressive national community. Democrats, spanning George Wallace to Edward Kennedy, find little ground for ideological cohesion and must seek unity of interest. Put differently, the ideological diversity of local community does not serve the Democratic Party's purposes.

In sum, the new political rhetoric (in its commonest stylistic-populist form) presents the citizenry with the ideology of character. Recall that I have argued the essential attraction of the new politicians is the appeal of citizen empowerment. The agency of this empowerment is the character of the candidate. The candidates feel and mirror the electorate's resentment against whatever object defines this incarnation of the New Politics. The parties maintain some ideological identity because each interprets the impulse of citizen empowerment differently. Each finds a different moral force reflected in their populist candidates. Admittedly, an increasing focus on agent and agency together with a decreasing focus on act and purpose make this ideological distinction more difficult to identify. Yet, as each party seeks to attract new constituencies (i.e., the so-called Reagan Democrats or the Hart yuppies), I suspect this is the very point.

Conclusions

In any sustained activity where interests conflict, there will be stories of the "new." Thus, each generation discovers a new ethic (New Age), a new order (New Economic Reality), or a new academic posture (New Rhetoric). William Jennings Bryan and Theodore Roosevelt brought progressive ideas to their respective parties and changed the prevailing sense of "The People" (Woodward 1983). Franklin Roosevelt's New Deal created a class-based coalitional discourse that defined the party's liberalism until the upheavals of 1968. A new oppositional politics spawned these historical electoral changes. Likewise, the present case is marked by the transition from coalitional to a new populist discourse. Moreover, this new populism ushers in a new vision of civic virtue.

Having characterized this particular manifestation of the "new," I am left with the task of providing some normative evaluation. After all, the practitioners of this New Politics insist on its moral efficacy in governing our affairs. Given such claims, the analyst is issued a mandate to judge the merit of these assertions. Because virtue is a functional concept, I will apply the new populists' own success criteria. First, does the new populist rhetoric actually have the potential to empower citizens? Second, does its discourse of community have the potential to create a vibrant community? Third, is truth-telling discourse itself honest? Finally, as a summary question, is this new discourse of virtue virtuous?

First, the new populism symbolically invigorates democracy by weakening institutions that give citizens influence. Because the rhetoric of citizen empowerment continually criticizes existing arrangements, political factions and their organizational manifestions—labor, agriculture, small business—are repudiated as mediating institutions that dilute the people's will.

Second, the new populists reject national community for faith in the progressive impulses of local community. Ironically, at a time when urban living has made neighbors strangers and mobility has extinguished the extended family, our politics celebrates the nurturing local community. At an earlier time, when most people lived in small towns and large families, our politics celebrated grand visions of national community. Perhaps in an age of television, when we all share the same political experiences, we want difference. In an earlier age when location, ethnic background, and economic circumstances determined our political experiences, we longed for unity. We wish for what we do not have. Politicians give us images of "ought" rather than "is."

Earlier agrarian demagogues attest to populism's often ugly legacy (Gunderson 1940; Lomas 1955; Smith 1959). Although the new politicians have not displayed the stridency of earlier populists, the same tension exists between pluralism and a discourse of citizen empowerment. The anti-elitism of the New Politics encourages the deprecation of legitimate groups that have historically made up the Democratic Party coalition. On the right, George Wallace portrayed the interests of minorities as antithetical to the concerns of ordinary white voters. Interestingly, similar charges have been made against social conservatism and its legitimation of a new racism (see Miller, Chapter 11). On the left, McGovern's populist discourse alienated whole blocks of the New Deal coalition (e.g., George Meany and labor).

As is everything else about the New Politics, this anti-pluralist strain is paradoxical. The new populists claim to bring everyone into the political community by rejecting the melting pot of the national community and embracing the quilt patches of local communities. Yet, inevitably the advocacy of *a* community's interest is against some interests in *the* community. Thought of in another way, pluralism defines "The People" in very concrete ways by identifying specific groups—religious, ethnic, social—whose values deserve respect. Pluralism creates "The People" by inclusion. On the contrary, populism defines "The People" in very universal ways by refusing to identify the included. Instead, populism creates "The People" by the exclusion of named enemies. A discourse of resentment hardly seems the desirable vehicle for empowerment in a multifaceted polity.

Third, the new populism deceives the public. To the extent that this populist vision responds to societal problems, it does so dishonestly. Recall I have argued that the interplay of situation and discourse give rise to this populist incarnation. In this claim, "situation" refers to new circumstances of party reform and not to a new assessment of the national interest. Earlier populists (and contemporary factional populists) responded to social upheavals, largely the excesses of industrial capitalism, which found relief in progressive leaders and platforms. In this case, however, stylistic populism serves as an apparent non-ideological—at least non-left/liberal—cover for candidates trying to win primary elections.

Finally, little virtue exists in the new populism. Recall virtues designate qualities of persons who effectively perform their social roles. Dysfunctional virtues are by definition not virtues. The central argument of this essay is that populism—particularly stylistic populism—creates terrible problems for governing.

Campaigning influences office holders' approach to governing. Presidential contenders challenge an incredibly exhausting obstacle course when they pursue their party's nomination. Ronald Reagan, for example, actively pursued the presidency for more than eight years. Preparation for the actual attempt may have begun a decade earlier. A relatively unformed politician—like Jimmy Carter—once in office will naturally continue to exhibit the rhetorical behaviors that got him elected. Yet, governing requires just those skills that party reform made unimportant in the nomination process. Presidents must bargain with elites to form coalitions (Polsby 1983, pp. 89-130). Successful executive-congressional relations, for instance, require such skills.

Historically, Americans view themselves as a pragmatic people. We grow up embued with the can-do *ethos* of our forefathers. Yet, in the past twenty years we have constructed a selection process that discourages appeals to unity, rewards empty appeals to candidate identification, and shuns the politics of civic action. Moreover, as the stridency of resentment increases, the fragile ethic of pluralism becomes increasingly vulnerable (see Gronbeck, Chapter 4; Miller, Chapter 11). Aristotle understood that rhetoric and politics—the twin arts of virtue and expediency—could equate the desired with the desirable and make virtue out of vice.

Notes

1. The exception to this generalization is a couple of articles that tried to explain some aspect of the changing electoral campaign. See Brock (1969) and Swanson

(1972).

2. Clark Clifford's famous memo to Truman on the 1948 election outlined this strategy of cooptation (Walton 1976, pp. 298-304).

3. For an account of the power of the campaign ritual to mute pointed discussion of grievances, see Bennett (1977). In addition, the effect of such activity is to attract reformist support away from opposition movements and leave the radical core isolated and vulnerable to legal repressions (Mauss 1971).

4. Edmund Pincoffs (1986) presents a clear, though somewhat technical, definition of virtue. He argues, "[V]irtues and vices are dispositional properties that provide grounds for preference or for avoidance of persons" (p. 79). Moreover, "dispositions ... are not just tendencies to act in certain ways but also to feel, to think, and to react and to experience `passions'" (p. 81). Finally, on Pincoffs' functionalist view, "it is the tensions, tendencies, pleasures, and pains of common life, including the engagement in practices, that lead us to value or disvalue this or that quality as responding well or ill to what we go through together" (p. 97).

5. Who, what, where, how, and why designate Burke's pentad of motives for human action. He employs the terms agent, act, scene, agency, and purpose (Burke 1969).

6. Theodore Lowi (1979) cites the address as a "turning point in the practice and theory" of America's public philosophy (pp. 274-275). Lowi's harsh critique of this view is interesting given that he edited Robert Kennedy's *The Pursuit of Justice*. This is even more intriguing given Robert Kennedy's own subsequent rejection of the New Frontier.

7. Extremists specify the virtuous and are particular about exclusion of the nonvirtuous. For example, in Hitler's discourse Aryans were virtuous and Jews nonvirtuous; in the Klu Klux Klan's discourse Protestant whites are virtuous and non-Protestant, non-European people lack virtue; and so forth.

8. I have not discussed the Old Right in this essay. The New Right has spent a good deal of energy distinguishing itself from this older Republican tradition; see Whitaker (1982).

4

Negative Political Ads and American Self Images

Bruce E. Gronbeck

Personalized attacks upon one's opponent have been a staple of American presidential politics almost from the start. The 1796 race was, in the words of historian Page Smith (1963, p. 898), filled with "newspaper polemics, pamphlets, and political rallies" that attacked and defended the characters of Thomas Jefferson and John Adams. He notes that, in Massachusetts, "[h]andbills denouncing Adams as an aristocrat and monarchist were nailed to gateposts, doors of houses, and posts ... and men were hired to ride through the state, their saddlebags stuffed with Anti-Federal broadsides" (pp. 901-902). Jefferson was depicted as a dupe of a foreign power, France, and Adams was accused of being an elitist with no faith in the people (Boller 1985). By the election of 1828, Jamieson (1984) found, electors favorable to the various presidential candidates were equally praised or vilified for their political preferences, and even sample ballots associating particular electors with particular candidates circulated in Pennsylvania that year.

The electronic presidential campaigning extended the reach of communications—and political acrimony. Radio came to presidential campaigns in 1924, when there were 500 stations and three million receivers in the U.S. That year it featured the 103 successive ballots at the Democratic National Convention required when "Klucks" (Ku Klux Klan members and sympathizers) took on "Turks" (anti-Klan forces) in the battle that saw Al Smith triumph over Gibbs McAdoo in a seventeen-day marathon (Becker & Lower 1962). The GOP's nomination of Calvin Coolidge was stunted by comparison, though later certainly Coolidge's ability to adapt his speechifying and evaluations of his opponent to radio contributed to his victory over Smith (Fleser 1966). By 1936, James A. Farley, chair of the Democratic National Committee and manager of Roosevelt's campaign, saw radio's reach in counterattack as cementing his victory:

The influence of radio in determining the outcome of the 1936 election can hardly be overestimated. Without the unrivaled medium for reaching millions of voters, the work of overcoming the false impression created by the tons of propaganda put out by foes of the New Deal would have been many times greater than it was, and, to be candid, it might concievably have been an impossible job [Farley 1938, pp. 318-319].

The power to present one's self and one's opponent in dramatic and highly contrasting ways, however, was not maximized until the arrival of television and computerized editing. The first TV ads came in 1952, when Dwight Eisenhower spent between $800,000 and $1.5 million on spots, somewhere between ten and twenty times the $77,000 spent by Adlai Stevenson. With music by Irving Berlin, animation by Walt Disney, and words by Ben Duffy of Batten, Barton, Durstine, and Osborn, the Eisenhower campaign drove America into the Unseeing Eye (*pacem* Patterson & McClure 1976) of candidate-sponsored video.

Even as late as Patterson and McClure's groundbreaking study of presidential TV ads in the 1972 campaign, forty percent of the ads had characteristics of documentary-style television, running five to thirty minutes (Kern 1989). By the 1980s, however, that had changed. In her study of the 1984, 1986 bi-electoral, and 1988 campaigns, Kern found the move to thirty and sixty second spots almost complete, with short spots presented in such density as to become a political information source able to overwhelm news coverage in terms of sheer facts, let alone feel-good and feel-bad images. She also documented the steady rise of negative political advertising in that decade, culminating in 1988 in what *Newsweek* (1988, p. 100) termed "one of the most negative national campaigns since the McCarthy era—so negative, at its worst moments, as to invite the suspicion that George Bush would say nearly anything to win"—with Michael Dukakis liable to the same comment.

As *Newsweek* suggested, negative campaigns come and go in this country, riding a kind of emotional sine wave through our electoral history. The present phase began in earnest, it would seem, in 1978, when pressure groups and political action committees (PACs) targeted a series of congressional and Senate seats for attack. That year, a web of New Right organizations took credit for attacking incumbents and seizing five "liberal" seats in the Senate: Gordon Humphrey winning in New Hampshire, Roger Jepsen in Iowa, Bill Armstrong in Colorado, John Warner in Virginia, and Alan Simpson in Wyoming. Another twenty-five conservative congressional representatives allegedly won that year thanks to PAC work (Viguerie 1980). From that beginning, the use of negative advertising continued to grow through the next decade.

In this chapter, we will take negative political advertising seriously. If we are to understand both its positive and its negative roles in electoral politics, however, we need to carefully define it; examine the argumentative and narrative structures of such ads into order to assay their rhetorical engines; discuss explicitly how it is that they both contribute to and detract from voter decision making as we understand that process within a democratic political framework; and, ultimately, to ask difficult questions about relationships between negative ads and America's conceptions of citizenship, political process, and political culture, especially in presidential campaigns.

Defining the Negative

Simply put, a "negative political advertisement" is one that creates unattractive or undesirable images of one's political opponents. This is a broader definition than many have offered in previous research; that broadening is suggested because some of the previous restrictions on this category of political messages make it all too easy to simply condemn them as harmful to political process and culture.

For example, Stewart (1975, p. 179) discussed "mud-slinging" and defined a mudslinger as a "person guilty of spreading rumors, making insinuations, perpetuating deceptions, telling lies, and calling names." Such a definition led him to deride the practice because its practitioners were seen by the public as "untrustworthy, dishonest, incompetent, unqualified, unlikable, not self-confident, and immature" (p. 285). Similarly, Trent and Friedenberg (1991, p. 84) discussed the "smear tactics and political hatch work" that candidates assign to "surrogate speakers" because "[d]emagogy is never viewed as an asset and normally backfires for the challenger who employs it." Diamond and Bates (1984 ed.) associated the so-called third phase of a political campaign with the "attack ad," which was characterized as "[n]amecalling, direct personal attacks, man-on-the-street, and symbolic attacks" used "to discredit the opponent" and "most frequently delivered by surrogate speakers" (Payne & Baukus 1985, p. 5).

Such terms as "mudslinging," "demagoguery," and "attack," of course, foster disparaging analyses in part by negative semantic loading. The words themselves suggest strong disapproval, and the definitions call up practices that run counter to the democratic ideal of the testing of candidates in the marketplace of political ideas. As well, they focus on the socially suspect motives and attributes of their users rather than the ways in which they shape their targets, the opponents, and their functions within the electoral process.

A more rewarding discussion may be possible if we neutralize for a bit the matter under discussion. Cragan and Cutbirth (1984) do just that in their attempt to rehabilitate the notion of *ad hominem* argument, urging us to consider the examination of personal circumstances of candidates not as a fallacy but as a way to understand a candidate's fitness:

> Although it is nearly axiomatic that candidates seek office by running 'on the issues,' it seems clear that a primary concern of the campaign is which person is best able to represent the voters. The policy questions that candidates address, while important, are far more transitory than is fitness for office. The candidate, as a human being, will be called upon to make decisions on behalf of the voters regarding issues which may be unclear at the time of the campaign. The primary message of the campaign must therefore be 'trust me rather than my opponent' [p. 229].

Such a viewpoint forces us to deal with character, competing *ethoi*, as central to political campaigning—even as the focus of issues and ways they are received when presented to the Led by would-be Leaders. The heart of campaigning, in this view, is the creation of arguments and stories that indicate to and show us why one should vote both for them and against their opponents (Tarrance 1982). In this view, negative ads are (potentially) merely the counterparts of positive ads, with both centering matters of political judgment on character judgment. To define the negative TV spot, then, as one that creates unattractive and undesirable images of one's opponent (1) potentially specifies a ground for political judgment (2) as portrayed in a multimediated message (3) attributed to a particular candidate even if constructed and purchased by another (such as a PAC or interest group). That is, to accept this definition is to believe that character is central to electoral activity, that mass-mediated, candidate-controlled messages carry the bulk of the electoral information used in electoral decision making, and that voters make few or no distinctions between candidates and supporting groups.

We will come back to those assumptions later in this chapter. For now, let us examine the argumentative and narrative structures of negative ads, to see how they function rhetorically.

Argumentatively Structured Negative Ads

The easiest way to begin an analysis of the rhetorical structure of negative ads is to look at a group that operates argumentatively. The standard attack ad asserts and often tries to illustrate an unattractive or undesirable characteristic an opponent is presumed to have. The attack is argumentative in that an assertion together with some kind of evidence is offered. That evidence may include factual or fact-like statements, visual depictions or illustrations, graphs, analogies, or icons (material symbols that have come to have positive or negative associations). The evidence is not always connected in traditionally rational ways to the assertion, though the structure is reason-like; that is, there is a kind of assumed or asserted inference connecting something evidence-like with something proposition-like to present us with a piece of discourse that is argument-like.

We can isolate three broad classes of argumentatively structured negative ads: (1) *The implicative ad.* Some negative ads work primarily by implication or innuendo. The focus of the ad is on a candidate him- or herself; the opponent's unattractive or undesirable characteristics are brought up only as contrasts, often with a phrase such as "unlike my opponent, I ... " (2) *The comparative ad.* Many, perhaps even most, negative ads within an argumentative genre depend upon an explicit comparison between the candidate sponsoring the ad and the opponent. (3) *The assault ad.* Some ads in this genre do almost nothing but attack opponents; in extreme cases, the people making the ads are present only in the mandatory credits. The ad is clearly centered on the opponent, not the candidate, and designed to create a negative image, to depict unattractive or undesirable character. When wholly focused on the opponent, it is called a "true negative" by Newhagen and Reeves (1991, p. 198).

To see these rhetorical structures, let us examine some ads from the 1984 senatorial races. These have been chosen in part because they have been gathered together on a large scale by the News Study Group of Emerson College (Payne & Baukus 1985 collection) and hence are a convenient body of discourse, in part because there is a good deal more variety in local than national elections, and in part because of the sheer size of the body of ads (eighty-one ads from twenty-six different races). Of the eighty-one ads in the package, twenty-eight—over a third—met the definition of "negative political advertisement" offered earlier in this chapter. If we can assume the Emerson College sample at least approximates the distribution of political ads across the 1984 senatorial races, we are dealing with a significant political phenomenon. Let us examine some sample attack ads of each type.

Implicative Ads

Consider a line from one of the ads for John Raese (R-WV): "We have politicians who have been too busy making promises to solve our problems." Or, one from a Thad Cochran (R) appeal to Mississippians, after listing all of the progress made on economic matters over the last few years: "None of that was true some years ago, and we don't want to go back to those days again." Another Raese ad asserts "We haven't had leadership for the past few years." Or, running for the Senate in Massachusetts, Ray Shamie (R) preached in one of his ads that "It's not time for government to grow— it's time for America to grow." This sort of comment can be made via an extended metaphor, as witness a quotation from Texas turncoat Phil Gramm.

Perhaps because he needed to make sure that his change of party during Reagan's first term was not seen as disloyalty, he had to attack the Democrats:

> While they're promising every special interest group in Texas that they're going to bring home the bacon for them in return for their vote, you and I have got to be out pointing out that all of this bacon they're using to buy votes with is coming out of the smokehouses of the working men and women of Texas [Payne & Baukus 1985 collection].

More subtly, candidate's slogans can intone innuendoes: "Judy Pratt [D-NM]—The *Honest Choice.*" "Tom Harkin [D]: A Senator Iowa Can Be *Proud* Of." "Carl Levin [D]: A *Proven* Fighter For Michigan." Note, too, how Sam Kusic, running in the West Virginia GOP primary by attacking Jay Rockefeller's big monied interests as a Rockefeller, chose an image-defining refrain: "United, hold up for all to see,/Mountaineers are *always free.*"

In each of these commercials, we are given a portrait of the candidate, firm of jaw, steely eyed, serious of purpose. Only in the Sam Kusic ads is there any direct mention of an opposing candidate. In most, the opposition in implicative ads is specifically ignored, being referred to negatively, yes, but only in general terms. The usual content of such spots is a recitation of sacred American values or a review of the candidate's previous record. In these commercials, the negative innuendos are never allowed to dominate or become too intrusive. They function more to define the edges of the candidate than to attack the opponent.

The Comparative Ad

The gold standard of negative ads is the comparative spot, those advertisements where some aspects of candidates' personae or some stands they have taken are depicted as important dividing lines between people. In 1984, both parties' senatorial campaigns made liberal use of these message forms.

Sometimes, the comparison is there only implicitly. For example, Alabama Democratic candidate Howell Heflin is accused of taking money from special interests and voting against railroad retirement legislation, the implication being that his opponent (Albert Lee Smith) would not. Even more subtle is an ad run by Republican candidate Nancy Hoch, examining Nebraska incumbent Jim Exon. After noting his earnings during his senatorial term—some $410,000—the ad tells us that, nevertheless, Senator Exon has sponsored only one bill (to create National Theatre Week), that he missed over half of the Armed Services Committee hearings, and that *Newsweek* calls him a "backbencher." The ad finishes with the assertion that "It's time we had a senator who does the job and makes Nebraska proud—

Nancy Hoch for Senate."

More common is the explicit comparison between the candidates. For example, Michigan incumbent Democrat Carl Levin ran such an ad. First, we see a *Detroit News* headline reading "Auto Jobs Disappear Despite Recovery." Then we are told that Levin was in Washington, fighting to strengthen the American auto industry, while his opponent Jack Lousma was in Japan, Toyota Hall to be exact, telling the Japanese he owned a Toyota—a near fatal admission for a Michigan politician. Phil Gramm also ran a classic ad of this type, which focuses explicitly on "Taxes—the Reagan-Gramm record versus the Mondale-Doggett record." It continues: "Phil Gramm wrote the Reagan economic program in Congress, which provided a *25% tax cut*. On his first day in Congress, Phil Gramm introduced a constitutional amendment to *balance the budget*. But in the Texas legislature, Lloyd Doggett voted *against* the balanced budget amendment. And, Doggett has joined Walter Mondale in committing to *raise our taxes*. Before you vote, think about how *they'll* vote on taxes."

Or, comparisons may attempt to show inconsistencies in some candidate's record. Both the Harkin-Jepsen race (Iowa) and the Simon-Percy race (Illinois) were swamped with attacks on inconsistencies. Charles Percy (R-IL) is attacked for voting in favor of the grain embargo but then taking the accolades when Reagan removes it. In turn, Paul Simon (D-IL) is assaulted in a clever set of "Simon Says" ads. Here is one of them:

> Compare what Paul Simon says with what Paul Simon does. The differ-
> ence is startling. Simon said, 'I am opposed to deficit spending,' but when
> Congress cut spending by $131 billion for the largest deficit reduction in
> history, Simon not only voted no, he called it a 'day of shame.' Simon
> introduced legislation saying 'A youth opportunity wage would encour-
> age employers to hire young people,' but after being pressured by special
> interest groups against the youth wage, Simon now opposes his own
> legislation he pushed for seven years. [A third and fourth example on
> federal spending and national defense is offered]. Simon says and Simon
> does. Stick with Percy. He's solid, effective. He's the Illinois Advantage
> [Payne & Baukus 1985 collection].

In comparative ads we have the sense of "real voter choice" being emphasized. Such an emphasis may even, in part, account for their lack of visual interest, as the stress is on a kind of reasonable judgment. These ads are unremarkable as a group: they tend to be in black-and-white and feature characters printed on the screen.

Finally, comparison ads can generate response ads. Incumbent Rudy Boschwitz (R-MN) ran an ad with his accountant telling fellow Minnesotans that Rudy does not use tax loopholes, gives twenty percent of his income to charity, and pays fifty-six percent of his earnings in taxes. The accountant then says: "Speaking for myself, those paid commercials questioning the integrity of Rudy Boschwitz are not only unwarranted but absolutely shameful."

In general, therefore, the comparative ad depends upon voters understanding themselves as rational decision makers, fully cognizant of their own power in the democratic electoral process. These ads suggest that voters have real choices, that clear choices exist in the characters and political programs of candidates, and that the record of actions of candidates speak for themselves, unaltered by manipulative advertising and campaign staffs. These assumptions may or may not have any basis in political fact; no matter, because they have a good deal of ideological power, and we will discuss that shortly.

The Assault Ad

We now come to the third and generally most unsavory class of negative argumentative ads: those directly assaulting the character, motivations, associates, or actions of an opponent, usually with little or no comparison to the candidate sponsoring the ad. The number of assault ads in the 1984 senatorial campaigns was legion, and can only be lightly sampled here, to illustrate four subclasses.

Attack on character. Paul Simon was attacked by the Percy campaign for writing "an official letter to the Ayatolla [of Iran] praising him as quote 'a just and holy man' unquote. Simon labels the seizure of sixty-three American hostages as merely a 'misunderstanding.' Is this the kind of foreign policy we want from an Illinois senator?" (This attack is occurring three years after the 1981 hostage release.)

Attack on motives. Following is a text of an ad run by the Helms for Senate (R-NC) Committee: "Got a pencil and paper handy? Take down this address: The New York Committee to Elect Jim Hunt [D], 230 Park Avenue, New York, New York. That's the *New York* Committee to elect Jim Hunt—doesn't that beat anything you've ever heard? And Jim Hunt is running TV ads all over North Carolina saying [show one] 'Well, you see, I think that the job of a senator from North Carolina—he's not the senator from New York or California somewhere—he's the senator from North Carolina.' Now, something's wrong here. Why is there a *New York* Committee to elect Jim Hunt? Where do you stand, Jim?"

Attack on associates. Not only does Jim Hunt catch it in Helms' ads for having a New York committee whose honorary chairpersons include New York Senator Daniel Patrick Moynihan, Governor Mario Cuomo, and Mayor Edward I. Koch. The person made the most guilty by associations in 1984 is Jay Rockefeller (D-VA); the beating is administered during the primary period by Sam Kusic. From several of his ads we learn the following: "Now, 44 percent of Democrats polled say NO to the Rockefeller family deception. They will not be bought." "This year, all of us in the family of West Virginia will be pitted against the forces of the New York international oil and banking interests of the Rockefeller family dynasty, trying to buy our U.S. Senate seat for themselves." "The Rockefeller family dynasty—the Standard Oil Company, Chase-Manhattan Bank, Citicorp Bank, international banks and oil companies conspiring to dominate the world through the control of energy, money, and information. Big Brother, imposing himself on the free will of the individual, upon the free will of a people, upon the free will of a state. 1984. Rally, mountaineers. Vote Republican Sam Kusic. Sounds like 'music' for the family of West Virginia. Sam Kusic for United States Senate. We can *win!*"

Attack on actions. Assaults on opponents' actions were numerous in 1984. In Alabama, Howell Heflin is attacked for the amount of special interest money he took and for voting against increases in the railroad retirement benefits. In Tennessee, Albert Gore (D) is attacked by Victor Ashe (R) for the amount of special interest money he accepted, for his "liberal" spending policies, and for generally being two-faced. In Iowa, Tom Harkin (D) is attacked by GOP incumbent Roger Jepsen for his attendance record, his failure to vote on the final passage of the railroad retirement bill and "the two bills to save Social Security," and his proposal for a domestic content bill. In Kentucky, Dee Huddleston (D) is attacked by Mitch McConnell (R) for "missing big votes on social security, the budget, defense, even agriculture," and for making "an extra $50,000 giving speeches" while missing those votes. In West Virginia, Raese uses quotations from what must be a letter to the editor in the *Wall Street Journal* to attack Rockefeller's "meager" accomplishments, to argue that he has "reneged on his major campaign pledge—jobs," and to threaten that "Rockefeller will attempt to buy the presidency." In New Mexico, there is even an implied attack on Pete Domenici (R) for being male, as Judy Pratt (D) says "We can no longer sit back and let men make *all* of the decisions which affect our lives. "Her husband agrees, saying "I'm ready for that—it's about time" (Payne & Baukus 1985 collection).

Assault ads, therefore, search out what presumably are flaws in opponents' character, motivations, associations, or actions, and then argue voters ought to make their electoral decisions by identifying whom they are against rather than whom they support positively. Those flaws thus presumably stand as evidence supporting a negative electoral proposition.

The Rhetorical Functions of Argumentative Negative Ads

Given variations in the races that comprised the twenty-six senatorial campaigns of 1984 we have reviewed, we cannot reasonably get into questions concerning the actual effect of these negative ads. Three conclusions, though, concerning rhetorical functions—how these ads work electorally—stand out.

1. In implicative, comparative, and assault negative ads, we have three different foci: the implicative ad focuses on self, the assault, on other, and the comparative, on both. As suggested, *ethos*, or what the campaign literature often calls style issues (Merelman 1976), centers campaigning and voter decision making. Therefore, s almost of necessity must have personal foci that can be reduced to "Vote for me" and "Vote against my opponent" (see Tarrance 1982).

2. More interestingly, though, underlying each type of argumentative negative ad is a different sociocultural rule or assumption. Underlying implicative ads is the assumption that differences between candidates matter, to be sure, but that voters are attempting to elect the person most closely aligned to themselves characterologically and politically. The comparative ads, as noted, stress the voter's right to decide in a situation of choice; ideologically, these ads most compellingly attempt to instantiate America's vision of its electoral process. And, assault ads rest on the assumption that we vote against rather than for representatives.

Regarding these sociocultural assumptions, we must note that all three may well be part of the voters' *actual* decision-making processes (see Boynton & Lodge, Chapter 10). That is, sometimes we seem to vote on the basis of perceived homophyly; sometimes we think we have enough information to make a reasoned choice; and sometimes we in fact do employ negative criteria to choices. Vice presidential candidate Richard Nixon was slipping badly in the polls before making the "Checkers speech" in 1952 to recover from the charge of a slush fund. George McGovern lost a tremendous amount of voter ground in the wake of the Eagleton Affair, where he had to dump his vice presidential candidate. Even Gerald Ford faced slumping public confidence following his gaffe about the freedom of Iron Curtain countries in the Ford-Carter debates of 1976. George Bush faced an "anyone but George" attitude that supplied votes to both Bill Clinton and H. Ross Perot in 1992. Such examples certainly demonstrate the power of negative thinking—about various personal characteristics and actions—to affect our preference polls action and, by extension at least, our actual votes as well.

3. While voters may actually use positive, comparative, and negative criteria in making electoral decisions, the fact remains that one class of argumentative negative ad—the assault ad—is terribly risky ideologically. Election to national public office in America involves a ceremony of elevation. In the electoral process a mere mortal, a person like us, is being transformed into a leader. We expect that leader to be better than us, to be trustworthy, loyal, helpful, friendly, and everything else associated with the scout law. To engage in negativistic character assassination as a candidate is to be caught stooping just when one should be looking upward. Voter

assessments of both candidates is likely to suffer (Basil, Schooler & Reeves 1991).

Implicative ads do not carry that risk, for their negative side is subtle, underplayed. Comparative ads certainly attack others, but in a rhetorically justified, "fair" sort of way; comparisons at least implicitly call for response and hence suggest a dialogue we believe is important to politics. That is, we could say that the attack in most comparative ads is exteriorized, is seemingly drawn openly from the world of human affairs. But, assault ads, with their attacks on character, motivation, associations, and personal behaviors, are more deeply interiorized; they attack not just the opponent's politics and political actions but very sense of self. The focus is less upon the political roles of individuals than upon their personal morality. To be sure, assessment of personal aspects of character is important, but when it drives out all other considerations—as it can in strongly negative campaigns filled with assault ads—then it distorts the electoral process.

We will return to these ideas after looking at negative ads structured in different ways—not argumentatively but narratively, less as propositions than as stories.

Narratively Structured Negative Ads

To adequately deal with ads that tell stories more than they directly argue, we need to complicate the analysis. So far, we have considered only what ads "said," without placing them in the context of a campaign. It is time to do some contextualizing. As all campaign junkies know, they run in roughly four phases: the first phase is the preannouncement time when candidates criss-cross the country seeing if they can raise hopes and money; primaries and caucuses fill the second phase as candidates jockey for position in the "horserace" against other party contenders; phase three comprises the summer of the conventions; and, the general election period starts sometime in mid-August (we used to say Labor Day) and runs to election eve.

All of this means that campaigns can be laid on a timeline and that we as an electorate have come to expect different sorts of political messages delivered to us at different times, even different ads: attention-getting messages in Act I, the rhetoric of expectations in Act II, the political myth-making and power-talk in conventions during Act III, and the argumentative thrusts and parries as well as sloganeering of Act IV (Gronbeck 1990). This timeline is important rhetorically for two reasons: (1) earlier campaign messages often condition and serve as context for latter ones, and (2) as a political culture we have come to expect different messages at different times. Regarding negative ads, we have come to expect them in the September-October period of general elections—after the vilification of the opposing party that went on in the national conventions and before the final weeks, when candidates normally return to the "high ground" of patriotic depictions of themselves and their civic virtues.

All of this means that we ought to be sensitive to the sequence of ads as well as their timing. To generalize this idea, we ought to be interested in what is said *in* an ad and *by* when and how it is told. The story told *in* a narrative ad is from time-past, focusing on the guilt or innocence of the story's characters; the story told *by* a narrative ad is in time-present, in the electoral contest, focusing on whom voters should prefer as a result of what they have learned. To put this in language of narrative performance theory (Maclean 1988), what polispot stories are about we can call the *énoncé*, the enunciated, while their broadcast at various times during the campaign is the *énunciation*, the saying or telling. Both the *énoncé* and the *énunciation* are narrative performances, the first, a story about past events, and the second, a story about a present telling of those past events. The *énoncé* is a story that purportedly describes some political happenings, an interpretive "what," while the *énunciation* is a story of the motivations of storytellers, that which we find out about them in their acts of telling this story here-and-now, an explanatory "why." The happenings thus are past matters to be interpreted; the tellings are acts to be understood in the "real time" of their performance, that is, acts within a campaign.

To see the import of these ideas, we will look at pairings between opposing negative narrative ads, what can be called *adversarial narratives*, and at changes in negative narrative ads over time, what will be identified as *sequel narratives*. Our focus will on some storied ads from Campaign '88.

Narrative Structures in Campaign '88

While the primaries showed us attack and counterattack in both parties, it was the interparty battle that stirred up the most political negativity. By June, Bush's pollster, Robert Teeter, showed him eighteen points behind Dukakis and sinking. Teeter used focus groups reacting to information about Dukakis's postulated liberalism to convince Bush that negative ads could work, should be started early, and should run throughout the campaign. It was an unusual strategy and one that bothered Bush, for it did not feature positively what he stood for—an important consideration for a man trying to separate himself from his popular predecessor. Finally, Bush's braintrust of Teeter, Lee Atwater, John Sununu, and Roger Ailes convinced him to "go negative," and the race was begun. Both candidates soon joined fray. We cannot follow all of the issues; exchanges over the environment, though, can nicely illustrate the adversarial and sequence negative narratives both parties used.

Adversarial stories. Boston Harbor was featured early on in environmental ads by both candidates, with Bush leading off:

> Michael Dukakis called Boston Harbor an open sewer. As governor, he
> had the opportunity to do something about it, but he chose not to. The
> Environmental Protection Agency called his lack of action the most
> expensive public policy mistake in the history of New England. Now,
> Boston Harbor, the dirtiest harbor in America, will cost residents $6
> million to clean. And Michael Dukakis promises to do for America what
> he has done for Massachusetts [Payne 1989 collection].

In an ad made on September 18, 1988, the Dukakis camp told its version:

> Now George Bush has attacked Michael Dukakis on the environment. The
> environment! For seven and a half years, George Bush tried to kill the
> Super Fund cleanup of toxic waste sites; twice supported vetoes of the
> Clean Water Act; ordered regulations weakened on corporate polluters;
> pushed for offshore oil drilling again and again. And, what's most
> amazing, George Bush doesn't think you'll even bother to look at the facts.
> That's politics [Payne 1989 collection].

Consider these stories. Regarding the *énoncé*, the GOP story is one of
executive shortsightedness that carried with it a $6 million pricetag. It is a
mini-tragedy, depending on the viewer's willingness to hold the man who
called Boston Harbor "an open sewer" culpable for its condition. The moral
of the story is ironic: "And Michael Dukakis promises to do for America
what he has done for Massachusetts." The force of the irony is to move
listener-viewers from the past to the present—out of the *énoncé* and into
Campaign '88 and its issues. Dukakis's presumed ineptitude and callous-
ness are presented as reasons for telling the story just after the Democratic
convention—as a corrective to things we heard there. Dukakis is depicted
as blameworthy because of the future difficulties he would cause if elected.

In response, the Democrats chose not to refute the GOP in an argumentative fashion, but rather told a story about the ruthlessness of Bush.
Melodrama's villain is hissed off the stage for slashing the Super Fund
budget, supporting vetoes of the Clean Water Act, weakening corporate
requirements, and championing offshore drilling. Moving from past-events
to Campaign '88, the ad finally makes the charge of cynicism explicit: "And,
what's most amazing, George Bush doesn't think you'll even bother to look
at the facts. That's politics." Bush's presumed villainy in the past thus is
transferred to the present campaign; we are asked to judge the *énoncés*
political, not environmental, consequences.

Both Bush's and Dukakis's basic ads on the environment, therefore,
while telling stories about past-fact ineptitude or villainy, signaled their
own storytellers and called attention to the *énunciation*. The Bush camp's

reference to Dukakis's "promises" and the Dukakis camp's final sentence, "That's politics," asked viewers to inscribe on the past act *ethos* fouls—to give Dukakis negative credibility points for his bungling and Bush, for his immorality and cynicism. By implication, those fouls were thought important enough to presumably govern the way Americans should vote.

A similar analysis could be done on Bush's attacks upon Dukakis's defense posture (the tank ads) and his crime policies (the infamous furlough and "Willie Horton" ads). In both cases, Dukakis's initial strategy was to counterattack Bush, sometimes with, often without, a defense of his own record and without policy statements. Little headway was made in the paired ads toward an understanding of goals and visions for tomorrow, though at least the ads featured a policy area.

Sequence narratives. More interesting were stories-in-sequence, the retelling of a single political story at different stages of the campaign. Granted, one ought to expect ads to change over time, as the voter has different expectations from stage to stage. Yet, the variations we find in later ads certainly are a function as much of previously aired ads as they are of campaign phase. As we move from ad to ad in sequences, we find heightened emotional states or more blatant attacks. Consider, for example, Dukakis's later retellings of Bush's environmental plots. Two weeks after their initial response to Bush, on October 3, the Dukakis campaign launched a series of ads called "Bush's False Advertising," including the following:

> George Bush is complaining about Boston Harbor. Bush's administration cut funds to clean up Boston Harbor. Bush's administration cut funds to clean up California's coast, from San Diego Harbor to San Francisco Bay. Bush opposed a crackdown on corporations releasing toxic waste. Bush favored a veto of the Clean Water Act, not once but twice. The nonpartisan League of Conservation Voters endorses Mike Dukakis. When you hear George Bush talk *about* the environment, remember [the word "Remember ... "on screen] what he did *to* the environment [Payne 1989 collection].

This ad thus followed the initial story rather closely, but added the endorsement—bringing in Dukakis as the good guy playing against Bush's bad guy—and the twist in the final sentence that turned the story from melodrama to irony. That is, new evidence was introduced in the narrative of past-facts, but, more important, when the storyteller brought us up to the present, we were asked to remember that things are not always what they seem in politics. Statements are ironic reversals of actions. Seeing and hearing are not believing in politics.

Somewhere about the same time (mid-October) and certainly after the presidential debates, "The Packaging of George Bush" series appeared with another story about the environment. Men presumably making ads for Bush had the following exchange at "2:25 p.m. Tuesday":

> A. "Geez, look at these poll numbers. People are really worried about the environment."
> B. "So do a commercial standing on a beautiful beach."
> C. "Give me a break! After seven and a half years of our boys taking apart the Environmental Protection Agency, James Watts—Bush personally got him to ease up on corporate polluters—that is on the record, and now we're going to say ..."
> D. "He's going to say he loves the environment, he's gunna make it clean and wonderful."
> E. "He's going to say that" [chuckles from everyone] VO/on-screen words: They'd like to sell you a package. Wouldn't you rather choose a president? [Payne 1989 collection]

The story of Bush's calumny has been expanded to include complicitious staff members who know the "facts" yet refuse to act in accordance with them as well as a completely malleable Bush, who obviously will say anything without regard for those facts. This forensic review of the actions of Bush's campaigners is tied to the present. The device used in "The Packaging of George Bush" series is something picked up from *Hill Street Blues*: a day and time reference, making both that-which-is-told and the telling acts presumably occurring somewhere about now and thus emphasizing the importance of making proper voting decisions at this time and on the basis of the immoral inconsistencies depicted in the story. Urgency is communicated in the collapse of past-fact and present-judgment. (For a close analysis of the whole "packaging" series, see Descutner, Burnier, Mickunas & Letteri 1991).

This ad, too, like the previous one, puts Bush's actions in conflict with his words and likewise questions his motivations; Bush's hidden moral sins—*rather than* his environmental policy per se—are taken to be the pivotal issues on which to make electoral decisions. By this point in the sequence of ads, there is little effort to pretend that one is assessing actual evidence even-handedly; rather, the center of the ad is not the environment at all, but the campaigners.

The crowning effort in the sequel narratives on the environment came from the last series of attack ads made by the Dukakis organization, the so-called "Future" or "Imagine" series. While *USA Today* was told these would be upbeat, the one on the environment, made on October 21, 1988, was a story that was a cross between *On the Beach* and *Bladerunner*. In black and white it showed future life in a totally polluted environment. Its words purportedly came from a television news broadcast, radio news, and a voiceover commentator:

[TV:] Exercise extreme caution, please remain indoors.

[RADIO:] Today the Republican administration promised a major new effort to deal with the growing environmental crisis. California beach pollution closed down the last remaining public beach. A Republican spokesman said today if you must go outdoors, use extreme caution and protect yourself from toxic air pollution [A young couple is sitting on the beach looking at a drilling rig; as they turn toward the camera, we see them wearing gas masks].

[VO:] Republicans and their failed environmental policies are destroying our way of life. If we don't make some changes now, imagine what it's going to be like in the future ["The Future" appears on the screen] [Payne 1989 collection].

The story told here is a dream of horror, of dehumanized life. In Northrop Frye's climatological genres of literature, we are in Winter, in the deepest of ironic narratives where the values of humanity are stood on their heads (Frye 1957). The forensic qualities of assessment are gone, and blame is so pervasive that even Bush is missing from the story; unidentified "Republican" personae are the faceless actors. There is not even villainy here, only death.

The sequence we find in the Dukakis 1988 negative narratives on the environment was paralleled in other sequences. His *énunciation* got shriller and shriller, attacking Bush for the federal government's furlough program and for the rape by a furloughed drug dealer of Patsy Pedrin, shouting his ineffectiveness as head of the federal anti-drug effort, and questioning his selection of Dan Quayle as follow-up chief of the anti-drug effort (Payne 1989). The education issue—no doubt thanks to Bush's theft of a traditional Democratic issue in statements about being an "Education President"— came up for the same treatment: it, too, had a "Future" negative ad that depicted an imagined twenty-first century with school closings and children unable to pursue their educational desires.

In most of the issue areas for which I have reviewed ads, the negative narratives in their sequels abandoned the pretense of assessing candidates' records and heightened issues in their political rather than social-institutional contexts. By the end, when the weapons of rhetorical assault had been dulled through overuse, attacks were removed from the campaign environment altogether in favor of dystopic visions of hell on earth. The negative ads in the last times generated apocalyptic visions of final states devoid even of political controversy; the rhetorical dialectics of politics gave way to the poetics of despair.

The Rhetorical Functions of Narratized Negative Ads

Even as cursory as this study of Campaign '88 is, it suggests some of the ways negative narratives can go bad in the campaign process:

1. Negative narratives wear out, and thus must be rebuilt. The Democrats, particularly, went time and again to the studio, retelling their tales of woe in order to keep fresh attacks before the voters. Political advertisement still is more of an art than science, and hence experimentation occurs during the runs of campaigns—especially by those who are behind.

2. Negative political campaigning is as much a defensive as offensive weapon. "Going negative" is something one does either when far behind (as Bush was when he started) or when one has been attacked personally—and successfully—by an opponent (as Dukakis insisted happened to him in the summer of 1988). Candidates are afraid of the power of their opponents' negative polispots and believe they need strong negative defenses for uses in cases of preemptive first strikes by the other party. As well, adversarial narratives—a direct countering of one jab with another—are presented to add excitement and to ward off any judgment of weakness. In 1988, Bush still carried the "wimp" label and Dukakis was seen as cool and emotionless; adversarial narratives gave them both chances to repair presumed character faults at the expense of an opponent.

Another consideration is worth contemplating. Voters are not very confident of their own knowledge of issues, nor do they think much of solutions proposed in the heat of a campaign. Character-based messages, thus, may have been the only grounds upon which most voters feel any degree of confidence when making electoral judgments. This certainly seemed the case in 1992; with both Bush and Clinton struggling on character issues, Perot shot up in the polls meteor in the late spring. Attack of an opponent's character as well as defense of one's own integrity (directly or by implication) ought, then, to be expected in a political campaign—though the mode and duration of attacks need be thought through carefully.

3. As negative narratives get reframed, political rhapsodies are obliged to tell darker and darker stories. If the assignment of evil to a candidate does not produce much movement in the polls, then the evil must be made even greater in the sequel commercials. Just as laundry soap advertisers constantly look for new ways to contrast their workalike products with those of other soap manufacturers, so do the attacks on the Brand Xs of politics gain in volume and sensation over time. On a seven-point scale of emotional intensity, the movement almost always is toward seven. Sequels get constructed to jolt inured voters—or so goes the rationale.

One should not take the comparison to laundry products too literally, however. Comparative ads for detergents are completed in a positive statement about one's own product; sales are presumed to depend upon affirmation. Negative ads in politics, however, frequently (almost always in 1988) are completed in denial or subversion of one's opponent. Their function is to destablize the voter support for the other, either increasing the undecideds (who presumably can be won by one's own candidate) or, as we noted in the opening paragraph of this chapter, even driving voters out of the electoral arena altogether in circumstances when one's candidate might be helped by a lower turnout.

4. What was especially bothersome in 1988 was the predominance of negative ads. A report on a study of Frank Biocca, director of the National Political Advertising Project, appeared in *USA Today* near the end of the campaign (Katz 1988). Biocca was convinced that voters' distaste for negative commercials had dissipated over time, even while the negative information of those ads was retained and hence an actionable part of voter decision processes; distasteful or not, he argued, negative polispots worked in favor of those who used them.

Yet, reactions to the voters who were tested seemed to belie those conclusions. The highest rated ads, those judged the most fair and those voters thought were most likely to affect their decisions affirmatively, were the positive rather than the negative ads. Those voters longed for more positive ads in 1988. Said one: "I liked the ones with the convention speeches because the music attracts my attention. The George Bush family things are really effective, but when he puts down Michael Dukakis, that really hurts him." Said another, reacting to Dukakis's relaxed discussion of young families and their problems, "To me, it means he has all of us in his heart. I just have a warmer feeling." And another: "For the young family with two people working, he seemed to get closeness by talking directly to them" (Katz 1988).

Now, we cannot put too much faith in such self-report data, for voters are notoriously bad at articulating the grounds for their decisions and even if memory of likable or unlikable images fades, the negative judgment can endure (Newhagen & Reeves 1991; cf. Lang 1991). Yet, the first social-scientific study done during 1988—a senatorial election study—confirmed that attacks were more effective with voters when launched against stands on issues than on the character of politicians (Pfau & Burgoon 1989; cf. West 1991). The most recent summary of research on attack ads in campaigns concludes that we cannot generalize their effectiveness (Johnson-Cartee & Copeland 1991). Even if we cannot directly connect expressions of sentiment with voting, we probably can take those sentiments as indicative of citizens' attitudes toward the campaign process—a topic we will take up shortly.

5. The relationship between voter feelings and actions can be explained partially by the relationships between the *énoncé* and the *énunciation* of its narratives. As one might expect, the *énoncé* tried opposition candidates for their various faults and sins; but, because those forensic stories were almost only assaultive and seldom comparative in their characterizations, they gave voters little to vote for, only images to vote against. Further, in emphasizing the politics of issue-manipulation and in presenting us with

negative portraits through the duration of the general election, the *énunciation* focused reasons-to-vote almost exclusively on political motive. What voters saw were stories of character defects that, in the final analysis, were offered within dyslogistic assessments of the political process itself.

The central stories featured assessments of personal morality, which, as we have known since Aristotle's *Rhetoric* (1378a), is but one-third of the bases of *ethos* or credibility. There was little concern for an opponent's good sense or good will, the other two bases, and, one might add, aspects of character highly relevant to assessments of political performance. Except for the initial negative ads that treated Dukakis's actual achievements as governor or Bush's actual votes when presiding over the Senate, no incidents in the attack stories showed relationships between candidates' actions and the quality of thought or the liberality of sentiment behind them. Rather, all issues were reduced to matters of ethicality of motive. The narratives were morality plays, wherein the sequences of actions depicted the principal player, the opposing candidate, as living out distasteful motives.

Within an articulation of a campaign process that emphasizes winning through destruction of opposition's moral base rather than through construction of one's own political agenda, voters were presented precious little to vote for. In Brown's understanding of interpretation and explanation (1987), in the 1988 polispots the past was reinterpreted primarily in terms of good-bad motives, not political action per se, while campaign organizations implicitly explained that public governance pivots primarily on personal ethics—on what the French called the Reign of Virtue in the late eighteenth century.

6. Narrative is preferred to argumentative discourse when the subject matter is morality. As we saw, one can build good arguments over whose voting record is more isomorphic with voter wishes, what someone did or did not accomplish while in office, and agenda for future actions needed to improve life in the collectivity. Bald assertions about someone's virtues and vices, however, can come off as whining, tattling, dull, or smug preachment if offered directly. When the subject is virtue and vice, the key to success is not argument but descriptions of actions. Again, to turn to Aristotle, "we praise a man for what he has actually done," more particularly in a sequence of actions where "we must try to prove that our hero's noble acts are intentional" (1367b)—or a villain's ignoble acts were likewise intentionally performed. This is what Osborn (1986) calls a rhetoric of presentation, where we are told how to look at the world, and a rhetoric of arousal, where we are instructed how to feel about what we see. Actions thus are related to each other, that is, cohere, through narrative structuration, and are made to signal a moral conclusion by the narrator's deliberate inscription of a particular interpretation on why we are being presented with what we see.

These six conclusions should help us toward a better understanding of the force for good or ill that negative polispots have in this country. What has been suggested is that adversarial stories, with their focus on character definition, function much like the comparative ads of the argumentative genre, and thus may have some redeeming features as campaign vehicle, but that sequel stories, because of their perhaps unavoidable movement toward the darker sides of life, put their focus character assassination: the unsavory pit of politics.

Negative Ads, Campaigns, and America's Self Images

Presidential campaigning in this country is a sociodrama writ large—extended over two or more years, dense in the amount and variety of discourse generated, and a multi-billion dollar enterprise. All of the time, effort, and cost combine to create a grand occasion for assessing this social order: the condition of the citizenry, the spray of our collective commitments, and the valuative foundations of our self images.

The most insidious aspect of assault ads and hypermoral sequel ads is their potential to create fissures in the social order. Normatively, campaigning should be a time of self-reflection and rededication. "A persuasive story and character," Fisher has maintained, should "not be merely subversive" (1989, p. 156). We have been taught to expect an affirmation of institutions in large-scale rituals of the kind campaigns are (Bennett & Edelman 1985). When leadership is personally attacked rather than reflected upon and campaigning as a process is taken to be more important than the policies that need to be examined and revalued, then collective affirmations may become impossible; when the *énoncé* is collapsed into a probe only of the personal, the *énunciation* becomes an exercise in "mere politics" that in turn subverts the objectives of campaigning in a democratic state: the testing and selection of leadership. When implicative, comparative, and policy-centered adversarial ads are left on the cutting room floor in favor of moral pieties and immoral character assassination, elections fail to fulfill their purposes.

Presidential candidates and their campaign committees, these days, are in most ways independent of party; having lives of their own, they are accountable to no other institution than themselves. If they have no stake in anything except winning, if they heed no call other than the pollster's or the money-changer's, they could become a serious threat to the purposes presidential campaigning ought to serve and they will accelerate this country's tumble toward minority elections; only 50.1 percent of our eligible voters cast ballots in 1988.

Now, party fraud and other abuses certainly were a part of presidential politics before the postmodern era, but at least some social institution could be held accountable for those abuses; no structure was responsible for the

Watergate break-in, and only individuals have been made responsible for the worst of the character assassinations of 1988. Worse, the collapse of party so far as national elections are concerned has taken away the voters' last direct tie to the process. A recent Kettering Foundation report, *Citizens and Politics: A View From Main Street America* (1991), explores the reasons for voter alienation. "They believe they have been squeezed out," says David Broder (1991), by "politicians, powerful lobbyists, and the media" who care little for connecting citizens and their government. Reducing political choices solely to questions of personality and personal morality likewise contributes to alienation, if only because it is much, much easier to attack someone else's faults than to demonstrate one's own virtues.

As Broder reacts to the Kettering Foundation's report, he says: "Disillusioned citizens are right in thinking that individuals are nearly powerless in a mass society's politics. This reports tells us, sadly, that they have entirely forgotten that parties existed to inform, to mobilize and to empower them— the very thing they want but no longer know how to get" (1991, p. 6A). Or, in the words of *Citizens and Politics:* "At the core of politics stands the citizen-public official relationship. Citizens seek public officials who are *not only* responsive to their needs, but who *include* them in the policy process and consult with them so as to understand and pursue the common good ... But citizens feel that they seldom interact with public officials—rather, they believe, public officials lecture them, talk around them, appease them, seek their blind support for initiatives, and sometimes even lie to them" (1991, p. 60). Given that elections represent our most intense and message-filled political process, we must look to elections for the rebirth of good government.

In this chapter, we have suggested that scrutiny of one's political opponents—their records, policies, fundamental *ethoi* or characters—should define presidential campaigning. In democratic theory, the testing of character is central to electoral contests. Only the degenerate forms of character testing must be avoided. As Wilson Carey McWilliams put it, "For both Republicans and Democrats, the election of 1988 indicates the need for a new civility, and for the kinds of word and deed necessary to affirm, for the coming century, the dignity of self-government" (Pomper et al. 1989, p. 200). Our politicians, media representatives, and citizens will hold only the most troubling images of campaigning until we refocus it.

Campaign '92 showed us some evidence that both the media and direct citizen input could affect campaign styles and the use of negative material. The regular presence of so-called truth boxes in the nation's newspapers, wherein the evidence and claims offered in specific ads were assessed, helped create a "good government" atmosphere during the campaign, as did televised stories showing faulty ads and the regular Thursday National Public Radio review of ads' contents. The public certainly played its part in public forums around the country, most notably during the second presidential debate in Richmond, Virginia, when an audience member poignantly asked all parties to dispose of attacks and cut to the run—the terrible issues facing the country. While the play lists of ads for the various candidates in 1992 are not yet available, causal observation in at least some markets around the country suggest that the candidates in fact did offer far more positive than negative messages in their advertising programs that year.

Campaign '92 seemed to demonstrate that standards of accountability could be laid on even seemingly all-powerful political entities such as presidential campaign commitments. Once the United States begins to believe collectively that citizens can make a difference, in spite of special interests and in spite of stockpiled campaign resources, they in fact will. That is the hope for tomorrow.

PART THREE

Mass-Mediated Images in Presidential Campaigns

Introduction

Mass-Mediated Images in Presidential Campaigns

Bruce E. Gronbeck and Arthur H. Miller

While many grumble about them and even find the notions repulsive, few would disagree with the claims that mass media frame the public sphere in our time and that television is the dominant medium in that sphere. The newspaper with the largest circulation in the United States, the *Wall Street Journal*, has a press run of 1.8 million. The *NRTA/AARP Bulletin* distributes the most U.S. magazines at 22.1 million, with the *Reader's Digest* next at 16.3 million and *TV Guide* at 15.6 million. *Time* leads the news magazines with a circulation of 4.1 million, while *Newsweek* and *U.S. News & World Report* follow at 3.2 million and 2.3 million respectively (World Almanac 1991). In contrast, television viewership for an event such as a presidential debate dwarfs such numbers; an estimated 80-100 million viewers saw each of the 1992 encounters. Such political activities as presidential convention acceptance speeches, inaugural addresses, and major press conferences are not far behind.

The relationships between mass media and the public sphere lead scholars interested in presidential campaigning into difficult, largely uncharted territory. Ever since the days of Columbia University's great Bureau of Applied Social Research studies of voting behavior in the 1940s and 1950s (Lazarsfeld et al. 1944/1968), we have been at some little loss to explain and rationalize the effects of mass media upon voters. Articulated by Joseph Klapper (1960), the "law of minimal consequences" recognized that but 5-7 percent of Lazarsfeld et al.'s respondents actually switched their preferences from one party's candidate to another's between May and October of an election year. In Klapper's explanation, other matters—people's selective use of media, their group norms and interpersonal relations, a community's opinion leaders, and an ideological middle-of-the roadism operative in American broadcasting—prevented mass media from reshaping our minds during electing time (Gronbeck 1985).

Such early research findings and summaries were startling because observers naively assumed that the mass (especially electronic) media were potential revampers of the world. Electronic media were thought of as weapons of manipulation capable of turning a 'tis into a 'taint via an arresting visual image, reassuring narrating voice, and soundtrack playing *Finlandia* or some equally patriotic symphony. Such media were feared because of their use of multiple (visual, verbal, acoustic) codes in combination with their coast-to-coast reach as well as their capability to present the same message simultaneously to the whole country (for background, see Czitrom 1982, Chapter 5). That the airwaves were apparently impotent was counter-intuitive.

By now, the law of minimal consequences has been more or less circumvented. One group of researchers has attacked its seeming anomalies by refocusing emphasis within it. Some have recognized that political campaigns ought not be thought of as events producing great realignments of political attitudes and behavior, but, rather, as large-scale reinforcement processes producing political stability. Such a view often asks, as well, that we focus less on message-makers than on mass media as dominant channels for campaign messages (e.g., see the work of Patterson 1980).

A second group of scholars has reframed Lazarsfeld's questions. Rather than asking "What are the effects of political campaign messages?" they ask "To what uses can political campaigns and messages be put by people?" The shift from effects questions to functions questions produces radically different kinds of information — about people's needs or desires when they consume mass-mediated discourse. The so-called uses and gratifications theory of mass communication frames this research (e.g., see Gronbeck 1978; Nimmo & Sanders 1981, pp. 11-36, 67-99).

Others extend such theorizing even farther, moving to critical or cultural views of campaign discourses and political culture. On the assumptions (1) that large-scale communication events reinforce political beliefs, attitudes, and correct behaviors, (2) that campaign messages are more enactments of what is politically needed and acceptable in a society than they are new, change-oriented solutions to old problems, and (3) that "political communication" thus includes not only speeches and other bundles of words but also complex behaviors and rituals to which voters assign meaning and significance. Cultural studies of politics have approached campaigning in symbolic terms, exploring the aspects of campaign rituals to which Americans attach social meanings (e.g., Nimmo & Combs 1980, 1983/1990; Trent & Friedenberg 1991; Gronbeck 1985).

One result of such moves from the law of minimal consequences to the view of campaigns as mass social rituals is a radical reconceptualization of relationships between mass media and campaign outcomes. We now understand that mass-mediated campaign messages are ubiquitous. On television you are fed video clips from speeches, candidate forums, biographical ads, issue ads, comparative ads, attack ads, God-motherhood-and country tableaux of candidates and their families, five-minute discussions of the "big" issues during the last two weeks of the campaign, half-hour biographies and campaign summaries on election eve, meet-the-press and talk-show appearances, morning show visits, and call-in shows wherein candidate phone banks can be utilized to flood the airwaves with the party line.

We also understand that the mass media are not mere conduits of candidate messages. Electronic and print media together control access (who gets to talk politics?), put campaign issues into hierarchies (whose agenda are emphasized, whose, minimized?), show party favoritism (who gets the good spots, the positive stories?), provide interpretation (whose actions are depicted positively, whose, negatively?), offer contextualizations (are a candidate's actions contextualized within issues, personal matters, remarks from dissenters?), and even recommend electoral actions (who gets endorsed by which media?). The mass media thus are centers of political communication and molders even of self images; they ought to be studied as such (Parenti 1993; Denton 1991; Bennett 1992).

Part III of this anthology illustrates a range of studies of mass media understood as a foundation of political symbolizations and collective images in presidential campaigns. We lead with a study by Cary Covington, Kent Kroger, and Glenn W. Richardson, Jr. examining Reagan's work to control press reports of his 1980 campaign through the "Issue of the Day" strategy for news conferences and through control of access to Reagan himself; their documentation of the press's independence in casting news and interpretations strongly suggests the need to view mass media as independent centers of communication messages in presidential campaigns. The chapter by David Woodard documents television coverage of campaigns over the last twenty years. Television news increasingly has concentrated its resources on the fifty-three primaries and caucuses in the first half of the electoral year; almost three quarters of television's news coverage of campaign is now expended before the fall general election contest begins. As well, the kinds and lengths of stories have changed significantly. In all, Woodard depicts an independent electronic medium playing highly significant roles of shaping and interpreting political electoral information for society.

David Birdsell probes relationships between the independent "debates" and voters' expectations of them. The debates over the debates fill newspaper and electronic commentary, and are signs that both the press and the citizenry are looking for more satisfying vehicles of political information during the late phase of the campaign. Dianne Rucinski completes the essays in this section, exploring politics, especially the odd-but-persistent beliefs that others are significantly affected by mass media more than we ourselves are. What this says about American self images provides Rucinski's readers with important matters to ponder.

The bottom line here was suggested earlier: in a country socially fragmented into two genders, multiple religions, generational strata, increasingly self-conscious ethnic groups, education-based enclaves, and sharply separated upper- and under-classes, the mass (especially electronic) media are our only town halls. As a society, we are wired together by the electronic media, which thus are forced to serve as the public sphere through which one can damn televisual politics only if one decides not to talk to other segments of the population; tilting with electronic windmills does no more good than did challenging wind-powered ones.

As scholars we must take up the challenges of media as primary symbolizers and sources of self images in political campaigns, exploring their power and modes of influence on outcomes. Part III pursues that task.

5

Shaping a Candidate's Image in the Press

Cary R. Covington, Kent Kroeger and Glenn Richardson

One of the most commented-upon features of presidential elections during the decades of the 1970s and 1980s has been the emergence of a new strategy that candidates employ to influence news coverage of their campaigns,[1] thereby enabling them to shape their public image. The strategy seeks to accomplish that goal by: (1) reducing the frequency of the candidate's contact with the media, (2) increasing the formality of those contacts, and (3) emphasizing a single campaign theme over an extended period of time. In this way, candidates try to limit the media's discretion in portraying them in terms other than those preferred by the candidate.

Understanding the respective roles of the press and the candidate in creating candidate images for the public is of considerable importance. Presidential campaigns are experienced directly by only a handful of citizens. For most people these are mediated events, that is, they occur through the media. If we are to understand how the public develops its images of presidential candidates, we must understand the process by and the extent to which the images that candidates intend the public to receive get communicated to the public through the news media.

Much has been written about candidates who have attempted to control the media's portrayal of them and the effects of those efforts. However, no clear conceptual or empirical definition of the media management strategy has been set forth, nor have systematic tests for its impact on the press depiction of a candidate been undertaken. A more precise definition of media management is needed before we can classify particular candidates' media strategies, which, in turn, is essential to any comparative analysis of candidates. The absence of an empirical test of the effects of the media control strategy on press coverage undermines our understanding of the roles that candidates and the press play in shaping the public's image of candidates.

These two issues form the focus for this chapter. First, we discuss the nature of candidate media management strategies by: (1) identifying the contrasting goals and resources of candidates and the press, (2) describing the dimensions along which a media management strategy is constituted, and (3) identifying the specific positions along those dimensions that define the "Issue of the Day" strategy, which we will study. Second, we consider the effects of the Issue of the Day strategy on the content of the media's coverage by: (1) providing a narrative account[2] of Ronald Reagan's 1980 presidential campaign and his use of the Issue of the Day (IOD) strategy to illustrate its use and assess its impact on the news media's coverage of Reagan's candidacy, and (2) conducting a content analysis of *The New York Times'* coverage of Reagan's campaign to evaluate hypotheses concerning the expected effects of the IOD strategy.

The Nature of the Media Management Strategy

Goals and Resources of Candidates and the Press

Any presidential candidate's media management strategy is predicated on the respective goals and resources of the candidates and the press. Presidential candidates and the news media often find themselves in conflict because of their competing goals. Candidates want to portray vote-maximizing *ideal* images to the public and they need the news media to convey those images. While political advertising forms a central element of any candidate's media strategy, most campaign strategists believe that coverage by the news media provides candidates with credibility that cannot be obtained through paid advertising alone (Arterton 1984).

In contrast, the news media wants to report information that is newsworthy and attractive to its consumers. These consumers of news want to be informed about the elections, and the press needs access to the candidates if they are to provide that information. Given the consumers' interest in controversy and the unusual, the information that reporters seek is often not sympathetic to the candidates. Even when it is, it may not conform to the candidates' desired images (Smoller 1990). Thus, candidates and the press are often at odds over how the candidates should be portrayed in the news.

Candidates and the news media employ different resources in their efforts to achieve their respective goals. The candidates' ability to cultivate their desired image rests on the control they exert over the content of the information they make available to the press (Fallows 1984). Campaign strategists believe the media prefers to report stories provided by the campaigns than to generate their own (Hertsgaard 1988). Thus, by shaping the content of the information provided to the media, a candidate can influence the content of the media's reporting.

The important and independent role played by the press rests on its power to select from the various stories present by a campaign those which it will report, and its power to interpret those stories (Broder 1975). The wider the range of topics on which to report and the larger the number of sources providing information, the more freedom the press possesses in choosing and interpreting stories.

Dimensions of a Media Management Strategy

A candidate's decisions about how to try to influence the press are structured along three dimensions. The first two dimensions concern the manner in which the candidate conducts relations with the media: (1) the *accessibility* of the candidate to the press and (2) the *formality* of their interactions. The third dimension concerns the contents of the candidate's messages to the media: (3) the *homogeneity* of the messages given to the press by the candidate.

Accessibility is defined as the frequency with which a candidate is available to the press, both personally and through staff members or other surrogates. While all candidates in the modern television era have been generally accessible to the media (McAvoy 1988, p. 12), significant variations can still be found across campaigns. Formality is defined as the degree to which the contacts of the candidate and his staff with the media are pre-arranged and highly structured. An informal relationship would be characterized by ad hoc interactions, conversations rather than formal questions and answers, and a lack of planning on the part of the candidate about the timing, placement, or content of the interaction. A formal relationship would consist of highly structured question-and-answer sessions, with considerable effort made to control who asks what questions.

Accessibility and formality each form an independent continuum of alternatives. As we shall see, the IOD strategy calls for high levels of formality and low levels of accessibility. However, a variety of other combinations is possible. Some candidates may be frequently available to the press, but limit the press's ability to solicit off-the-cuff remarks. A heavy reliance on "photo opportunities" would exemplify this strategic mix. Incumbent presidents often employ this approach. Alternatively, candidates can have few interactions with the press, but still be quite informal during those rare contacts. Early in his 1980 campaign, for instance, Ronald Reagan was criticized by some of his staffers for indulging in this approach. Finally, candidates can opt for a strategy of frequent and informal contacts. Early in the primary season, candidates seeking more extensive press coverage and public name recognition may adhere to this approach.

The IOD strategy's combination of low accessibility and high formality has been employed in different forms by candidates other than Ronald Reagan. Richard Nixon used versions of this approach in 1960 and especially in 1972. Gerald Ford in 1976 and Jimmy Carter in 1980 employed the "Rose Garden" strategy, which was designed to structure and limit the press' contacts with the candidate and constrain the press' ability to question the candidate (Schram 1977, p. 342). In 1988, both George Bush and Michael Dukakis, at certain times during the campaign, used this approach. Both employed guidelines that prevented any staff member from speaking with the press without prior approval, mandated that no announcement was made to the press without prior clearance, and required that every encounter between the candidate and the press was "structured to create a positive image" (McAvoy 1988, p. 12).

The homogeneity of a candidate's messages is defined as the degree to which the messages delivered to the press over some period of time are unified in content and intent, creating a single, easily identifiable and consistent theme.

Campaigns since 1960 have exhibited substantial variation in their degree of homogeneity. For example, the 1968 Hubert Humphrey campaign was widely acknowledged to lack a coherent campaign theme until the last few weeks of the campaign (White 1969, p. 445). Michael Dukakis refused to adopt a well-defined thematic campaign plan, despite constant pleas from his key aides to do so (Black & Oliphant 1989). In contrast, Ronald Reagan's campaigns in 1980 and 1984, and George Bush's 1988 campaign were all characterized by the presentation of a series of internally homogeneous campaign messages.

The reason for a homogeneous message is simple. As Theodore White (1982) explains: "say what you have to say clearly, say it again, say it over and over, until the theme strikes home" (p. 161). A single, repeated message has the greatest chance of influencing the public's image of a candidate. A variety of messages may deter any single message from being retained, and may combine to create a confused and less persuasive image.

Characterizing the "Issue of the Day" Strategy

The IOD strategy consists of press relations that are formalized and infrequent, and messages that are focused on the same subject matter over several days at a time. It is designed to minimize the press's control over the content and interpretation of campaign stories by restricting the variety of subjects raised and the settings in which they are discussed by the campaign. The candidate hopes to force the media to cover preferred stories in a favorable manner.

The IOD strategy helps the candidate promote the preferred image in three ways. First, continued repetition of a single issue by the candidate maximizes the likelihood that the public will learn about those things that the candidate considers important. Second, the highly structured and infrequent interactions minimize the likelihood of the unexpected glitch or mistake. Finally, the emphasis on a single issue prevents competing campaign messages from masking or diluting the candidate's preferred message.

The IOD strategy has evolved over time. Early variants consisted of simply limiting the press's opportunities for unstructured access to the individual. Thus, instead of free-form press conferences, Richard Nixon delivered addresses but took no questions, or tried to create the appearance of a question-and-answer session with the audience, when in truth those asking the questions had been carefully screened and prompted to ensure that only the *right* questions were asked (McGinness 1968). Later candidates further refined the strategy. In its pure form under Reagan, the IOD strategy allowed the press access to Reagan once each day, and permitted him to speak only to the issue identified for general promulgation for that day. Moreover, all his campaign surrogates spoke only to that issue as well (Hertsgaard 1988).

Use and Effects of the Issue of the Day Strategy: Ronald Reagan in 1980

Why Study Reagan in 1980?

We will use the 1980 Reagan campaign for our empirical examination of the use and effects of the issue of the day strategy. This campaign is particularly appropriate for use as a case study for two reasons.

First, the strategies Reagan used in his dealings with the press can be identified with confidence. The ideal source for describing a candidate's press strategy would be the campaign's manager or media advisers, who could authoritatively state what strategy was employed and when. In fact, three of Reagan's top strategists did just this when they laid out their approach to the media in a post-election discussion of the campaign (Wirthlin, Breglio & Beal 1981). This article provides an insider's perspective on the campaign. While the authors' assessments of the efficacy of their efforts may be influenced by self-interest, their description of the types of strategies used should be fully reliable.

Second, over the course of the campaign, the Reagan campaign exhibited variation along all three dimensions that define a media management strategy. They shifted several times between the homogeneity of the IOD strategy and the more traditional stump speech, which addressed a variety of topics. There was also significant movement along the formality and accessibility dimensions, as Reagan moved towards a pure form of the IOD strategy over the course of the campaign. Thus, this case study allows us to identify shifts in Reagan's media management strategy and to look for the anticipated changes in the character of the media's coverage of the campaign during those periods.

A Narrative Account of Reagan's 1980 Media Management Strategy

This case study examines four phases of the Reagan campaign to describe the characteristics of the variety of press strategies employed by Reagan and the differences in the effects that each version had on the coverage that Reagan received.

Issue of the Day I: Defense and Foreign Policy Week. Reagan launched his general election campaign at a press conference on August 16th, 1980. From that date until August 23rd, Reagan strategists attempted to coordinate the messages of Reagan, Bush and other campaign surrogates to create a clear Reagan profile focused on defense and foreign policy issues (Kessel 1988, p. 197). By using "defense week" as its opening salvo of the campaign, Reagan was attempting to reconfirm to his committed followers that he would be strong on defense.

On August 16th, Ronald Reagan and George Bush appeared together at a press conference in Los Angeles to announce that Bush would spend the week in China while Reagan would tour the country talking about foreign policy and defense issues. In that press conference, Reagan was queried on past statements unrelated to defense, such as his claim that the New Deal was "based on fascism" or that "trees cause air pollution," both of which he dismissed as distortions of his actual statements. More critical to his attempt to emphasize foreign policy and defense issues, Reagan was asked to explain previous statements regarding his desire to officially recognize Taiwan. Without fully distancing themselves from Reagan's earlier stances, both Reagan and Bush assured the press that their message of the need to stop Soviet expansion and open up U.S.-Chinese trade would be well-received in Beijing, and that Reagan's clarifications on Taiwan would "sit very comfortably with the Chinese" (Raines 1980a, p. 22).

Reagan spent the rest of that week addressing the issue of defense and foreign policy in a number of forums. Over the same time period, Reagan surrogates held press conferences and released issue papers documenting Reagan's assertions (*Public Opinion* 1981, p. 9). In his first public address of the week, Reagan gave a speech to the Veterans of Foreign Wars (VFW) in Chicago. The speech was designed to emphasize Reagan's "peace through strength" policy and the decline of the U.S.'s position in the world due to Carter's "inconsistency, vacillation and bluff" (Raines 1980b, 1A, D7). Shortly before the speech, Reagan and his aides inserted a reference to the Vietnam War as a "noble cause" (Germond & Witcover 1980). Reagan's statement was intended to please the VFW, but the blunt and off-the-cuff remark reignited concerns that he was too amenable to entering into another war. It contributed to his campaign's "stumbling start" (Abramson, Aldrich & Rohde 1982, p. 40).

However, Reagan continued to be plagued during this first week by his statements regarding a possible "two-Chinas" policy. Even before Bush arrived in China, the Reagan campaign was criticized harshly by China's most influential newspaper, *The People's Daily*, which accused Reagan of "interfering in China's internal affairs" and called his stance on Taiwan "brazen and absurd" (Tharp 1980). On his arrival in China, Bush was pressed by reporters to clarify previous Reagan remarks regarding Taiwan. Bush said he would clear up the matter with his hosts before giving a statement to the press. At the end of Bush's visit, China's official New China News Agency released a scathing indictment of Reagan's "two Chinas proposition," and made it clear that Bush had been unable to convince the Chinese government that U.S. relations with China would not worsen under a Reagan administration. Bush tried to assure the Chinese and the press that it was "habit and not conviction" that led Reagan to refer to Taiwan as "the free Republic of China," but largely to no avail. Reagan campaign aides told the press that all Reagan wanted to do was highlight the "shabby treatment" Carter was giving Taiwan, but by the end of the first week of campaigning, they acknowledged that their attempt at "foreign policy and defense week" had been a strategic blunder (Raines 1980c, p. 28). Finally, at a press conference on August 25th, Reagan conceded that he had made misstatements on Taiwan and that he would abandon any plan to create an official U.S. liaison office in Taiwan. The Reagan retraction was given front page coverage by *The New York Times*, which concurrently ran an editorial critical of Reagan's Taiwan stance.

"Foreign policy and defense week" had begun as the Reagan campaign's first attempt at the IOD strategy. By their own standards they failed to maintain the correct focus. Reagan's press secretary, Lyn Nofziger, attributed at least part of the strategy's failure to the press's access to Reagan during press conferences. By the end of the week he had imposed a new limit on the number of press conferences Reagan would hold in the future (Raines 1980c, p. 28). Other aides felt criticisms of Reagan in the press resulted from his other, informal contacts with the press. To impose some structure, they placed Stu Spencer, an experienced campaign operative, on the campaign plane to ensure that Reagan, who was known to become too "informal" when chatting with members of the press, kept to the script (Germond & Witcover 1980, p. 209). The education of the Reagan campaign had begun and the first lesson was to keep the candidate away from the press by reducing the number and increasing the formality of their interactions.

Issue of the Day II: The Stealth Bomber Criticism. On Labor Day, in a speech intended to attack Carter's economic policy, Reagan ad-libbed that he was glad to see Carter was starting his campaign "down in the city that gave birth to and is the parent body of the Ku Klux Klan." The next day, Carter quickly pointed out that he was in Tuscumbia, Alabama to denounce the Klan. Moreover, the Klan had actually originated in Pulaski, Tennessee (T. Smith 1980, B-8). What had been intended as a solid week of attacks on Carter's economic record, became instead a series of Reagan clarifications and apologies for his Klan remark.

Reagan's advisors decided they needed to deflect attention from Reagan's mistakes by creating a new attack on Carter. They tried to put Carter on the defensive by criticizing his revelations during the previous week of a new and secret U.S. weapons system: the "stealth" bomber. Back on August 20th, Defense Department officials had announced that the U.S. government had developed and flown an experimental aircraft designed to evade Soviet radar. The officials said the disclosure was made to clarify a recent story in a trade journal about the same project. Sources in Congress immediately suggested that the Carter administration was revealing the stealth program in response to Reagan's earlier criticism of Carter on national defense (*The New York Times* 1980, A-1, A-20). A week later, Representative Samuel Stratton (D-NY) charged the Carter administration with being more interested in "convincing the public that it is doing a great job than in keeping our secrets from the Soviet Union" (Burt 1980a, A-16). The unusual timing of the stealth disclosure and the subsequent skepticism about its motivation made the issue a prime target for a Reagan attack.

In a September 4th speech in Jacksonville, Florida, Reagan accused Carter of compromising national security with the stealth disclosure. The next day, Reagan appeared with Henry Kissinger, who said the Ford administration had been able to avoid leaks on the stealth project, and echoed the charge that Carter had misused the powers of his office to further his election prospects. On September 6th, the Carter administration announced a new security classification system to stop the disclosure of national secrets (Burt 1980b, A-1, 27). Later, Carter charged Reagan with playing "cheap politics" and patently denied that his administration had harmed national security by revealing the existence of the stealth program. During this same time period, in contrast to the earlier uses of the IOD strategy, access to Reagan was noticeably reduced (Germond & Witcover 1980). Thus by hammering away at Carter and refusing to address other subjects, the Reagan campaign shifted the focus away from Reagan's misstatements to Carter's own liabilities.

Dropping the IOD Strategy: The Basic Stump Speech. Again, the lesson learned by the Reagan campaign was the need to keep the candidate under close supervision (H. Smith 1980, E-2). Beginning on September 7th and continuing through October 17th, the Reagan campaign implemented a new media management strategy. It dropped the homogeneous approach for a more traditionally wide-ranging message. It was designed to promote his experience as governor of California and his moderate policy stances towards Social Security, the role of the federal government, and the economy

(Germond & Witcover 1980, p. 259; Kessel 1988, pp. 198-200). During this time he spoke on a variety of subjects. He presented his five-year plan to balance the budget, reduce taxes, and restore national defenses. He declared his support for the Civil Rights Act of 1964 and proposed to liberalize immigration. He gave public assurances that he would protect social security, he pledged not to end price supports for farmers, and he promised to put a woman on the Supreme Court. Reagan was attempting to present himself as a competent and moderate man who could appeal to independents, union members and ethnic voters. But most importantly, he sought to avoid making any more verbal miscues (Wirthlin et al. 1981).

Issue of the Day III: Direct Attacks on Carter. By October 19th, Reagan began to launch direct and negative attacks on Carter's defense and foreign policies (Wirthlin et al. 1981, p. 48). On that date, he appeared on CBS-TV to give an address on those subjects. The speech emphasized Reagan's priority on maintaining peace, following a bipartisan foreign policy, and pursuing a "peace through strength" defense policy. From October 19th to October 22nd, the Reagan campaign returned to the homogeneous message, only this time the organization was better prepared to keep Reagan from deviating from the planned issues: they limited the media's access to Reagan, and pressured Reagan to avoid unnecessary informalities with the press (Kessel 1988, pp. 203-205; Wirthlin et al. 1981, p. 48; Germond & Witcover 1980, p. 266).

As the final week of campaigning began, Reagan and his surrogates returned a final time to a more heterogeneous message. They crisscrossed the country attacking Carter's economic policies, his competency, and his weak defense and foreign policies. The Reagan campaign intended to make the 1980 election a referendum on Carter. The Reagan strategists conclude that this was in fact the interpretation one should give the 1980 election results, and that the outcome was partially the result of the ability of Reagan strategists to keep the press' coverage tuned to the Reagan agenda (Wirthlin et al. 1981, p. 49).

Assessing the Effects of the Issue of the Day Strategy

Data Base and Measurement of Variables. To determine the effect, if any, of Reagan's evolving press strategy on how he was covered by the news media, we have analyzed a sample of *The New York Times'* reporting of the 1980 presidential election campaign. By analyzing the content of *The New York Times'* election stories, we can begin to determine the extent to which the IOD strategy achieved its intended objectives.

The New York Times was selected because it is one of the most widely read and influential newspapers among societal elites (Weiss 1974), and has a modest agenda-setting effect on public opinion (Winter and Eyal 1981). The potential influence of *The New York Times* makes it a prime target of candidate efforts to shape the coverage received.

We analyzed news stories from four distinct periods of the 1980 Reagan campaign: (1) the first "defense and foreign policy week" of August 16-23, (2) the "stealth bomber criticism" period of September 4-8, (3) a week (October 12-18) selected at random from the period during which Reagan used a traditional stump speech, and (4) the final salvo of attacks on defense and foreign policy that occurred October 19-22. These time periods were selected to maximize variation along the independent variable of the Reagan press strategy, while maintaining a substantive focus on defense and foreign policy issues.

The first period (August 16-23) is characterized by a highly homogeneous message but fairly frequent and unstructured contacts between Reagan and the press. This period scores low on formality and high on access, and so we consider it a weak implementation of the relational dimensions of the IOD strategy.

The second period (September 4-8) maintains the homogeneity of the first week, but is distinguished by the campaign's conscious decision to increase the formality of Reagan's relations with the press and to reduce its access to him. Thus, on the dimensions of formality and access, this version of the strategy qualifies as a moderate usage of the strategy relative to the other periods under study.

The third period (October 12-18) was randomly chosen from that period of the Reagan campaign when the organization used a stock campaign speech that touched on a variety of topics, while retaining a relationship with the press characterized by low accessibility and high formality. This week is our control week against which our other weeks can be compared in terms of homogeneity of the message.

The final period (October 19-22) was characterized by the Reagan campaign's return to the IOD strategy with high message homogeneity, high formality and low accessibility. We consider this final phase to be a period of strong implementation of the IOD strategy on all three dimensions.

Our basic unit of analysis was the paragraph. For each of the four periods, we selected for analysis all those stories that satisfied one of four criteria: (1) stories whose headline mentioned Reagan, (2) stories dealing with the issue of the day topic, (3) stories entitled "News Analysis," that dealt with the election, and (4) any editorials or commentary concerning the 1980 campaign.[3]

Every selected paragraph was coded on four characteristics: the day and date of the story, whether the paragraph involved the intended issue of the day topic, and whether the paragraph involved reference to a Reagan misstatement, or "gaffe." In addition, those paragraphs in Weeks One, Two, and Four that involved the issue of the day or a Reagan "gaffe," as well as all paragraphs in Week Three were coded for: the *substance* of the paragraph, the *primary source* of the information, the paragraph's *placement within the paper* (front page or not front page), the paragraph's *placement within the story* (first five paragraphs or not), the *type of story* within which the paragraph appears (straight news, editorial, or news analysis), and the *tone* of the paragraph (favorable, unfavorable, or mixed). The variables used in this study were:

Week. This variable identifies in which of the four weeks under study the paragraph was printed. This variable allows us to identify the condition of the independent variable. Each week exhibits variation in some combination of message homogeneity, candidate accessibility, and formality of meetings.

Issue of the Day (IOD). Is the paragraph about Reagan's issue of the day? For all three weeks under study in which the strategy was used, the issue of the day was defense/foreign policy. Therefore, in Week Three (in which there was no IOD), all paragraphs coded as dealing with defense or foreign policy were coded as being about the IOD.

Reagan Gaffe. Is the paragraph about a personal blunder by Reagan? Those reported on during these weeks were his claim that the Vietnam War was a "noble cause," his statement of support for a "two Chinas" policy, and his remarks regarding Carter and the Ku Klux Klan.[4]

Paragraph's Tone. The crucial question being examined by this variable is whether the issue of the day is being reported as the candidate presented it, or in some other, unintended manner. Seven categories were initially created to capture the interpretive tone of the paragraph.[5] For the purposes of this analysis, those paragraphs given any of the three negative codes described in footnote 4 were collapsed into a single category defined as "negative interpretation" (coded -1) and those paragraphs with any of the three positive codes were collapsed into a single category defined as "positive interpretation" (coded 1). Paragraphs with a 0 code in the seven-category coding scheme were defined as "mixed interpretation" and retained their 0 coding.

Type of Story. The final variable categorized paragraphs according to whether they came from a "straight news" story, a "new analysis" story, or an "editorial."

Hypotheses. The intended effects of the IOD strategy can be stated in three hypotheses. The first concerns the effects of the strategy on the homogeneity of the press's coverage; the second addresses the effects of the strategy on the interpretive balance of the press's coverage; and the third assesses the effects of the strategy on the campaign's ability to prevent reports based on Reagan misstatements:

1. *The Homogeneity Hypothesis*: When Reagan's campaign presents a

single message over an extended period of time, the homogeneity
of the stories reported by *The New York Times* will be greater than
when the campaign presents a variety of messages.

2. *The Tone Hypothesis*: As Reagan's campaign presents a single message over an extended period of time, increases the formality of the
Reagan's contacts with the press, and reduces the frequency of
those contacts, the percentage of paragraphs that reflect favorably
on Reagan's election campaign in *The New York Times* will increase.

3. *The Gaffe Hypothesis*: As Reagan's campaign presents a single message over an extended period of time, increases the formality of
Reagan's contacts with the press, and reduces the frequency of
those contacts, the percentage of paragraphs written about candidate mistakes in *The New York Times* will decrease.

Findings

The analysis of the contents of *The New York Times'* coverage of the
Reagan campaign reveals mixed effects for the IOD strategy. The strategy
appears to have accomplished some but not all of its objectives.

The Homogeneity Hypothesis. This hypothesis provides some insight
on the extent to which the press reports what it is given by the candidate
rather than developing its own stories. Table 5.1 reveals that in Weeks One
and Two, a period during which the Reagan campaign was still learning
how to use the IOD strategy, and the press was allowed fairly easy access to
Reagan, about one-third of the paragraphs written in *The New York Times*
dealt with the issue of the day.

In contrast, during Week Three, when there was no IOD strategy at
work, the subject of national defense and foreign policy took up only 20.1%
of the paragraphs written. When, at the end of the campaign, the Reagan
organization returned to the IOD strategy and used it to its full effect, fully
two-thirds of the paragraphs written about Reagan dealt with his chosen

TABLE 5.1 Effects of the Homogeneity Component of the IOD Strategy on the
Homogeneity of *New York Times* Coverage of Reagan's 1980
Campaign

Week	Homogeneity Component in Use?	Percent of Paragraphs with "Issue of the Day" Content
One	Yes	38.6%
Two	Yes	33.9%
Three	No	20.1%
Four	Yes	67.6%

Source: Author's analysis of *New York Times* coverage.

TABLE 5.2 Temporal Patterns in Homogeneity of New York <u>Times</u> Reports on
Reagan's 1980 Campaign

Number of Days IOD Strategy was Employed	% of Paragraphs on IOD (total number)			
	Week 1 (9/17-9/24)	Week 2 (10/5-10/9)	Week 3 (10/13-10/19)	Week 4 (10/20-10/23)
1	27.9 (43)	51.1 (45)	2.2 (46)	84.3 (70)
2	20.0 (5)	50.0 (40)	0.0 (00)*	52.6 (38)
3	50.0 (20)	49.4 (83)	5.3 (95)	60.2 (88)
4	26.3 (19)	5.6 (54)	1.7 (59)	68.4 (76)
5	52.2 (23)	11.5 (52)	26.2 (61)	---- ----
6	86.4 (22)	---- ----	31.2 (77)	---- ----
7	10.9 (46)	---- ----	35.0 (140)	---- ----
8	44.2 (86)	---- ----	---- ----	---- ----

* On October 14th, there were no stories in the *New York Times* that met our
criteria for inclusion in our analysis. There were indeed stories on the
election, but none pertaining directly to Reagan. This is the only day from
our sample for which that was true.

Source: Author's analysis of *New York Times* coverage.

subject. Thus, using Week Three as a baseline, the data suggests that the IOD
strategy was increasingly effective at setting the news media's substantive
agenda during the campaign.

Of course, even during Week Four, when the IOD strategy was
apparently most effective, one-third of the press's coverage of Reagan did
not involve the issue of the day. During the other two weeks in which the
strategy was used, almost two-thirds of the coverage dealt with other
subjects. This indicates that the press does find other things to report, even
when the candidate is trying to focus attention on a single issue. Thus, the
homogeneity component of the IOD strategy appears to influence, but not
dictate, the contents of the press's reports.

A subsidiary line of inquiry considered whether the homogenizing

TABLE 5.3 Effects of Homogeneity Component of IOD Strategy on "Tone" of
Coverage of Reagan's 1980 Campaign

Interpretation of Paragraph	Type of Week	
	3 IOD Weeks with Homogeneity Component	1 Week without Homogeneity Component
Favorable	50.7	46.9
Mixed	3.7	14.6
Unfavorable	45.6	38.5
Number of Paragraphs	377	96
Favorability Bias*	5.1	8.4

* Favorability Bias = (%Favorable Interpretation - %Unfavorable Interpretation)

Source: Author's analysis of *New York Times* coverage.

effects of the IOD strategy dissipated over the course of the periods when it was used. That is, given that the IOD strategy has some observable effects, are they concentrated in the first few days of the strategy's use, and then weaken as the story becomes less newsworthy and the press has time to develop other stories?

Table 5.2 shows no systematic support for a dissipation effect. The percentage of paragraphs dealing with the issue of the day fluctuates substantially and without pattern from one day to the next during Week One. Given the tentativeness with which the IOD strategy was implemented during Week One, this is the time period when a dissipation effect would be most likely to appear. In Week Two, there is a bifurcation in IOD paragraphs which supports the hypothesis: in the first three days, the IOD gets about one-half of all the coverage, while in the last two days there is a precipitous drop-off. However, in Week Four, while coverage of the IOD was highest on the first day, it remained at about fifty percent throughout the period, and rose rather than fell after the second day.

The Tone Hypothesis. Candidates seek to encourage a more favorable interpretation of their message by controlling the content and character of their relationship with the press. Tables 5.3 and 5.4 show that the strategy has little effect on the interpretation that the press puts on those messages.

Table 5.3 tests for the effects of the homogeneity of the messages on the tone of the coverage provided. Since Week Three used a multi-topic stump speech rather than a single issue approach, it provides a baseline for estimates of the homogeneity component's effect on the tone of press coverage. We looked for such an effect by comparing the distribution of favorable and unfavorable paragraph interpretations for the three IOD weeks with the same distribution during Week Three. The distributions are very similar. During the three IOD weeks, 50.7% of the paragraphs favorably interpreted Reagan's messages, while 45.6% provided negative interpretations. Week Three's results are comparable: 46.9% favorable and 38.5% unfavorable. A "favorability bias" variable that estimates the net balance of press interpretation can be calculated by subtracting the percentage of paragraphs with unfavorable interpretations from the percentage with favorable interpretations. Contrary to our expectations, the favorability bias is larger for the week when the homogeneity component was not in use than for the three IOD weeks when it was, 8.4% to 5.1%.

Table 5.4 examines whether the increasing formality and reduced frequency of contacts that characterized relations between Reagan and the press over the course of the campaign improved the interpretation that Reagan received. If that trend had a favorable effect, then the percentage of paragraphs with a favorable interpretation should increase over time while the percentage with unfavorable interpretations should decrease. Table 5.4, which breaks down Table 5.3 into the weekly distribution of favorable and unfavorable paragraphs, shows no discernable pattern. The highest percentages of unfavorable paragraphs occur in the first and last weeks of the study, and the favorability bias coefficient is lowest in the last week, when the strategy should have had its greatest effect. Thus we conclude that, while the IOD strategy may help shape the content of the message that the public receives, it does not improve the "spin" that is put on that message by the press.

TABLE 5.4 Effects of Access and Formality Components of IOD Strategy on "Tone" of Coverage of Reagan's 1980 Campaign

Interpretation of Paragraph	Week			
	One	Two	Three	Four
Favorable	48.0	58.1	46.9	48.4
Mixed	7.0	1.1	14.6	3.3
Unfavorable	45.0	40.9	38.5	48.4
Number of Paragraphs	100	93	96	184
Favorability Bias*	3.0	17.2	8.4	0.0

* Favorability Bias = (%Favorable Interpretation - %Unfavorable Interpretation)

Source: Author's analysis of *New York Times* coverage.

TABLE 5.5   Interpretation of Paragraph by Type of Story: An Aggregate
             Analysis

Interpretation of Paragraph	Type of Paragraph		
	Editorial	Straight News	News Analysis
Favorable	24.7	54.6	60.0
Mixed	4.9	6.4	2.9
Unfavorable	70.4	38.9	37.1
Number of Paragraphs	81	357	35
Favorability Bias*	-45.7	15.7	22.9

* Favorability Bias = (%Favorable Interpretation - %Unfavorable Interpretation)

Source: Author's analysis of *New York Times* coverage.

We also investigated a second line of inquiry concerning the tone of the paragraphs: In what types of stories does the press criticize or praise the candidate, and do those patterns vary when the IOD strategy is in use? Table 5.5 shows a distinct pattern regarding where the kudos and criticisms get expressed. Across all four periods of time, 70.4% of all editorial paragraphs were negative and only one-fourth were positive. In contrast, clear majorities of both the straight news and news analysis paragraphs were positive.

Table 5.6 examines the effects of the IOD strategy on that pattern. The three IOD weeks elicited much higher rates of negative opinion in editorial and news analysis stories, (80.8% and 50%, respectively), than did the week without the homogeneity component of the strategy—Week Three (51.7% and 20% respectively). Similarly, the percentages of paragraphs with favorable contents was higher for the non-IOD week (37.9% and 80%) than the three IOD weeks (17.3% and 45%). This resulted in favorability bias coefficients for those two types of stories that clearly favor the non-IOD strategy. For the IOD weeks, editorials had a -63.5 bias, and news analyses had a -5.0 bias. In contrast, the non-IOD Week Three had only a -13.8 bias on editorials and a +60.0 bias on news analyses. Thus, in those stories in which reporters are most likely to feel comfortable expressing an opinion, Reagan's attempt to limit the content of message given to the press corresponded with reporting that was, on balance, much more negative than when he was giving reporters a range of topics on which to report.

However, limiting the content did appear to pay off on the type of story with the most numerous paragraphs: the straight news story. On straight news paragraphs during the three IOD weeks, 56.7% of the straight news stories during Week Three had favorable interpretations. The favorability bias coefficient for the IOD weeks was three times the size of the coefficient for Week Three: 17.4 vs. 5.8.

Thus, the homogeneity component of the IOD strategy appears to have created an interesting tradeoff for the Reagan campaign. Editorials and news analysis stories make up a small proportion of the total coverage given to a campaign when compared to straight news stories. They composed less than 20% of the total number of paragraphs written about Reagan during the IOD weeks. On those relatively infrequent types of stories, Reagan did less well when he imposed homogeneity than when he did not. However, on the overwhelmingly more numerous straight news stories, Reagan did markedly better by controlling the content than when he presented a variety of stories. Thus, the candidate appears to have chosen to go with a strategy that results in better news coverage, and pay the price for it when the reporters felt free to express their own views.

The Gaffe Hypothesis. The final hypothesis considers the effects of structuring and minimizing the candidate's interactions with the press on the reporting of candidate mistakes. Weeks Two through Four each showed an increase in the formality of Reagan's relationship to the press and a decrease in his accessibility relative to the preceding week. Moreover, for the purposes of this hypothesis, the homogeneity of the message is not an important determinant of the frequency with which the press reports Reagan making a campaigning mistake. Thus, we consider the four weeks to constitute an ordinal ranking of formality and accessibility, with Week One scoring lowest on formality and highest on accessibility, and Week Four scoring highest on formality and lowest on accessibility. Given this pattern in the independent variable, what changes in the dependent variable can we

TABLE 5.6 Interpretation of Paragraph by Type of Story: Effects of IOD Strategy

Type of Strategy Employed	Interpretation of Paragraph			Number of Paragraphs	Favorability Bias*
	Favorable	Mixed	Unfavorable		
IOD:					
Editorial	17.3	1.9	80.8	52	-63.5
Straight News	56.7	3.9	39.3	305	17.4
News Analysis	45.0	5.0	50.0	20	-5.0
Non-IOD:					
Editorial	37.9	10.3	51.7	29	-13.8
Straight News	42.3	21.2	36.5	52	5.8
News Analysis	80.0	0.0	20.0	15	60.0

* Favorability Bias = (%Favorable Interpretation - %Unfavorable Interpretation)

Source: Author's analysis of *New York Times* coverage.

TABLE 5.7 Effects of IOD Strategy on Coverage of Reagan "Gaffes" During 1980 Campaign

Week	Percentage of Paragraphs Concerning Reagan "Gaffe"
One	33.0%
Two	19.0%
Three	0.6%
Four	0.0%

Source: Author's analysis of *New York Times* coverage.

observe?

Table 5.7 shows a strong influence of formality and accessibility on the frequency with which mistakes were reported. Week One documents Reagan's "stumbling start" (Abramson et al. 1982, p. 40), as fully one-third of the paragraphs dealt with Reagan's misstatements. That drops off to 19% in Week Two (the week Stu Spencer joined the campaign staff to limit Reagan's contacts with the press), and virtually disappears thereafter (0.6% in Week Three and 0.0% in Week Four). Thus, the Reagan staff was overwhelmingly successful in preventing Reagan from shooting himself in the foot with off-the-cuff remarks, by eliminating the opportunity for such unplanned statements to be made.

Conclusions

The findings reported suggest a degree of caution in our assessment of the efficacy of the IOD strategy. Even Ronald Reagan, the "Great Communicator," was unable to fully control the image of his candidacy that the press presented to the public. Reagan's campaign did appear to increasingly control the content of the messages provided by the press. However, even in the final weeks of the campaign, one in three paragraphs written about Reagan were unrelated to his intended message.

The strategy was also effective at minimizing press coverage of Reagan "gaffes." Two alternative explanations of the decline in such coverage are possible. On the one hand, Reagan may have become more adept in his meetings with the press, so that the actual number of misstatements would have declined regardless of the nature or frequency of his conversations with the press. On the other hand, he may have continued to make mistakes, so that their very frequency would have made them "old news" (Fallows 1984).

Neither alternative is particularly persuasive. Given Reagan's penchant to misspeak himself after he took office, the first interpretation seems unlikely. Rather, when he spoke with the press in an unstructured situation, there continued to be a significant chance that he would say something controversial. The second alternative is implausible because election campaigns occur over a relatively short time frame and have as one of their clear functions the evaluation of the candidate's character. In those circumstances, it is doubtful that Reagan's mistakes would have become less newsworthy simply because of their frequency.

Thus, we conclude that the strategy of reducing Reagan's contacts with the press and reducing the opportunities for dangerous off-the-cuff remarks by formalizing those contacts, appears to have been highly successful in limiting the likelihood that Reagan would commit a verbal gaffe in the presence of the press. In this regard, the strategy was very successful.

However, Reagan's efforts at shaping the tone of the coverage that he received went relatively unrewarded. Increasing the homogeneity of the messages and the formality of contacts, and reducing the frequency of contacts had no apparent net effect on the press' tendencies to give Reagan a positive or negative assessment. The IOD strategy did encourage more favorable reporting in straight news stories, but it did not appear to limit the press's ability to independently interpret the substance and merits of the candidate's remarks in editorials and news analyses.

Thus, we conclude that the process of creating a public image for a presidential candidate is a three-player game involving the candidate, the public, and the press. The press continues to play an important and independent role in the construction of candidate images in the minds of the public.

Notes

1. For the purposes of this paper, the terms "media," "news media," and "the press" are used interchangeably.

2. This case study is not a comprehensive account of Reagan's entire 1980 election campaign, or of every change in its media management strategy. Rather it focuses on the four phases in the deployment of that strategy that form the subject of our subsequent content analysis of news reports. It describes how the various versions of the strategy worked and how the press responded.

3. Transcripts of speeches or press conferences were not coded. In fulfilling its role as the "news of record," *The New York Times* publishes complete transcripts of major speeches and news conferences, independent of any editorial discretion.

4. Please note, we are not making the substantive judgement that Reagan mispoke himself, or that what he said was foolish or naive. Rather, we are identifying those Reagan remarks that the news media described as errors on Reagan's part.

5. The six category codes were as follows:
-3 = Negative interpretation by the journalist's language

-2 = Negative interpretation by independent source
-1 = Candidate's defensive reaction to criticism
0 = Mixed/Undiscerned
1 = Reporting candidate's message favorably
2 = Positive interpretation by independent source
3= Positive interpretation by the journalist's language

While this variable is coded as if it were an interval level variable, we have used it only as a nominal variable.

The -3 score identified paragraphs in which the journalist used language that cast the candidate's message or campaign in a critical light. For example, Howell Raines began a story on Reagan's "Taiwan" problems with the paragraph: "The Ronald Reagan campaign has, to borrow from the terminology of nuclear mishaps, developed its own China syndrome (Raines 1980, A18 [emphasis added]). The journalist was describing problems of the Reagan campaign by using a metaphor with negative connotations.

Paragraphs coded with a -2 identified paragraphs in which information was supplied that was contrary to or critical of Reagan's message. Paragraphs in which the press reported about the Carter campaign's attempt to refute a Reagan claim, or in which experts challenged Reagan's message fit into this category.

Paragraphs were coded -1 if the point of the paragraph was to assert that Reagan was on the defensive regarding his own message, as occurred with the Taiwan issue early in the general election campaign.

A neutral category (coded 0) was added to account for paragraphs that gave a conflicting or unclear interpretation of Reagan's messages.

The final three categories are largely the reverse of the first three negative categories. Paragraphs in which Reagan's message was printed verbatim or with minimal interpretation were coded +1: "Mr. Reagan called peace his 'number one priority ... but it must not be peace at any price'" (Raines 1980, A1). This is what in other studies might be considered "neutral" reporting. Thus the paucity of 0 codes should not be interpreted to mean the press was rarely neutral. Rather, it means that few paragraphs had mixed or unclear reports. The traditionally "neutral" reports were categorized as +1 to reflect the fact that the press was covering the candidate as the candidate intended. Likewise, those paragraphs in which independent sources of information were used to advance Reagan's message were coded +2, and paragraphs in which the journalist used language supportive of Reagan's message were coded +3. These latter two codes capture what might more routinely be understood as favorable interpretations, over and above simply reporting the candidate's message as it was presented.

6

Coverage of Elections on Evening Television News Shows: 1972-1992

J. David Woodard

Political power in the American democracy comes from winning elections, and nothing has changed the nature of those elections in the past thirty years more than television. Today television is the main source of news, and twice as many people trust what is broadcast on television more than what is reported by other media (Ranney 1983, pp. 13-15). Yet after all these years of televised election coverage, little is known about how an American presidential campaign appears to the viewing, and voting, public and how that coverage has changed over time.

Today candidates recognize that citizens have become consumers, who prefer to function as an audience of observers rather than as participants in political contests. Presidential elections are like "horse races," (Patterson 1980) where candidates vie with one another before a television audience trying to improve their appeal and convince voters of their ability to win. The natural question given a casual audience watching a race on tv is how do the horses run? How do we know when someone is ahead, and how will we measure their lead?

Coverage on the evening news is a desirable outcome for candidates, today's campaigns are scheduled around television. Speeches are written for sound bite editing, rallies are organized to give the illusion of support for the candidate. Candidate staffs are trained to put the best "spin" on a story. One test of candidate success is the amount of television coverage a campaign receives relative to that of the opponent. A large portion of the candidate strategy involves trying to attract coverage, and an equally large amount of the media time involves projecting winners and losers against the backdrop of expectations created by earlier news stories.

Understanding the roles the press and candidate play in campaign coverage is of considerable importance because only a handful of people experience the candidate first hand. If we are to understand how the public develops its images of presidential candidates, it is important to understand how television coverage changes from primary, through the party conventions to the general election.

The implications of television coverage are the grist of much political science research, the bulk of which deals with political images in elections (Robinson 1981; Robinson & Sheehan 1983; Patterson 1980; Nimmo & Savage 1976; Nimmo & Combs 1983; Miller et al. 1986). The frequency and quality of candidate coverage has been a special focus because they can be crucial to a candidate's success or failure. Investigations of political campaigns usually focus on post-Labor Day coverage or episodic events during primary contests (Lichtner 1987). No comparisons have been made across elections, and "relatively few studies of media impact on elections have analyzed media content systematically" (Graber 1991, p. 100). This research widens the scope of inquiry by examining coverage from campaign announcement, through the primaries, conventions, and to the contest between party nominees in the fall. Comparisons are then made between and among the various campaigns for which comparable data are available.

Previous Studies

There is strong evidence that television news plays a powerful role in shaping public opinion (Iyengar & Kinder 1987). Studies of television coverage in recent presidential elections reveal an emphasis on personal attributes such as trustworthiness, strength of character, leadership abilities and compassion on the evening news shows (Weaver 1981; Graber 1986; Robinson & Sheehan 1983). Such qualities are especially amenable to the intimacy television offers to viewers, but the brevity of the medium requires bold pictures to reinforce verbal messages. Content analysis of the network evening news shows indicate that they pay little attention to the issue stands and qualifications of the candidates. Instead it is the hoopla, rallies, noise and excitement that are covered (Patterson & McClure 1976). As a result, around each candidate there has grown a coterie of advisors who handle the image of the aspirant (Sabato 1981).

While much has been written about candidate attempts to control the media reporting, we lack clear conceptual and empirical explanations about the ebb and flow of television coverage and its impact on voters. On a priori grounds the impact of television might be expected to be greatest during the primary elections phase of the presidential selection process. The ambiguity and complexity inherent in the primaries would seem to facilitate television's capacity to introduce candidates and sort out issues. In a 1976 study, Alrich, Gant and Simon (1978) argued that primary election results affected campaign momentum, poll standing, contributions and media attention. Brady and

Johnson (1987) examine the information given the voters and the amount of learning which takes place in the early presidential primaries and conclude that "citizens are informed during the primary season ... [and] There is a substantial amount of serious coverage of the candidates."

The results of primaries and caucuses are interpreted in light of how candidates are "expected" to perform, and these expectations are generated by the candidates and the media. The quest for the presidential nomination is in part a psychological battle and television can be influential in creating momentum, which can in turn influence the election outcome. At the nominating convention the role of television becomes paramount. The effects of television coverage are especially important for aspiring vice presidential candidates and party leaders who want to have a voice in future decisions. Conventions have been streamlined to be more attractive to the television audience. Paletz and Elson (1976) examined NBC's coverage of the 1972 Democratic convention and found that television coverage left conflict and disorder as impressions of the event through the procedures of network reporting.

The general election campaign is a better defined situation than the primaries and party convention. The chances of media intrusiveness are less because the networks try to balance their coverage between the party candidates. Television coverage emphasizes who is going to win, how the candidates are doing and how their campaign reflects their capacity to govern. In 1976 Thomas Patterson found about sixty percent of television coverage and fifty-five percent of newspaper coverage in the general election was devoted to the campaign contest (Patterson 1980, p. 45). Robinson and Sheehan's (1983) analysis of the *CBS Evening News* during the 1980 election found that five out of six stories emphasized the competition, little time was spent on issues of policy. Research on the effects of media have difficulty untangling such effects from other influences. This is especially true in elections, when compared to the voters' party allegiance, psychological characteristics, or past and current experiences and information, the effects of mass media coverage appear minimal (Neuman 1986, p. 156). Even so, the rise of electoral consultants coupled with the establishment of television as a trusted source of information, along with the steady decline of party influence in elections, has led to a continued interest of media influences on voting (Nie et al. 1976; Patterson & McClure 1976; Shaw & McCombs 1972; Jamieson 1984).

Methods and Data

This research differs from previous studies in that it examines election coverage from start to finish, and compares coverage across campaign years. Every story aired on the presidential election by the three major networks on any day was coded into the data set. The source of the news stories was the Vanderbilt *Television News Index and Abstracts* of the daily newscasts. News stories were coded on the basis of their principal subject matter, the length of the story, their placement in the broadcast and their general content for approximately a two year period before each presidential election. When filmed interviews with candidates, sympathizers or consultants were broadcast, the coding scheme allowed for the recording and analysis of on-camera interviews. Weekend stories were included, but sometimes they were upstaged by sporting events. To be included in the study a story could be on any aspect of the election.

The Vanderbilt Television News Archive began recording evening news broadcasts in August of 1968, so the election held that year is ignored here. At the inception of this project, the goal was to utilize the Vanderbilt archive data to examine the coverage of presidential election campaigns from 1972 through 1992. Unfortunately, the Vanderbilt Archive has been experiencing financial difficulties since 1990, thereby making it impossible to incorporate, in a timely fashion, any empirical evidence on the 1992 campaign. The analysis presented here will be restricted, therefore, to the period from 1972 to 1988, but comments on the 1992 race will be included whenever possible to do so despite the absence of Vanderbilt data.

The typical way of measuring television news coverage has been to count the number of stories broadcast by the major networks for a certain period of time.[1] Often stories must be of a certain length (usually at least thirty or forty-five seconds) to be included in the study. Occasionally, researchers have tried to incorporate the importance of lead stories, but calculating their value relative to the other stories is difficult. Each evening news show consists of roughly twenty-two minutes of news and slightly less than ten minutes of commercials. A typical broadcast has four commercial breaks, the important stories appear early in the show with lesser stories trailing through the subsequent commercials. In this study the stories were included if they had at least ten seconds of air time.

The rank order of the stories is used as an indicator of their significance, and the relationship between the length of the story and its place in the news lineup is taken as an indication of its importance and visibility.[2] Every television news story has both a timed length and a rank order in the evening broadcast. Using commercial breaks as a dividing line, a measure of news story "salience" is computed based on the placement of the story in the broadcast line-up multiplied by its timed length. Story "salience" is a measure of television coverage using the dictionary definition of the "noticeable, conspicuous and prominent" importance of a story. This measure assumes that stories at the head of the broadcast are more important than those at the end of the show, and that longer stories are more important than shorter stories.[3] A comparison of television evening news show coverage showing the salience measure for all three networks is shown in Table 6.1 for the data in the study. There are 12,537 stories in the data set for all the stories in election years 1972 to 1988.

The highest amount of television coverage on the evening network news programs was in the 1976 election, followed by the 1980 election and the 1988 election. These three elections offered exciting contests and new faces to the voters, as such they were especially attractive to the television medium. The amount of attention lavished on the 1976 and 1980 contests is partly a function of the changing nature of American politics and the structure of electronic journalism at the time. The evening networks were unrivaled in their coverage of presidential candidates; cable news and the competition of syndicated afternoon shows which draw viewers away from the network news was a feature of television still years in the future. Every year since 1979 fewer people have watched what the networks air. By 1990 the combined share of the TV audience which the networks enjoyed had plunged from a peak of more than ninety percent to sixty-two percent. Evening newscasts experienced a twenty-one percent drop in viewership during this period.[4]

The salience measure combines the rank-order attention given various election stories with story length. In 1976 there were a thousand more stories broadcast than in the election of 1988, but the higher placement of stories in the broadcast que for 1988 meant that the salience figure for that year approached that of the earlier contest. It is also interesting to compare coverage in 1984 and 1988 because the number of stories is about the same in both years, but the placement of the stories in 1988 meant that the salience

TABLE 6.1 Comparison of TV News Coverage

Election Year	Number of Stories	Salience
1968	677	-
1973	2,433	941,880
1976	2,949	1,198,920
1980	2,617	1,185,750
1984	1,915	960,690
1988	1,946	1,126,680
Total	12,537	

Source: Vanderbilt Television News *Abstracts.* Stories were coded if there was a designation by the networks that the story subject was the presidential election or campaign.

figure in that year was much higher. Even though the number of stories broadcast about presidential elections is decreasing, beginning in 1988 the stories on the evening news were placed higher in the broadcast line-up emphasizing the election more and raising the salience score.

To better analyze the amount and type of coverage given the election by the major television networks the nearly two-year time period of the presidential election campaign is divided into four segments. The first stage is called the preprimary period, and stretches from January the year before the election year until the first primary stories are filed by correspondents in the field. The second period examines press coverage of the presidential primaries, from the first stories broadcast in Iowa and New Hampshire, through key states which illustrate vote-getting ability in strategic regions, until the nomination is clinched by one of the major party candidates. The third period examines the television coverage of political conventions, which attract huge amounts of media attention in an election year. The final stage is the general election, from its beginnings usually around Labor Day until the final vote in November. Table 6.2 compares the coverage by the three networks for these phases of the presidential election. The Table exhibits the number of stories in each time period, the salience figure for that time period and the percentage of the total election coverage devoted to that phase of the campaign.

The figures in Table 6.2 are for the number of stories, salience score and duration of that phase of the campaign. The row percentages show that television coverage of presidential primaries increased dramatically in 1976 as the primary phase of the campaign became the major focus of network coverage in the election. In the years since the 1976 election, the primaries have received more TV attention than the fall general election. In 1972, stories about primaries began in January. In 1988 the first primary story was in November of 1987, nearly four months before the Iowa caucuses. The Iraq war delayed primary coverage in 1992 until December, but the initial coverage was still nearly four months before the crucial New Hampshire primary. A look at the length of the television primary phase of the election campaign shows that it has expanded from about twenty weeks in 1972 to about thirty weeks in 1988 and 1992.

Part of the explanation for increased media attention to presidential primaries lies in the number of primaries in 1988 and 1992 as compared with those twenty years earlier. In 1968 there were seventeen primaries, in 1972 twenty-three, in 1988 thirty-eight and in 1992 thirty.[5] But the differences in television coverage involve more than the number of primaries. A comparison of the 1972 and 1976 campaigns in Table 6.2 shows that the total length and number of stories for the two presidential campaigns was about even, yet the attention given to the primary contests in 1976 was nearly twice that of

TABLE 6.2: Comparison of TV News Coverage: The Phases of a Presidential Election

Election Year	Preprimary	Primary	Convention	General Election	Total
1972	n = 343 (116,870) weeks 01-54 12%	n = 606 (213,160) weeks 55-76 23%	n =874 (389,400) weeks 77-88 41%	n = 610 (222,450) weeks 89-98 24%	n = 2,433 941,880 100%
1976	n = 363 (134,280) weeks 01-53 11%	n = 1,279 (503,370) weeks 54-76 42%	n = 621 (260,350) weeks 77-86 22%	n = 686 (300,920) weeks 89-97 25%	n = 2,949 1,198,920 100%
1980	n = 475 (187,880) weeks 01-51 16%	n = 893 (389,260) weeks 52-79 33%	n = 562 (269,040) weeks 76-85 23%	n = 687 (339,570) weeks 86-97 29%	n = 2,617 1,185,750 100%
1984	n = 176 (65,850) weeks 01-46 7%	n = 769 (374,450) weeks 47-76 39%	n = 464 (244,490) weeks 77-86 25%	n = 506 (275,900) weeks 87-97 29%	n = 1,915 960,690 100%
1988	n = 183 (100,810) weeks 01-45 9%	n = 768 (439,210) weeks 46-76 39%	n = 417 (241,200) weeks 77-86 21%	n = 578 (345,460) weeks 87-98 31%	n = 1,946 1,126,680 100%
AVERAGE 1972-1988	n = 308 (121,138) weeks 0-50 11%	n = 863 (383,890) weeks 51-76 36%	n = 588 (280,896) weeks 76-86 26%	n = 613 (296,860) weeks 87-98 27%	n = 2372 (1,082,784) 100%

Source: Vanderbilt Television News Abstracts.

1972. Why was there so much more primary coverage in 1976? Part of the explanation may lie in the nature of the contest that year, both parties had a tight race for the nomination.

The length may also be explained by advances in media technology which had improved to the point where the networks could get more and better film from the field for presentation on the evening news. What may be in evidence in Table 6.2 is the influence of economics on evening news coverage. In the 1970's vast encampments of network reporters accompanied candidates from primary to primary. In the 1992 race not one of the networks assigned a reporter to each major candidate during the primary. Instead of following the candidates with reporters, the networks provided film and commentary on the race from desks in New York and Washington. The primaries are attractive to the networks because they are where the controversy and contest is in American politics. The networks are competing with one another to gain an edge and give the party nominee to viewers as early as possible. They are the place to "scoop" the competition, and every year since 1976 primaries have remained as the focus of network coverage.

At one time decisions about the Democratic or Republican nominees were made in deliberations at the convention hall, but now the delegates merely ratify the choices already made in the primaries. About the only suspense at the convention is the choice of the vice-presidential nominee and whether the party will be united for the upcoming election. Television coverage has always featured the political conventions; coverage of the conventions rates as the highest weekly salience score of any event in each two-year election cycle. The percentages in Table 6.2 show that about one-fourth of the television coverage since the 1972 election is focused on the conventions.

The last phase of the campaign, the general election, is a time when candidates engage in debates, while reporters speculate as to how the two candidates are faring with the voters. At this stage of the contest, no issue is more important than television "exposure." In the general election it is hoped that with evening news broadcasts will come a better understanding of the candidate and the campaign's themes. Research on political campaigns focuses on the events of the general election even though the majority of television time concerning candidates has already been completed. This last phase of the presidential campaign occupies roughly 25% to 30% of the total election coverage. The salience scores in the last few weeks of the fall general election campaign reflect the attention given party nominees before and after presidential debates (weeks 88-98).

An average of the salience scores is shown in the last row of Table 6.2. The figures show that coverage is incidental in the preprimary stage, rising to a crescendo in the primary period. The coverage in February and March is especially high. Coverage diminishes in the early summer, but rises for the conventions in July and August. The general election features coverage which varies with debates and controversy, but rises in the week before election day. The pattern holds regardless of contestants, issues or events; the amount of coverage seems to be determined more by programming schedule than political events. Since the most important finding in Table 6.2, is the rise in attention given to intra-party primary contests, it is to that subject that the research next turns.

Primary Elections

The controversy which once inhabited the convention hall and the smoke-filled rooms of nearby hotels, is now reserved for presidential preference primaries. Today primaries mean media exposure, money pouring into the coffers of the perceived front-runner, and the likelihood of a stump speech gaffe which is suitable for replay on television. Primaries convert the selection of party candidates into highly visible, sometimes bitter, competition among people in the same party who must eventually come together in public to back the party nominee. Controversy is everywhere apparent in primaries and usually the subject of television journalism.

Nowhere is the speculation richer than in the early primary contests where some candidate can be declared the winner or loser with only a fraction of the total potential vote. Iowa, as the first primary, has become the place where candidates are potentially first sifted. Especially for Democrats, the Iowa contest has become a place where "outsiders" can ride the magic carpet to success. George McGovern ran unexpectedly close behind Ed Muskie in 1972, and Jimmy Carter used a caucus victory there to get wind in his sails for 1976. In 1984 Iowa gave Gary Hart six percent more of the vote than expected and the press immediately declared a "two-man race" as a consequence. In 1992 favorite son Tom Harkin's candidacy made the Iowa primary less important, so the focus on television coverage was on the subsequent New Hampshire contest. The media have made the primaries, and especially the early primaries, the litmus test of presidential success.

Early primary contests, especially Iowa's importance in this transformation and its place as a media state, is seen in Table 6.3. The Table measures the salience attention based on the number of stories originating there in the elections of 1972 through 1988. The figures in Table 6.3 are the percentages of total television time in the primary phase of the election contest devoted to candidates and voters in thirteen states that held primaries in each election between 1972 and 1988. In the 1972 and 1988 presidential elections, primary television coverage in these thirteen states accounted for roughly two-thirds of the total attention given the period. In the other three elections, the amount of television attention to these primaries shrank

TABLE 6.3 Media Coverage of Presidential Candidates in Primary States

State	1972	1976	1980	1984	1988
Iowa	1.7%	1.2%	6.6%	8.2%	33.7%
New Hampshire	10.5	8.6	9.3	8.0	14.8
Wisconsin	9.5	2.0	2.9	-	3.4
Pennsylvania	4.0	5.0	4.0	4.4	1.3
Massachusetts	1.9	5.6	3.2	3.2	-
Indiana	2.4	2.2	-	-	-
Ohio	3.1	-	1.9	-	-
West Virginia	-	-	-	-	-
Florida	12.2	4.5	2.4	4.5	1.5
Oregon	6.7	1.0	-	-	-
California	13.9	2.9	2.9	4.2	4.2
New Jersey	-	1.0	-	-	-
Illinois	2.1	4.3	6.5	5.6	4.6
Other	32.0	61.7	60.3	61.9	36.5

Source: Vanderbilt Television News *Abstracts.* Stories were coded if there was a designation by the networks that the story subject was the presidential election or campaign.

dramatically, nevertheless they still accounted for roughly forty percent of total primary attention. In 1988 the television coverage devoted to Iowa and New Hampshire alone accounted for nearly half of the coverage given candidates in the primary period. "Calendar bias" reflected in the coverage of the early primaries, and a general fascination with how candidates appear as media celebrities, characterizes television today. As a subject Iowa has expanded rapidly in comparison with other states and New Hampshire attracts a consistent, and less variable, amount of primary coverage. In 1992 Bill Clinton faced considerable criticism of his private life before the New Hampshire primary and many pundits had written him off because of this. But, his second place finish in New Hampshire established him as the "come-back kid", thus giving him a much needed boost toward the frontrunner position and his subsequent presidential victory.

With the exception of the early primary states, the percentages in Table 6.3 are uniformly decreasing across time. All states lost in media attention with the increasing number of primaries, including some which played dramatic roles in determining eventual party nominees. For example, in 1976 the Pennsylvania primary was the climactic contest in the Democratic selection process, but it only attracted 5% of the total primary coverage. States with large populations, and an impressive number of electoral votes, do not attract a commensurate amount of attention on the evening news. The Illinois primary has a fairly steady record of coverage, but Wisconsin, Pennsylvania, Massachusetts and Florida have very uneven records. Victories in these states, with their diverse geography and populations, are crucial to proving vote-getting ability, yet they fail to garner a proportionate amount of television coverage.

California, which has twenty percent of the electoral votes needed to win the presidency, only receives about four percent of the television coverage given to candidates in the primary phase of the election. The demise of California is easily explained by "calendar bias" since television is attracted to the early story. The subsequent story, no matter how profound, escapes notice. While it is true that more states are having primaries, and that the primary season is longer, these are not the reasons for more primary coverage. Instead, the agenda for primary television coverage is driven by the calendar and the organizational patterns of news gathering. The early primary contests are easily scheduled and anticipated, the subsequent primaries, even though they may be critical to the election outcome, usually get attention only in the week before the voting. The 1988 election was a time when the early contests in Iowa and New Hampshire were subjects for speculation and exaggerated importance, as a result they captured half of the television coverage given primaries in a year when primaries were the major focus of television coverage.

Democrats and Republicans

In the twentieth century political parties have grown steadily weaker because they have lost control over candidate nominating procedures. Television has expanded a politician's ability to deal directly with the public and minimized the role of parties in the electoral process. If pictures and time on the air count for improved standing, then the Democrats should have an advantage in presidential elections since they had contested primaries more often than the Republicans during the period investigated here. Of the five elections in this study, the Democrats have been the incumbent party only once, in 1980 when Jimmy Carter lost to Ronald Reagan. In three of the five elections (1972, 1976 and 1984) there was an incumbent GOP president in the contest, and George Bush had many advantages of incumbency in 1988 when he was vice-president.

Percentages in Table 6.4 show the coverage Democrats and Republicans receive during the four phases of a political campaign. The amount of the coverage, rather than the tone, is the focus here. As expected higher figures are generally found for Democrats in the preprimary and primary stages of the election. The anomaly in the Table is the 1976 election where a disproportionate amount of attention was heaped on the Reagan and Ford contest even though Ford was an incumbent officeholder. Aside from the lead Republicans had in the 1976 preprimary period, Democrats uniformly received more attention at the preprimary, primary and convention stage of the election contest.

In the general election, the amount of coverage has favored Republicans in both incumbent and non-incumbent years. While in some years this advantage has been slight (i.e., 1972 and 1984), at other times the advantage has been significant (i.e., 1976 and 1980). In 1988 the Republicans had a respectable edge in coverage. The striking finding here is that Republicans turn the tables on their Democratic opponents in the all important general election period. These measures are for the amount of television coverage only, no consideration for topic or slant of the story is coded in Table 6.4.

Why do Republicans enjoy advantages over Democrats in terms of the amount of coverage in the general election? One reason may be the power of incumbency Republicans enjoyed during most of the time of this study. Another explanation may lie in the dominance Ronald Reagan always evinced where the media was concerned. The explanation may be as simple as the fact that Republican debate gaffes (Ford in 1976, Quayle in 1988) as well as debate and advertising successes (Reagan in 1980 and 1984, Bush in 1988) attracted subsequent television replays. For whatever reason, the figures in Table 6.4 show a reversal of the dominance Democrats generally enjoy prior to the general election period.

Filmed Stories and Commentary

Television is an entertainment medium, and as such it seeks to attract viewers by focusing on personalities. Television presents news in a point of view format because viewers identify more strongly with people than with abstract ideas. TV news favors interesting visuals of important people saying important things; the story should be short, have exciting pictures and a clear plot. In a presidential campaign the events of each campaign day, the appearances before select audiences and the themes of prepared speeches are all set with the local and national news shows in mind.

The television news format does not provide detailed, substantive information; instead, it focuses on visuals that cut to the core of the conflict. The technology of television news is aimed at increasing the visual presentation of people and events.

TABLE 6.4 Campaign of Television Coverage: Democrats and Republicans in Campaign Phases

Incumbent Republican	Preprimary	Primary	Convention	General Election
1972	Democrats: n=203 (70,610) 60% Republicans: n=81 (26,120) 22% Other: n=59 (20,100) 18%	Democrats: n=488 (180,980) 85% Republicans: n=56 (12,730) 6% Other: n=62 (19,450) 9%	Democrats: n=519 (242,280) 62% Republicans: n=229 (91,720) 24% Other: n=126 (55,400) 14%	Democrats: n=206 (83,040) 37% Republicans: n=226 (84,140) 38% Other: n=178 (55,270) 25%
1976	Democrats: n=109 (41,920) 31% Republicans: n=190 (76,490) 57% Other: n=64 (15,870) 12%	Democrats: n=654 (245,790) 49% Republicans: n=408 (181,770) 36% Other: n=217 (75,810) 15%	Democrats: n=222 (87,610) 34% Republicans: n=355 (156,350) 60% Other: n=44 (16,390) 6%	Democrats: n=160 (81,850) 27% Republicans: n=257 (123,460) 41% Other: n=269 (95,610) 32%
1984	Democrats: n=110 (43,430) 66% Republicans: n=34 (12,650) 19% Other: n=32 (9,770) 15%	Democrats: n=567 (283,200) 75% Republicans: n=66 (31,700) 9% Other: n=136 (59,580) 16%	Democrats: n=268 (149,970) 62% Republicans: n=114 (61,680) 25% Other: n=82 (32,840) 13%	Democrats: n=192 (102,920) 37% Republicans: n=187 (104,050) 38% Other: n=127 (68,930) 25%

(continues)

TABLE 6.4 (continued): Campaign of Television Coverage: Democrats and Republicans in Campaign Phases

	Preprimary	Primary	Convention	General Election
Incumbent Democrat 1980	Democrats: n=328 (139,570) 74% Republicans: n=111 (39,110) 21% Other: n=36 (9,200) 5%	Democrats: n=362 (161,150) 41% Republicans: n=356 (157,130) 40% Other: n=166 (70,980) 19%	Democrats: n=268 (135,650) 50% Republicans: n=256 (117,170) 44% Other: n=38 (16,220) 6%	Democrats: n=204 (107,030) 32% Republicans: n=295 (146,520) 43% Other: n=188 (86,020) 25%
No Incumbent 1988	Democrats: n=125 (73,410) 73% Republicans: n=49 (21,660) 22% Other: n=9 (5,740) 5%	Democrats: n=374 (216,920) 49% Republicans: n=286 (161,890) 37% Other: n=108 (60,400) 14%	Democrats: n=212 (126,600) 53% Republicans: n=171 (97,770) 41% Other: n=34 (16,830) 6%	Democrats: n=181 (108,960) 32% Republicans: n=212 (125,330) 36% Other: n=185 (111,170) 32%

Source: Vanderbilt Television News *Abstracts.* Stories were coded if there was a designation by the networks that the story subject was the presidential election or campaign.

Throughout the period covered by this study the typical election news story has remained stable, averaging around two minutes; but the number of interviews, especially filmed interviews, sandwiched in such a story has increased. In 1972, only 20.7% of campaign stories had filmed interviews, by 1988 slightly more than half (52.1%) of the stories carried interviews. This was largely due to the widespread use of newer technology and the tendency of television to reduce the sound bite of a news story to accommodate more film and a faster pace on the evening news show.[6]

As the capacity of television has expanded to present film of diverse events, so too has the tendency of television news stories to present controversy. Real life is usually not dramatic, and most events do not have a neat or easily understood story plot, but television demands conflict and drama for each presentation. The medium itself asks that pictures be supplemented with controversy. Election stories are frequently simplified to candidate versus candidate, or a Democrats versus Republicans format to supply balance and create drama or disagreement. News coverage of a single event, like the result of the Iowa or New Hampshire primary, is frequently reformulated into the "who's the front-runner" format to add excitement to the race. The political nature of an election campaign means that any statement is subject to interpretation, so television manufactures conflict by asking for an on-camera comment from an opponent or competitor. The advancing technology makes candidate statements and announcements subject to instant commentary. How better to spice up the "who's the front-runner" story than with some comment by a candidate who did better or worse than predicted?

Table 6.5 gives the number of stories in the general election phase of a campaign when a member of an opposing campaign, or the nominee of a contesting party, was allowed on-camera commentary. The figures show that Republicans have a slight edge in responding to Democrats, and that the tendency of television reporters is to include more stories of this type. While less than six percent of the total number of filmed stories were conflictual and the total is not a large number of stories, the inclusion of these stories coupled with more film of daily campaign activities means that viewers are exposed to an increasingly complex visual menu.

Conclusions

There have been substantial changes in the way television presents pictures of the American presidential election; such changes may help account for some of the recent concerns about voter apathy, negativism and dissatisfaction with government. First, there is the very nature of the television presentation. The rhythm of five election campaigns is seen in a comparison of the amount of attention given elections and the placement of those stories in the news line-up. There are fewer television stories broadcast on the election contest today, but they are given more play by news producers in the evening news line-up. The subject matter of these stories is increasingly centered in the primary campaign. By looking at the television coverage over the nearly two year period the attraction to primaries becomes evident. States with early primaries profit from the desire of television to be first to give the viewer the eventual party nominee. The unstructured nature of the primary season allows television to intrude with an explanation and prediction about the outcome. This research confirms that more and more television stories are devoted to the coverage in primaries. The build-up to the early primaries is followed by diminished attention to subsequent state primaries which might be crucial to determining the party nominee.

After the early primaries, television stories build to the party conventions. The conventions are often devoid of issue content, but high in the human drama and personal conflict familiar to television audiences. Democrats get more coverage than Republicans in the early going of a campaign. Once the fall general election begins both major party candidates rely on the television evening news shows to present their case for election. In 1992 the candidates all engaged in a new media tactic aimed at extending their media exposure during the general election phase of the campaign by appearing on the talk show circuit, especially the *Larry King Live* program. Despite this new strategy, even in 1992 the rise and fall of their media coverage and attention during the general election campaign period was very much a consequence of their debate performances. Very important from a television standpoint is the fact that nearly three quarters of the total network media time given to a presidential election has been expended before the fall general election begins.

Second, the powers of presidential incumbency, at least where television is concerned, should not be exaggerated. In the fall campaign media attention is often more a consequence of the debate schedule. Each party nominee is treated as a viable candidate, but Republicans do slightly better in terms of the amount of coverage in the general election phase. Despite the 1976 and 1992 primary challenges to incumbent Republicans, the quarrels among Democrats generally occupy the early television agenda, by contrast Republicans appear as slightly favored co-stars mainly in the fall.

Third, the nature of the television election story has changed to where more film is used with more quotes and opinions by diverse commentators. The candidate comments are reduced, and subject to analysis and interpretation by a host of on-camera interviews. The stories which appear on television screens are characterized by film which emphasizes conflict, the contest and political opinions. To the viewer at home, the presidential election campaign is a visual collage of opinionated snippets which feature more and more filmed attacks on an opponent and opinions about his

TABLE 6.5 Filmed Reaction Stories*, 1972-1988

1972	Democrats to Republicans	n=14	1.2% of all filmed stories
	Republicans to Democrats	n=05	
1976	Democrats to Republicans	n=12	1.1% of all filmed stories
	Republicans to Democrats	n=12	
1980	Democrats to Republicans	n=32	2.8% of all filmed stories
	Republicans to Democrats	n=55	
1984	Democrats to Republicans	n=46	3.9% of all filmed stories
	Republicans to Democrats	n=68	
1988	Democrats to Republicans	n=76	5.6% of all filmed stories
	Republicans to Democrats	n=94	

* Reaction stories are stories where an opposing point of view is presented on film in the broadcast

Source: Vanderbilt Television News *Abstracts*. Stories were coded if there was a designation by the networks that the story subject was the presidential election or campaign.

motives.

Television presentations emphasize controversy in the contest, with film and explanations for success or failure. Such a menu can appear to be negative on its face. Although research on the political media has emphasized its minimal effects, there are those who think television contributes to the growth of political cynicism and malaise. Of all the explanations about voter apathy, or rising voter disillusionment with elections, none has yet treated what is suggested here—that the nature of the television presentation is such that it treats voters to a boring two year mini-series with tired actors and predictable outcomes. To spice up an otherwisely dull plot, television keeps controversy alive by playing filmed interviews, attacks and commentary. The nature of the presentation is such that what appears as negative may be justified as better television coverage.

What is the portrait of American democracy that is conveyed by news coverage of the presidential campaigns? The television emphasis on primaries moreso than the general election conveys an image of a conflict laden political system where intra-party divisions and disarray dwarf inter-party differences. The specific focus on conflict between candidates suggests that political leaders are more eager to undercut each other than to offer substantive solutions to public policy problems. Also, given that news coverage of the primaries tends to concentrate on the horserace, the overarching emphasis of primaries conveys the impression that American politics stresses strategy over substance. We would expect that the net result of such coverage would be to leave the citizen feeling like a spectator rather than a participant in the political process.

Notes

1. For elections the research of media coverage tends to focus on the general election phase of the presidential campaign, from Labor Day (i.e. early September) to the November election date. Some coverage is given to candidates in the primary stage of the campaign. Here stories were selected if they had a network election designation, usually by a "Decision 1980" or "Election '76" or some similar tag.

2. The assumption of rank order influence is based on the research of S. Iyengar & D. R. Kinder (1987). *News that matters.* Chicago: University of Chicago Press.

3. An example of the salience calculation is a story broadcast by CBS on Wednesday, May 4, 1988. After the first commercial, a two minute and 50 second story was run on Michael Dukakis' strategy for winning the Democratic nomination. Stories before the first commercial were multiplied by five, after the first commercial by four, after the second commercial by three, and so on throughout the broadcast. There was a time when ABC had six commercial breaks in their broadcast, with the first one occurring just seconds after the introduction of the evening news show. For these ABC stories the first break was ignored. The formula for calculating salience is:

placement	x	time	=	salience
4	x	170 seconds	=	680

As a comparison of the salience measure the same CBS story would have the following salience scores in different placements within the broadcast:

Before the first commercial:	5	x	170 seconds	=	850
After the first commercial:	4	x	170 seconds	=	680
After the second commercial:	3	x	170 seconds	=	510
After the third commercial:	2	x	170 seconds	=	340
After the fourth commercial:	1	x	170 seconds	=	170

The rough equivalents of the salience scores for this story are that as a lead story, or a before the first commercial story, the salience score of 850 for a two minute and fifty second story is equal to a story of four minutes and forty seconds in the third position. To equal the 850 salience figure a story after the fourth commercial would have to run for fourteen and ten seconds.

Coding was fairly staightforward. A lead coder coded stories for a particular year, then an investigator would select random days to check for reliability. There was 93% coding agreement in the year before an election, and 99% with the election codes during the election year. Length, placement, subject matter, location, and content variables were all over 94% for all election years. The coding of speakers and actions in filmed interviews was less precise, but still averaged 87% for all the election years.

4. J. Katz. (1991 June 27). Say goodnight, Dan ... *Rolling Stone*.

5. J. Havick. (1992 July). *American democracy in transition* (p. 117). New York: West Publishing Company.

6. D. Hallin. (1990). *Sound bite news: Television coverage of elections, 1968-1988*. Woodrow Wilson International Center for Scholars, Washington, DC.

7

What Should Debates Be? Standards of Public Discourse

David Birdsell

Editorial responses to presidential debates configure an activity requiring either an ingenious balancing act or a high tolerance for contradiction. The candidates must be serious but not ponderous, relevant but not pandering, succinct but not glib, smart but not intellectual, and understandable but not simplistic. The formats must be wide-ranging but probing, engaging but never merely entertaining, revealing of character but not at the expense of policy discussion, and short but thorough. Questioners and moderators must keep candidates honest but cannot intrude themselves into the debate, be available when the debate gets out of hand but invisible when the candidates can be left to themselves, and know a great deal but not make the audience aware that they do.

Of course, few debates or debaters can meet such exacting requirements. Dissatisfaction with debates—or grudging acknowledgment that there are no useful alternatives to an imperfect form—has been a staple of political analysis in both popular and academic literature since the Kennedy-Nixon series in 1960 (Auer 1962). Some commentators believe that formats are the principal issue (Bitzer & Reuter 1980; Hellweg, Pfau & Brydon 1992). Others focus on press involvement and coverage of the events (Madsen 1991; Morello 1991). Still others fault candidates for failing to take seriously an opportunity for open political dialogue. Though diverse in their diagnoses and prescriptions, all of these debate doctors share the goal of improving the circulation of information in the body politic. Each wants the citizenry to know better what he or she thinks central to sound political decision making.

Taken as a whole, this body of commentary is itself a sustained discussion of the role of political discourse in electoral politics. Criticizing a given debate performance for its failure to generate memorable moments or its emphasis on irrelevant sound bites assumes a set of values regarding what we should know and how we should know it. In that sense, the debate over debates can be understood as a microcosm of the debate over political culture: a contained forum for championing different standards of public expression.

In this essay, I will first examine two divergent if not contradictory expectations of presidential debates that illustrate the difficulty and raise questions about the desirability of ever arriving at a single, universally satisfying debate format. Second, I will argue that (1) wider candidate availability through forums other than debates and (2) innovations in debate formats provide an opportunity to improve not only formats, but our discussion about them. Finally, I will offer two recommendations—further experimentation with formats and improved public education—designed not to shape debates that more efficiently serve a single purpose, but rather to enrich the process by which we render decisions about candidates and the vehicles we choose to evaluate them.

Polar Expectations

General election presidential debates command audiences of tens of millions of people, more than large enough to make mistakes costly and victories meaningful ("Special Issue" 1992, pp. 88-91). Further, they may be more influential than other campaign media events in shaping some voter's decisions (Fouhy 1992; Drew & Weaver 1991). However, because there are usually so few debates during the period of the general election, each debate takes on an apparent significance that it cannot bear. Not only is the relative importance of each event increased, but the amount and kind of material covered is more pressured as well. One, two, or three debates must be made to cover the gamut of policy issues from health care to foreign policy, the range of character traits from resolve to sensitivity. No format can attend to all of the legitimate questions about a candidate, so some critics are bound to walk away unhappy.

The result is a tension in the coverage and criticism of campaign debates that mirrors the tensions in the events themselves. Divergent expectations abound, but I will narrow to two here: first, the difficulty of satisfying the demands that debates be both thorough discussions of issue positions and memorable projections of character, and second, the requirements that debates must be engaging but avoid entertainment. These categories overlap considerably, suggesting the difficulties involved in drawing clear guidelines for assessing what happens in debates. I will illustrate claims with examples drawn from coverage of the 1992 primary and general election debates.[1]

Memorable Characters, Satisfying Policies

The compressed formats, broad audiences, and high stakes of debates pressure candidates to phrase their positions as poignantly (if as unspecifically) as possible and journalists to try to get beyond the prepared material. Many observers feel that the process is therefore terminally tainted, given over to media agenda that demean the presidency itself, let alone the quality of political discourse in election campaigns. Christopher Lasch recently summarized his version of this position in *The New York Times*. He believes that the requirements of television force candidates to "rely on their advisers to stuff them full of facts and figures, quotable slogans and anything else that will convey the impression of wide-ranging, unflappable competence. Only ideas are missing from their arsenal, understandably enough in view of TV's aversion to consecutive thought." For Lasch, minor tinkering with the form of debates is beside the point. The only responsible thing for a candidate to do is to refuse to appear. "A refusal to play by the media's rules would make people aware of the vast, illegitimate influence the mass media have come to exercise in American politics. It would also provide the one index of character that voters could recognize and applaud" (Lasch 1992, A-19).

Defending televised presidential debates, Tom Brokaw argues that network sponsors have achieved the twin virtues of arranging debates that are "dignified but lively" (Brokaw 1987, p. 74). In rough translation: he believes that while the networks do not demean candidates, journalists nonetheless find ways to chew over the politicians' dissembling and inconsistencies. Apparently sharing Brokaw's debate aesthetic, *The New York Times* praised NBC's first primary debate of the 1992 campaign as an imperfect but credible effort to serve "the ideal goal of any such exercise ... to dig more than one answer deep, to get past the easy oratorical pearls that competent candidates can polish on demand on any subject" ("Digging Past Political Pearls" A-20). These two assessments reflect what seems at one level to be a fairly clear expectation on the part of news organizations: a debate has not succeeded unless it moves its participants off of their prepared material. The result is less given to the sound bite, and consequently more "substantive."

Though disdain for canned speech is a consistent editorial response to debating, newspaper coverage sometimes reveals a rather different orientation. R.W. Apple's story on a 19 January 1992 Democratic candidates' debate, also appearing in the *Times*, leads with disappointment over the failure of the event as drama, then dutifully recounts the very tag lines decried in the editorialists' vision of debating ideals:

> Everybody had an angle in Sunday night's debate among the Democratic Presidential candidates. Stirring political theater it certainly was not, but

it gave some clues about what each of the five will be trying to do in the weeks ahead.

Governor Bill Clinton of Arkansas portrayed himself as the tribune of the middle class. Former Senator Paul E. Tsongas of Massachusetts said his economic program was more highly regarded by experts than those of his rivals. Senator Bob Kerrey of Nebraska talked a lot about health insurance. Former Gov. Edmund G. Brown, Jr. of California rolled out a whole new tax plan. And Senator Tom Harkin worked hard to justify his claim to be the "the only real Democrat" in the lot.

No one fell on his face. Each managed to score a point or two at the expense of his rivals. And a few ideas, usually about as common at such shindigs as unfilled jobs in New Hampshire (*sic*), actually found breathing room (Apple, "Debate" A-19).

No one who wants to find out what those ideas might have been could get help from this article. The criteria framed in the first paragraph, that political theater and rumblings about campaign strategy are what really matters, control the entire piece. In fact, nothing else in the article elaborates in any way on what occurred in the debate. Harkin's stalest sound bite is the only line in the debate deemed worth space in the paper.

In a story appearing some six weeks later, following a series of three Democratic debates, Apple quotes candidate Bob Kerrey ripping Bill Clinton for "giving 'a baloney answer' on health care" (Apple "Candidates" A-12). However, a more forceful phrase-fest captures Apple's sustained attention:

[T]oday's debates were relatively mild. Nothing was nearly as personal as the melee on Saturday night in Denver, when Mr. Tsongas and Mr. Clinton tore into each other with a fury that dismayed many senior party officials. The trigger was Mr. Clinton's assault on Mr. Tsongas' limited support of nuclear power.

"No one can argue with you, Paul; you're always perfect," Mr. Clinton said sarcastically, looking to the audience for confirmation.

Mr. Tsongas replied: "I'm not perfect. But I'm honest" (Apple, "Candidates" A-12).

Here the energy issue is only the backdrop for the personal clash. The political theater on display in Denver meets the dramatic requirements sought in the earlier article, and receives its due in the coverage. Ignoring the flip meanness of this exchange, the paper's editorial staff later praised the primary debates overall for gradually evolving "the fact, and spirit, of a round table" ("The State of the Debates" p. 24).

Apple's pieces cited here are political roundups that situate particular campaign events in terms of their importance to each candidate's agenda. It is then especially curious that the stories reflect not at all the supposedly changed character of debates celebrated in the editorial pages. For Apple, the debates distill to what has always garnered attention, the bite-fest and the bickering (Diamond & Friery 1987). Editorial enthusiasms and report-age do not connect.[2] The phenomenon is not unique to *The New York Times* or Apple. In a study of editorials concerning presidential debates, John Morello found that editorials are not only poor guides to general newspa-per content, but poor guides to the standards used in constructing the editorials themselves (1991). Morello found the editorialists intellectually inconsistent—for example, insisting on evidence as a standard for infer-ence but offering none themselves, or bemoaning the problems of unelaborated argument but resorting to catch phrases of their own—making more difficult a sustained, cogent evaluation of debates.

While newspapers should perhaps police their own argumentative houses, consistency is not the major issue here. The divergence between editorial opinion and coverage speaks to fundamental problems in cover-ing and commenting on debates. Sound bites by definition are designed to be memorable; if they are hard to recall, they can scarcely count as the stuff of slogan. They are also, for the same reasons, easier to report. To get beyond the bite means getting into the policy arguments. Even papers willing to provide considerable detail on a comparison of policy posi-tions—*The New York Times* is certainly one of them—are unlikely to do so every time a candidate, in debate or elsewhere, raises a given issue (Bennett 1988, pp. 23-25). What is new in the news, barring major shifts in program, is the presentation, and the presentation is often the sound bite. Journalists committed to pushing candidates past the bites will get either an extended, hard-to-cover elaboration of the "bited" position or an evasion, which, without an enormous expenditure of explanatory effort, can only be labeled as such before moving onto the next point. Neither the full position nor a detailed account of how a candidate was unresponsive is likely to be reportable, much less memorable, beyond a small, highly motivated (often academic) audience.

When journalistic commentators are provided with policy-focused, solidly reasoned cases, they are not necessarily happy with the result. After the 15 December 1991 Democratic debate, *Boston Globe* staff member Robert L. Turner liked Bill Clinton and Paul Tsongas because they "gave the strongest, most coherent answers." Still, he found Clinton less than rivet-ing; the Governor's "self-assured performance was undercut by its bland-ness—its failure to produce a memorable moment" (Turner 1991, p. 23). Following a 16 February 1992 Democratic primary debate, Dick Williams complained in *The Atlanta Journal and Constitution* that "The debate Sunday night among the five Democratic presidential candidates was so polite, so thoughtful and so boring that it might have been a debate among candidates for governor in a medium-sized state" (Williams 1992, p. 37). In a similar vein, Marvin Kitman, writing in *Newsday*, found little solace in the prospect of a PBS-sponsored debate:

> When MacNeil/Lehrer do the debates, I would expect they'll stay longer on each issue, with fewer issues. They will put more emphasis on economic issues. On PBS it will be the Debate That Dares to Be Boring, more coma-inducing than usual. But it will be what they call in society a Good Thing. I predict the Good Thing proponents at PBS will dare to take the High Road on Friday night, heroically boring to death the great American public (Kitman 1992, p. 44).

These commentators may want to get past the oratorical pearls, but they also want something to shine. Policy specifics are not their principal interest; fully elaborated issue postures would not satisfy their prescriptions for debates. Ross K. Baker, a Rutgers University political scientist writing in the *Los Angeles Times*, suggests that the missing element is passion. He found the first 1992 primary debate, "a dreary performance sodden with political scholasticism[,] ... eloquent testimony to the Democrats' descent from being our most passionate public people into a collection of sublimated errand boys for the party's special interest groups" (Baker, "Simply Put" B-7).

The dissatisfactions of Turner, Williams, Kitman, and Baker bring the contradictory pressures of memorable character and issue depth full circle. Candidates and the formats in which they operate will be vilified for pandering should the evening focus around slogans and shouting, but more detailed discussions are not likely to be found engaging the first time around, or reported the second. In Baker's words, they become "too damned presidential" (Baker, "Simply Put" B-7). Any given debate might produce a golden mean, but no format could guarantee it and no candidate could reproduce it on every outing.

The net effect of these contradictions is to shift attention to character because character is so often offered as the handle for grasping an issue position. Walter Mondale sees this problem as inherent in the nature of presidential debates, which he thinks of primarily as opportunities to glean insight into a candidate's character. "This is why," he writes, "the public is eager to get past the campaign handlers and the managed messages. It is why we so avidly watch the Presidential debates, searching for any clues of what really moves the candidates" (Mondale 1992, A-21). Sound bite avoidance becomes a test of character for those who would focus on policy while those inclined to look at the candidates more directly want their character unleavened by the more troublesome aspects of policy. Because the linkages between policy and personality are at best mysterious and at worst unfathomable, all but the most dedicated proponent of policy-pure debating will likely recur to some element of personal style in order to make a comment about a candidate's capabilities rather than the soundness of a given position. Even the *Times* editorialists, in their enthusiasm for ABC's "round table" debate, illustrated the improvements in form with examples drawn from candidates' personal styles ("The State of the Debates" p. 24). Of course, issue abandonment has its character implications as well. Ross Perot's quixotic career in 1992, its first phase in particular, is ample evidence that character can stand alone no more than can issue. All of this leaves debates in a bind. Candidates and sponsors must choose between attention with a smirk and a pat on the back with a yawn.

Entertainment v. Engagement

Most commentators would agree that debates need to be engaging even if they would disagree on what constitutes engagement. No one actively wants to be bored and policy wonks genuinely *like* policy. That presidential debates should actually be entertaining, however, occasions considerable discomfort in the editorial community, and that in turn reopens the question of what entertainment means or could mean in the context of presidential debating. Entertainment is, according to many, beneath the dignity of the office that presidential debaters seek; consequently, a debate that entertains is not a debate that aspires to the deeply serious context of a presidential campaign. Debates are then pressured into yet another difficult balancing act: they must command attention, but not too much; the audience must turn off the television set feeling edified, but not particularly like they have had a good time. *Nation's* foreign editor, George Black, sums up a typical reaction to "entertaining" politics in his preview of the Democratic primary debates:

> American television, as currently structured, does not allow for the kind of public service pre-election programming that is commonplace in Western Europe. The network execs also bear a heavy responsibility for the declining quality of political discourse over the last decade. It is their choices that have eroded the boundaries that used to divide news programming from entertainment. And there is no shortage of people in network TV whose idea of a spruced-up debate would be to subject each candidate to a session with Geraldo Rivera and a studio audience (Black 1991, B-5).

Wary of the entertainment label, Marvin Kalb defended the format offered in his "9 Sundays" proposal by insisting that, "These debates need not be entertaining, just informative" (Kalb 1991, A-25).

Of course, debates that do not attend sufficiently to honest engagement are likely to be written off as hopelessly boring exercises in the soporific arts. Ross K. Baker sniped at the Democrats for conducting a "mannerly and oh-so-decorous" primary debate in New Hampshire, a debate that focused on "another circular firefight over arcane policy distinctions" (Baker 1992, B-7); no one need worry about entertainment here. Marvin Kitman's attack is more global: "The word 'debate' itself can clear a channel from the screen faster in the average American TV home than anything since the invention of the term 'public TV'" (Kitman 1992, p. 19). As if to prove him wrong, Muppets Miss Piggy and Gonzo took to their podiums for a "campaign" debate on 18 February 1992, televised on ABC's *Good Morning America*. This contest left no question and made no apologies about its entertainment value.

Televised debates suffer from at least two problems in navigating between the Scylla of boredom and the Charybdis of genuine entertainment. The first is the fact of appearing on television, where the closest visual and verbal analogue for the most common formats may be the TV game show. Susan J. Drucker and Janice Platt Hunold have provided a detailed comparison of the arrangements at the 8 October 1984 Reagan-Mondale debate and find them strikingly similar in many respects to the appearance, pacing and activities one might find on a game show (Drucker & Platt Hunold 1987, pp. 202-206). The analogy reappears in journalistic literature. For example, praising a MacNeil/Lehrer format over more typical debate formats, *The Washington Post* celebrates the absence of "funny little game-show separate podiums, which tend for some reason to make the candidates look forlorn and ridiculous" ("Debates '92,'" A-20). The marketing emphasis and overall goofiness of the television game show prompt the kind of associative distaste that causes Black to wrinkle his nose at the notion of candidates appearing with Geraldo: television is not serious.

This is a problem rooted in the twinning of entertainment and television, the notion that all television entertainment (and by extension, all television programming) must entertain in the same way. "Entertainment" in this sense means *Wheel of Fortune*, or *Beverly Hills, 90210*. The absence of analogues more appropriate to serious debate is unfortunate, because in order to be successful, debates at some level must be entertaining. To say as much is not to say that debates must debase themselves. Turning away from presidential contests for the moment, public debates on college campuses are popular events, often drawing large audiences. From their earliest employment in public forums, debates were expected to be entertaining, often precisely because audience members could see fine argument in action (Bode 1968, p. 101). In the last century, even political debates were certifiably engaging, events that few citizens would want to miss. To say of these debates that they were entertaining is in no way to suggest that they were unedifying. Lincoln and Douglas entertained the crowds that assembled to hear them, and those crowds benefitted as a result (Jamieson & Birdsell 1988).

The second problem regarding debates and entertainment, then, is a pejorative, limited notion of entertainment. Hair-shirt standards of debating that actually *aspire* to be merely informative are a recent development, a reaction against the too-easily-trivialized products of television. Debates were happily entertaining and intellectually satisfying for hundreds of years. They have prompted chagrin over the possibility of generating genuine enthusiasm only since 1960. This is a situation that may be changing with the profusion of non-debate formats in the 1992 campaign, about which I will have more to say in the next section.

Of course, the audiences that once found debates stimulating and were not embarrassed to say so were educated differently from those watching debates today. They were accustomed to listening to much longer speeches and to following those speeches closely. They also consumed their debating in person, creating a shoulder-to-shoulder sense of the public—and at least a theoretical chance to interact directly with the debaters—that does not apply to the way that the vast majority of Americans see debates at the end of the twentieth century. What they saw as entertainment might be hard to sell as even listenable to an audience today.

Candidate Availability and Format Diversity

The 1992 campaign saw a profusion of candidate appearances on talk and call-in shows. While no one appeared with Geraldo, Bill Clinton, George Bush, and Ross Perot went just about everywhere else. The morning talk shows held numerous interviews and call-in sessions. *Larry King Live*, the birthplace of the Perot campaign, hosted the other two candidates as well. Clinton and Bush even appeared on MTV.

Reaction to these appearances has been very positive in some quarters and guarded in others. Marvin Kalb calls the massive increase in candidate availability "revolutionary" (Kalb 1992, A-25). He believes that by allowing candidates to speak more or less directly to the voting public, the talk show formats have fundamentally changed the nature of political television. The *Chicago Tribune* editorialists write that the current surge of appearances has already outdistanced academic recommendations for improved election programming:

> Lo and behold, the networks have already gone beyond the Nine Sundays concept. They are clamoring to get the candidates on TV, and not just for a few minutes. They have turned over as much as two hours to questions and answers with the candidates and have done so without taking a

financial bath ("Tune in" 1992, p. 22).

Writing in *The Christian Science Monitor*, Hunter compares debates unfavorably with the newer kinds of candidate appearance:

> No institution has been more symbolic of this radical change than the presidential TV debates in the fall. The networks have turned them into the superbowls of presidential politics, hyping them into make-or-break moments in the campaign. Yet they tell us virtually nothing of value about competitors for president ... But now ... the talk shows [have] provided at least a partial answer: unending public exposure, uncut and unedited (Hunter 1992, p. 19).

Less enthusiastic have been those who argue that the Larry Kings and Phil Donahues are not as adept at pressing difficult political questions as their counterparts in the mainstream press. Candidates who appear on talk shows can avoid the issues that they do not want to discuss and focus on their own agenda without much fear of contradiction from the interviewer/host. Leslie Stahl, for example, contrasts a *60 Minutes* segment on Ross Perot's charges of GOP harassment with a later Larry King interview. Stahl said that *60 Minutes* could not find "anything to corroborate the wiretap or the dirty tricks." That absence of corroboration was the focal point of her interview with Perot. Nevertheless, "a few days after our interview and after Lisa's [NBC correspondent Lisa Myers] piece and after Mort Dean's piece, Ross Perot went on the Larry King show and repeated each and every charge word for word, and Larry King did not challenge him once" (Stahl 1992).

Though it is too early to tell which effect may be the more important, supporters and critics of candidate appearances alongside non-journalistic media personalities both have a point. Few would support a model of access that denies the opportunity for the kind of close scrutiny that trained members of the press can provide on a regular basis. On the other hand, some of the work of simple introduction, of familiarity with a candidate's face and principal positions—however polished and puffed up—can be done well on the talk shows. By providing such information, the talk shows in effect take pressure off of debates. Debates were not, in 1992, the only major, comparatively unscripted public events. Though they were not always made to do so, they could have been used to pick up where the talk shows left off, to explore more deeply the matters of evidence and program that are not covered adequately on *Donahue*.

The implications could be quite significant for reinvigorating the debate form. Rhetorical scholar J. Jeffrey Auer defined a traditional debate as "(1) a confrontation, (2) in equal and adequate time, (3) of matched contestants, (4) on a stated proposition, (5) to gain an audience decision"

(Auer 1962, p. 146). While all of these "rules" have been bruised by recent formats, "equal and adequate time," in the sense of too few debates, and "on a stated proposition" have taken the worst drubbing. The paucity and brevity of debates (and in the primaries, the number of contestants) have made impossible sustained attention to much of anything, let alone a clear proposition. So while we have had debates that address general topic areas, such as "the economy," we have not seen debates that addressed a full-fledged proposition. Propositions (debaters would call them "resolutions") could easily be drawn from pressing campaign issues, such as, "Resolved: That the federal budget deficit should be eliminated before any new domestic spending initiatives are begun." Quite apart from the strategic considerations appropriate for any given candidacy, it would be impractical to spend an hour or two on such a focused topic when the debate presents one of the only opportunities of the entire campaign to see how a candidate thinks. As a result, propositions have remained unstated and we have had more diffuse discussions of about the candidates programs and capabilities.

Talk shows and other forms of access reduce this pressure, what columnist Hunter referred to as the "Superbowl" trappings of presidential debates. Instead, debates can do the things they are designed to do more neatly because they need not shoulder the entire burden of unscripted access. This is, however, an opportunity that must be actively pursued to be realized. It will not spring naturally from developments in context, but must be inculcated into expectations of the form.

Happily, in addition to distant historical precedent, there are as well very recent grounds for optimism that such a framework might evolve. The 1992 campaign compressed four debates (three presidential, one vice-presidential) into a nine-day period, October 11-19. Each of the debates used a different format. The first was similar to the traditional press panel; the second employed a moderator to choose questions from an audience of citizens; the third was a hybrid with the first half of the debate conducted by a single moderator and the second half by a press panel. The vice presidential debate was conducted by a single moderator. The rapid juxtaposition of debates and styles drew attention to form and to performance across form. Rather than harking back four years to the last presidential debate for an analogue, viewers could think back to the debate of two to four days before. Ed Fouhy, the producer for the Commission on Presidential Debates, said that the net result was to build attention over the week, involving the American people in a collective experience (Fouhy 1992).

Particularly interesting was the second presidential debate, held in Richmond, Virginia, on October 15. There, 209 citizen-participants, undecided voters selected by the Gallup organization, served as audience and questioners for the candidates (Fouhy 1992). ABC correspondent Carole Simpson moderated the program. Two questioners spoke directly to issues of campaign discourse, asking candidates to stop attacking one another and to talk about issues instead.[3] The questions were phrased in terms of discourse norms: how positions are presented and the possibility for compromise. Importantly, they were voiced not by members of the media, but by citizens who had found a route into a hitherto alien process.

The importance of these exchanges was not so much what was said or the candidates' responses, but the fact that the debate focused, however briefly, on the nature of debating itself. The questions arose from arguably the least professional, academic, or otherwise arcane sources in the course of the campaign. Watched by over 88 million viewers, this debate projected the citizenry directly into arguments in which they had a stake.

The first question was the less well publicized, but the stronger of the two. A woman said, "Yes, I'd like to address all the candidates with this question. The amount of time the candidates have spent on this campaign trashing their opponents' character and their programs is depressingly large. Why can't your discussions and proposals reflect the genuine complexity and the difficulty of the issues to try to build a consensus around the best aspects of all proposals?" ("Transcript" 1992). Clinton's response addressed most directly implied questions about discourse. "Let me say, first of all, to you that I believe so strongly in the question you ask that I suggested this format tonight. I started doing these formats a year ago in New Hampshire. And I found that we had huge crowds because all I did was let people ask questions and I tried to give very specific answers. I also had a program starting last year. I've been disturbed by the tone and the tenor of this campaign" ("Transcript" 1992). As he spoke, Clinton moved into a camera shot with the questioner, then stood at the front of the stage and addressed his opponents. Through strong verbal identification with the format and his physical movement toward the audience orientation, Clinton in effect joined the audience in challenge to his opponents, a tactic he repeated often during this debate.

My point here is not that citizens are better questioners than members of press panels or that Clinton's movement was necessarily a laudable development in presidential debating. Rather, I am saying that the citizen questioners are able to call attention to format in a way that journalists cannot, and that Clinton took advantage of the question to offer a format— a format he had insisted upon in debate negotiations (Fouhy 1992)—and hence discourse as an index of character. This kind of attention is necessary to any serious evaluation of the nature of presidential debates. The Richmond format suffered from many problems, particularly from a lack of follow-up. As an exclusive format for debates it would be a poor choice. It did, however, help bring particular kinds of questions to the fore and authorize a public role through direct participation.

Though commentators discussed the format differences in their post debate reviews, not enough was done during the 1992 cycle to exploit the juxtaposition of the debates. No questioner, for example, started a question by pegging a candidate to an answer in a prior debate. Themes reemerged, but in content terms, each debate might have been an event by itself, completely detached from its highly relevant and very recent context.

Conclusions

Solving the problems of the Richmond format as well as capitalizing on its advantages requires that we continue to experiment with a variety of debate formats, not with an eye to choosing the best one, but to ensure that different kinds of questions continue to be asked of the candidates who run for president. The specific arrangements are important, but not moreso than the democratic principles represented by their variety: no single format can do what needs to be done, precisely because each format produces a comparatively limited, and hence skewed, kind of information. The United States' historical ambivalence about the qualities of leadership and how best to ascertain them in a given politician requires flexibility. Robert Denton observes that "The institution of the presidency is largely undefined. The Constitution is alarmingly vague on the responsibilities, dimensions and roles of the office" (Denton 1982, p. 2). Significant campaign events must remain sufficiently flexible to speak to a variety of meanings. They must also remain open to a variety of viewers. Policy elites may not be comfortable with some aspects of access or inclusion, but different approaches and tones must be attempted if more people are to feel a part of an evolving process. To ignore any of these constituencies is to reduce presidential politics to a more or less certain cipher, an framework that may be inimical to the nature of the office itself.

In 1988, Kathleen Jamieson and I recommended that campaign discourse be actively promoted as a unified whole, so that speeches, press conferences, debates of any sort, and even advertisements could be brought more easily to bear upon one another. Central to a useful vision of variety is to draw, as often and as thoughtfully as possible, the necessary links between the different activities. Linkages of this sort provide a bulwark against the kind of popular "forgetting" that allowed Ross Perot to trumpet a discredited conspiracy theory on Larry King's program. Let the candidates on Larry King, by all means; let them debate with average citizens, but hold them accountable before and after with professional news analysis.

Because the process of gathering these fragments of campaign communication around a tight nucleus of careful thought about politics and governance has as much to do with the public as with candidates or the media, my second recommendation has broadly to do with education. It is no longer acceptable to concentrate on written forms of communication to the exclusion of other media. If we to protect people against potentially misleading images, we should do it the same way that we protect them against misleading words: teach them enough about the form(s) to gain a some critical distance. Ideally, we could teach them to use the form(s) themselves. In these senses, public education must look forward.

Though this is a frequent argument with respect to political advertising (Jamieson 1992), it has received less attention in relation to presidential debates. A number of scholars have commented on the visual dimensions of political debating (Keplinger & Donsbach 1987; Messaris, Eckman & Gumpert 1979; Morello 1988; Tiemens 1978; Tiemens, Hellweg, Kipper & Phillips 1985; Tiemens 1989), but visual considerations either have been neglected or treated non-seriously in media reactions to debating. In 1992's Richmond debate, Clinton's skillful use of position to command camera angle went largely unremarked. Tactics of this sort must be identified and discussed, preferably by a public consciously versed in the visual logics of television.

We must also, however, look backward, to relearn what can be accomplished orally and what cannot. Editorialists who take television to task time and time again for failing to elaborate complex policy positions are applying a print standard to a medium that is not only visual, but oral. Speech is marginalized for what it can do because of what it does not do well. That serves neither the media nor the political process.

Though I am framing this recommendation as a matter of education, I do not mean to suggest that it should remain in the schools. It should start in the schools, but these lessons should be woven into the fabric of routine political analysis as well. Adults are at least as important an audience as children, and the media can be helpful in promulgating new standards and frank discussion of the implications of political discourse.

The debate about debates is an important forum for determining what does and what should matter to the nation, but the discussion is not as clear as it could be. Just as formal debates work best with stated propositions, so too will the debate over norms of political discourse be most effective when the terms can be made clear. The first step is to speak clearly and directly about the commitments and confusions entailed by words such as "character" or "substance."[4] The second is to know how the choice of medium, form, and arrangement shape the stakes in the process. The recommendations I have outlined here are ambitious, but the are also necessary if our democracy is to remain participatory in any meaningful way. Further, by relocating the debate from formats to first principles, we would make clear that the issue at hand is not anyone's short term political advantage, but rather the intellectual and symbolic covenants upon which all such advantages must ultimately rest.

Barbara Kellerman defines "political culture" as "those enduring and widespread ideas, habits, norms, symbols, and practices that are politically relevant, especially as they pertain to the legitimate use of power" (Kellerman 1984, p. 4). Assuming that the campaigns are relevant to legitimacy and that legitimacy is remade in accordance with the press of circumstance (Neustadt 1980), not only debates, but the debate about debates must be sufficiently reflexive to be able to mould norms of public discourse as well as respond to them. Only then can politicians and analysts join the argument head on rather than obliquely, in the process elevating it to a central role in the assessment of candidates and campaigns. Treated this way, the evaluation of debates can frame a discussion more neatly civil than merely nomian.

Notes

1. While nominating debates are different from general election debates in several respects, I have chosen to consider the two in tandem because in 1992, both employ or respond to several innovations unusual in earlier campaigns. Most importantly, the 1992 debates have taken place against a backdrop of greater candidates accessibility to the public via the media (I am distinguishing here between accessibility to reporters and presentations directly to the public) and diminished use of press panel questioning formats. Further, all of the general election debates featured three candidates rather than the one-on-one format of past campaigns, eliminating one of the central structural difference between general election and primary debates in the 1984 and 1988 election cycles.

2. *The New York Times* did run a variety of debate articles during the primary season in 1992. In particular, a series of pieces by John Tierney took a longer and more variegated look at debating than did R. W. Apple's horserace coverage. These pieces did not, however, follow every debate, and the disjunction between the *Times'* other coverage and its stated editorial posture remains dramatic.

3. The second question was, "If I may, and forgive the notes here, but I'm shy on camera. The focus of my work as domestic mediator is meeting the needs of the children that I work with by way of their parents, and not the wants of their parents. And I ask the three of you, how can we as symbolically the children of the future President, expect the two of you, the three of you, to meet our needs: the needs in housing and, and, and in crime and, doctrism, and your political parties" ("Transcript" 1992).

4. There is a large literature on presidential character and related perceptions. In order to gain a sense of the difficulty of arranging a forum that consistently and satisfactorily addresses complex notions such as character, it is important to treat seriously the multiple meanings of the word (which are routinely ignored in both popular and academic commentary). On character generally, see Kaster & Zukin (1982), Kellerman (1984), and Wayne (1982).

8

Media Influence in Presidential Campaigns: A Caveat

Dianne Rucinski

One of the more striking political paradoxes in the late twentieth century is that while Americans overwhelmingly supported democratic movements abroad, in the 1988 General Election only half of those eligible to vote opted to do so. In applauding Polish trade unionists as they battled the Polish government, thus forging the first eastern block break with Soviet authority, and in glorifying the bravery of Chinese students as they stood firm in their demands for greater freedoms and democracy in China, Americans were reassured that democracy was the ideal form of government. It seemed to be taking hold in even the darkest corners of the globe. That people in desperate straits would strike against the government, stand firm in the face of tanks, and so blatantly flirt with death confirmed in minds of Americans that it was naturally right that all people would welcome the prospect of self-government and would be willing to die for that opportunity. Such fundamental shifts in political ideologies proved that the American experience of effective self-governance was unique, that we had successfully led, rather than followed, the patterns established by other nations. During the same period, in contests at all levels, vote turnout continued to decline in the U.S.

At first glance this yawning contradiction might simply be a political application of the parental dictum "do as I say, not as I do." However, it underscores and reminds us of the fundamental division individuals perceive, separating themselves from others in how we as individuals reconcile the divergence of principle and practice. We often desire our fellow citizens to possess stronger commitments to rationality and the obligation of citizen participation in democratic life than we believe is achieved. Similarly, many of us would like to be better democratic citizens, knowing we should vote, should pay more attention to politics, and should devote more energy to exploring political problems than we do.

The difference is in how we reconcile the divide between principle and practice for ourselves and for others. In short, we are much less generous to and forgiving of others than we are of ourselves. We explain our own deficiencies in meeting our principles by citing a host of situational factors that frustrate our intentions. We often perceive others to be much less capable than we are when it comes to sorting through the barrage of campaign messages and making decisions. Others are easily persuaded by the flimsiest political rhetoric and moved to irrationality or even violence by the slightest provocation, but we believe ourselves to be relatively immune from manipulative political messages. As we will see, this is especially true for intentionally and overtly persuasive messages, like political advertisements and other forms of propaganda. We personally think that we can recognize it when we see it and dismiss it as such, but that others are vulnerable. In the minds of both citizens and elites, the power of mass media in charting the country's political future is tremendous, yet selectively so.

Yet there is more to the peculiar relationships among politicians, media, and citizens as campaigns unfold than easily explained differences in attribution. In this chapter I argue that expressions of dismay over the conduct of presidential campaigns speaks to and of American's continuing anxiety about the wisdom, health, and vitality of our experiment with electoral democracy. It is a nagging and awkward reminder that our surface belief that all citizens are political equals, even if they are not social or economic equals, betrays an underlying contradictory belief that we really are not. Further, these conflicting beliefs, coupled with particular types of campaign messages, produce exaggerated claims for the power of media effects while simultaneously masking what genuinely ails us, hindering debate about constructive reforms, and thwarting attempts to bring about concrete change.

Beginning with a selective review and brief analysis of the comments of elites and common citizens about the conduct of the most recent presidential elections, I follow with a discussion of perceptions of media effects generally and perceived effects of distinct types of political messages. The tendency for individuals to attribute powerful media effects on others while believing that they personally are immune from such influence, a phenomenon Davison (1983) labelled the "third-person" effect, suggests we carefully re-examine statements made about media effects in election campaigns. Arguing that we view discrepancies in perceived effects as a derivation of a general cognitive process, I demonstrate that particular discrepancies between attributed media effects on the self and on others and perceptions of harm of those messages vary with perceptions of mediated political communications; and furthermore, these divergent perceptions have implications beyond perceived effects.

The voiced consternation with the seemingly unbounded trend toward greater negativity in campaigning, or at least in particular types of negativity (see Gronbeck & Miller, Chapter 1), the sense that contemporary campaigns are less about issues than about the management of candidate images (see Covington et al., Chapter 5; Morreale, Chapter 2), and doubts that the press is successfully performing its watchdog function register not only tangible problems with the election process, but more pervasive concerns with the wisdom of the systems of electoral democracy and mass media. Rather than interpreting current debates about the conduct of modern American presidential campaigns narrowly as evidence of changes in the information environment, we should more properly understand these debates as expressions of apprehension with the process of representative democracy and the quality of government elections produce. In short, this chapter does not attempt to establish whether or how much presidential elections have changed, but rather suggests reinterpretation of such discussions.

Powerful Media Effects in Recent Presidential Elections

Like negative campaigning, anxiety over the conduct of presidential elections is not new. Complaints about political attacks in speeches, pamphlets, and newspapers have existed throughout America's electoral history. The criticism has not abated but has expanded to include different mass media as their use has spread through the general population. While the particular characteristics and subtleties are often treated as specific to particular elections, they can be categorized as falling into one of two general types. The first type is criticism of the "professionalization" of political campaigns, meaning the growing involvement and presumed wizardry of commercial consultants. The second is concern about the impact of media content generally and distinctive types of content on both election outcomes and on civic participation.

Criticism by elites of recent elections has focussed on the extent of manipulation and management of the press by political consultants and the role of television in this process (McGinnis 1968; Arterton 1984; Jamieson 1984; Hallin 1991). Common citizens appear to share the same types of concerns. In a poll taken during the 1984 election campaign, 52% of those polled worried that campaign commercials made "candidates look the way campaign managers want[ed] the candidate to look, instead of the way the person really is" and a solid majority (82%) expressed a preference for fewer commercials and more live appearances (Harris Survey October 11, 1984). Since this criticism is discussed at length in the Covington et al. chapter, I will emphasize the second type of criticism.

Appraisals of the conduct of presidential campaigns are often coupled with a resigned acknowledgement that whatever else they are, unscrupulous politics in the form of mudslinging advertisements and heavily stage-crafted appearances are "effective." As we shall see, not only are political ads deemed extremely effective in influencing attitudes and opinions, but often are thought to be exclusively responsible for election outcomes. In a press release circulated two weeks before the 1988 election, Louis Harris reported "A substantial 71-25% majority of voters are disturbed by the negative campaign, especially the TV commercials which have been used by both candidates," noting that a clear majority (approximately 70%) thought both Bush and Dukakis advertisements were either far too negative or somewhat negative and reported that 39% were "fed up" with political advertisements because they were too negative.

Yet in the same release, Harris opined: "The simple story of the election is that the Bush commercials *have worked* and the Dukakis commercials have not" (Harris Poll October 23, 1988, p. 1, emphasis added). Harris provides two forms of evidence in support of this claim. First, he cites changes in perceptions about Dukakis and intimates that the changes are solely the result of Bush's campaign efforts. The report cites an increase from 52% to 63% among those who perceived that Dukakis was soft on crime. This change is directly linked to the prison furlough advertisement. Other support for the effectiveness of Bush's campaign effort include a shift from 34% to 49% of those who thought Dukakis was "too liberal in his views" and a jump from 54% to 69% among those who thought that Dukakis was not qualified in foreign affairs.

Harris's second form of evidence comes from opinions about the perceived effectiveness of campaign advertisements by members of the public. In the press release distributed one week before the general election, Harris claims: "The pivotal role of this television advertising is further pointed up by the fact that voters rate the Bush advertising effort as effective by 61-30%, while the Dukakis ad effort is judged effective by a lower 53-41%. The eight point gap is roughly comparable to the spread in the voting preference" (Harris Poll November 1, 1988, p. 1). The implicit assumption of a causal link cannot easily be avoided. When asked about the furlough advertisement specifically, a 49-42 split thought that the ad was "effective as far as [the respondent is] concerned," but was judged unfair by 63% of the respondents (p. 2). What is crucial to understanding points about the use of polling data here are that shifts in public opinion are tied directly to specific political ads with scant discussion of alternative explanations, and that perceptions of media effects, by both "experts" and citizens, are treated as the equivalent of effects.

From highly disputable yet seductively elegant causal arguments made by Harris and the voices of common citizens as they attempt to diagnose the ills of contemporary politics emerge a picture of a menacing and powerful mass media. Further supporting the notion of powerful media effects comes in the selective acknowledgement by some members of the media that the responsibility for cleaning up the campaign environ- ments was, in part, their own. Writing in the *Washington Post*, David Broder went so far as to argue that the press should cast off the mantle of objectivity in simply reporting what was said by whom, which was failing the democratic process. Instead, Broder advocated treating "every ad as if it were a speech" and "not being squeamish about saying in plain language when we catch a candidate lying" (January 14, 1990). The solution for the press was to deconstruct political ads, bit by bit, assessing the veracity of each claim. Although the format varies, "truth boxes" are printed in newspapers and stories are broadcast at some point during the campaign; they refer to specific ads, which are usually analyzed only once. To date, there is no mechanism to correct for the fragmentary nature of news or to counteract the repetition of the advertisements, which often plays a signifi- cant role in the effectiveness of any message.

One underlying assumption made by journalists in deconstructing political ads is that citizens do not recognize, are unaware, or forget that political advertisements are like all advertisements in that they are, by definition, pieces of advocacy. By "policing" televised political ads, these members of the media not only reveal an assumption that the ads are effective or influential, but also expose beliefs essential to understanding perceptions of media effects on others. In short, the decision to police television political ads demonstrates the following convictions concerning media effects:

1. In the superior power of television to influence attitudes and beliefs, since direct mail pieces, newspaper ads, and radio ads were not policed in the same manner;
2. That intentionally and conspicuously persuasive messages are more effective than so-called "objective" information in influenc- ing attitudes because news articles, which are often directly based on information provided by campaign organizations, and candi- date debates were not subjected to similar scrutiny;
3. In the selective influence of the ads on the "masses," for reporters "privately scoffed at their simple messages" (Rosenstiel October 4, 1990).

All of these beliefs can be tied to what Davison (1983) called the "third- person effect," which is a derivation of Fritz Heider's (1958) influential research on attribution and causal explanations.

Accounts of Media Effects on the Self and on Others

The contributions of Fritz Heider to our understanding of how people make sense of human action have proved indispensable to generations of social investigators. From Heider's early observations, it is considered psychologically axiomatic that when it reflects positively on them, individuals attribute their actions to relatively enduring factors such as personality or style, and to situational factors when it reflects negatively on them. When asked to explain behaviors of others, individuals are more likely to attribute actions to enduring individual factors, whether these attributions reflect positively or negatively on others.

The varieties and textures of these differential judgments we make when comparing our own actions to those of others have been widely investigated. The tendency to attribute our own failures to external factors and our successes to personal factors has been explained as a mechanism used to maintain a healthy, positive self-concept. It has also been argued that this tendency is an indicator of self-knowledge over time in that we have a historical awareness of our own behaviors over time, and as the result of our focus of attention in a field of action. The most prominent explanation given for the tendency to attribute behaviors of others to enduring personality factors regardless of the judgment of the behavior is that it is a *general tendency*, a predilection. In other words, it is only for the self that we make exceptions to the general tendency.

Within the context of mass communications and public opinion, this phenomenon has been labelled the "third-person" effect (Davison 1983). While social scientific investigations of media effects have not uncovered massive, uniformly applicable media effects, Davison asserts that the "powerful media effects" paradigm lives on in that individuals continue to believe that media messages can and do have a strong influence on others. For contemporary scholars, what is critical about this difference in perceptions is not whether people overattribute effects on others or underattribute effects on themselves, for social psychologists addressed the issue long ago. What is critical, argues Davison, is that the perception of powerful effects has implications for other beliefs and for behavior. To support his argument Davison cites several historical cases in which perceptions of media effects on "others" led some individuals, especially those in positions of power, to act forcefully and decisively to curb presumed media impact.

He cites as an example the decision of U.S. military officials to withdraw black soldiers from the Pacific during World War II based on perceptions that black soldiers would be unduly influenced by leaflets dropped on the troops by the Japanese. The message of the leaflets was that blacks should not fight the "white man's war" and urged blacks to desert.

There was no evidence that the leaflets had the intended effects; rather, the perception that blacks would respond led U.S. military officials to act. It is worth noting at this point that all troops exposed to propaganda were not withdrawn. Specifically, white troops, who also received healthy doses of Japanese propaganda, were not removed from combat.

Beliefs that certain types of media content exert a stronger influence on people is not an idiosyncratic quirk of policymakers. Evidence of such beliefs comes from public opinion research on levels of tolerance for the expression of unpopular political beliefs or reprehensible opinions. While there is some debate about whether Americans are becoming more or less tolerant of specific political groups (Mueller, 1988; Sullivan & Marcus, 1988), from the 1940s up to the present public opinion polls have shown that a significant portion of the population believes that certain groups and individuals should be prevented from expressing their opinions and beliefs publicly. Throughout the 1940s and 1950s from 25% to 40% of those questioned thought that the Socialist party should not be allowed to publish a newspaper and from 39% to 75% thought that members of the Communist party should be prevented from speaking on the radio (Mueller 1988). As recently as 1979, roughly 30% of respondents to national survey thought that right-wing groups perceived to be harmful to the nation, such as Nazis and members of the Klu Klux Klan, should be prevented from appearing on television (cited in McClosky & Zaller 1984); 60% believed that a radio or television station that regularly provided a voice in support of only one political group and spoke against other groups should be required by law to present a more balanced view; and 51% thought that books that advocate the overthrow of the government should be banned from libraries (McClosky & Brill 1983). While these opinions are only occasionally held by a majority, they suggest that substantial numbers of citizens believe that certain political messages, especially when mass mediated, can be powerful enough to be justifiably restricted.

Direct assessments of the public's beliefs about the power of mediated messages also come from recent research on the third-person effect. A series of investigations of the third-person effect demonstrates the self-other discrepancy in the general population or segments of the population across a variety of media content types including dramatic programming (Lasorsa 1989), news content concerning foreign affairs (Perloff 1989), libelous messages (Cohen, Mutz, Price & Gunther 1988; Gunther 1991), and presidential election campaign news, advertising, debates, and polls (Rucinski & Salmon 1990). In laboratory studies using students as research participants, Cohen, Mutz, Price and Gunther (1988) and Gunther (1991) found that libelous messages are thought to have a stronger influence on the perceptions of others but little or no impact on the self.

In a campaign context the same discrepancy between perceptions of media influence on the self and on others appears. In a study conducted during the final weeks of the 1988 election, Rucinski and Salmon (1990) found a self-other difference when respondents were asked how much influence they thought five different types of campaign content had on their own voting decisions and on the voting decisions of "most Americans." For each type of campaign content—news, debates, negative political ads, general, non-negative political ads, and polls—respondents thought that "most Americans" were more strongly influenced than they themselves. The largest chasms in perceived influence existed for negative political ads and polls, while the narrowest gap was for news and debates.

However, the types of campaign content generally derided by journalists and other critics of contemporary campaigns—negative political ads and polls—were ranked lowest by respondents in their perceptions of overall impact. In other words, even though respondents thought that all five types of content were more instrumental in forming the vote decisions of others, negative political ads and polls were judged to be the least influential compared to other types of messages. In fact, news and debates were judged overall to be the most influential.

At this juncture, the picture is on powerful media effects—on other people. Complicating the picture is the finding that respondents thought that negative political ads and polls, the materials scorned most by critics and journalists, had less influence than debates and news. The key to understanding this puzzle may lie in what accounts for the discrepancy. In examining factors that might influence the discrepancy in perceived effects on the self and most Americans, Rucinski and Salmon (1990) hypothesized that education should be positively related to differences in perceived effects. This is precisely what they found: the higher the level of education, the less likely respondents would report influence on themselves and the more likely they were to report influence on the voting decisions of most Americans.

Media Effects and American Self Images

First Amendment and other abstract values of free expression notwithstanding, the history of mass media in the United States is replete with demands from various interest groups that certain types of media content be regulated. Demands for restrictions are often based on arguments alleging powerful effects, and occasionally are accompanied by claims of distinctive or unique vulnerability of special audience members, such as the limitations on advertising targeted to children. At other times, demands do not carry any argument of special vulnerability but rest on an assumption of powerful media effects—on others, the masses, or "them."

It is striking that social investigators and policy advocates rarely, if ever, concede any influence of media messages on themselves personally, even among those who spend thousands of hours immersed in examining the content. Perhaps a "critical consciousness," "reflectivity," or objectivity inoculates social investigators, as a unique understanding or special knowledge of politics allows journalists to "privately scoff" at the simplicity of negative political ads. This privilege is not extended to the great unwashed.

This chapter deliberately has not assessed or presented any evidence that supports, opposes, or otherwise evaluates the effectiveness of negative political advertisements or any other type of campaign material. Indeed, they might be extraordinarily effective, but questions about authentic or genuine influence can never be answered by asking people how effective they believe messages to be.

This chapter has focussed on differences in perceptions of message effects because those perceptions reflect fundamental beliefs about ourselves and about others. Seemingly contradictory sets of beliefs, one for ourselves and one for others, allow us to reconcile splits between principle and practice, to cheer on democratic movements abroad while tuning out politics at home, to demand politicians do the will of "the people" while disdaining and disregarding opinion polls. In part, the coexistence of these divergent sets of beliefs for ourselves and for others protects us from our own hypocrisy, providing justification for our outrage at the messages produced in contemporary campaigns without admitting that we think that freedom of expression—to speak and to hear—should not apply to everyone. According media content powerful influence on others allows us to make messages the focus of our attacks while disguising the roots of our discomfort. Cloaked in the rhetoric of benevolent concern for the political process is our elitism, unbecoming and anathematic to a democratic state founded on the principle that all people are created equal. The split grants us a way of intimating what would be otherwise an unpalatable opinion: Perhaps we aren't all equal, equally capable of decoding and deconstructing media messages, and by extension, of making rational, informed political choices. And, if this is so, then maybe the practice of electoral democracy really isn't such a good idea.

By attacking the messages, while insisting that they have no influence on us personally, we betray our darkest thoughts of our fellow citizens, and come to grief at the prospect that perhaps the American experiment with self-governance is failing, that our experience is really not unique, that we too will follow instead of lead. As much was expressed in a story about his own interpretation of 1988 campaign when journalist Paul Taylor mused "[t]here is an anxiety in the national psyche that underlies all the others: Are we still the chosen people?"

PART FOUR

Images of the Voter-Citizen in Presidential Campaigns

Introduction

Images of the Voter-Citizen in Presidential Campaigns

Bruce E. Gronbeck and Arthur H. Miller

In classic democratic theory, citizens are witness-participants during electoral campaigns. They watch, probe, evaluate, and judge what they are told and by whom, and then, on the bases of their perceptions of the problems, the policy solutions, and political promises, they reason their way to a particular vote. In classic democratic theory, citizens operate at a dispassionate distance from the events of the campaign so as to make reasonable, calculated, and serious decisions.

But, of course, classic democratic theory faces two practical problems in accounting for actual voting behavior in the United States. For one thing, this country periodically has had large sectors of *disenfranchised* citizens. The original Constitution allowed only propertied white males to vote; it took most of the nineteenth century to let into the electorate non-propertied white males and black males, and it was not until 1920 that women were added. Next came a period of disenfranchisement, as the electorate shrank after 1896, thanks to decline in party confrontations and increases in registration statutes. The 1960s saw the confrontation in several southern states over voter qualification and testing laws that led, once more, to an expansion of the electorate. American history thus has been punctuated by swings toward both enfranchisement and disenfranchisement at various times (Piven & Cloward 1988).

The second matter of importance to our understanding of citizen activity is social-psychological, or more broadly, *rhetorical*. Not only can there be institutional barriers to or rewards for voting, but also important attitudinal-behavioral factors affecting voting participation. In summary of research on this thesis, Piven and Cloward (1988) note:

[T]he key to the puzzle of why so many people do not vote lies in one or another of their attitudes and preferences, or their lack of necessary

resources. Thus, people fail to vote because of a sense of political ineffectiveness, or they lack a sense of civic obligation, or they feel little partisan
attachment, or they possess few educational resources, or they exhibit
some combination of these factors (p. 113).

Such explanations stress especially individualized psychological reactions
to situational stimuli in the political environment. We would suggest that
voting or non-voting is not simply an individual matter (though it is that),
but also a more generalized matter of voters in blocs or groups who perceive
themselves and their place in society in particular ways. When citizens do
not participate, it is because they see themselves as outsiders. Ways of seeing
the world and citizens' orientations toward that world are constructed
rhetorically, in the languages or symbols generated by candidates and their
staffs, by the press and other sources of popular discussion of politics in the
public sphere, and even by citizen-voters themselves.

The image of the citizen-voter as decision maker in the electoral process
can be interpreted in a similar vein. Again, classic democratic theory offers
the icon of the well informed, issue oriented, utility maximizing voter
selecting between candidates in a calculating fashion (Downs 1959). Others
have challenged this conception demonstrating that the classic model
presents an unrealistic image of both the voter's cognitive abilities (Herstein
1981) and the individual-level cognitive processes involved in the making
of an electoral decision (see Boynton & Lodge, Chapter 10).

Further, it has been demonstrated that voters respond more to candidate character and candidate-generated symbols than to their statements
articulating policy alternatives (Kinder 1986; Miller & Wattenberg 1985;
Miller, Wattenberg & Malanchuk 1986). Many voters also have been found
to base their candidate choice and partisan identification on how they feel
about other blocs of voters and the connections they perceive between
political candidates and particular groups or interests in society. In short,
the image of voter as decision maker must be framed in a series of interre-
lated, symbolically constructed realities.

To state this more baldly: *the idea of the "voter" or "citizen" is socially
constructed in symbolic ways*. Indeed, all of our social roles—as father or
mother, aunt or child, professor or plumber, Catholic or agnostic, Midwest-
erner or Nigerian—have been constructed discursively, that is, via language
(admonition, instruction) or significant acts (positive or negative, meaningful sanctions for "proper" or "improper" actions in particular situations).
Our understandings or interpretations of social behavior in particular
settings are conditioned by such socially constructed roles, and that behavior is guided by social rules—etiquette, catechisms, licensure requirements,
expectations, etc.

"Citizenship" is subject to the same sorts of symbolic specifications. The duties of citizens in political documents or institutions have been specified; to be sure, there are rules and regulations regarding who can vote, when, and how. The ebb and flow of voting behavior, however, more intriguingly are controlled by popular perceptions of the political system:

- Are outcomes, through some conspiracy or power base, preor-dained? Will my vote "count" or not?

- To whom should I listen—and why—as I seek guidance in casting my vote?

- In what ways will my life be improved or threatened by voting in particular ways?

- Against whom am I voting when I vote (or not) in a certain pattern? Who comprises the Other or the Enemy in an election?

- Should I vote for the most likely winner (the so-called viable or electable candidate) or for someone else on some other basis?

- Will I think better of myself for voting or for staying out of the electoral mess? (On these matters, see Campbell et al. 1960; Wolfinger & Rosenstone 1980; Schaffer 1981; Miller & Somma 1988).

Such perceptions, we would argue, are created discursively, in the verbal and non-verbal messages directly and indirectly created by candidates and their staffs, the public prints, and even people's self reports as encoded in public opinion polls. Citizen-voter roles, our understanding of the "the people" at any given time (McGee 1975), are built out of thousands of messages that flow through the duration of a campaign. Those visions of citizen-actors affect electoral behavior in important ways.

In this view, then, the three centers of symbolic activity we have identified—candidates and their staffs, the mass-mediated discourses in the public sphere, and voters' themselves—vie with each other in a struggle to control citizen-voters' views of themselves and their actions during electing time. This section of the book examines some of those struggles.

Dan Merkle and Peter Miller open the section with a discussion of the role of public opinion polls—our explicit picture of ourselves that we construct statistically at regular intervals during campaigns—in depicting voters for all citizens. The essay by G.R. Boynton and Milton Lodge examines the idea of voter images more microscopically, using computer modeling as a tool to understand voter self perception and decision-making processes. Arthur Miller offers the third essay, assaying from presidential elections survey data the ways in which racially loaded messages are constructed indirectly and the degree to which they are correlated with voting patterns.

The fourth essay, by Harold Zullow, puts a particular spin on the idea of American exceptionalism, one tied to the sense of hope voters often feel during campaigns; he explores the mechanisms whereby hope is created and the ways in which that sense of hope translates into electoral activity. Finally, Monica Bauer explores the association of money and political activity: our democratic bias against the influence of money on politics and our struggles to control (or not) the relationship between money and electoral outcomes.

Thus, for this section we have assembled essays that probe the citizen-voter image itself, some of the factors that affect its particular features, and ways those images interact with both specific themes (e.g., money and electoral results). We will come back specifically to what we have learned about citizen-voters in Part V, where they will be the central focus of American self images.

9

Campaign Polls and America's Sense of Democratic Consensus

Daniel M. Merkle and Peter V. Miller

In the popular culture of presidential elections, public opinion polls are a ubiquitous, potent, and often times harmful force. Polls are assigned responsibility for everything from rapid campaign discourse and superficial press coverage to diminished or wrongheaded political participation. Press critics have argued against the burgeoning use of polls by the media. Though it is unlikely in the United States, polls during election campaigns—due to their presumed negative influence—are government controlled in a number of democracies, and the European Community is now discussing the standardization of such regulations across the member countries.

The potential effects of polls on the public and political process are many. These include both direct and indirect effects. Direct effects concern the impact of polls reported by the mass media on individuals' perceptions, attitudes, and behavior. Indirect effects include the way polls affect important elites in the political process, whose actions ultimately affect the public at large; the effect of polls on the campaign strategies employed by political candidates; the impact of poll information on the way reporters cover the election campaign; and the effect of poll results on financial contributors and volunteers for campaigns. This chapter explores both the direct and indirect effects of public opinion polls in order to better understand how they help construct our self images and our sense of democratic consensus.

Direct Effects of Polls Reported by the Media

During the 1992 presidential campaign it was hard to escape the constant barrage of media poll reports and discussions about what they meant. The most recent campaign is a vivid reminder of how the number of polls reported by the news media has dramatically increased in the past two decades. Research has identified three main trends at the heart of the proliferation of polls in the media. First, most large media organizations, and many smaller ones, now sponsor or conduct their own polls (Ladd & Benson 1992; Holley 1991; Demers 1987; Rippey 1980). This clearly wasn't the case, for example, in 1972. Second, not only are more media organizations conducting polls, but the number of polls conducted by each organization has increased tremendously (Ladd & Benson 1992; Lewis 1991; Gollin 1987). Finally, there has been a trend toward more prominent placement of poll stories in the media (Keenan 1986; Broh 1983). This is not surprising; as media organizations spend more money on their own polls, it is in their self-interest to highlight the results more (Ladd & Benson 1992).

The widespread reporting of opinion polls by the news media underscores the importance of considering the impact of these polls on the public. If polls do have direct effects on individuals, then these effects become more important as the number of polls reported in the media increases. We can think of polls affecting people in various ways. First, polls can influence people's perceptions of the opinion climate. These perceptions are then thought to influence people's attitudes and behaviors, a notion we explore in a review of research on bandwagon versus underdog effects and on the spiral of silence.

Perceptions of the Opinion Climate

For public opinion polls to have an impact on individuals' attitudes and behavior, they first must influence perceptions of the opinion climate. We use the term opinion climate here to refer broadly to the distribution of aggregate opinion or level of consensus on a given topic. Obviously, polls provide information about the aggregate opinion of a defined population and the extent to which it changes over time. But individuals must first believe that polls accurately reflect aggregate opinion if polls are to influence perceptions of the opinion climate. They must think that polls are accurate.

In general, however, surveys find that public confidence in the accuracy of polls is less than overwhelming (Lavrakas, Holley & Miller 1991; Roper 1986; Hastings & Hastings 1984, p. 304). Roper (1986), with a more positive slant, states "that although there is skepticism among the public about polls, few people are entirely negative" (p. 10). In addition to general perceptions about the accuracy of polls, it is common for people to make judgments of poll accuracy on a poll by poll basis. An individual's own view on issues is one factor that has been found to influence judgments of poll accuracy for a specific set of poll results on issues such as abortion and the death penalty (Merkle 1991b; 1992; 1993). Poll consumers judge a public opinion poll to be more accurate if the results show majority rather than minority support for their own position.

Surveys showing that people tend to be somewhat skeptical about the accuracy of polls in general, as well as research on how prior attitudes affect judgments of poll accuracy for a specific poll, suggest there are situations in which individuals will not believe poll results. They instead may think that public opinion in general corresponds to their own view (see further discussion of this phenomenon below). But this doesn't necessarily mean that polls can't influence perceptions of the opinion climate.

It is likely that skepticism about poll accuracy will be diminished in situations where numerous polls yielding similar results are reported over time. Presidential campaigns in which polls consistently show one candidate leading the other (like the 1992 campaign after the Democratic Convention) fit this description quite well. In such situations, it becomes more difficult to escape the consistent message of the polls and hard for supporters of the trailing candidate to selectively interpret the polls in their candidate's favor. On the other hand, when the polls are contradictory or show the margin between the candidates to be small, it is easier for voters to selectively find support for their respective candidate. Therefore, polls are less likely to have an impact on individuals' perception of the opinion climate in these circumstances.

Research by Lewis-Beck and Skalaban (1989) suggests support for the notion that polls are more likely to affect perceptions of the opinion climate when presidential races are lopsided. For the presidential election years 1956-1984, they found that voters' accuracy in predicting who would win the election was positively related to the actual margin of victory. For example, the proportion of voters correctly forecasting the election outcome was much higher in 1964, 1972 and 1984 than in 1960, 1976 and 1980. Since Lewis-Beck and Skalaban (1989) only looked at actual victory margins, a comparison of pre-election polls from 1980 and 1984 is illustrative. In 1980, pre-election polls showed the race between Carter and Reagan to be fairly close even though Reagan actually won by 10 percent. In 1984, various pre-election polls predicted that Reagan would win by between 10% and 25%, and the actual margin of victory was 18% (Kagay 1992).

There has been very little research focusing directly on the question of whether polls influence perceptions of the opinion climate. Granberg and Brent (1983) and Crane (1982) analyzed data from the 1980 National Election Survey and found that respondents' perceptions of who was leading in the latest polls was moderately related to whom they expected to win the election (r = .34). But these researchers also found that individuals' candidate preference was a much stronger predictor of expected electoral outcome than was the perception of which candidate was leading in the latest polls.

Thus, we conclude that polls can influence individuals' perceptions of the opinion climate. The impact of polls on perceived consensus can extend beyond simply telling people whether their own opinion is in the majority or minority and how aggregate opinion is changing over time. Polls also provide information about the issues that are important to the public, societal norms, the mood of the country, expectations of the future and evaluations of the past.

However, the influence of polls on perceptions of the opinion climate is not inevitable. When attitudes are strongly held, when poll findings are isolated, or when the results of multiple polls are equivocal, individuals are likely to selectively interpret the results in a manner that is consistent with their predispositions—projecting their own view to construct a subjective opinion climate. Conversely, if prior attitudes are weak and poll findings are multiple and consistent, we would expect a greater effect of poll information on individuals' estimate of opinion climates.

Bandwagon and Underdog Effects

For well over fifty years, it has been suggested that the reporting of public opinion poll results can have a direct impact on the public's attitudes and voting behavior (e.g., *New York Times* 1936; Lewis 1940; Pierce 1940; Katz & Cantril 1937; Allport 1940). Recent public opinion surveys indicate that a sizable proportion of those interviewed believe that polls reported by the mass media influence voters (Opinion Research Service 1989, pp. 1103, 1106; Hastings & Hastings 1987, p. 275; 1984, p. 303), interfere with or are harmful to the political process (Lavrakas, Holley & Miller 1991; Kohut 1986), or are "bad" for the country (Traugott 1991).

The terms "bandwagon" and "underdog" have been traditionally used to describe the impact that public opinion polls are purported to have on the public. As originally conceptualized, the bandwagon hypothesis predicts that individuals tend to vote for the frontrunner in election polls (i.e., jump on the leader's bandwagon) because they want to vote for the winner, don't want to throw away their vote, or want to go along with the crowd (Institute for Propaganda Analysis 1940; 1937). The counterpart to the bandwagon idea, the underdog effect, seemingly occurs because people are sympathetic, and it is human nature to root for the underdog. Regardless of the underlying motivation, shifts in opinion caused by polls are hypothesized to be either consonant with majority poll opinion (bandwagon) or dissonant with it (underdog). The research in this area on the effects of polls on individuals' attitudes and voting behavior, which dates back to the 1930s, can be classified by the three main (increasingly sophisticated) methodologies used: sequential poll results, survey self-report, and experiments.

Sequential Poll Results. Early on, researchers used sequential poll results to study the impact of polls on public opinion, and this method continues to be used (e.g., Robinson 1937; Gallup & Rae 1940a; Gallup & Rae 1940b; Klapper 1964; Mendelsohn & Crespi 1970; Gallup 1972; Roll & Cantril 1972; Beniger 1976; Kavanaugh 1981; Marsh 1984b; McBride 1991). What these researchers do is look at poll results from independent samples to see if the front-running candidate's lead increases or decreases over the course of the campaign. The idea is that if the bandwagon hypothesis is correct, one would see the candidate leading in the first poll forecast increase his or her vote percentage in subsequent polls and in the election outcome. But a number of these sequential poll studies find a trend in the direction opposite the bandwagon hypothesis (see Merkle 1991a). In other words, the polls tend to show that the leading candidate's vote percentage tends to actually decrease as the election approaches.

It is very difficult to interpret these data as evidence of poll effects (e.g., an underdog effect) because there are a number of other alternative explanations that could account for this result. For example, this pattern of findings may be accounted for by a regression effect. Oftentimes, the candidate who is far ahead in the polls has nowhere to go but down. Also, shifts in aggregate opinion during election campaigns can be caused by any number of factors, only one of which is public opinion poll results (e.g., see Cantril 1991, p. 215). By using sequential poll results it is impossible to separate the effects of these various factors and hence to specify the cause of any shifts in aggregate opinion.

Another problem with sequential poll results is the often-mentioned argument that if bandwagon and underdog effects do occur, it is likely that they occur at the same time and thus cancel each other out in the aggregate (e.g., Klapper 1964; Mendelsohn & Crespi 1970; Navazio 1977; Marsh 1984a; Marsh 1984b; Lavrakas 1990; Lavrakas, Holley & Miller 1991). Since competing shifts in opinion are hypothesized, it makes little sense to look at aggregate measures of opinion for evidence of these effects.

Survey Self-report. Survey questions have also been used to document the impact of opinion polls on individuals. Respondents are simply asked if public opinion polls have influenced their voting decisions. After the 1984 general election, Sussman (1985) found that 3.8% of the respondents in a national survey were willing to admit that the polls had helped them decide to vote for Reagan, while 3.7% indicated that the polls had helped them decide to vote for Mondale. The remainder of the respondents said the polls did not effect their vote preferences. Similarly, polls conducted in Canada and Great Britain have also found that 2 to 11% of those interviewed are willing to admit that they had been influenced by the results of public opinion polls (Hastings & Hastings 1990, p. 393; Hastings & Hastings 1985, p. 273; Crewe 1982; McAllister & Studlar 1991).

There are two obvious problems with assessing the impact of polls on persons' opinions by asking for self-reports. First, research indicates that individuals may not be able to accurately describe what has influenced their opinions (Nisbett & Wilson 1977). Secondly, even if individuals were completely aware of factors influencing their opinions, social desirability pressures (e.g., Nederhof 1985; DeMaio 1984) would make it unlikely that they would admit to being influenced by poll results.

Experiments. The two methods just mentioned are clearly inadequate if we want to establish a causal relationship between exposure to a public opinion poll and some preference shift. As has been noted previously by others, the best way to establish causality in studies of poll effects is through the use of an experimental design (Campbell 1958; Marsh 1984b, p. 572; Lavrakas 1990).

Experiments on poll effects have been conducted in a variety of contexts including classrooms, discussion groups, cafeterias, in people's homes and on the telephone (the last two as a part of surveys). Both voting intentions and issue preferences have been studied. The most common type of experiment (or quasi-experiment) is a post-test only design comparing sometimes randomly assigned experimental and control groups. Members in each group are asked for their opinions using an identical question; in the experimental group the question is immediately preceded by a presentation (either orally or in written form) of poll results on the topic in question.

Studies using this method have yielded mixed results. Some results are consistent with the bandwagon effect (Cook & Welch 1940, study one; Hall, Varca & Fisher 1986; Mutz 1990, study three; Marsh & O'Brien 1989), while others find no significant differences between the experimental and control groups (Dizney & Roskens 1962; Navazio 1977; Tyson & Kaplowitz 1977; Roper, cited in Cantril 1980, p. 53; Lavrakas, Holley & Miller 1991). Still other studies have yielded results consistent with the bandwagon effect in some circumstances but not others. Results consistent with the bandwagon effect have been found for low-commitment but not high-commitment issues (Kaplowitz et al. 1983), after exposure to information about the trend of opinion but not current static opinion (Marsh 1984a), and among "high self-monitors" but not "low self-monitors" (DeBono 1987).

Unlike sequential poll studies, the randomized experiments that measure between-group effects can attribute any reliable difference to the experimental treatment. But the experimental studies just discussed share one characteristic with the sequential poll method; both methods focus on group level shifts in opinion rather than individual level effects. This design permits making reliable distinctions between the two groups but ignores the possibility of individuals shifting in opposite directions. Another body of experimental evidence looks at the effects of poll information at the individual level.

Atkin (1969) found both consonant and dissonant shifts at the individual level among college students responding to issue and voting questions in 1968. When comparing the magnitude of the shifts, Atkin (1969) found that the consonant shifts were larger than the dissonant shifts. A more recent experiment, also using college students as subjects, was conducted during the 1980 presidential election by Ceci and Kain (1982). The first part of the study was conducted in the students' discussion groups. The subjects in the experimental group were asked which candidate they preferred after either being told that one of the candidates was leading in a recent poll (Carter or Reagan). Students in the control groups were not given any poll information. Later that same week, confederates, pretending to be conducting a telephone survey, called each of the students. Prior to asking the subjects for their current vote intention, the interviewer supplied those in the experimental group with results from a recent poll as had been done earlier in the discussion groups.

Although Ceci and Kain (1982) found both consonant and dissonant shifts at the individual level, the overall tendency was for subjects to shift their vote preferences away from the candidate depicted as dominant in the polls (dissonant shift). They interpreted this finding in terms of the oppositional reactivity hypothesis. Ceci and Kain explained that "dominance information caused [the] subjects to react oppositionally toward the dominant candidate without actually becoming more favorable toward the underdog even though superficially that is what appears to have happened" (p. 240). This shifting was most pronounced among the undecided, as well as those who weakly supported either Carter or Reagan.

In Canada, Cloutier, Nadeau and Guay (1989) used a sophisticated quasi-experimental panel design to measure individual level opinion movement on the issue of North American Free Trade. They too found individual level opinion shifts in both directions, interpreting these shifts as evidence of bandwagon and underdog effects. In this study, the consonant shifts occurred with greater frequency than the dissonant shifts leading the authors to conclude that "bandwagoning occurs more frequently than underdoging" (p. 213).

Finally, Lavrakas, Holley and Miller (1991) conducted a split ballot experiment as part of a telephone survey conducted during the 1988 presidential campaign. Overall, there was not a significant difference between the experimental and control groups. In an attempt to look at individual level effects, the authors conducted a discriminant analysis predicting vote preference in the control group using a number of demographic characteristics. Then, applying this model to the experimental group, Lavrakas, Holley and Miller (1991) report that 11% of those who were predicted to support Dukakis expressed a preference for Bush (bandwagon effect) and 18.5% of those who were predicted to support Bush expressed a preference for Dukakis (underdog effect), resulting in a net underdog effect.

Summary of Bandwagon and Underdog Research

The empirical evidence for the so-called "bandwagon" effect is at best mixed. The effect is often not found, and some researchers have reported an "underdog" effect. But the research evidence comes from studies that are either flawed or suffer from various conceptual and design limitations. Many of the studies consist of post hoc examinations of sequential poll results from independent samples making it next to impossible to determine the cause of any shifts in aggregate opinion. Overall, the experimental studies have yielded inconsistent results and are seriously limited in terms of construct and external validity given the subjects used (e.g., college students), the settings in which the studies are conducted, and the way in which the independent variable manipulations are presented to the subjects.

The cumulative effects of polls may be much more important in election campaigns than the impact of a single poll. But experimental studies have been limited to studying the effect of single polls. Many of the experimental studies focus only on net effects and ignore the question of individual level effects. Studies that have reported information about individual level effects report opinion shifts in both directions, with consonant shifts dominating in two of the studies (Atkin 1969; Cloutier, Nadeau & Guay 1989) and dissonant shifts dominating the other two (Ceci & Kain 1982; Lavrakas, Holley & Miller 1991). In sum, studies of the bandwagon hypothesis do not offer strong support for it, and this lack of support is buttressed by research on projection effects in campaigns.

Projection Effects in Election Campaigns

An alternative to the bandwagon hypothesis—the idea that perceptions of others' views shape individual attitudes—is that individuals' attitudes have an impact on their perceptions of others' views. In election campaigns, the term "projection" is used to describe "the tendency of respondents to ascribe their vote intentions to others" (Klapper 1964, p. 37). A similar effect has been found to operate for issue preferences and is referred to as "looking-glass perception" in sociology (e.g., Fields & Schuman 1976) and the "false consensus effect" in social psychology (e.g., Mullen et al. 1985).

An early study by Hayes (1936) conducted during the 1932 presidential election demonstrated that supporters of both Hoover and Roosevelt believed their candidate would win the election. Similar projection effects have been found in numerous election studies since (e.g., Thomsen 1941; Lazarsfeld, Berelson & Gaudet 1948; Berelson, Lazarsfeld & McPhee 1954; Carroll 1978; Brown 1982; Crane 1982; Lemert 1986). Granberg and Brent

(1983) conducted an extensive analysis of the eight presidential elections, 1952-1980, and found that "people tended to expect their preferred candidate to win by a ratio of about 4:1" (p. 477), with the correlation between candidate preference and expectation concerning the election outcome ranging from .42 to .68 (see also Pratkanis 1989, p. 80) for similar findings from Gallup polls).

Using panel data collected during the 1940 presidential election, Lazarsfeld, Berelson and Gaudet (1948) suggested that both bandwagon and projection effects accounted for the correlation between vote intentions and expectations, although they thought the bandwagon effect was more important (p. 168). Berelson, Lazarsfeld and McPhee (1954) tempered this conclusion after analyzing their data from the 1948 presidential campaign and reanalyzing the 1940 data. Their new conclusion was that both bandwagon and projection effects occurred and were of equal strength (p. 289).

The analyses for these conclusions did not receive detailed treatment in their respective books (Lazarsfeld, Berelson & Gaudet 1948, p. 168; Berelson, Lazarsfeld & McPhee 1954, p. 289; but see Lazarsfeld, 1972). For this reason, Klapper (1964, p. 36) reanalyzed the data. His analysis indicated that the projection effect was stronger than the bandwagon effect, although he conceded that the original authors may have used a different type of analysis that he was not able to replicate because it was never fully described. Granberg and Brent (1983) also reanalyzed the 1940 data and found the projection effect to be larger in magnitude than the bandwagon effect, although the difference was not statistically significant (see also Campbell 1963).

More recent studies suggest that projection effects occur to a greater extent than do bandwagon or conformity effects. Bartels (1985) used two-stage least squares to estimate simultaneous, reciprocal bandwagon and projection effects for data collected during the 1980 presidential primaries. His results indicated that the projection effect was twice as large as the bandwagon effect for Carter during the early phase of the campaign, while the bandwagon effect was twice as large as the projection effect for Bush during this same time period. Two other analyses conducted at a later stage of the primaries found the projection effect to be substantially larger than the bandwagon effect for both Carter and Reagan. Bartels (1985) concludes: "The most reasonable interpretation of the general pattern of these results is that projection is a quite persistent behavioral phenomenon, varying little in impact across the range of campaign settings represented in the 1980 data" (p. 813) (see also Brady & Johnston 1987; Abramson et al. 1992).

In sum, research on projection effects conducted during election campaigns finds a tendency for individuals to expect the majority to vote in line with their own preferences. Studies that focus on whether preferences influence expectations or vice versa support the conclusion that projection effects are stronger and more common than bandwagon effects.

Spiral of Silence

Another area of research in which perceptions of the opinion climate are thought to influence behavior is Noelle-Neumann's spiral of silence theory (1991; 1985; 1984; 1977; 1974). However, in this perspective the focus is not on voting intentions but rather on individuals' willingness to express opinions in public. The spiral of silence is a conformity based theory predicting that individuals have a fear of isolation and, therefore, continuously monitor the opinion climate. Individuals who perceive the opinion climate to be consistent with their viewpoint are more likely than those in the minority to openly express their opinions in public. This theoretically changes the climate of opinion leading to a spiraling process where the majority viewpoint appears to get stronger and stronger because the proponents of this viewpoint are more likely to express their views publicly. Simply stated, the perception of opinion climate affects people's willingness to express their own view.

The mass media provide relevant information about the opinion climate in the form of polls. But surprisingly, Noelle-Neumann (1984, p. 41; 1979, pp. 147-148; 1977, p. 149) ascribes little influence to polls reported by the media. Rather Noelle-Neumann argues that people assess the climate of opinion using a "quasi-statistical sense," which is assumed to operate for "hundreds of issues" (Noelle-Neumann 1984, p. 14) independently of published poll reports. In a review of the spiral of silence theory, Salmon and Kline (1984), take what seems to us to be a more reasonable position: "What is most likely is that polls are a sufficient but not necessary mechanism through which individuals can perceive the opinion climate" (p. 18).

Noelle-Neumann's (1991; 1985; 1984; 1977) research in Germany provides much of the empirical support for the spiral of silence theory. But other researchers have found the evidence for the idea less convincing, as Price and Allen (1990) note. As was true with bandwagon and underdog research, the less than satisfactory empirical support for the theory could, in part, be attributable to inadequate operationalizations of the theoretical constructs and to limitations of the methodologies employed. But, in addition to these possibilities, criticisms of some of Noelle-Neumann's key assumptions point to serious problems with the theory itself (e.g., Price & Allen 1990; Salmon & Kline 1985; Merten 1985).

The most serious criticism, which is applicable to arguments about the bandwagon effect of polls as well, is that the spiral of silence overemphasizes the pressure of conformity and majority influence and fails to consider important implications of research on minority influence (Price &

Allen 1990; Moscovici 1991). In addition, in the spiral of silence theory, the "group" that is hypothesized to exert the conformity pressure is aggregate opinion in the country as a whole, which is quite removed from the individual. As Price and Allen (1990) argue, "it is not at all clear whether diffuse collectives such as 'the public at large' can hold out the same negative sanctions or threats of rejection that smaller face-to-face groups can" (p. 381).

In spite of these criticisms, the spiral of silence provides a plausible alternative to the bandwagon effect of polls. Instead of changing one's opinion or voting behavior in the face of conformity pressure, an individual can simply retain his or her beliefs and keep quiet.

Poll Effects Revisited

Our look at the research on the direct effects of opinion polls on attitudes and behavior has discounted the power of poll information and accentuated the power of individual attitudes. But is it fair to say that poll effects do not exist? It seems to us that such a conclusion—even though it fits the current research evidence better than the opposite view—is unwarranted. Given the problematic nature of the bandwagon research reviewed here, the difficulties with causal inferences as well as construct and external validity, it is wise to keep an open mind about poll effects. Further, we can easily envision some circumstances in which information about public opinion can have an impact on voting decisions.

Hickman (1991) sets out some conditions under which poll results are more likely to influence attitudes and behavior. According to his template, polls will have an impact on individuals who (1) have a strategic orientation, (2) cannot predict the outcome of the election based on other information, (3) must make an immediate decision about which candidate to support, (4) have little or no commitment to any of the candidates, (5) have existing predispositions that are consistent with the poll results, and (6) perceive the poll results to be accurate.

Contrary to what might be inferred from the bandwagon literature reviewed earlier, these conditions are increasingly likely to be met—even in presidential election contests. The volatility of the presidential race poll data in May and June of 1992—when Perot, Bush and Clinton all were shown to be "leading" at one point or another—signals the fact that many voter preferences were not grounded in a firm attitudinal base. When opinions are not crystallized, the potential for poll effects is greater.

Additionally, in circumstances where there is a multicandidate field, for example during primaries or the general election period when there is a third party candidacy, strategic voting becomes a factor (e.g., Abramson et al. 1992). Previous bandwagon effect studies have been conducted during presidential elections involving races with only two major candidates and in elections where prior attitudes were more likely to play an important role in vote choice. We would expect to see more signs of poll effects in presidential primary and general elections where there are three or more candidates and less-than-firm voter attitudes. In such circumstances, votes may be cast for the "viable" as opposed to the "preferred" candidate.

Black and Black (1993) present data from exit polls conducted by Voter Research and Surveys suggesting that Perot's perceived lack of viability in fact did cost him votes. Thirty six percent of the exit poll respondents indicated that they "would have voted for Ross Perot if he had a chance to win" (p. 16) and another four percent actually voted for Perot but failed to answer this question. Obviously public opinion poll results were one of the sources of information about Perot's lack of viability in the final months of the 1992 campaign. Whether polls were a major determinant of Perot's viability cannot be determined given his withdrawal from the race, his unsubstantiated claims about Republican "dirty tricks," and his selection of James Stockdale as running mate, all of which undoubtedly played a role.

Indirect Effects of Polls

We have reviewed evidence on the most publicized possible effects of polls—direct impact on attitudes and behavior. Compared to this evidence, relatively little attention has been paid to the various indirect effects of polls. These indirect poll effects involve influences on political actors and media professionals whose actions ultimately may affect the public at large. The indirect effects on the public to be considered here include the effect of polls on campaign strategy, the impact of polls on contributors and campaign volunteers, and the impact on political reporting. These effects tend to receive less attention than direct effects because they occur behind closed doors. They are the subject of anecdotal accounts and inferences made by campaign professionals and reporters, not the focus of systematic empirical research. The following discussion recounts some of the lore of campaign insiders and its implications for the development of America's self image.

Polls' Effect on Political Campaigns

Political pollsters play a very important role in presidential election campaigns. They often serve as key strategic advisers to the campaign in addition to measuring voter sentiment and the "horse race." (Moore 1992; Levy 1984). Political pollsters use their data to help determine the most effective strategies for marketing their product, the candidate (Honomichl 1984, Chapter 5). *Advertising Age* recognized the important role of the pollster in politics when they named Richard Wirthlin Advertising Man of the Year because of his role in designing Ronald Reagan's successful marketing plan in 1980.

Altschuler (1982) outlines a number of ways that polls are used by political candidates and their campaign staff. First, politicians use polls to help them decide whether they should declare their candidacy. Among the factors to be considered in such polls are the name identification and positive or negative evaluation of the prospective candidate and his or her opponents. If the candidate sponsoring the poll is contemplating a run against an incumbent, the office holder's record is apt to be scrutinized in poll questions. Measurements of support among various constituencies also may be important. The data are not only used in deciding whether to run and in plotting initial strategy, but also in soliciting funds and other support. Poll numbers can offer legitimation for a budding candidacy; without the quantitative demonstration of viability, contributions and volunteer or in-kind support may not be available, effectively making it impossible to become viable.

During the campaign itself, polls are used to measure the positive and negative images of the candidates in the race. These data have important implications for campaign strategy. For example, in the early stages of the 1988 presidential campaign, George Bush had much higher negative ratings than did Michael Dukakis. This was one of the primary factors leading the Bush campaign to begin attacking Dukakis on a number of key issues (Moore 1992; Goldman & Mathews 1989). Bush's advisors knew it would be easier to increase Dukakis' negative ratings than it would be to decrease Bush's. The same strategy was employed by the Bush campaign after the Republican Convention in the 1992 race, attacking Bill Clinton on what came to be called the "trust" issue. This approach again met with some success—at least Clinton's support did lessen—but not enough to win Bush re-election. The "trust" attack may have been the result of private polling within the Bush camp, but not necessarily so, since public media-sponsored polls (e.g., CBS-New York Times) were available and showed Clinton to be vulnerable on this factor.

Polls on less character-based issues also play an important part which formulating campaign strategy. Although in some cases poll data might play a role in determining what side of an issue the candidate should take, more commonly polls are used to determine what issues and themes to stress during the campaign. Issues are addressed by the candidate if they are thought to increase his or her chances for electoral success. Candidates identify public concerns in polls to which they can lay claim and communicate back to the public as "what the election is about." The process of selecting issues, however, relies not on measurement of any and all public concerns, but on finding those issues that are most beneficial for the candidate's "positioning." The candidate must pick areas of strength (or weakness for the opponent) from those that are available. Reinforcing those particular themes to garner the support of persuadable voters becomes the job of campaign advertising and "earned media." Campaign messages based on polls, then, are attempts to establish a consensus on what the election is about and who is best able to deal with the defined matters.

Though they may have been surprising to many Americans, the winning "consensus" issues of the 1988 election—patriotism, toughness against the Soviet Union, prison furloughs, the evils of the ACLU, "no new taxes"—achieved hegemonic status through effective campaign message execution after being identified in research (Blumenthal 1990). These matters may have seemed odd concerns upon which to contest the election, given other possible issues such as the collapse of the Soviet Union, the immanent failure of the savings and loan industry, the enormous federal budget deficit, the manifest failures of public education, or the loss of U.S. global competitiveness. The selection and promotion of the winning definition are testaments to the Republicans' ability to identify areas of strength among "base" and "swing" voters in strategic states—however peripheral the issues might have been to the "real" problems of the country—and to the "stay on message" during the campaign. In 1992, after the dissolution of the Soviet Union, the Clinton campaign's selection of the economic issue, its pre-emption of attacks on traditional Democratic weaknesses (on welfare and crime, for example), and its power in staying on the economic message in the face of the Republicans' character assault showed that Democrats too could use research to frame an election and keep the focus long enough to win.

In addition to polls, focus groups have played an important role in framing messages and issues before they are used by the campaign. Focus group research involving New Jersey and Georgia voters by the Bush campaign in 1988 helped identify a few issues such as the pledge of allegiance and furloughs that were used effectively to increase negative perceptions of Dukakis (Moore 1992; Goldman & Mathews 1989). Similarly, Stan Greenberg's focus groups involving so-called Reagan Democrats in Macomb County, Michigan, provided information on how Bill Clinton should position himself for the 1992 presidential race.

In addition to deciding on message strategy, polls affect decisions about how to allocate campaign resources (Altschuler 1982). Polls provide information about the candidate's chances for success in each state. Precious campaign resources such as money for advertising and the candidate visits to the state can be utilized to achieve the maximal benefit. Statewide "horse race" polls by campaigns track the effectiveness of tactics in states where the campaign is believed to be competitive (see e.g., Moore 1992).

Polls in Journalistic Accounts of Elections

Measuring the horse race in journalistic accounts of elections is a tradition that precedes by many years the advent of scientific polls. The partisan press of the 19th century printed straw polls submitted by readers who conducted polling exercises while, for example, travelling by train (Herbst 1993). The horse race poll is in part a reader response device, a feature believed to be popular with audiences and thus a commercial venture, and in part a method for journalists to cover a traditionally important topic—the state of the public mind. Media-sponsored polls are by now an established feature of election campaigns that shapes journalistic coverage and thus helps to develop consensus and paint our self image.

Like campaign-sponsored polls, media polls influence the course of campaigns by highlighting candidate strengths and weaknesses and by establishing candidate viability or lack of it. Media polls can be very influential with potential campaign contributors or volunteers. Additionally, independent of any effect on contributors or voters, polls offer a convenient frame for reporters' discussions of campaign developments, as their summaries of "how things are going" for the different candidates provide a backdrop for coverage of current strategy. Phrases such as, "Candidate A, lagging in the polls, today announced ... " are common features of campaign stories. These summary statements, in fact, may be more important in forming beliefs about candidate viability than are the polls upon which they are based. As these phrases diffuse throughout the journalistic community, a candidate may undergo coronation or defeat prior to the election. In the 1992 campaign, for example, a familiar theme was the statement that "no candidate with Bush's negative rating has ever won." By contrast, a news magazine's coverage of Bill Clinton late in the campaign focused on what he would do in the White House after the election. Whether or not such coverage creates direct effects on voter behavior, it is evident that polls shape the story of the election and thus the consensus in the press about the meaning of the contest. In closer races, of course, such consensus-building is much more difficult, and polls are then the subject of dispute about "why they disagree." Such was the case early in the 1992 race before Ross Perot decided, prematurely, not to run.

Conclusions

We have looked at ways in which polls may directly and indirectly influence the public, ranging from voter behavior to the construction of America's self image. We have noted that the many avenues of potential poll influence are incompletely and obliquely addressed by empirical research. The impact of polls is probably not best judged by brute comparison of poll results and voter behavior, but by tracing the influence of the research through the formation of campaign strategy and journalistic treatment of the race. Polls can be viewed as offering parameters within which campaign teams and the press view the nature and conduct of elections. In doing so, polls may constrain and focus debate, enabling the construction of political meaning. This is not to say that polls create phony issues, but that they necessarily treat only some of the many possible issues and images that might be considered. When information from polls is then applied—strategically or unreflectively—by political elites in campaigns and the press, the interpretations they construct will perforce shape political discourse. The effects of this process on the electorate may or may not be observable in the course of an election campaign, and certainly are not likely to be static. Though George Bush appeared to benefit from public opinion research that focused his campaign message of 1988, that choice of discourse, so roundly criticized subsequently in the press, became an albatross around his neck in the election of 1992.

What, then, can we say about the relationships between the reporting of polls and American self images? Combining the direct and indirect influences of polls on the public, we can conclude that perhaps we are what we say we are to pollsters. Insofar as polls constrain and focus the public debates over character issues and insofar as polls are becoming *a*—perhaps even *the*—principal journalistic story, especially in the last month of a campaign (Ratzan 1989), then they likely are significant implements for constructing American self images during election time.

Democracy theory posits the idea of virtual representation to describe public opinion in the eighteenth century. Edmund Burke, especially, was clear on the role of the representative as acting in the best interests of— rather than on the commands of—his constituents (E. Burke 1963). By the late nineteenth century, the system of tribalism and clientism (Piven & Cloward 1988), whereby one's ethinic patron or downtown boss traded protection and services for politcal clout and patronage, made public opinion a tradable commodity. The Catholic vote or the Tammany Hall vote could leverage contributions and shape legislation. And now, in the late twentieth century, public opnion is etched on computer printouts, constructed from samples overnight, and readied for next morning's front page and the *Today Show's* news segment. We are able to construct images ourselves—our beliefs, attitudes, values, and rationales for behaviors— with social science as the medium: numbers, statistical comparisons, graphs, time lines, and appropriately low sampling errors.

As Martin notes (1984, p. 15), "The idea of collecting, summing, and averaging the opinions of a population, as opposed to culling the wisdom of a community by listening to the sages who cared to comment and by achieving a consensus, developed gradually, " but come it did. Its development was perhaps inevitable once the technology for such collecting and averaging was available. Public opinion polls reduce us to simple yes-no categories, five-point attitudinal scales, and standard demographic segments. The sheer ubiquity of public opnion polls during today's presidential elections guarantees us many statistical snapshots of ourselves. But, despite their abstractness and inflated number, their importance can scarcely be overestimated, for they dominate our family album. Those snapshots are major products of presidential elections showing who we think we are every four years.

10

Voter's Image of Candidates

G. R. Boynton and Milton Lodge

The campaign began with John Williams' statement that the federal deficit had to be reduced even if it meant spending less for social programs. The messages of the campaign—about positions on issues and the groups supporting the candidate—shared much with other campaigns. Candidates frame their messages to appeal to voters (see Morreale, Chapter 2; Lee, Chapter 3; Gronbeck, Chapter 4). They employ elaborate strategies to insure that the mass media carry the message the candidate wants (see Covington et al., Chapter 5 and Woodard, Chapter 6), sometimes successfully and other times unsuccessfully, because media people have their own agenda in presenting candidates to their audiences (see Rucinski, Chapter 8). An election campaign is this interaction of message, media, and *voters*.

Candidates have the greatest control over the messages they generate, less control over what the media does with and to their messages, and even less control over how the messages are heard. When two voters read that Williams supported a strong defense one heard an affirming message: "We need to stay strong; help primarily ourselves; defense spending means more jobs; and defense spending only to defend democracy not to conquer [the] world." The other person heard something very different, a disaffirming message: "Major cuts in defense spending are essential; we do not need all the warheads we have; we do need a stronger economy; we should be the lender not the debtor; Bush raises taxes." Arguments about defense policy that have played a major role in American politics and presidential election campaigns for several decades became part of what they heard when Williams spoke. From such meager bits and pieces of information about candidates, voters construct full blown images of the politicians seeking their votes.

Our knowledge of voters' ability to construct candidate images, on the spot, sometimes appears at odds with other knowledge we have about voters and their interactions with election campaigns. Most voters have a sparse image of presidential candidates and their images of other candidates is even leaner (Conover & Feldman 1989; Powell 1989; Miller 1991). Although little may be remembered about the policy positions of candidates, they normally vote for the candidate who is most compatible with their own views about politics (Graber 1988).

This puzzle is a triangle. Voters can construct a full blown image of a candidate on the basis of very little information, which implies a considerable knowledge of politics. Yet voters can remember very little about the policy positions of candidates, which implies little knowledge of politics. Yet they vote for the candidates who share their views on the issues of the day, which implies they act as though they know the policy positions even though they cannot recall them. How can the three sides of the triangle be held together? How do voters participate in, or interact with, the campaign such that all three findings can be true?

The campaign we study to tease out a solution to this puzzle is a quasi-experimental survey. John Williams is a candidate presented to the *voters* in the questionnaire with a campaign "fact sheet". That John Williams is a fictitious candidate is important for the research because we know everything the voters know about him; what they know about John Williams is what they learned from the questionnaire. Hence, there is no question about what they may have seen, heard or read about the candidate, that we do not know about, to confound the conclusions. The theory we employ is a theory of information processing; the process by which voters attend to campaign messages and convert them into impressions or images of candidates. The process outlined in the theory is embedded in a computer program that is our model of the theory. In the paper we work back and forth between the voters' reactions to Williams, the theory, and the program to show how the puzzle may be pieced together.

Constructing Images of Candidates and Spreading Activation in Memory

The first "fact sheet" statement about Williams was:

"WILLIAMS sees the federal deficit as a major problem facing the country and calls for cuts in social programs to reduce the deficit."

What one voter heard was:

Probably under pressure from a variety of industry captains not to cut the defense budget.

Probably Republican—trying to appease his conservative constituents.

Probably supportive of general Reagan-Bush domestic policy.

Probably sees the former Soviet Union as still being a substantial threat to world peace and western livelihood [sic] Probably himself at least moderately wealthy—thus out of touch with the real problems of the U.S.

Notice that the very first reaction puts Williams' statement into the context of defense, which *is not* mentioned in the policy statement. The first two responses construct "pressures" on the candidate from the captains of industry and conservative constituents. The third response generalizes the position-statement to the entire "Reagan-Bush domestic policy." The next response adds a perception of the former Soviet Union to the construction. Finally, the subject adds wealth to constructed-candidate-Williams as a way of explaining why the candidate is "out of touch with the real problems of the U.S." On learning that Williams is pro-life, from a later policy statement, the subject *fills in* a position on capital punishment and euthanasia.

We have employed 'heard' beyond its ordinary usage because we understand 'hearing' as spreading activation through a network. Hearing is not something done to you, the disturbance of airwaves, but is a process of understanding the current message in terms of an organized network of ideas (called a schema by some researchers) about politics. The replies from the voter illustrate the network of beliefs that form their image of Williams. In the campaign statement candidate Williams is connected to "federal deficit requires cutting social programs," and for this voter "federal deficit requires cutting social programs" was previously connected to a moderately elaborate set of the ideas, including fears about the former Soviet Union and beliefs about wealthy people. The spreading connections between the ideas *defines* Williams' message.[1] This person is quite explicit about the tentativeness of the construction of candidate Williams, employing "probably" in each statement. However, if the one campaign message was all the person had to go on for John Williams, then this is who he would be. Other subjects were not as explicitly cautious in their construction of Williams.

In order to determine the knowledge structure network that gave meaning to the voters' understanding of Williams, each subject was given the following instructions:

A policy statement made by candidate **John Williams** is printed inside the box on each of the following pages. For each policy statement we provide spaces for you to write in the first five **associations** that come to mind when you read about a candidate who takes this issue stand.

1. WILLIAMS sees the federal deficit as a major problem facing the country and calls for cuts in social programs to reduce the deficit.
2. WILLIAMS opposes the busing of school children as a means to enforce racial integration in the public schools.
3. WILLIAMS is critical of Israel's handling of the Palestinian problem.
4. WILLIAMS opposes major cuts in defense spending, believing that recent changes in the Soviet Union and Eastern Europe may not be permanent.
5. WILLIAMS is endorsed by various environmental groups as being pro environment.
6. WILLIAMS is a pro-life advocate who favors a constitutional amendment to ban abortions, except in the extreme cases of rape or incest.
7. WILLIAMS favors the death penalty for premeditated murder.
8. WILLIAMS supports deregulation of the coal industry.
9. WILLIAMS is opposed by women's groups.

The subjects were asked to provide the "first five *associations* that come to mind" when they read each of nine brief statements of policy position or group support from the candidate, Williams. "Associations that come to mind" is a very non-directive instruction permitting a wide range of responses. With one or two exceptions these were *au current* matters of public argument. The federal government budget deficit, race, gender, the environment, and the others were issues occupying the headlines about national politics at the time of data collection. The policy position least in the news, deregulating the coal industry, also generated the fewest responses.

If each subject had produced five "what comes to mind" for each of the nine statements it would have produced a cognitive network in which John Williams, the candidate, is the central node, and attached to him via the statements are nine policy positions and group commitments. Extending out from each node-as-statement are five other nodes picturing "what comes to mind" for that node. Only a few of the subjects had five associations for each of the nine policy positions. The mean number of responses was 3.7. On average, the nine questions elicited thirty-two responses per subject; summed over all subjects it was just over a thousand responses to the question. The responses were brief, typically using less responses to the question. The responses were brief, typically using less than the single line provided for each response. The number of words per response was 3.4, with many one word responses.

This is our operational version of knowledge structures or associative networks. It is not a technique of data generation that has been employed by other researchers, to the best of our knowledge. It shares some features with all open-ended questions, but it is not simply an open-ended question. It is a specific type of question/probe. And, as with any new *tool*, there are many questions we cannot answer about how the tool structures the matter it is put to work on. Our first look at the responses lead us to believe it is producing responses consistent with our expectations.

There is a coherent structure to the responses that extends well beyond the specific statement of policy or group support. Our findings are similar to Miller's (see Miller, Chapter 11) analysis of racial attitudes where he shows how they are related to attitudes about other groups and policy positions. We need an explanation of how the responses can have this intertextual, coherent-structure character; an explanation to help understand how the triangle, which is our puzzle, can be held together.

The theory of cognition we use to account for the character of the responses traces its roots to the work of Newell and Simon (1972) and John Anderson (1983). Two important commitments in the theory are 'process' and 'bounded rationality' (Simon 1957). Understanding communication and cognition as process is an understanding that emphasizes action. 'Hearing' is understood as inter-action rather than something happening to you. *Noticing* that a noise is a message, a sentence for example, and that another noise is the sound of an automobile, which may or may not be treated as a message, is the action of the hearer. There is no place for a "blank slate on which is written" in this conception of communication and cognition.

Bounded rationality is the other side of the process coin. The cognitive capabilities of human beings are finite; we cannot attend to everything that might be attended to at any moment, and we cannot bring everything we know to bear on what we are attending to. Some of the limits of human information processing can be specified quite precisely, for example, the time required to encode new information in memory. This seemingly technical constraint becomes important for understanding what the activity we call hearing can be. For example, the finding that people who know more about a subject remember more from a communication than do people who know less about the subject.

Memory plays a central role in contemporary theories of human information processing, and in these theories memory is treated as two functional components: (1) long-term memory; and (2) working memory. Long term memory is everything we know, and working memory is that small slice of what we know that is being consciously attended to at the moment. The distinction is not between two places, as if there was a physical location for long-term memory and another physical location for working memory. Instead, the distinction is between levels of activation; working memory is the part of what we know that is most active at any moment.

A basic finding of research on long-term memory is that much of what we know is organized associatively, in "packets" of conceptual knowledge and associations (Rumelhart & Norman 1983; Rumelhart & Ortony 1977; Schank 1982). The fact that what we know is structured semantically accounts for much of the speed and coherence of human thought, as well as many of the systematic biases that result (Lodge, Mcgraw & Stroh 1989). These semantically bundled units are typically pictured as nodes linked together as associative networks.

Working memory corresponds to that set of things we are actively attending to at any given moment (Anderson & Hubert 1963; Fiske 1980; Belmore 1986). Two characteristics of working memory make it a *bottleneck* in human cognition. First, we are able to attend to only a limited part of what we know at any moment; perhaps the "magic number" seven plus or minus two chunks of meaningful information (Miller 1956). The second constraint is the serial nature of conscious processing; 'considering' is one cognitive action at a time. Because of these two limitations the depth and breadth of considerations that can be taken into account is limited when making judgments (Payne 1982).

The dynamics of what is being attended to and what is not being attended to is provided by spreading activation. In the most straightforward case a person encounters a message, and attending to the message generates spreading activation through the associative network that is long-term memory. The nodes relevant to the subject of the communication become most active and others are not activated in the process. When a person reads that John Williams is in favor of capital punishment that activates associations with euthanasia. Reading that John Williams wants to reduce the federal deficit activates a range of other associations such as the belief that he favors the death penalty, wants to cut defense, is pro-life and opposes busing. Reading, then, is spreading activation through a semantically organized network, which is our specification of how reading can have the intertextual and coherent-structure character that permits constructing candidates *whole* on the basis of little information.[2] If the question is: How do individuals construct a *whole* candidate from the bits and pieces of information available to them? Our answer is spreading activation through a semantically organized network. While this answer addresses one leg of the triangle of our knowledge of voters it does not illuminate how the associative network comes into being and why it is what it is and not something else.

Campaigns as Learning: Remembering, Forgetting, Organization

Jimmy Carter was unknown outside of Georgia when he began his run for the presidency. In only a year Michael Dukakis jumped from obscurity to household word—and back. The learning that must occur in a presidential election campaign may start at a quite rudimentary level. Name recognition is the first hurdle and all candidates for the presidency surmount that hurdle, though many persons seeking the nomination do not. Name recognition is important for candidates, but it does not take us very far toward understanding what Bruce Gronbeck (Chapter 4) points to as what we need to know about what is and is not learned in campaigns. In this section we lay out how an associative network—an understanding of politics—may result from a campaign.

Remembering and Forgetting

When most citizens first heard Jimmy Carter's or Michael Dukakis' name, spreading activation drew a blank; there was no node, he was unknown. Spreading activation through a network of nodes is measured in milliseconds, but adding to what we know, creating a new node in the network, is measured in seconds (Simon 1979). Thus, focus of attention may shift more quickly than learning can occur. We have all experienced reading, listening, or watching and afterward not being able to recall the *details* even though we paid attention to all of the details when we were reading or watching. Something more than *exposure* is required for the learning to occur that involves remembering. Either repetition in the message or a goal of learning the name of the candidate can keep the candidate's name active long enough for it to become something we know, a new node in the network. These two conditions come together in a presidential election campaign. The message is repeated—over and over; ordinary citizens see and hear the names of the candidates many hundreds of times in the nine or ten months that is the current presidential election campaign (Graber 1988). And our interest in who is going to be the new president peaks during this period; almost all of us set a goal of learning the names of the presidential candidates.

It is important to notice that we can process information without being able to remember it later (van Dijk 1988). Remembering and forgetting are important elements in any understanding of human cognition. What is less apparent but equally important is cognitive processing that does not involve forgetting because the message was never *remembered*. Hearing a message is a spreading activation process, and it does not necessarily follow that having understood a message we will remember it. The learning that involves establishing a new node requires an extended focus of attention devoted to the message—at least on the millisecond time scale of cognitive activity—and most hearing is a faster process.

Learning is more than establishing a node in the network, however; it is also remembering and forgetting. Memory fades, and our theory specifies the fading as a function of node strength. Nodes decay at the same rate; two nodes of the same strength at one time would be equally remembered or forgotten at some later point, but two nodes of unequal strength would be remembered or forgotten unequally at the later point. This is relatively easy to demonstrate when the time-scale is measured in days, but it also is plausible on a longer time-scale. Who was the Republican candidate for the presidency in 1976? Who was his running mate? It is likely that many people who can remember Gerald Ford's candidacy do not remember that Robert Dole was the Republican vice-presidential candidate. It is very unlikely that people who can remember Dole's candidacy for the vice-presidency do not remember Ford's candidacy. Being able to remember Ford's candidacy and not being able to remember Dole's candidacy can plausibly be attributed to the difference in node strength accumulated for the two Republican candidates in 1976, though it does not completely rule out an unequal rate of forgetting.

The Ford and Dole candidacies also illustrate how nodes are strengthened. Once a node is learned it does not have to be re-learned, but it is strengthened by subsequent messages. Ford's name did not have to be learned in 1976 (Conover & Feldman 1989), but Dole's surely did by much of the American public. And the greater newsworthiness of the actions of presidential candidates meant his name was heard and read many more times. Learning—encoding a node in memory—is not simply a function of exposure, but once it is learned node strength is a function of exposure.

Organization

When one of the subjects read that Williams favored a strong defense, this is not all that was noticed. Reading is spreading activation through a network. Nodes do not come into being in isolation but are embedded into a network. The single node is important in the way it is connected in the network. It is the pattern of connections in the network that give very different readings of the same message. If you live on Long Island, defense and jobs are connected via Grumman. If you live in Iowa, jobs are connected to agriculture but not defense. If Williams was speaking to Iowans his strong defense message would call a somewhat different set of associations to mind than if he was speaking to Long Islanders. We will call the pattern of connections, which make different readings possible, the organization or structure of the network.

Activation spreads through the network depending on the strength of linkage between the nodes. Nodes that are strongly linked will be activated together; it is this conjoint activation that provides "what comes to mind." The organization of the network, or the pattern of linkages, depends on the relative strength of the nodes that are linked. For example, if two nodes were linked to a third node the strength of the connection between each of the two nodes and the third node would be its strength relative to the other node. If node one was stronger than node two then its link to node three would be stronger. In this simple case there appears to be no distinction between node strength and linkage, but in even a small memory model, such as our model, there is a substantial distinction because nodes are linked to many other nodes and the relative strength of each node varies depending on which other nodes are linked in each configuration.

Specifying the linkage between nodes in terms of relative node strength gives an account of how the messages of a campaign can re-organize the network that is a person's understanding of politics. A campaign in which two issues are emphasized and are consistently linked, for example, can change the pre-existing linkage. Issues that were previously un-linked become linked; issues that were linked fade because they are not emphasized. The result is a network quite differently organized after the campaign than at its start.

In the 1980s and in 1992 the civil rights argument has frequently been equated with "quotas." Republicans say 'tis; Democrats say 'tain't.[3] How the bundle of ideas we pull together as 'civil rights' has changed over time is a concrete case of change in the organization of a network. In 1960 the image of civil rights was Martin Luther King's letter from the Birmingham jail. Even the most dedicated segregationist had difficulty denying the discrimination practiced against blacks (Matthews & Prothro 1965). By 1988, what civil rights brings-to-mind for white citizens had changed dramatically (see Miller, Chapter 11). The change cannot be traced to first hand experience. White persons do not apply for a job and find that a person of another race is always better qualified for the job. White persons do not seek housing and find that the only apartments and houses available are in black neighborhoods. White persons do not find that they are asked to pay a higher price for an automobile. As the beneficiaries of discrimination we have few means of finding out about the practice of discrimination other than through public debate. And the public debate has been about quotas—not about discrimination. The result is two-thirds of whites believe there is little or no discrimination being practiced (see Miller, Chapter 11). Civil rights and discrimination were linked in the 1960s. Discrimination has faded as civil rights has become linked to quotas. Writing in 1965, Matthews and Prothro (1965) told us what the result would be:

the power of the Negro vote increases to the *extent that whites perceive the issue as involving matters of fairness and impartiality*. One of the greatest resources of Negroes in their struggle for equality is the obvious congruence of many of their demands with the "democratic" and "good government" ethos. Reforms that can be justified by simple and clear appeals to the whites' sense of fair play and impartiality have a relatively good chance of being adopted. Thus nondiscrimination in public hiring practices is far easier to achieve than a policy of compensatory opportunities that seems, on its face, to discriminate in favor of Negroes (p. 480).

Summary

Creating, organizing and reorganizing associative networks is one of the principal forms of learning in presidential election campaigns. No one would deny that presidential election campaigns are important arenas in which American citizens learn about their polity and their own citizenship. But political scientists have had difficulty finding the learning that has resulted. At least part of the difficulty is due to the conception of learning that informs the way the research has been conducted. Our theory specifies three ways learning may happen: (1) reinforcing what we already know or adding to node strength; (2) adding new knowledge or new nodes to the network; and (3) reorganizing the links between nodes producing different paths for the flow of activation.

Reinforcing what we already know, as a form of learning, is an excellent example of the difficulty of studying learning in election campaigns. The stability of the themes across election campaigns (see Morreale, Chapter 2; Lee, Chapter 3) is a pattern of messages ideally designed to produce this form of learning. However, only if you have some conception of what the network would be if the themes were not repeated can you determine how the network is structured because of the campaign. Our theory can address this question because, unlike most theories of voting, a conception of decay or forgetting is central to the theory, and we have a method for tracing change in the network.

Our theory also specifies how learning does not occur where political scientists have most often looked for it—citizens knowing the policy positions of the candidates. An example: In 1960 John Kennedy *won* one of the debates with Richard Nixon largely because of his answer to a question about Quemoy and Matsu. Very few of the listeners had heard of Quemoy and Matsu before the question, and only the most committed of listeners bothered to learn where the islands were located. When asked, after several weeks, almost no one was able to recall Kennedy's answer (van Dijk 1988), even though they had been impressed at the time. How voters could not remember Kennedy's *policy* on Quemoy and Matsu is easily accounted for:

person sets a goal of learning will new information be learned. This, then, is our answer to the second leg of the triangle, the puzzle with which we started. New nodes will be added to a network only if there is great redundancy in the communication or if the person has the goal of learning. How a candidate's answer to policy questions become part of voters' impression of him is the topic we turn to next.

Affect and Impression Formation

Social scientists, especially cognitive scientists, normally distinguish cognition and affect—what you know and what you like —and they conceptualize and study them separately. But the language of the responses to "what comes to mind" does not fit this bifurcation. It is both cognitive and affective.

For example, one subjects' impression of candidate Williams' pro-life position was:

Absolutely wrong.

Who is he to make such decisions for other people?

How many adopted children does he have?

Will he ever have to give birth? (of course not)

That alone is a very bad position for him.

The language is affect laden. There is no mistaking the impression of Williams' position; Williams is "absolutely wrong." You can almost hear the sneer in "Will he ever have to give birth? (of course not)." The person knows and uses the arguments against the pro-life position: a private sphere that government should not enter; adoption is an alternative in argument rather than in practice; males should not be setting the rules for females who must bear the child. But to notice only what the person knows is to miss the affect in which this knowledge is embedded. The impression of Williams is an affect-loaded impression. We will follow Abelson (1968) in calling it "hot cognition," as a way of uniting cognition and affect. We understand cognition as spreading activation through a semantically organized network with learning and forgetting as operations on the network. Following Abelson's lead, we need a reasonable way to get affect into the network.

From the research on person perception or impression formation we draw three points on which there is broad agreement in the research community. First, forming an impression of persons is normally an 'on-line' activity. Norman Anderson (1989) makes the point quite emphatically when he says, "Life is on-line." On-line is contrasted with what might be a sequential process. Not on-line would be learning something about a person and then reflecting on what you had learned to form an impression of the person. On-line is forming the impression of the person as you are learning—on the fly, so to speak. We are able to do both, of course (Cohen 1981; Hastie & Park 1986; Lichtenstein & Srull 1981; Ostrom, Lingle, Pryon & Geva 1980). But there is evidence that forming impressions of persons is so much a part of our everyday life that we do it without thinking about it or do it un-self-consciously (Newman & Uleman 1989). Lodge, McGraw and Stroh (1989, 1990) have shown that on-line is how impressions of candidates for political office are often formed.

The second point we take from research on impression formation is: the impression formed, or the evaluation, of a person depends on the prior evaluation of what you are learning about the person. The easiest way to explain the point is to describe the type of experiment used to justify the claim. Ask subjects for their feelings about a large number of policies and groups at time one, without mentioning a candidate. At time two, some weeks later so the first interview will be a blur in their minds, give the subjects a fact sheet describing a candidate with a subset of the policies and groups asked about at time one. After reading the fact sheet the subjects are asked to give their impression of the candidate. Compute a score for each subject based on what they said they liked and disliked about the candidate in the time two interview. If the score based on the time one feelings about the issues and policies does a better job of predicting the subjects' impression of the candidate than does the score based on what they said they liked about the candidate in the time two interview that is taken as justification for this point. The results consistently favor the pre-existing evaluation of what is learned about the person over what can be remembered. (Lodge, McGraw & Stroh 1989; 1990).

This point is important because it specifies where to locate the affect in the network. The candidate node has to have more than a name tag. It must also have an affective tag; a way of computing the assessment of the candidate. But so must the other nodes; issues and groups are "hot" as well. It is on the basis of the person's assessment of those nodes that what is learned about the candidate becomes an assessment of the candidate. Just as the network may be thought of as a pattern of activation or node strength, so may it be thought of as a pattern of affect.

Third, the impression formed of a person is cumulative. Your current impression of a person is based on the memory of your past impression plus the current information you are encountering. Impressions are remembered, added to and subtracted from, or adjusted in light of subsequent experience (Park 1989).

This point is important for understanding how impressions are formed in an election campaign that takes many months from start to finish. What you learned about a candidate at the beginning of the campaign, much of which you can no longer recall, as well as what you learned recently are bound up in your current assessment of the candidate.

With these three points we have a theory of political cognition that is thoroughly affective—hot cognition.

Images are multi-faceted. One person heard strong defense as defending democracy, high technology and jobs. Another heard it as deficits, taxes and the U.S. international trade deficit. When John Kennedy talked to Americans about Quemoy and Matsu he was confident, knowledgeable and he was not going to let the Chinese take advantage of the situation. Wherever Quemoy and Matsu were and whatever needed to be done he was the person you wanted in charge. Spreading activation was united with a positive impression on all of these dimensions. You did not need to learn his specific proposals to be impressed. The resulting generalized affect became more important than the specific facts. Hot cognition is how that is possible.

Conclusions

Presidential election campaigns are a time when we focus attention on politics. Messages abound—in the campaign oratory, in campaign advertisements, in the media and in conversation. We are inundated with messages. What the messages are, and how they are what they are, is recounted in many of the chapters of this book. In this chapter we have outlined a theory about how messages may become images.

John Williams' campaign was simple—only nine statements. The images, the associations that come to mind, were more elaborate, more multi-faceted than the original messages. They were images of policy and character, argument and affect. The images reflect the broad stream of messages of American electoral history. But each person put together his or her individual combination; no two were exactly alike.

We have suggested how that can happen by outlining a theory of cognition—of hot cognition. Imagining is understood as spreading activation through a semantically organized network. Learning and not learning, remembering and forgetting, and reorganizing the way we think about politics were explained as the interaction of messages and what we already know. Finally, we showed how affect could be as much a part of the network as the cognition.

While outlining the theory we also investigated some images of ourselves—how images of voters' knowledge of politics can be understood. The ability to imagine a full-bodied candidate Williams was explained as spreading activation through an organized semantic network of ideas about politics. The ability to like best the candidate with whom one agrees while not being able to remember the agreement was explained as impression formation that does not require the sustained and focused attention needed for learning.

Notes

1. There are a number of ways to arrive at this understanding of 'hearing.' For example, in mid-century logical positivisits attempted to define `sense data' as an independent datum on which cognition could operate; it was an attempt to give a coherent account of how sensation and cognition could be differentiated. But the Wittgensteinian arguments overwhelmed the position. One line of argument following from Wittgenstein's work is quite explicit about 'hearing' as occurring through an associative network (Bloor 1982; Hesse 1974). Cognitive science is another way to arrive at this understanding of hearing. Work on perception and parsing both indicate that they cannot be effectively understood as first hearing then understanding (Dyer 1983). Wittgenstein's argument starts with a social theory of knowledge (Bloor 1983) whereas cognitive science is more individualistic in orientation. There are many other lines of argument, some more social and some more individualistic, that lead to the same result. The conception of communication we take from these lines of argument is spelled out more fully in Boynton (1990). In this paper we want to take the point for granted and develop from it rather than make a general argument for an active theory of 'hearing.'

2. There is, of course, much more to the story than we are able to summarize here: what kind of information is stored in memory; pattern matching that identifies these nodes as relevant and others as not relevant; productions that structure the step by step consideration of the message; and much more. We rely heavily on John Anderson's (1983) account of cognition in our theorizing.

3. See *The Washington Post* (1991 July 30) p. A-4 for the standard discussion of how much Democrats and Republicans will be helped and hurt electorally by quotas without any mention of discrimination either as a campaign issue or as it is being practiced in society.

11

Social Groups as Symbols in America's Sense of Democratic Consensus

Arthur H. Miller

> When the official subject is presidential politics, taxes, welfare, crime, rights or values ... the real subject is race. Race is no longer a straightforward, morally unambiguous force in American politics; instead, considerations of race are now deeply imbedded in the strategy and tactics of politics, in competing concepts of the function and responsibility of government, and in each voter's conceptual structure of moral and partisan identity. Race helps define liberal and conservative ideologies, shapes the presidential coalitions of the Democratic and Republican parties, provides a harsh new dimension to concern over taxes and crime, drives a wedge through alliances of the working classes and the poor, and gives both momentum and vitality to the drive to establish a national majority inclined by income and demography to support policies benefiting the affluent and the upper-middle class (Edsall & Edsall 1991).

The social diversity of America provides a bountiful source of both positive and negative political symbols for presidential campaigns. Republican presidential candidates, we are told, were successful in the elections of the eighties because they exploited a new racism rampant in America (Sears 1988; Kinder & Sears 1981; McConahay 1986; Edsall & Edsall 1991). This modern racism is not blatant. Unlike traditional racism, it makes no direct mention of blacks and other minorities as inherently inferior or socially undesirable, and thus deserving of legal segregation or regulation. The last presidential campaign to witness a discussion that appealed to traditional racism occurred when Johnson and Goldwater openly disagreed over the 1964 Civil Rights Act.

The new racism which has become increasingly relevant since the 1964 election is subtle and indirect. The politicians who evoke racial prejudice among the populace, according to the new racism theorists, do so by reference to topics that are not explicitly racial in nature. Rather than addressing racial issues directly, they discuss issues such as law and order, traditional values, the family, crime, drugs, joblessness, welfare fraud, patriotism, and sexual conduct, all of which indirectly trigger underlying racist predispositions and reactions among whites (Edsall & Edsall 1991, p. 61).

While it is clear from previous work (e.g., see Carmines & Stimson 1989) that race and race-related issues have influenced party fortunes at the presidential level as well as the orientation that Democrats and Republicans take on civil rights liberalism, the new racism argument is limited for a number of reasons. First and foremost, it is too narrowly conceived as a description of the role that social groups play in presidential campaign politics. The new racism can be construed more generally as part of a new conservative egalitarian populist ideology (see Lee, Chapter 3) that extends well beyond issues of race-related civil rights. Modern racism as part of a broader ideology of social conservatism focuses attention on differing American images, hopes, and fears reflected in the campaign rhetoric of the two parties. On the one hand there is the image of conservative egalitarianism. It stresses traditional values such as loyalty to the larger community and patriotism; family and parental responsibility; respect for authority, religion and rules; and the work ethic, sexual restraint, and social stability. People who express this orientation are opposed to special treatment not only for blacks, but also for unions, gays, feminists, or any other liberal groups. They are likely to believe that discrimination is a past phenomenon, and very likely to attribute success or failure in life to personal responsibility. They fear that there is a growth in drug use, crime, homosexuals, and welfare recipients occurring in the country. On the other hand, there is the liberal-oriented ideology of those who champion the rights of individuals and promote programs to compensate for the past discrimination against various groups seeking empowerment in society.

Second, the new racism argument tends to focus attention exclusively on the social extremism of the left. According to this argument, blacks and groups demanding the protection of their rights have done so through such liberal policies as promoting affirmative action, protecting criminal defendants, and easing restrictions on welfare recipients. In the abstract these policies may be seen as progressive and humane, but in reality the white, middle class sees them as programs for black people who are irresponsible, morally corrupt, and too lazy to better themselves through hard work. And on top of this, the white, middle class is paying for these programs with their hard-earned tax dollars. Given this set of beliefs, the angry white, middle class turns out in elections to vote against any Democratic candidate who supports such liberal policies. No matter how accurate this description may reflect the beliefs of middle class whites, it ignores the possibility that there are negatively evaluated groups on the conservative right that can also evoke a strong voter reaction that is detrimental to Republican candidates.

Third, the modern racism argument is limited because it suggests that little old-fashioned discrimination or outright group animosity, whether racial or in any other form, is evident in American society today (Sniderman & Tetlock 1986, p. 148). According to the new racism argument, racist predispositions today are evoked indirectly, through symbols that have no apparent racial connection. The response is associated with racial animosity, but the cuing symbol, at least on the surface, has no obvious racial implications.

Clearly there are numerous examples that fit the modern racism argument. The 1988 Bush campaign television ad labeled the "revolving door" showed convicts going in and almost immediately coming out of prison through a turn-stile. The ad was critical of the Dukakis program in Massachusetts that allowed some criminals to go home on weekend leave. Because a number of the individuals going through the revolving door appeared to be African Americans and Hispanics, some people charged that the ad was intended to connect racial animosity and fear of crime.

We fully agree that indirect symbols can activate negative group sentiments. Nevertheless, to focus entirely on presumed indirect cues ignores those situations where the group connections are less subtle and where certain groups themselves become the symbols that add meaning and organization to how the individual thinks about politics. For example, to talk of Willie Horton, a convict who committed rape and murder while on a weekend leave from a Massachusetts prison in 1988, is to turn Willie Horton into a symbol of lawlessness. Printing a picture of Willie Horton, who is black, as part of a campaign ad criticizing the furlough program, however, appeared to some as a direct attempt to connect racial attitudes and fears of crime.

There is a growing literature that presents evidence supporting the contention that social groups themselves act as the symbols that add meaning and organization to how the public conceives of politics (Lau 1986; Hamill, Lodge & Blake 1985). There is also increasing evidence that evaluations and cognitions involving social groups influence a variety of associated political attitudes including political ideology and policy preferences (Brady & Sniderman 1985; Sears et al. 1980), evaluations of government economic performance (Conover 1985), beliefs about the distribution of power and equity in America (Sears et al. 1986; Dennis 1987) and party evaluations (Miller et al. 1991). In general, all of this research demonstrates that a substantial proportion of the citizenry organizes its thinking about politics in terms of groups rather than issues or candidates. Given these findings, the perceived intergroup connections and the vote impact of these connections deserve more attention than is provided by the writings on modern racism.

Finally, as an explanation for election outcomes, the modern racism theory clearly had some difficulties with the outcome of the 1992 election. If Edsall and Edsall (1991; 1992) were correct in arguing that the outcomes of elections in the 1980s were a reflection of new racism sentiments, then we must ask what happened in 1992? Surely the answer could not be that racist predispositions had suddenly disappeared or that there were no symbols available in the 1992 campaign that could be used as subtle cues to evoke those predispositions. Perhaps the answer is as straightforward as that suggested by Edsall and Edsall themselves, namely that in a year when the economy becomes the number one issue it overrides the power of modern racism, which depends on social rather than economic issues to divide the public. Whatever the explanation, the new racism theory suggests that the group animosities influencing the elections of the 1980s did not affect the outcome in 1992—a point we return to later.

The purpose of this chapter is to address these limitations of modern racism theory. The intention is not to critique new racism ideas per se, but rather to examine certain aspects of the theory that have received little empirical attention and to demonstrate how modern racism is more potent, both theoretically and empirically, if it is incorporated as part of a broader conception of how we construct our social identity.

The chapter proceeds by first looking at historical shifts in where the public stands on government assistance to minorities as well as shifts in their perceptions of where the candidates for the two parties stand on this policy issue. Next, the connections between racial attitudes and certain nonracial issues that were presumed to act as symbols evoking racial predispositions in the 1988 election, namely, taxes, crime and traditional values, are investigated. This analysis helps us to understand both the importance and limitations of new racism.

After assessing the limitations of new racism as an ideology and an explanation of election outcomes, we turn to an alternative conceptualization that focuses on social groups as symbols. We demonstrate how the associations between group affect and party assessments have changed over the recent past, and how group ties affected the 1988 and 1992 elections. Finally, we end with a discussion of what was both similar and different when the 1992 election is compared with earlier elections, and the implications of this for future politics and self-images in America.

Reexamining New Racism

According to new racism arguments, three elements are necessary for racial attitudes to influence vote outcomes. First, the voters must perceive that there is a difference between the race-related policy positions of the two parties and their respective candidates. Without this difference, racial attitudes, no matter how subtle or obvious, will not get translated into election outcomes. Second, even if negative affect towards blacks is not directly related to the electoral choice, it must have at least an indirect influence through its association with race-related issues. If a basic dislike for blacks is not associated with race-related policy preferences, those preferences may simply reflect liberal or conservative differences rather than racial animosity. Third, new racism assumes that there is a significant degree of attitude consistency or ideological constraint underlying the public's attitudes toward race-related policy issues, black affect, and a set of policy issues that, on the surface, are not obviously race related but yet presumably act as subtle cues of racial predispositions. Each of these three

TABLE 11.1 Respondent, Candidate and Party Positions on Government Assistance to Minorities

	1972	1976	1980	1984	1988	1992
Respondent						
Pro-Assistance	34.0	34.3	21.8	31.8	26.4	25.9
Neutral	23.5	21.7	29.5	30.7	24.0	27.8
Anti-Assistance	42.5	44.1	48.7	37.5	49.5	46.3
Mean	4.2	4.3	4.5	4.1	4.5	4.4
Democratic Candidate						
Pro-Assistance	73.0	61.5	58.3	60.6	59.7	41.0
Neutral	16.0	20.6	21.3	21.6	22.0	28.1
Anti-Assistance	11.0	17.9	20.4	17.8	18.3	30.8
Mean	2.7	3.2	3.3	3.2	3.2	3.8
Republican Candidate						
Pro-Assistance	32.1	40.3	16.5	25.2	15.2	17.0
Neutral	30.3	25.1	25.5	21.9	25.6	26.5
Anti-Assistance	37.6	34.6	58.0	52.9	59.3	56.5
Mean	4.1	3.8	4.7	4.3	4.8	4.7

Source: National Election Studies (NES) 1972-1988; Iowa Social Science Institute 1992 (ISSI).

points are examined in turn.

New racism proponents argue that historical shifts in the positions that the two political parties and their presidential candidates take on race related issues has contributed to an increased association between racial predispositions and policy and vote preferences. Prior to the early 1960s the majority Democratic party was perceived by the public to be slightly more conservative on questions of racial policy than was the minority Republican party (Carmines & Stimson 1989). After the mid-sixties, however, the perceived orientation of the parties reverses, with Democrats becoming perceived as increasingly more liberal (pro-civil rights) and Republicans increasingly more conservative (anti-government involvement in promoting civil rights). While Carmines and Stimson present data only through 1980, the evidence in Table 11.1 confirm their findings through 1992.

In addition, the data of Table 11.1 demonstrate that Ronald Reagan and George Bush were perceived by the public as far more negative toward government assistance to minorities than were earlier Republican presidents Richard Nixon and Gerald Ford. Furthermore, the evidence from 1992 reveals that Clinton was perceived as more moderate on the issue than were previous Democratic candidates.[1] Nevertheless, in every election year, including 1992, the Democratic candidate was perceived as more favorable toward government aid to minorities than was the Republican candidate. Moreover, in every election (including 1992) the Republican candidate was perceived as closer than the Democrat to the policy position preferred by the average citizen (note the differences between the means for the candidate and the respondent). In short, the data fit the criterion of perceived party differences assumed by the new racism theory.

The second assumption of new racism theory also enjoys some support from available data, although it is less convincing than that found for perceived party differences. The role of black affect, that is a basic dislike of blacks, in new racism theories has been quite controversial. For example, Kinder and Sears (1981) define symbolic racism as the combination of racial prejudice (anti-black affect) and traditional American values. But Sniderman and Tetlock (1986, p. 136), argue that Kinder and Sears fail to demonstrate this association outright, claiming that "if symbolic racism does not involve dislike of blacks, it is far from clear in what sense it can be said to be racism at all." Similarly, Carmines and Stimson (1989) failed to demonstrate that race-related policy ideology incorporates negative black affect. In fact, their factor analysis revealed that preferences on race-related policy and racial affect were independent of each other (Carmines & Stimson 1989, pp. 124-125). In all their anecdotes about public sentiments against government spending programs to help blacks, Edsall and Edsall (1991, 1992) also fail to determine if this is a reflection of anti-black affect. After all, as Sniderman, Piazza, Tetlock, and Kendrick (1991, p. 425) point out, "Oppo-

TABLE 11.2 Correlation of Black Affect and Racial Attitudes with Non-racial Issue Attitudes[a]

	Black Affect	Liberal/ Conserv.	Spending	Taxes	Crime	Patriotism	Family Values
1988							
Black Affect	----	.07	.21	.03*	.11	.06	.02*
Aid Minorities	.21	.18	.35	.04	.12	.08	.09
Racial Equality	.26	.19	.24	.01*	.14	.17	.20
Quotas	.22	.16	.25	.12	.11	.10	.18
1992							
Black Affect	----	.04*	.13	.06	.03*	.06	.16
Aid Minorities	.21	.13	.17	.02*	.07	.15	.18
Racial Equality	.23	.24	.26	.07	.13	.16	.23

[a]Table entries are Pearson r correlations. All scales have been coded in a consistently liberal to conservative direction to produce correlations.
* Not significant at $p < .01$ (2 tailed).
Source: 1988 NES; 1992 ISSI

sition to government spending may be inspired not by racism but rather by a person's conservatism."

The correlations presented in Table 11.2 reveal the strength of association between black affect and a variety of policy questions, one's liberal to conservative orientation, as well as attitudes toward crime, patriotism, and traditional family values (see Chapter Appendix for specific measures used in each index). Not surprisingly, affect toward blacks is moderately correlated with public preferences on policy questions that are obviously related to benefits for blacks, such as government aid to minorities and affirmative action programs. The correlations between black affect and attitudes on issues that appear to be non-racial, such as liberal/conservative, taxes, crime, patriotism, or family values, however, are noticeably weaker. The only moderate sized correlation is that which occurs between black affect and attitudes on government spending. In general, these weak correlations raise doubts about the extent to which affective predispositions and prejudice toward blacks are cued by campaign themes focused on taxes, crime, patriotism, or family values.

Of course, the anti-black sentiment could be cued indirectly, which is the third point made by new racism arguments. Presumably there is some degree of ideological constraint underlying the broader set of racial policy questions and other less obviously race-related issue areas. Indeed the correlations between the racial items and the other indicators are stronger than those found for black affect alone. Anti-black affect, therefore, may get indirectly triggered through the connection between racial policy preferences and other issues that have no obvious racial connection such as taxes, crime, or family values. That is, crime cues concerns about racial policy, which in turn cues racial prejudice.

The correlations in Table 11.2 between attitudes on race-related issues and other issues are certainly stronger than those between anti-black affect and the non-racial issues. Only the question on taxes produces relatively weak correlations with the racial issue questions, a particularly interesting result given that Edsall and Edsall argue strongly that the revolt against taxes is a critical aspect of new racism ideology. Attitudes toward government spending, on the other hand, are consistently correlated with both black affect and the race-related issue questions. In this regard, the Edsall and Edsall (1991) argument that the public see "too much middle-class money going to blacks and the poor" (p. 55) is given support by the data in Table 11.2. It should be noted, though, that liberal/conservative orientation is also more strongly correlated with the race-related issue measures than with black affect. The consistently stronger correlations, therefore, could be a reflection of attitudes toward the size and role of government rather than racial bias.

In short, the data of Table 11.2 provide at least some support for the new racism view that when candidates discuss topics such as crime, government spending, patriotism, or family values, what they really are invoking are racial predispositions. But the most important aspect of this argument, yet to be tested, is that these indirectly cued racial predispositions influence voting and the outcome of elections. To test this part of the theory requires a multivariate analysis examining the impact of race-related attitudes on the vote after controlling for other plausible explanations such as economic anxiety, partisanship, or liberal/conservative ideology.

The results of the multivariate analysis, presented in Table 11.3, reveal little direct impact of either anti-black affect or race-related policy attitudes on candidate evaluations or the vote. In 1988, anti-black affect and the attitudes toward racial equality did have a statistically significant effect on candidate evaluations, but none of the race-related variables had a significant, independent direct impact on the vote choice. Candidate assessments and the vote decision were clearly dominated by concerns about crime, government spending, patriotism, liberal/conservative ideology, and partisanship. If the public's concern about crime was increased by the 1988 Willie Horton ads, the impact of that concern on the vote certainly went well beyond any simple expression of racial animosity.

The 1992 analysis presented in Table 11.3 indicates even less impact of race-related attitudes, especially as a predictor of candidate evaluations. In part, this may be a reflection of the fact that Clinton deliberately distanced himself from Jesse Jackson and other black activists during the campaign. As a result, the public perceived him as more moderate on race-related policies than any previous Democratic candidate in the past two decades (recall the data in Table 11.1 on perceived candidate positions). Of the three race-related predictors in the 1992 equations, only the racial equality index was significantly related to candidate assessments and weakly (.05 level of significance) associated with the vote. As may have been expected, given the deep recession of 1991-1992, the economic variables—government spending, taxes, concerns about the national economy—were relatively more

TABLE 11.3 Multivariate Analysis Predicting Candidate Evaluations and Vote Choice, Whites Only

	Candidate Evaluations		Vote	
Predictor	1988	1992	1988	1992
Black Affect	.07(.00)	.01(.31)	.01(.60)	.03(.10)
Aid Minorities	.01(.74)	.01(.40)	.01(.64)	.03(.12)
Racial Equality Index	.06(.00)	.07(.00)	.02(.27)	.04(.05)
Quotas Index	.03(.13)	----	.03(.12)	----
Spending Index	.06(.00)	.14(.00)	.08(.00)	.21(.00)
Taxes	.07(.00)	.03(.22)	.02(.26)	.08(.00)
Crime Index	.17(.00)	.12(.00)	.21(.00)	.14(.00)
Patriotism Index	.08(.00)	.06(.00)	.06(.00)	.06(.00)
Family Values Index	.05(.01)	.05(.00)	.04(.03)	.11(.00)
National Concerns Index	.05(.01)	.07(.00)	.04(.04)	.16(.00)
Liberal/Conservative	.06(.00)	.06(.00)	.09(.00)	.04(.05)
Party Identification	.20(.00)	.16(.00)	.33(.00)	.27(.00)
Adj. R^2	.60	.62	.65	.70
(N)	(1184)	(1803)	(1001)	(1476)

Table entries are standardized coeffecients with significance level in parentheses.

Source: 1988 NES; 1992 ISSI

important in 1992, but that did not appear to be the reason for the weak impact of the race-related variables, since they were also weak in 1988.

In summary, the evidence presented in Tables 11.1-11.3 reveals that the public perceives Democratic and Republican candidates to take distinct stands on race-related policies. Anti-black sentiments and race-related policy preferences, however, have little direct impact on the choice of a presidential candidate. Of course, given that these race-related attitudes correlate somewhat with all the other nonracial variables in the Table 11.3 equations, racial sentiments have at least indirect effects on candidate assessments and the vote. In other words, when a voter casts their ballot largely on the basis of concerns about spending or crime, they are doing so partly because of the racial predispositions that are associated with attitudes toward crime or government spending. Indeed, it may be argued that new racism theory is better represented by data that show racial attitudes as having no direct impact on the vote, but only an indirect impact through association with issues that are not obviously racial in content. This indirect effects model may be closer to the subtle, indirect cuing situation described by new racism theorists.

When examined more closely, however, the analysis reveals some telling limitations to this argument. First, the indirect ties, empirically speaking, are quite weak and tenuous. The overall level of attitude constraint, indicated by the strength of the inter-item correlations among the various measures assumed to capture, either directly or indirectly, the new racism ideology (see Table 11.2) is no greater than the size of the correlations found among a general set of policy questions (Jennings 1993, p. 426). Second, the definition of group cleavages solely in terms of race ignores numerous other social groups that individuals may use as indirect cues when organizing their thinking about politics, or when defining their self image and their image of American society.

Reference Groups as Political Cues

An alternative approach is to not assume that race forms the major social cleavage in American politics, but rather to treat it as an empirical question. A major limitation of new racism theory is its singular focus on race as the only critical cleavage in America. This is not to deny the importance of that cleavage; rather it should be seen in the broader context as a reaction to the empowerment of more groups in society than just blacks. We need to determine what set of social groups are used by the public when organizing their thinking about the world of politics, how the public perceives the political parties associated with these groups, and the extent to which a positive or negative identification with the groups determines political behavior.

New research demonstrates that a substantial proportion of citizens organize their thinking about politics in terms of groups rather than issues or candidates (Lau 1986; Hamill, Lodge & Blake 1985). This group orientation to politics makes a good deal of sense because social groups are very visible actors in the political arena. Indeed, some research suggests that groups have played an increasingly important and visible role in politics since the start of the seventies. Walker (1983), for example, has documented a dramatic rise in public interest groups during recent years. Likewise, changes in election laws regulating campaign financing have contributed to an explosion in the number of organized interest groups, and made PACs a household word in the process (Sabato 1985; Schlozman & Tierney 1986). Also, there is growing evidence that evaluations and cognitions involving social groups influence a variety of political attitudes, including political ideology and policy preferences (Brady & Sniderman 1985; Sears et al. 1980), evaluations of government economic performance (Conover 1985), and beliefs about the distribution of power and equity in America (Sears et al. 1986; Dennis 1987). In general, all of this research reveals an important influence of social groups on political attitudes and behavior in the United States.

The theoretical treatment of social groups in recent research differs substantially from that which appeared in the literature of the sixties. The early treatment of reference groups placed a great deal of emphasis on face-to-face interactions and group cohesion (see Lau 1983 for an excellent review of the relevant literature). More recent work focuses on information processing and treats social groups as categories that provide a source of identification for group members or information cues for nonmembers (see among others Tajfel 1972, 1978; Fiske & Taylor 1984; Lau & Sears 1986). Within this newer theoretical framework there is no longer the need for the very restrictive assumption of face-to-face interaction for the group to influence individual behavior. Merely the perception that one is or is not part of a group is sufficient to differentiate how people will act towards ingroup and outgroup members (Brewer 1979; Jackson & Sullivan 1987; Tajfel et al. 1971; Wagner et al. 1986; Lau 1989).

In brief, the major components of the theory can be summarized as follows. The world of politics is one of complexity that must be simplified and organized if it is to have relevance and meaning. In dealing with this complexity and everyday flow of information individuals sort objects, people, and events into broad categories that are then used as short-cuts for efficient processing of subsequent information in a coherent rather than a piecemeal fashion. Social groups regularly serve as important and relevant categories that influence one's self concept as well as one's understanding of social and political relations. Social groups are not only visible actors in the political arena, but power struggles between competing groups in society are salient to the public.

Some groups are more visibly involved in and salient to politics than others. Over time citizens forget about the specific details of political interactions between various groups, but they develop a general sense of those groups they share common concerns with and those that are less similar to their own political orientation. Generally, people are more positive in their evaluations of groups with which they share common concerns and relatively more negative towards those with which they have less in common. Groups are perceived to be connected, with varying degrees of intensity, to different political parties. Theoretically, if people like certain groups and they perceive those groups as aligned with a particular candidate or party, they should evaluate the politician and party more positively. Similarly, if they dislike the group, it should have a negative impact on their judgment of the party and candidate.

Change in partisan strength and alignment, according to the theory, occurs in three possible ways. The groups connected with each party could change, either through the rise of new groups or because of shifts in the salience of already existing groups. Public evaluations of the groups connected with each party could change; assessments of some groups could become more positive while others became more negative. Finally, the number of people who identify with a group could change, either increasing or decreasing, thus influencing the party's fortunes despite stability in the perceived connection of the group to the parties or evaluations of the group.

The Structure of Party-Group Connections

Recent research demonstrates that the public does associate certain clusters of social groups with each political party, although the particular group associations are not stable over time (Miller, Wlezien & Hildreth 1991; Miller & Wlezien 1993). Factor analyses of the group thermometers for 1972, 1984, and 1988 indicate that the structure of party-group connections changed over that period, particularly for the groups the public associated with the Democratic Party. In the early seventies, Democrats were defined in terms of the poor, blacks, unions, the middle class, Catholics, and liberals. By 1984, however, the set of groups the public associated with the Democratic party had narrowed and included such "fringe" groups as black militants, the women's movement, people on welfare, gays, and lesbians. These activist groups displaced, at least in the public's perception, certain more moderate groups of the traditional Democratic coalition, such as Catholics and the middle class. The groups that were perceived to be newly associated with the Democratic party were less positively evaluated by the public than the more traditional groups (on average, by 20 degrees on a 100 point rating scale), thereby partially explaining the decline in identification with the Democratic party evident after the mid-seventies.

During the same period of time, a shift also occurred in public perceptions of the groups associated with the Republican party. Unlike the Democrats, the change in the groups that the public associates with the Republican party did not involve displacement of some groups by others. Rather, an increased connection developed between traditional Republican groups—big business, wealthy people, and conservatives—and "fringe" groups, on the right, specifically anti-abortionists and evangelical groups active in politics. These Republican fringe groups were also less positively evaluated than were traditional Republican groups. Through 1988, however, the correlation between evaluations of Republican fringe groups and feelings about the Republican party were substantially weaker than the connection between affect toward Democratic fringe groups and Democratic party assessments (e.g., in 1988 the average Republican correlation was .13 as compared with .34 for the Democratic groups).

Group Attitude Constraint

But to what extent does positive or negative affect toward one sociopolitical group get transferred to feelings about another group? Similarly, to what degree does this broader group affect get connected with policy issues?

Jennings (1992, p. 426) raises doubts about the level of ideological consistency underlying sociopolitical group evaluations. He reports that the average inter-item correlation among the ratings of eight sociopolitical groups was only .12 in 1980. The groups included in the analysis were big business, labor unions, women's liberation movement, blacks, conservatives, liberals, the moral majority, and environmentalists. The problem with the Jennings analysis is that he computed the average intercorrelation among all of these groups together. However, as the research by Miller, Wlezien, and Hildreth (1991) demonstrates, there are two sets of sociopolitical groups here, those that the public associates with Democrats and those perceived as Republican groups.

In order to obtain a meaningful estimate of the magnitude of attitude constraint, the two sets of correlations must be evaluated separately. After all, we should expect that the correlations between the two sets of groups would be very low and possibly negative. Indeed, when the average intergroup correlations reported by Jennings are recomputed for the two separate sets of groups, we discover an average of .33 for the Democratic groups (unions, women's liberation movement, blacks, liberals and environmental-

TABLE 11.4 Correlations Among Ratings of Sociopolitical Groups Associated With Democrats

	1988				
	BL	CRL	PW	FEM	G & L
Blacks (BL)	----	.53	.35	.27	.23
Civil Rights Leaders (CRL)	.43	----	.39	.54	.32
People on Welfare (PW)	.32	.36	----	.28	.22
Feminists (FEM)	.24	.40	.32	----	.32
Gays & Lesbians (G & L)	.29	.42	.33	.44	----
	1992				

Note: Correlations are Pearson r. The upper matrix is for 1988, the lower for 1992. All correlations are significant at p < .01 (2 tailed).

Source: NES 1988; ISSI 1992

ists), and .37 for the Republican groups (big business, conservatives, Moral Majority). These correlations are much higher than those Jennings reports for a set of seven issues (.12) or ratings of eight political leaders (.23). In short, when the analysis is correctly carried out, the results suggest stronger attitude constraint for group evaluations than either issue positions or candidate evaluations.

Data from the 1988 National Election Study (NES) and the Iowa Social Science Institute (ISSI) 1992 election survey also reveal substantial attitude consistency in group ratings. For example, the correlation between ratings of evangelical groups and anti-abortionists was .35 and .43 in 1988 and 1992 respectively. Similarly, among the Democratic sociopolitical groups the average inter-correlation in 1988 was .34 and .35 in 1992 (see Table 11.4). Clearly, someone disliking any one of these groups also tends to dislike the others. Similarly, anyone feeling positive about one group tends to be positive toward the rest of the groups. Affect towards blacks and civil rights leaders certainly plays an integral part in the overall cohesion of these group ratings. Nevertheless, a reference to some other groups, such as feminists or gays and lesbians, could also act to trigger racial feelings and vice-versa.

The fact that all of the inter-group correlations are consistently strong suggests that there is some fundamental dimension underlying all of the ratings. The underlying commonality may be that some people see all these groups as fringe groups whose actions are unacceptable and thus negatively evaluated, while others see them as groups striving for empowerment and thereby deserving of support. The same interpretation could also apply to the Republican groups. Some people may think that anti-abortion and

Evangelical political groups are acting to promote a morally correct position and thus rate them positively. Other people, however, may react negatively because they dislike the political tactics of these groups or feel that the issues they articulate, such as abortion or prayers in schools, should be dealt with privately and not by the government. Alternatively, the underlying dimension could simply be liberal to conservative ideology, a point we return to momentarily.

A significant degree of attitude constraint was also evident in the correlations between evaluations of the sociopolitical groups and preferences on a variety of issues. Table 11.5 presents the correlations between the average rating each respondent gave the Democratic groups (all those in Table 11.4; labeled DEMGRP) and Republican groups (evangelicals and anti-abortionists; labeled REPGRP), and the various race-related and non race-related issues from Table 11.2. All of the correlations in Table 11.5 are statistically significant, thereby suggesting more ideological consistency than when racial prejudice alone is assumed as the underlying predisposition as in Table 11.2. Indeed, on average the correlations in Table 11.5 are much higher than those in Table 11.2. Perhaps most surprising is the fact that the correlations of DEMGRP with the race-related measures—aid minorities, racial equality, and quotas—are noticeably higher than the correlations obtained when using a measure of affect toward blacks.

Clearly, issues that some new racism theorists perceive as only race-related topics appear to tap broader sociopolitical group cleavages. Moreover, the positive correlations found between DEMGRP and the various issues, as opposed to the negative correlations obtained with REPGRP

TABLE 11.5 Correlation of Democratic and Republican Group Affect Measures with Racial and Non-racial Issue Attitudes

	Aid Minority	Racial Equality	Quotas	Liberal/ Conserv.	Spending	Taxes	Crime	Patriotism	Family Values
1988									
DEMGRP	.29	.42	.31	.27	.38	.13	.26	.09	.22
REPGRP	-.07	-.12	-.14	-.23	-.10	-.07	-.14	-.17	-.26
1992									
DEMGRP	.33	.41	----	.22	.23	.08	.13	.08	.38
REPGRP	-.08	-.11	----	-.27	-.34	-.10	-.37	-.14	-.16

All correlations are significant at p < .01 (2 tailed)

Source: NES 1988; ISSI 1992

measure, reveal a degree of polarization or "us" versus "them" aspect to this cleavage. Respondents who were positive toward the Democratic groups were also systematically more liberal in their issue preferences, while those who were relatively more positive toward the Republican groups preferred conservative issue positions. Indeed, the correlations with liberal/conservative self identification demonstrate that evaluations of the two sets of groups reflect an underlying ideological orientation. This conclusion is further supported by the finding that how people respond (positively or negatively) to the term "liberal" was strongly correlated (.54) with ratings of Democratic groups in both 1988 and 1992. When a politician is labeled as a "liberal," as Bush did repeatedly to Dukakis in 1988, it could trigger group sentiments.

Again, some critics would argue that the strong connection between group affect and liberal/conservative ideology is simply a reflection of differences in political orientation rather than anti-group prejudice per se. This is a reasonable argument, and just as in the case with anti-black affect it can be examined empirically. One way to test this argument is with a multivariate analysis examining the impact of anti-group attitudes on candidate evaluations and the vote choice after controlling for liberal/conservative orientation. If political ideology accounts for anti-group sentiments, then we should find no direct impact of group evaluations on candidate assessments or vote choice after controlling for political orientation and issue preferences.

Comparing the 1988 and 1992 Elections

The results of the multivariate analysis that includes the Democratic and Republican group affect measures, as well as all the issue measures used in the earlier regressions comparing the 1988 and 1992 elections (from Table 11.3), are presented in Table 11.6. The most striking finding from the multivariate analysis is that the group affect measures were not only statistically significant after controlling for liberal/conservative ideology, policy preferences and party identification, but were among the strongest factors influencing candidate evaluations and the vote choice. The combined impact of both Democratic and Republican group affect was equal to the impact of the strongest issue concerns. For example, in 1988 the impact of group affect was equal to that of concerns about crime, the most important issue in that election. Similarly, in 1992 the group measures had a combined impact that was slightly more powerful than concerns about government spending, which was the single most important issue of that election. In short, taking a broader perspective on group cleavages reveals far more direct impact of group prejudice on election outcomes than when anti-black affect alone is examined.

Another very important result of the multivariate analysis is that it reveals a reversal in the relative impact of Democratic and Republican group affect for 1988 and 1992. In 1988, how people felt about the Democratic groups had approximately twice as much impact on their vote as did their feelings about the Republican groups. The relative impact for the two sets of groups reversed in 1992, although the impact of Republican groups was only marginally greater than that of the Democratic groups. Nevertheless, the 1992 impact of Republican groups was virtually double what it had been in 1988.

The change in the relative impact of affect toward Democratic and Republican groups in 1988 and 1992 reflects differences in the dynamics

TABLE 11.6   Multivariate Analysis Including Democratic and Republican Group Affect to Predict Candidate Evaluations and Vote Choice, Whites Only

	Candidate Evaluations		Vote	
Predictor	1988	1992	1988	1992
Democratic Group Affect	.17(.00)	.08(.00)	.13(.00)	.10(.00)
Republican Group Affect	-.06(.00)	-.12(.00)	-.07(.00)	-.14(.00)
Aid Minorities	.01(.81)	.01(.44)	.01(.68)	.02(.19)
Racial Equality Index	.05(.03)	.06(.00)	.02(.36)	.04(.02)
Spending Index	.05(.02)	.12(.00)	.08(.00)	.18(.00)
Taxes	.07(.00)	.02(.35)	.04(.09)	.07(.00)
Crime Index	.16(.00)	.10(.00)	.20(.00)	.13(.00)
Patriotism Index	.08(.00)	.06(.00)	.06(.00)	.05(.01)
Family Values Index	.04(.05)	.05(.00)	.03(.16)	.11(.00)
National Concerns Index	.06(.00)	.07(.00)	.04(.05)	.15(.00)
Liberal/Conservative	.04(.07)	.01(.43)	.07(.00)	.02(.23)
Party Identification	.19(.00)	.17(.00)	.34(.00)	.30(.00)
Adj. R^2	.63	.65	.69	.74
(N)	(1192)	(1796)	(1008)	(1468)

Table entries are standardized coeffecients with significance level in parentheses.

Source: 1988 NES; 1992 ISSI

of the campaigns for those two years. In 1988 the Democratic candidate Michael Dukakis was easily labeled by the Republicans as a "liberal," associated with feminists and black extremism of some form (Willie Horton). In 1992, on the other hand, Bill Clinton resisted the liberal label and distanced himself from black extremism (for example, by criticizing rap singer Sister Souljah). As a result Clinton successfully cast himself as a moderate Democrat in the eyes of the public (recall Table 11.1). Moreover, on an issue that was critical in 1988 and somewhat important in 1992, namely fears about crime, Clinton was perceived as far more strict than Dukakis had been four years earlier. Indeed, in 1992 people believed that Clinton would be relatively tougher on crime than would Bush (41% saw Clinton as tougher than Bush, whereas 25% saw Bush as tougher). In 1988, however, 49% thought Bush would be tougher on criminals than would Dukakis, and only 21% thought that Dukakis would be tougher. Given these differences between perceptions of Clinton and Dukakis, it was difficult for the Republicans to label him as just another liberal. Also, he effectively distanced himself from feminists and blacks in the public's perception, but yet did not alienate these types of people among the voting population.

In addition, when it came to issues regarding gays, the one liberal group that Clinton was associated with somewhat in the public's perception (although not as much before the election as after), those opposed to gay rights, split their vote between Bush and Perot. While Clinton was able to distance himself somewhat from unfavorably assessed Democratic groups, the Republicans, on the contrary, became much more closely identified with the conservative fringe in 1992 than they were in 1988. In fact, the correlation between Republican group affect and ratings of the Republican party went from a mere .12 in 1988 to a robust .39 in 1992. This shift most likely reflects the greater presence of visible conservatives, such as Pat Buchanan and Jerry Falwell, during the primary campaign and at the Republican party convention. The increased impact of attitudes toward the Republican groups may also reflect the greater emphasis given to pro-life and traditional family values during the Republican convention and the early phase of the fall election campaign. Certainly Vice President Dan Quayle's criticism of Murphy Brown (a TV character played by Candice Bergen) increased public perception of Quayle as extremely conservative. Murphy Brown, as part of the program script, becomes pregnant out of wedlock and decides to give birth rather than have an abortion, thereby becoming a single, working parent. Although Brown did what pro-life groups would prefer, the Vice President was still critical saying that the "cultural elite" were promoting a "poverty of values" in America by glamorizing single parenthood. While the Vice President probably meant this criticism to show his commitment to the "traditional" family, it backfired because many people saw it as an example of being out of touch with the problems of ordinary people, and as an attack on working mothers more generally.

In addition to the shift in relative impact of the Republican and Democratic groups, a significant change also occurred in the overall ratings of these groups between the 1988 and 1992 election. In 1988 the average rating for the Democratic groups (using a scale that ranged from 0 as most negative to 100 as most positive and 50 as neutral) was 48.2, but by 1992 that evaluation had increased slightly to 50.8. When the individual groups in the Democratic set are examined, it is evident that the increase came from a significant rise in the evaluation of gays and lesbians, from only 28.5 in 1988 to 36.6 in 1992. Clearly this sociopolitical group is not highly liked by the public; nevertheless the increase in positive sentiment was significant. The increased positive evaluations of gays, however, was somewhat offset by a slight decrease in the ratings of people on welfare (from 49 to 45) and feminists (from 53 to 49). The net result on average, however, was the slight increase in positive evaluations of the Democratic groups mentioned above.

Public ratings of the Republican groups also changed between the two elections, but in a negative direction. The average rating of the two groups (46.7) was slightly negative in 1988, but noticeably more negative in 1992 when the mean rating stood at 40.4. Public evaluations of both Evangelical political groups and anti-abortionists declined during the four years (Evangelicals from 53.6 to 45.3, and anti-abortionists from 39.7 to 35.8). This decline may have resulted from various personal scandals that continued to plague the Evangelical ministry, and a rise in extremist tactics used by some pro-life organizations when picketing abortion clinics. Whatever the cause, the result was that fewer Americans identified positively with these groups in 1992. But more importantly, because the changes occurring in evaluations of the Democratic and Republican groups were in opposite directions, the net difference between the two sets of group ratings was much larger in 1992 than four years earlier; hence, group affect had a greater overall impact on the 1992 election outcome. In sum, all of the differential shifts associated with evaluations of the groups were disadvantageous for George Bush.

All of this emphasis on the election impact of group affect is not meant to suggest that this was the only factor undermining the Bush reelection effort. The regression analysis reported in Table 11.6 also demonstrates that economic related factors—concern that the national economy had worsened, the feeling that government spending was out of control, and that taxes needed readjusting—had a greater impact on the election in 1992 than in 1988. All of these economic attitudes also contributed to the Bush loss. But, contrary to what many journalists and pundits have suggested, the economy was not the only factor determining the election outcome. The impact of attitudes toward the family also increased in 1992, and while that may have helped Republicans during the elections of the 1980s, in 1992 it appeared to trigger closer scrutiny of the Republican fringe groups.

In summary, the state of the economy was certainly "the" issue of the 1992 election, but it was not the only determinant of the outcome. Group prejudice also had a major effect on the dynamics of the 1992 campaign and the eventual outcome, just as it had in the elections of the 1980s. The difference was that the Democratic fringe groups had played the major role in the earlier elections. In 1984, feminists were most visible with the vice presidential candidacy of Geraldine Ferraro. In 1988, Jesse Jackson's candidacy and the Willie Horton ads called attention to black activists and raised fears of black criminals. The result was that Democrats defected to vote for Republicans because in the public's perception they were not associated with extremes (see Miller et al. 1988). However, in 1992 Bush was perceived as more closely linked with the Republican fringe than Clinton was with the Democratic fringe. The net outcome helped spell defeat for the Republicans.

Moreover, when the overall impact that group affect had on the election is assessed, it is important to consider both the direct and indirect influence. How people feel about groups influences their reactions to various issues, including economic issues (Brady & Sniderman 1985). Public beliefs about who will benefit from some government policy, or the fairness of the policy, are partly formed on the basis of group associations and group affect. When Bush became more closely connected, in the public's perception, with the Republican fringe it reinforced the growing belief that Bush was less concerned with middle America, and thus less likely to promote interests with which they identified whether the issue was one of economics or morality. In short, when both direct and indirect effects are considered, it is evident that group prejudice played a significant role in the outcome of the 1992 election.

Conclusions

The analyses presented above have implications for both new racism theory and American self images. The analysis results do not disprove new racism theory—that was not the purpose—but they do reveal the limitations of the theory. Social competition in America involves more than racial differences or prejudice. The social identity theory proposed here incorporates symbolic racism as part of a broader conceptualization of social competition. The broader theory treats the 1992 election outcome as part of

a general phenomenon, whereas new racism theory treats it as an exception. How people feel about sociopolitical groups acts as a heuristic for
structuring and organizing political thinking and decision making in a
schematic fashion similar to that described by Boynton and Lodge in
Chapter 10. The important point demonstrated here is that a broader set of
sociopolitical groups, including African Americans, but also groups from
both the left and the right, form social schemata that people use when
making political decisions.

Considerable controversy exists in the literature over whether these
group comparisons reflect responses to perceived threats to the economic
well-being of one's group or symbolic factors such as group stereotypes,
political orientation, and cultural values (Kinder & Sears 1981; Bobo 1983;
Sears 1988). The analysis presented here reveals that group affect was
related to both preferences on government economic policies that have
resource redistribution implications as well as questions regarding life style
and cultural values, which are largely symbolic factors. Certainly the
connection between evaluations of some sociopolitical groups and perceived demands on the government treasury are more straightforward than
for other groups. For example, finding a correlation between feelings
toward people on welfare and attitudes on government spending is not
surprising. A similar correlation between spending preferences and evaluations of feminists, gays, or evangelical political groups, on the other hand,
is surprising and certainly not straightforward. This set of correlations
apparently involves an inferential process through which individuals connect concerns about values with concerns about spending. In short, if an
individual does not identify with the moral and cultural values they
associate with the groups they perceive attached to a particular political
party, they subsequently infer that the spending policies of that party will
also be unacceptable. In other words, symbolic factors, not economic
concerns, were the critical element in producing the observed correlation.
Furthermore, the substantial direct impact of Democratic and Republican
group affect on the vote choice, after controlling for economic self interest,
demonstrates that good old fashioned group prejudice still plays a major
role in determining political outcomes in America.

One aspect of American self images implied by the above findings is
very reminiscent of a conclusion reached by Ron Lee (Chapter 3) in his
discussion of pluralism versus populism. As Lee suggests, the mobilization
of some groups seeking an inclusionary empowerment can be characterized
rhetorically in exclusionary terms. The politics of social group competition,
as practiced in the 1980s and early 1990s, is very much a politics of exclusion.
This form of politics tends to define America rhetorically in terms of what
we are not, rather than what we are. The image of America as reflecting the
values and life styles of social groups associated with either the extreme left

or right is anathema to most voters. Yet, since the mid-sixties the United States has been experiencing a period in which a number of sociopolitical groups have been seeking their own unique form of empowerment. It is not simply that racial minorities have been challenging for greater political and economic equality in a system that promotes considerable inequality; rather, it is that numerous sociopolitical groups of the left and the right have been demanding an equal voice. This drive for empowerment has created a major dilemma, especially for the Democrats. How could liberal-oriented subordinate groups be encouraged in their efforts at ending discrimination and gaining empowerment, when the very act of mobilizing on behalf of their own interests put the reform efforts and electoral fortunes of the broader coalition in jeopardy?

The former ideal of America as a melting pot with its emphasis on assimilation has given way to the notion of cultural diversity and group empowerment. This new cultural image has forced middle America to confront its prejudices and stereotypes. But, it also has given politicians a social environment in which they can practice the rhetoric of exclusion, which thrives on messages invoking fears that the dominant life style may be threatened by the unacceptable values and practices of some undeserving fringe groups in society.

Beginning with the civil rights legislation of the mid-sixties, the Democrats became the protector of rights and freedoms. However, the impression this created for many Americans was that the Democratic party had become a moralist preacher: Not a moralist preacher of family values, prayer in schools, patriotism, or the work ethic of white, majoritarian America, but rather the champion of minority rights and fringe group empowerment. In short, many people saw the Democrats as telling them what was still wrong in society, rather than what was right, thereby supporting a conclusion reached by Morreale in Chapter 2. The vision of tomorrow conveyed by the Democrats may have projected the ethical, moral vision of virtue, but it was not a positive, inclusionary vision that middle America was ready to embrace. Rather, it was a vision that provided considerable material for the conservative, exclusionary populism of the Reagan and Bush campaigns.

Considerable attention has been given by the voting behavior literature to the question of whether citizens vote for a particular candidate, or vote against them. For example, it is often said that the outcome of the 1980 election reflected a vote *against* Jimmy Carter not a vote *for* Ronald Reagan. The above discussion and analysis extends this concept of negative voting beyond a consideration of the candidate to a consideration of certain constituents as well. The social identity theory proposed above suggests that the public, in voting against a particular candidate, is actually voting against certain constituencies. Who those negative constituencies are shifts with time and historical circumstances, but the campaign focus on specific groups is largely shaped by the candidates, in particular as part of their negative ads (see Gronbeck Chapter 4, as well as Miller & Wlezien 1993).

In 1992, Clinton was able to compile a winning margin partly by distancing himself from some sociopolitical groups, and partly by crafting a campaign message that appealed to the resource interests of the broader community rather than the empowerment of multiple minority constituencies. His emphasis on middle class concerns such as health care, tax reform, and international economic competitiveness was effective in reducing fragmentation among Democrats and providing a broader majoritarian appeal. But, it should also be remembered that two other group-related elements contributed to Clinton's victory. First, the anti-gay vote split between Bush and Perot. Second, the Republicans made a mistake in 1992; they became the moralist preacher presenting in their sermon, as epitomized by Pat Robertson and Pat Buchanan's Republican Party convention address, a view of traditional family values, patriotism, and a life style that was also an unacceptable image of society for middle America. It would be a mistake, therefore, to conclude that the 1992 election signaled an end to exclusionary politics. On the contrary, as long as America remains a mosaic of competing interests, candidate appeals using exclusionary discourse remain a potent strategy of American politics.

Notes

[1]The 1992 data are from The University of Iowa Social Science Heartland Poll because the University of Michigan National Election Study data were not yet available at the time that the chapter was being completed. The Heartland Poll involved 2,100 interviews conducted by phone immediately after the 1992 election. The fact that the 1992 data for the individual's own position and the perceived position for Bush are similar to the 1988 NES estimates suggests that the ISSI data are a reasonable alternative data set to use in 1992.

Appendix

The following questionnaire items were used to construct the various indices employed in the statistical analysis. The items were selected using exploratory factor analysis (utilizing Kaiser's criterion and verimax rotation) of the 1988 NES data and confirmatory factor analysis of the 1992 ISSI data. The variable numbers from the NES study are also indicated for easier replication. All analyses were based on white respondents only.

Racial Equality Index

V845   Speed of Civil Rights: Do you feel that civil rights leaders are trying to push too fast, too slow, or at the right speed?

V865   Fair Treatment of Blacks: Should the government in Washington see to it that black people get fair treatment or is this not their business?

V925   Equal Rights: We have gone too far in pushing equal rights.

V961   Favors to Blacks: Blacks should overcome prejudice and work their way up without any special favors.

V963   Blacks Should Try Harder: If blacks would only try harder they could be as well off as whites.

Spending Index

V349   Spending on Food Stamps: Should federal spending on food stamps be increased, decreased, or kept the same?

V385   Homeless Spending: Should federal spending be increased, decreased, or kept the same?

V381   Spending on Programs for Blacks: Should federal spending be increased, decreased, or kept the same?

V323   Jobs: the government should ensure that every person has a job; each person should get ahead on their own.

Crime Index

V634   Which candidate is tougher on crime and criminals--Bush or Dukakis?

V394   Which candidate do you think will do a better job of solving the drug problem--Bush or Dukakis?

Taxes

V354   Which party is more likely to raise taxes; the Democrats, the Republicans or wouldn't there be much difference between them?

Patriotism Index

V968   Flag Flying: Does seeing the American flag flying make you feel extremely/very/somewhat/not very good?

V970   National Anthem: Does hearing the national anthem make you feel extremely/very/somewhat/not very emotional?

Family Values Index

V953   Family Values: This country would have many fewer problems if there were more emphasis on traditional family ties.

V954   Lifestyles: The newer lifestyles are contributing to the breakdown of our society.

Quotas Index

V857   Affirmative Action: Favor/oppose preferential hiring and promotion of blacks.

V870   Quotas: Favor/oppose colleges reserving openings for black students.

12

American Exceptionalism and the Quadrennial Peak in Optimism

Harold M. Zullow

Reach into your wallet, and look at the left reverse side of a U.S. dollar bill. Inscribed on the Great Seal, around the pyramid, is "Annuit Coeptis": Through the years, rebirth. The Founding Fathers' aim was that the United States should perpetuate itself through the periodic reinvigoration of elections. Another aim was unity: the Great Seal also bears the motto "E pluribus unum" ("Out of many, one"). Every four years, the presidential election enables this rebirth by drawing the electorate's attention to shared values and concerns. How this rebirth manifests itself in the public's optimism for the nation, and in a preference for optimistic candidates, is the focus of this chapter.

An election campaign can reinforce shared ultimate goals and values at the same time it affords an opportunity for debate over specific policies, and thus ease acceptance of the defeat of one's own issue positions. Without this collective glue, mobilized groups might respond to defeat of their positions with protest or violence (Hibbs 1973).

A set of conditions can be proposed under which elections will reinvigorate an electorate:

- Awareness of shared values, national self-images, and superordinate goals (e.g., Sherif et al. 1961).
- Shared belief in the equity and advancement potential afforded by the social structure.
- Blurring of ethnic, linguistic, and socioeconomic differences.
- Shared positive events and victories, which can facilitate self-esteem, identification with and esteem for the group (Hirt et al. 1992).

When these conditions are present, an election should stimulate confidence in the nation's future. This, in turn, has ramifications for a government's ability to govern, to forge consensus, and for the economy's well being (Katona, 1980). In the United States, the blurring of ethnolinguistic and socioeconomic differences (exemplified by the "melting pot" metaphor) and certain national self-images and beliefs should be conducive to forging a sense of renewal.

Two aspects of the American self-image are especially conducive. One is that Americans view their country as one of unlimited horizons and unique mission. They want to feel in control of their destiny—that problems can be solved. According to the well-known Turner thesis (1893), the frontier of the westward expansion of the United States shaped this self-image. Max Lerner (1957, pp. 28-29) called it "American Exceptionalism."

> The versions a culture has of its own strength and success are as important parts of its tradition as the versions it has of its origins or mission. Some of the early historians believed they saw the hand of God operating exclusively in American history ...

> Stronger than the impulse to see America as a Chosen People is the impulse to see it as a unique historical experience. The idea of American "exceptionalism" is valid if you take it in the sense that America has its own civilization pattern, which does not follow the pattern of others and is not linked by any inevitable destiny to their doom ... America has been favored by geography and historical circumstance.

> Another variant of the theory of exceptionalism is the argument from pluralism—that American greatness derives from its special blend of ethnic, religious, and linguistic strains ...

Dynamism is part of this exceptionalism—a spirit that "is inclusive rather than exclusive, optimistic rather than fear-ridden, dynamic rather than obsessed with order and hierarchy" (Lerner, p. 47). Recent election-year surveys indicate that Exceptionalism is one of the most widely, strongly held value systems by the majority of voters (Robinson 1988). Sixty-five to seventy per cent endorse such soaring statements as: "I don't believe that there are any real limits to growth in this country today," "We can always find a way to solve our problems and get what we want," "America is unique in its mission" and "limitless in its possibilities."

The Horatio Alger story reflects another important collectively held belief—an individualistic side of American Exceptionalism. The belief in the possibility of personal advancement through effort makes elections a contest about how best to facilitate individual opportunity, rather than a battle over allocating resources. It mitigates against a zero-sum view of political contests.

An impending presidential election should reinforce the shared political culture. In accord with this, content analysis of campaign rhetoric of the last hundred years shows that Americans have elected presidential candidates whose speeches voice the greatest optimism about solving the nation's problems (Zullow & Seligman 1990a). Because voters are wooed by these optimistic messages, the campaign should activate spreading attitudes of optimism and exceptionalism.

It can also re-focus the public's attention on public, rather than private, concerns—which, as Tocqueville worried (Sennett 1979), might ebb in a democracy dedicated to "the pursuit of happiness." Orienting the public toward communal concerns and values can be called a sociotropic function of elections. Voting is more closely linked to national than personal economic evaluations (Kiewet 1983; Kinder & Kiewet 1981). Elections may remind citizens that they are part of something larger than the self, and satisfy a need for belongingness (Maslow 1954; Murray 1938). An electoral cycle of optimism for one's nation, stronger than optimism for oneself, would be an indicator of sociotropism.

In considering the hypothesis of an electoral optimism cycle, first we will examine the argument that changes in the public's expectations can be attributed strictly to economic conditions. Second, we shall review evidence that Americans vote for the more optimistic-sounding presidential candidate. Third, we shall examine whether the electorate prefers optimistic candidates regardless of its own mood or of economic conditions.

The Quadrennial Peak in Collective Optimism

Since the 1950s, we have had an ongoing measure of the American public's optimism—monthly since 1978, and quarterly before then. The University of Michigan has surveyed representative nationwide samples regarding: (1) optimism for the nation's economy; (2) optimism for one's own financial situation; and (3) satisfaction with one's current financial situation. These items are combined into an Index of Consumer Sentiment, which predicts changes in consumer spending and economic growth. In a Mertonian self-fulfilling prophecy, optimistic consumers spend discretionary income more readily, which contributes to economic growth. Consumer optimism is used by the U.S. Commerce Department as a leading economic indicator, and begins to decline nine months on average before a recession (Katona 1960; 1980). Some economists believe it can be explained as a reaction to the economy (Shapiro 1972), but a significant amount of the variance in optimism cannot be accounted for by economic indicators (Adams & Klein 1972). Thus, we may seek to understand part of its variance in psychological causes: for example, the impact of non-economic current events on consumers' moods.

The non-economic event proposed here is periodic: the presidential campaign and election. Optimism about the nation's economy is used here as a proxy for generalized optimism about the nation. This usage is supported by the fact that in other nations, generalized hopes fluctuate in harmony with economic hopes (see Noelle-Neumann 1989). In the U.S., survey data allow us to test for forty years the hypothesis of an election cycle.

Using this data (*Surveys of Consumers* 1992), we can examine whether the economy is expected to be better or worse in the next five years. This item best taps optimism for the national rather than personal situation. Its time frame corresponds to the tenure of the administration about to be elected. The predictions are: (1) It should reach its highest point during the greatest attention to the presidential election: i.e., from the end of the nominating conventions (August) to the time of the election (November). (2) It should remain at a peak only in the case of a president's first inauguration, when the hope for a fresh start is still present. (3) It should then decay as a function of time since the last election (time for disillusionment to set in), and rise again as a function of time remaining till the next election.

For the ten election cycles between 1951 and 1990, the average optimism in the August-to-November months of the presidential election year (mean optimism of 96) increased significantly over the corresponding pre-election year months (reaching an average of 108). It dropped significantly in the post-election year (on average down to 92) and bottomed out during the mid-term Congressional election year (an average of 86).

To the extent that the election peak reflects the anticipation of a fresh start, optimism should continue into the early months of a new administration. To test this, I averaged optimism in the January-to-July months of the presidential election year and the post-election honeymoon year, comparing it to the pre-election and mid-term Congressional election years. Optimism increased significantly from the pre-election year to the primary and nomination phase of the election year. It increased further during the first half-year of the honeymoon, but dropped thereafter.

Figure 12.1 shows the semi-annual changes in optimism during the ten election cycles from 1951 to 1990. Scores are displayed for the first half of each year (January to July) and the second half (campaign months of August to November). A peak in expectations during the presidential election years (shaded areas) is evident. Expectations plummet after the election, or after an average of six months' honeymoon when a new president is inaugurated. Kennedy was a notable exception to this fall from grace.

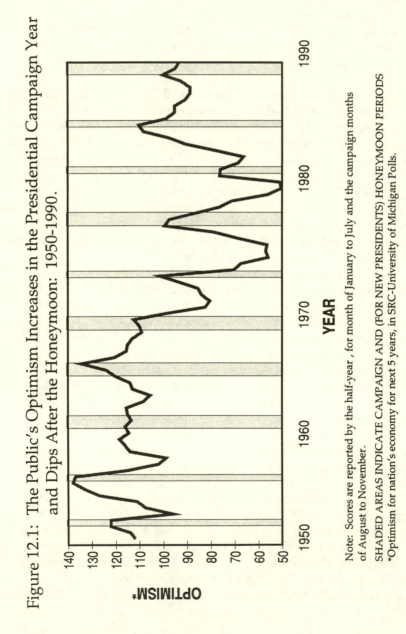

Figure 12.1: The Public's Optimism Increases in the Presidential Campaign Year and Dips After the Honeymoon: 1950-1990.

Note: Scores are reported by the half-year, for month of January to July and the campaign months of August to November.

SHADED AREAS INDICATE CAMPAIGN AND (FOR NEW PRESIDENTS) HONEYMOON PERIODS

*Optimism for nation's economy for next 5 years, in SRC-University of Michigan Polls.

A ratcheting down in the average level of optimism occurred during the 1970's and early 1980's. This was the period of inflation, recession, Watergate, energy crises and malaise. Yet even in this era, optimism still climbed to a relative peak at the time of elections in 1972, 1976, and 1980. As we shall see, optimistic candidates continued to run and win.

What makes the public so optimistic during campaigns? One explanation has nothing to do with national self-image. Optimism might simply result from the income growth in those years, with voters aware of the personal economic benefits they are reaping.

If election-cycle fluctuations reflect a self-centered perception that conditions are salubrious for one's personal finances—rather than a national feeling—then optimism about one's finances should increase more than optimism about the nation. Quite the opposite, the peak is more pronounced for national optimism. It exceeds personal optimism more so in presidential election years than any other years. This complements findings on the "sociotropic" voter, that voting is more closely linked to perceptions of the national economy than of personal finances (Kiewet 1983; Kinder & Kiewet 1981). The electoral optimism cycle and sociotropic voting argue for a sociotropic function of elections. They are evidence for a spirit of community, of people acting based on collective values—a "Gemeinschaft" (Tonnies 1887/1988).

Furthermore, the year of the electoral cycle is quite significant as a predictor of optimism, but non-significant as a predictor of real disposable income, indicating that shifts in optimism are more closely linked to the election cycle than are shifts in income. Controlling for income growth, the effect of year is strong though just missing significance as a predictor of optimism. Finally, there is a reciprocal prediction between optimism and income growth: each may fuel the other. The temporal variance in consumer expectations cannot be fully accounted for by economic predictors, and is associated more closely than economic variables with the election calendar (cf. Hibbs 1987 on robustness of the "political business cycle").

A trough rather than a peak occurs for optimism during mid-term Congressional elections, which may help explain the short coat-tails of presidents. Therefore, the quadrennial peak is probably in part due to a special feeling Americans have for the presidency, and about having a say in who occupies it. There are four reasons why this should be true:

1. *Optimism is intrinsic to the American self-image.* The presidential campaign is an occasion to reaffirm this self-definition.
2. *The presidential election is a chance for a fresh start.* In a catharsis from the disappointment of recent administrations and events, elections offer the chance for voters and candidates to pledge allegiance to values and policies. Elections are fought on the battleground of

what the next four years will look like. They are inherently a prospective as well as a retrospective judgment (Fiorina 1981).

3. *Americans identify with the president unlike any figure.* As a symbol of national power and prestige, the opportunity to join in selecting the occupant of the Presidency may empower voters with a sense of heightened control. That the Presidency occupies a special position in voters' hearts is suggested by its high ratings as an esteemed institution compared to the Congress—even though Congress is also elected by the people.

4. *During the presidential campaign, optimistic rhetoric from the candidates (Zullow & Seligman 1990a) may exert a contagious influence on the public.* Hearing optimistic rhetoric may reinvigorate the public's sense of American Exceptionalism, dramatize the prospect of a fresh start, and renew our symbolic identification with the presidency.

How do candidates' optimism affect the public? Unfortunately, we cannot submit them to psychological testing of their optimism. However, content analysis permits us to quantify their rhetoric. We can study presidents from Washington on, using a content analysis measure I developed for "pessimistic ruminations," based on research on depressive and coping styles of thinking.

Content Analysis of Optimism and Pessimistic Rumination

Two kinds of optimistic thinking have been well studied. One is "explanatory style": how we explain the causes of problems. Seeing the cause of a problem as temporary, specific, and situational is an optimistic view. On the other hand, explaining the cause as long-lasting, global, and one's own fault is pessimistic in its implication for what one expects in the future (Abramson et al. 1978). Optimists are more resistant to depression, and persist and achieve in the face of obstacles (Peterson & Seligman 1984). Another kind of thinking is the extent to which people ruminate about problems aside from their solution. Pessimistic ruminators dwell on problems, wondering "Why has this happened?" Their answer is: "It's my (our) fault; it's going to continue and affect everything we do."

To assess explanatory style, causal explanations for negative events are extracted from the text. They are rated by independent trained raters—blind to the speaker's identity—along three dimensions, according to strict criteria (Peterson 1992; Zullow et al. 1988). Seven-point ratings along these dimensions are summed and averaged to derive a speech's score:

- *Stable-Unstable*: Will the cause persist, or is it temporary? "We are greedy for immediate gratification" is a fairly stable cause for a low savings rate, while "Tax laws discourage individual incentive and savings" is a relatively unstable cause.
- *Global-Specific*: Is the cause general, or specific to this one case? For example, a global cause for a war would be "Human nature is aggressive." A specific cause is "Iraq covets Kuwait's oil." The former explanation would lead one to expect that wars will occur in many situations, since human nature is omnipresent. The latter explanation would lead one to expect wars only when one nation seeks another's resources.
- *Internal-External*: Is the cause inside of ourselves, or in the situation and other people? "We are not producing good products" is an internal cause of a trade deficit. "Other countries restrict the importation of American goods" is an external cause.

Rumination is also rated by independent trained coders, according to strict criteria, for phrases that dwell on a negative situation other than how to resolve it (Zullow 1985). The resulting score, for percentage of sentences that contain ruminations, can range from 0 to 100.

These content analysis scores yield high and satisfactory inter-rater reliability compared to other psychological content analysis instruments. To measure a candidates' tendency to be high in pessimism and rumination, transformed scores for both variables are summed to create an index of "pessimistic rumination."

We must be wary about inferring candidates' traits from their words. However, to the extent that we are interested in the resonance of an optimistic rhetorical style with Americans' self-image, one need only demonstrate that the style exists and that it is consistent across speeches.

Candidate Optimism and the Election of the President

If American Exceptionalism is central to the electorate's value system, voters should on average prefer candidates who express greater optimism for solving the nation's problems.

Hofstadter (1963), in *Anti-intellectualism in American Life*, chronicled the history of voter rejection of intellectual candidates, epitomized by the 1952 contest between Stevenson and Eisenhower. Is this rejection motivated by the desire for a leader who embodies our self-image, and does not brood about his ability to control events?

TABLE 12.1 Scores of Presidential Candidates on Content Analysis and Election Variables, 1900 to 1992.

Year	Candidate	Party	Pessimistic Rumination_a	Pessimism_b	Rumination_c	% Support in Early Polls_d	% of the Vote_e
1900	McKinley	Rep	-0.02	10.00	23.0	--	53.2
	Bryan	Dem	-1.53	8.24	53.7	--	46.8
1904	T. Roosevelt	Rep	1.28	9.17	15.9	--	60.0
	Parker	Dem	-2.80	10.90	45.3	--	40.0
1908	Taft	Rep	-0.03	9.15	30.1	--	54.5
	Bryan	Dem	-1.69	9.78	42.7	--	45.5
1912	Taft	Rep	0.08	9.05	29.8	--	40.0
	Wilson	Dem	0.69	8.25	29.8	--	60.0
1916	Hughes	Rep	-0.06	7.06	47.7	--	48.3
	Wilson	Dem	0.58	8.98	25.0	--	51.7
1920	Harding	Rep	-0.35	9.30	32.3	--	63.8
	Cox	Dem	-2.49	9.93	50.0	--	36.2
1924	Coolidge	Rep	0.79	9.43	19.0	--	62.7
	Davis	Dem	-0.96	9.37	38.3	--	37.3
1928	Hoover	Rep	1.07	8.77	21.4	--	58.7
	Smith	Dem	0.14	8.74	31.7	--	41.3
1932	Hoover	Rep	-0.19	10.14	23.6	--	40.9
	F. Roosevelt	Dem	0.24	8.03	36.5	--	59.1
1936	Landon	Rep	-0.49	9.25	34.2	--	37.6
	F. Roosevelt	Dem	-1.24	9.05	43.9	--	62.4
1940	Willkie	Rep	-1.21	9.86	36.9	--	44.6
	F. Roosevelt	Dem	-2.09	11.48	32.9	--	55.4
1944	Dewey	Rep	-0.76	9.60	34.2	--	46.2
	F. Roosevelt	Dem	-1.56	12.33	20.1	--	53.8
1948	Dewey	Rep	-1.27	12.10	19.0	56.4	47.4
	Truman	Dem	0.98	7.21	35.4	43.6	52.3
1952	Eisenhower	Rep	2.27	8.67	9.4	53.8	55.4
	Stevenson	Dem	-2.96	12.55	33.3	46.2	44.6
1956	Eisenhower	Rep	1.12	9.75	12.8	55.9	57.8
	Stevenson	Dem	-0.47	9.67	30.5	44.1	42.2
1960	Nixon	Rep	-0.76	11.64	17.3	53.2	49.9
	Kennedy	Dem	1.17	7.60	30.1	46.8	50.1
1964	Goldwater	Rep	0.60	8.61	27.8	31.0	38.7
	Johnson	Dem	0.86	10.50	9.4	69.0	61.3
1968	Nixon	Rep	1.76	8.72	14.5	58.1	50.4
	Humphrey	Dem	1.94	8.63	13.3	41.9	49.6
1972	Nixon	Rep	1.56	8.96	14.6	62.9	61.8
	McGovern	Dem	-1.58	11.97	23.3	37.1	38.2

TABLE 12.1 (continued): Scores of Presidential Candidates on Content Analysis and Election Variables, 1900 to 1992.

Year	Candidate	Party	Pessimistic Rumination$_a$	Pessimism$_b$	Rumination$_c$	% Support in Early Polls$_d$	% of the Vote$_e$
1976	Ford	Rep	1.23	8.97	18.1	40.0	49.0
	Carter	Dem	1.59	8.05	21.8	60.0	51.0
1980	Reagan	Rep	0.60	8.11	32.0	49.4	55.3
	Carter	Dem	0.24	9.00	28.4	50.6	44.7
1984	Reagan	Rep	1.30	7.46	29.8	55.9	59.2
	Mondale	Dem	-1.15	10.25	33.0	44.1	40.8
1988	Bush	Rep	1.04	8.67	22.6	52.2	54.0
	Dukakis	Dem	1.68	9.22	11.2	47.8	46.0
1992	Bush	Rep	0.31	8.50	31.8	55.3	53.1
	Clinton	Dem	0.54	8.92	25.9	44.7	46.9

Note: Scores are based on content analysis of the nomination acceptance speech.

a A sum of the z scores for pessimism and rumination. Lower scores indicate more pessimistic rumination.

b High scores indicate greater pessimism.

c Percentage of sentences in the speech which contain rumination about negative events. Higher scores indicate a higher percentage of rumination.

d Percentage of the two-party support obtained in the Gallup Poll at the end of the August convention.

e Percentage of the two party support obtained in the election.

The Presidential Elections, 1900-1984

To test this, nomination acceptance speeches of every Republican and Democratic presidential candidate from 1900 to 1984 were content-analyzed for pessimistic rumination (Zullow et al. 1988; Zullow & Seligman 1990a). These speeches are quoted widely in the media and, since 1948, broadcast on TV (Frank 1988). They are a rite of passage in which all candidates must outline their hopes and fears. They are delivered at a comparable career point: having won the nomination, but with the fall campaign ahead to woo the voters. Eleven candidates in this century were nominated more than once. The rank-order correlation between pessimistic rumination at the time of initial and re-nomination was .74 (p < .02). This is evidence that it is a stable feature of candidate rhetoric—as must be the case if the style manifested in the acceptance speech influences the autumn election outcome.

In 18 of 22 elections, the candidate lower in pessimistic rumination won. This was significantly greater than the 11 of 22 expected by chance alone, and the correlation of the victory margin with the margin of advantage in pessimistic rumination was .61 (p < .001). Controlling for incumbency using a dummy variable did not alter this finding, so the results cannot be attributed to an advantage of incumbents.

The four exceptions were Nixon's victory over Humphrey in 1968, and Franklin Roosevelt's re-elections. Humphrey's optimism score was better than Nixon's by an unreliable margin. In accord with this near-match, he overcame a 16-point deficit in the polls to come within a hair's breadth (0.8%) of winning. As for FDR, who was both very ruminative and action-oriented, he presided over an era when ruminating about problems may have been necessary to face the crises of depression and war. Table 12.1 shows candidates' scores for pessimism and rumination, how they fared in early trial heat polls (since 1948), and the election results.

Since 1948, early trial heats have indicated the candidates' standing at the time of their acceptance speeches. In three cases, the underdog at the time of the conventions was more optimistic than the odds-on favorite. This happened in: 1948, when Truman was more optimistic than Dewey; 1960, when Kennedy was more optimistic than Nixon; and in 1980, when Reagan was more optimistic than Carter. Each time, the underdog gained support and pulled off an upset victory. When the overdog was much lower in pessimistic rumination, he held on to a lead and widened it, to win a landslide. This happened in 1952 and '56 (Eisenhower over Stevenson), 1964 (Johnson over Goldwater), 1972 (Nixon over McGovern) and 1984 (Reagan over Mondale). The correlation between an optimism advantage in the convention speech and the gain in support was .73 (p < .02).

Does optimism indicate merely that odds-on favorites and incumbents perceive they are likely to win? The come-from-behind victories of optimists such as Truman, Kennedy, and Reagan argue against this possibility. Optimism did not correlate with an early advantage in the polls at the time of nomination. Controlling for the early advantage and for incumbency, optimists were even likelier to win.

Another account offered for these results holds that a thriving economy makes incumbents optimistic, and that candidate optimism is epiphenomenal to the vote (Greenstein 1990; Masters 1990; Simonton 1990). This was tested using the election-year increase in real per capita disposable income, a correlate of the election outcome (Tufte 1978). Pessimistic rumination correlated non-significantly with this indicator of economic well-being, and predicted the election controlling for changes in income (Zullow & Seligman 1990b). Candidates' optimism may thus mediate between economic change and election outcome. Their explanations for economic conditions may affect voters' explanations, which in turn affect the vote (Feldman & Conley 1991; Winter 1990). When Carter blamed the bad economy on "my mistakes" in 1980, voters agreed with him.

A final alternative account of the present results holds that candidates who are congruent with voters' issue positions will be optimistic because of positive reinforcement from audiences, but it is issue congruence and not optimism which elicits voter approval (Greenstein 1990; Masters 1990; Simonton 1990). Rosenstone (1983) asked political scientists to rate candidates from 1948 to 1980 for issue congruence with the contemporary electorate. Candidates' pessimistic rumination correlated moderately but non-significantly with Rosenstone's measure of issue congruence. Pessimistic rumination was a stronger predictor of the election (controlling for issue congruence) than issue congruence was (controlling for pessimistic rumination).

Thus, candidate optimism may moderate between issue congruence and electoral outcome, but is unlikely to be a mere proxy for issue congruence. It predicts the vote, controlling for issue congruence *and* the economy (income growth) in a master regression. Issue congruence also predicts winning, controlling for candidate optimism and income growth. Income growth *does not* significantly predict the election, controlling for candidate optimism and issue congruence. This three-variable model accounts for a striking 95% of the variance in the vote.

Four mechanisms consistent with the value system of American Exceptionalism can explain this. One is that depressive people are poorly-liked and evoke avoidance (Coyne & Gotlib 1983). This mechanism can be tested by comparing polls of how well voters personally like the candidates.

A second is that pessimistic ruminators should respond passively to setbacks. If voters like dynamic candidates, as exemplars of American Exceptionalism, then the more vigorous campaigner should gain support. This can be tested by whether pessimistic rumination correlates with the number of campaign stops visited per day.

The third mechanism is that optimistic non-ruminators should engender more hope in voters: this can be tested by subjects' reactions to speeches that differ in pessimistic rumination.

The fourth mechanism is that voters may seek candidates who match their own values or those of the times (Gibb 1969; Hollander 1985). Winter (1987) found that presidential candidates whose speech profiles of power, affiliation, and achievement motives were congruent with the electorate's (assessed by content analysis of contemporary popular culture) won by margins proportional to their congruence. Similarly, an electorate increasingly optimistic at election time may prefer a candidate whose style accords with exceptionalism.

We can begin to test these mechanisms. Are pessimistic ruminators less well-liked? The University of Michigan National Election Studies have queried prospective voters since 1948 on what they like and dislike about candidates. The number of likes relative to dislikes has strongly predicted the vote (Kelley 1983). Pessimistic rumination correlated highly with a preponderance of dislikes for elections through 1976, due to the fact that ruminators were disliked.

More active campaigning by optimists is another possible mechanism. The number of campaign stops per day was culled from published itineraries for 1948 through 1968 (Runyon et al. 1971) and 1980 (West 1983). Pessimistic rumination correlated highly with the difference in stops between the candidates, due to a relationship between optimism and activity. Controlling for campaign stops reduced the correlation between pessimistic rumination and the election outcome, suggesting that vigor is a mechanism linking optimism to victory. Truman, Kennedy, and Reagan had the greatest advantage in campaign stops over their opponents, and all won upset victories. Truman's 1948 whistlestop tour was the most famous example of an underdog waging a vigorous campaign.

In summary, candidate optimism is related to the economic context (changes in voters' income) and political context (issue positions) in which elections occur. It may mediate between these contextual factors and the election outcome. Candidate activity level and voter liking of the candidates are also likely mediators between optimism and the election outcome. This is consistent with Americans' preference for candidates who exude confidence and dynamism.

The 1988 and 1992 General Presidential Elections

Before the 1988 Iowa caucuses, the presidential candidates' stump speeches showed that Bush and Dukakis were favored in their respective parties, with Bush more optimistic than Dukakis. Substituting their scores into a regression equation based on optimism in the elections of 1948 to 1984 yielded a forecast, as of early February, for Bush to defeat Dukakis by 7%.

Bush and Dukakis won the nomination, as forecasted, and delivered nomination acceptances more optimistic than the 20th century average. This was the apex of Dukakis' optimism, surpassing Bush. A reversal occurred during the fall debates, as the advantage returned to Bush and persisted in the weeks after the debates.

Substituting the average pessimistic rumination for Bush and Dukakis during the fall campaign (debates and stump speeches) into a regression equation based on past elections, the collapse in Dukakis' style during the fall translated into a 9.2% expected victory margin for Bush. This was closer to the actual result (8%) than any major pre-election poll (Zullow 1988).

In every other year with televised debates, the more optimistic nomination acceptance was associated with the more optimistic debate performance. What happened in 1988?

Ted Sorenson, Dukakis' speechwriter hired specially for the nomination acceptace, had also crafted John F. Kennedy's "New Frontier" acceptance speech. Dukakis' acceptance occurred shortly after the first report of the present studies on candidate optimism appeared on *The New York Times* front page. His effort to harmonize with American values in the nomination speech may have been a style he was unable or unwilling to sustain.

The 1992 campaign was a more straightforward case. The optimism of Bill Clinton, "The Man from Hope" (Hope, Arkansas), surged past George Bush's in June. His lead in the polls crystallized the following month. Bush's optimism would have been stronger were it not for his tone on the economy. He vacillated between denying the existence of economic problems, and catastrophizing and taking blame for them.

The pattern of the public's optimism in 1992 was unusual. As with most of the last ten election cycles, expectations began to rise after the mid-term Congressional elections (November 1990). In accord with the hypothesis that positive collective events should foster optimism for the country, the Gulf War victory resulted in the largest one-month increase ever in consumer expectations. This was clearly a sentiment for the nation's well-being, since expectations for the economy rose far more than for personal finances.

However, expectations stalled and fell later in 1991. In 1992, the rise in optimism resumed at an unusually late time and steep pace. It did not fully manifest itself until November and December, when Clinton had been elected the new president.

The dour mood of 1992, snapped only by Clinton's election, was reminiscent of 1980. Both times, a malaise of the national spirit had set in two years earlier. Both times, a surge in optimism occurred only in November, instead of building up in the months before the election.

When the national self-image of optimism fails to assert itself during a campaign, the only avenue for many voters to feel hopeful may be voting against the incumbent. The late spurt in optimism at the time of the 1980 and 1992 election implied that voters were better able to pin their hopes on a specific individual (Reagan and Clinton) than on the political system more generally.

Optimism, Exceptionalism, and Elections: A Uniquely American Connection?

The aim of the Founding Fathers that the nation should be reinvigorated every four years is realized in the quadrennial peak of public and presidential optimism. Holding constant other factors such as incumbency, fund-raising, an early lead in the polls, and congruence with voters' issue positions, the candidates who voice the most optimism get elected president. Is this true holding constant the public's optimism and economic conditions? The public's optimism might affect the incumbent, yet it could be the public's and not the incumbent's optimism which affects the vote. Another possibility is that a strong economy makes the public and the incumbent optimistic, but it is the economy and not optimism which affects the vote. Candidate optimism *does* strongly predict the vote, controlling for the election-year public's optimism and changes in disposable income. The economy does not predict the vote, controlling for public and candidate optimism. When public perceptions of the current personal financial situation are substituted for the public's optimism into the equation, economic perceptions join candidate optimism as a strong predictor of the vote (cf. Shapiro & Conforto 1980). This strictly psychological model accounts for 92% of the variance in the vote.

This is in contrast to findings on the economy's importance in presidential election outcomes (Fair 1988; Tufte 1978). It suggests that the economy's impact is via people's perceptions.

This also affirms that optimistic campaigns succeed with the voters, holding constant voters' own optimism. Optimistic themes accord with our cultural value of American exceptionalism. The candidate who evokes pessimistic themes stands in critique of the culture and its values. A candidate can run a successful campaign in critique of the nation's *current condition* while embracing exceptionalism, but to do so he must ruminate optimistically about problems.

Five post-war candidates did this successfully. Ironically, Truman as an incumbent was one of them. He threatened to call a "do-nothing" Congress back into session from its summer recess, and to "make them like it." Kennedy's theme was a "new frontier." The image he painted was a still-pioneering nation, ready to tackle unsolved problems after the stasis of the Eisenhower years. Carter's 1976 slogan was "Why not the best? A government as good as its people." He distanced Watergate from the national self-image, portraying it as an aberration from the goodness of the people. Reagan's themes in 1980 were "Let's make America great again," and "Are you better off than you were four years ago?" He blamed Carter and liberal economic policies for problems, and proposed a supply-side economic medicine and strong foreign policy. Clinton's mantra, as "The Man from Hope" (Hope, AK), was "change," "hope", and "I want to be an agent of change."

Those who ran in critique of the nation's current condition without evoking optimism ran in critique of exceptionalism. Stevenson bemoaned the staggering burdens of the presidency and the overwhelming problems of the world. Carter preceded his re-election campaign with the famous "malaise" speech of 1979. Dukakis adjudged the U.S. on a par with Nicaragua and other nations—a comparison pounced upon by Bush. These candidates failed to develop an important bond that Americans have with their leaders. Other intellectuals such as the Roosevelts and Kennedy made exceptionalism central to their rhetoric. They successfully drew attention from personal to collective matters, even in times of widespread personal trauma.

Sociotropic voting, based on national rather than personal evaluations, has been interpreted as either altruism toward one's fellow citizens, or a rational calculus that national economic conditions indicate the president's potential to help one's own situation (Kiewet 1983). The present account offers a radically different interpretation: individuals have a need for belongingness to a larger entity than the self (Maslow 1954; Murray 1938), derive self-esteem from that identification (Hirt et al. 1992; Luhtanen & Crocker 1992), and will act to promote the well-being and values of that entity. Presidents are powerful reinforcers, for mere exposure to their rhetoric can make us feel potent and united in our collective identity and goals (Winter 1967). Experimentally priming voters with statements about the individualistic component of exceptionalism actually reduces ideological differences between liberals and conservatives in their judgments about the economy (Rasinski & Tourangeau 1991). Perhaps this process was at the root of the so-called era of the "end of ideology" in the mid-1950's, when national optimism reached a zenith.

Presidential campaign rhetoric is one likely contributor, then, to the enhanced optimism of the public in election years. As Santayana (1920/1956, p. 105) wrote of American optimism in *Character and Opinion in the United States*: "What maintains this temperament and makes it national is social contagion or pressure—something immensely strong in democracies." Other paths of contagion deserve study. Do Americans talk more among themselves about national affairs during election years (Berelson et al. 1954)? Do the media promote optimism then? In *Time* magazine covers since 1955, content analyzed for another study (Zullow 1991), rumination was less likely to occur in the cover story captions during presidential election years.

It is a pervasive web that supports the cycle of expectations. To my knowledge, the present findings are the first of such cyclicity in public opinion. We can learn as much about how collective values are propagated by studying elections in which the cycle is less pronounced as those that conform to the typical pattern. I have ventured a few factors that would undermine the sociotropic impact of elections: ethnolinguistic fractionation, socioeconomic inequality, and events that weaken national perceptions of control. These might accentuate disillusionment and inhibit the renewal of confidence.

Comparative study of other nations can help clarify these issues. Tufte (1978) found that only some of the world's democracies showed an association between elections and the business cycle. If exceptionalism underlies the quadrennial peak in optimism, then only electorates with a similar self-image should manifest a cycle. Any brand of exceptionalism should not suffice: only the myth of a pioneering spirit, of can-doism. Nations have different myths of their strengths. Russia's is in suffering with stoicism. In Poland, it is devout religiosity. One wag has said that Canada suffers from "Can-notism." Other nations such as Israel, built by pioneers amidst hostile conditions, or Britain with its tradition of democracy and the "sun never setting," might display more of an electoral optimism cycle.

If inequality or fractionation inhibit optimism for the nation, then other democracies more afflicted with these ills should not manifest a cycle, and might subsist at lower average levels of optimism. Japan is ethnolinguistically homogeneous, while Canada has been split.

A fascinating cross-cultural question is whether election cycles of optimism, and shared values of exceptionalism, help sustain a greater long-term economic vigor and optimism. By reinvigorating our hopes, elections may fulfill the ideal of "Annuit Coeptis."

13

Money and Politics: In Pursuit of an Ideal

Monica Bauer

It is to be regretted that the rich and powerful too often bend the acts of government to their selfish purposes. Distinctions in society will always exist, under every just and good government. Equality of talents, of education, or of wealth, cannot be produced by human institutions ... but when the laws undertake to add to these natural and just advantages artificial distinctions, to grant titles, gratuities, and exclusive privileges, to make the rich richer and the potent more powerful, the humble members of society—the farmers, mechanics, and laborers—who have neither the time nor the means of securing like favors to themselves, have a right to complain of the injustices of their government. There are no necessary evils in government. Its evils exist only in its abuses (Walker 1976, p. 69).

These are the words of Andrew Jackson, delivering to Congress his 1832 veto message of the National Bank bill. In these words we see some of the contradictory impulses in American political culture concerning money and politics. On the one hand, America is the place where the talents of individuals will allow them to rise above their fellows, and no attempt should be made to disparage the achievements of those whose talents have led them to wealth. On the other hand, America is also the place where every voter is supposed to have an equal say in the election of leaders; and the political system is not a commodity that should go to the highest bidder. The ideal type of democracy is one that embodies the most celebrated line from Lincoln's Second Inaugural: government "of the people, by the people, and for the people." This ideal is the standard all American reform movements have used to judge American politics.

A central tension in American life is between freedom and equality. Freedom means that citizens have the freedom to buy what they desire. What if the thing most desirable to own is political influence? Yet, the American political culture values the democratic. The trend in American

history has been an ever-increasing demand for egalitarianism. The movements in American history ranging from reduced property qualifications
for voting in the post-revolutionary period to the Voting Rights Act of 1964
show a steady increase in the demands for political equality. How can "one
person, one vote" be a slogan in our political ideology if the wealthy are able
to buy political influence disproportionate to their numbers?

In this essay I examine the historical roots of the continuing struggle for
campaign finance reform, a struggle that reflects America's self-image as a
nation "of the people, by the people, and for the people." After a historical
overview of money and politics, I will look at the present incarnation of
campaign finance reform. I will argue that, despite recent reforms, the
influence of money is never far from American presidential elections. The
question is, can a democracy that celebrates capitalism and the creation of
wealth successfully separate money and politics?

Fighting the "Money Power"

The use of wealth to buy political influence is a feature of American
political history, as has been the fight against the power of the wealthy in our
politics. It was displayed in the words of a petition to Congress in 1878, "The
Petition of Nine Millions of Citizens for the Abolition of the `Political
Machine' and the redress of Other Grievances":

> upon the day of election we find ourselves compelled by force of circum-
> stances to make a choice between only two men for each office, both of
> whom by large expenditures of money have purchased the privilege of
> representing our parties, and have been selected by interested agencies
> through manipulation, deception, trickery, and bribery. Under such cir-
> cumstances, thousands of us refuse to vote .... The expense of party
> machinery is paid by the contractors, lobbyists, office -holders, monopo-
> lists, bankers and railroad kings, who manage it in their interests (Walker
> 1976, p. 114).

The 19th-century belief that politics was corrupted by the influence of
the "interests" was not based on unfounded rumor. The 1876 dramatic
capture and return to America for trial of Boss Tweed "brought to light some
of the more spectacular episodes in municipal graft" (Walker 1976 p. 109).
"Dollar Mark" Hanna raised millions from the new railroad and utility
owning class to fund the successful campaign of McKinley, and the Guilded
Age came to a close with the sensational revelations of the Teapot Dome
political money scandal. In this context, the reform movements—the Farmer's
Alliance, the Grange, the Populist Party—struggled with one goal in mind:
to overthrow the "money power."

By the twentieth century, a vocal and organized segment of American society proclaimed that politics had become so corrupted by the wealthy that only the people, governing directly, could fulfill the American democratic vision of a government. The Progressive movement assumed that representative government and even the presidency had been subverted by the corrupting influence of big business and therefore demanded a direct method for citizens to pass laws. Thus the ballot initiative and referenda were created.

A 1914 pamphlet on the initiative and referenda system states the case bluntly:

> It is not the people who defeat reform. The people want honest government .... It is the power of money and corporate influence and official interest that check-mate progress .... The referendum will be the death of the lobby. It will be impracticable to lobby them because of their number. And it will be useless to lobby legislators, for they cannot deliver the goods (Walker 1976, p. 165).

These sentiments were not confined to a small number of obscure reformers. The Progressives were successful in achieving a number of their goals, including the direct election of senators, open primary elections, antitrust legislation, and numerous other reforms. Their ranks included presidents such as Theodore Roosevelt, Woodrow Wilson, and Franklin Delano Roosevelt. The ire of the Progressives was aimed at corporate donations to campaigns, and in 1905 Roosevelt said that "All contributions by corporations to any political committee or for any political purpose should be banned by law" (Gardner 1976, p. vi).

In 1907, 1910, 1911, and 1925, Congress, responding to the Progressives, passed the first campaign finance reform laws in its history (Gardner 1976, p. vi). They limited expenditures for members of the House to $5,000 and $25,000 for those seeking the Senate, and, significantly, banned corporate contributions. These laws were put on the books and promptly ignored. Soon the nation's reformers were caught up in the New Deal and the influence of big business on American politics seemed as dead as Herbert Hoover's political career. Yet, the issue of money and politics remained to be addressed at a later date.

After the death of Franklin Roosevelt, money and political influence were revived again in the 1952 controversy over Richard Nixon's "slush fund." Eisenhower was appalled to read press reports of money passed on to Nixon from a group of California businessmen, and there was serious talk of dropping him from the ticket. So powerful was the sentiment against such a mix of money and politics in the American people that Nixon went on television to explain why he had accepted such monies. This was the famous

"Checkers" speech, where Nixon assured the voters that his wife wore a "good Republican cloth coat" and that one of the "donations" had been a little dog for his daughters. Nixon managed to quell the furor about his finances not so much with facts but with a demonstration of his own sense of morality. Money in politics is suspect, linked to corruption; only by constructing an image of a personal morality could Nixon disarm his critics.

Campaign Technology Fuels Need for Greater Amounts of Money

With the advent of television advertising in the 1952 Eisenhower campaign, politics entered a new era where the need for massive amounts of money took on a new urgency. The old party-centered politics was giving way to candidate-centered politics, driven in part by the new technology that enabled candidates to reach over the heads of party leaders and appeal directly to the electorate. Where presidential campaigns had once been exercises in getting out the vote of the party faithful, by 1960 they had become elaborately planned media campaigns. This was a much more expensive way of doing politics. The cost of presidential elections more than tripled between 1960 and 1968.

Both parties needed to respond quickly to the change in conditions. Yet Democrats continued to use the old methods of big labor contributions added to the checks of a few "angels," while Republicans, at the nadir of their power in 1964, were forced to find a way to raise new funds from small donors through direct mail. When Richard Nixon finally won the White House in 1968, a pro-business party was once again in power. Large donations began rolling into the coffers of the Republican party. One party had solved its money problems. But the manner in which the Republicans solved their problem triggered another round in the cycle of campaign finance reform.

The Modern Reformers Common Cause

The reform spirit emerged again in the form of a group calling itself "A Citizen's Lobby." Common Cause was founded by John Gardner as part of the reform impulse of the 1960s, the same era that gave birth to grassroots community action programs, environmental and anti-war groups, and the Public Interest Research Group of Ralph Nader. All these organizations held in common the shared vision of more citizen involvement in American politics and public policy. The Jacksonian, Populist, Progressive, and New Deal reforming instinct found expression once again in these movements to bring "Power to the People."

Common Cause was designed to be a non-partisan group promoting "good government" in the tradition of the Progressives. An issue that

Common Cause focused on, in part because of the highly publicized explosion in the costs of campaigning for office, was the elimination of special interest money in American politics. Their initial frustration had to do with proving their case. Common Cause suspected that big business and big labor donations were being given, in part, to influence politics. But there was no means to force any candidates to disclose where their money came from and in what amounts. So, in 1971, Common Cause sued the Republican and Democratic National Committees under the 1925 Federal Corrupt Practices Act. It was the pressure of this lawsuit, based on laws never before enforced, that prompted Congress to write a new campaign finance reform law. This was the birth of the Federal Elections Campaign Act of 1971 (Gardner 1976, p. vi).

The FECA act sets limits on campaign contributions, and set up a mechanism for disclosure of the sources of campaign money for all federal elections. This set off a panic in both political parties; but the Republicans, with an incumbent president seeking re-election, were poised to be more successful with their last-minute fundraising. Since the law was passed in 1971, but slated to take effect on April 7, 1972, Nixon's campaign fundraisers labored to beat the day the law would take effect.

The founder of Common Cause, John Garder, described the Committee to Re-elect the President's fundraising as "the most effective, remunerative, and disastrous fundraising performance in political history ... They swept through the nation's top corporate offices like Sherman marching through Georgia, and vast sums of secret money poured in (Gardner 1976, p. viii).

The CEO of American Airlines, George Spater, was among the corporate executives in 1974 who testified before the Senate Watergate Committee. He was asked to contribute $100,000 to the Committee to Re-elect the President and he complied with the request. When asked why he knuckled under to the CREEP's solicitation of so large an amount, Spater replied: "There were two aspects. Would you get something if you gave it, and would you be prevented from getting something if you didn't give it" (*All the President's Donors* 1990, p. 22).

These funds and their illegal sources were uncovered when in September 1972 Common Cause sued the Committee to Re-elect the President under the still operative 1925 Corrupt Practices Act for failing to report the amounts and origins of these slush funds. While CREEP had been consumed with the need to raise their money before the new FECA law was to take effect, the Committee was unprepared to face a suit under the old law. Because of this suit, monies that ended up financing "some of the most unsavory aspects of Watergate" were traced to corporate bank accounts and according to Gardner this "led to many guilty pleas and convictions of corporate executives who had made illegal gifts" (Gardner 1976, p. viii).

The Watergate Crisis of Confidence and the Context of Reform

Sam Ervin, the "simple country lawyer" who presided over the Senate Watergate hearings, wrote in 1974 that "Watergate has become a symbol for corruption in government. It has thus contributed to a growing cynicism in the American people about those elected to public office. I consider Watergate to be one of the great tragedies of our history" (Ervin 1974, p. vii). The Watergate hearings cemented in the national memory the tie between "dirty" fundraising and "dirty" politics. In the immediate aftermath of these hearings, with their disclosures of checks laundered through Mexican banks to pay hush money to burglars, the 1974 amendments to FECA were passed and signed by President Gerald Ford. The new amendments called for complete public financing of presidential general elections, limited severely the amount individuals or groups could give to candidates, and imposed spending ceilings.

The spending ceilings were attacked by an odd consortium of politicians on the left and the right. Republican Senator James Buckley and Democratic Senator (and former candidate for President) Eugene McCarthy joined together in a suit against the Justice Department, Buckley v. Valeo. The Supreme Court ruled that individual candidates and groups acting independently of the candidates could not be restrained in their spending, as political money was used as an expression of political speech. The Congress could only limit expenditures by those accepting federal matching funds. The Court agreed that Congress had the right to limit some avenues of political fundraising: "In this case the Congress was legislating for the 'general welfare' --to reduce the deleterious influence of large contributions on our political process, to facilitate communication by candidates with the electorate, and to free candidates of the rigors of raising money" (Gardner 1976, p. ix).

The reform impulse in America has been the strongest in response to national trauma. Populism grew during the depressions of the 1870s and Progressive reform was motivated in response to the need to mitigate the worst features of laissez-faire capitalism: child labor, the killing of labor activists, and the stranglehold of monopoly power on utilities. The New Deal responded to the Great Depression. The reformers of the 1960s and 1970s were responding to a crisis in public confidence in the nation's political system.

There are many books that detail the context of the 1960s and 1970s reform movements; assassinations, race riots, and a divisive war in Vietnam all added to a kind of national nervous breakdown. This can be charted by following the response to a group of questions used in the National Election Surveys and aggregated to form a measure of the people's trust in their government. The percentage of whites who score in the medium or high range for trust in government drops from seventy-two percent in 1958 to forty-five percent in 1974; "the sharp decline in political trust between 1972 and 1974 almost certainly reflects the impact of the Watergate affair" (Abramson 1983, p. 234).

The Effects of Campaign Finance Reform: New Rules and New Methods

Some scholars contend that the campaign finance reforms passed immediately after the Watergate hearings were designed more to help Democrats than to repair the lost sense on the part of the electorate that presidential campaigns were fair and democratic. The 1974 amendments to the 1971 Federal Elections Campaign Act outlawed large campaign contributions, which had permitted the Republican party to spend so much more than the Democratic party in the 1968 and 1972 elections (Alexander and Bauer 1991). Contribution limits were set at just $1,000 per person per election, and $5,000 per outside political committee, soon to be labelled as Political Action Committees or PACs.

How would presidential campaigns raise the millions of dollars needed to run for president in the media age with only small donations? The answer was the use of federal matching funds in the pre-nomination contexts and full federal financing of the post-nomination phase of presidential elections, to be undertaken with donations collected by means of a one dollar check-off on income taxes. Big money donations would be illegal, donors' names would be disclosed to the public, and candidates in the pre-nomination contests would be encouraged to raise money through small donations, with only donations of $250 or less matched by the federal government.

The newly-created Federal Election Commission enforced the disclosure requirements under the FECA, so that every individual who gave over $100 to a federal candidate would be on the record, for all to see. Federal matching funds would be given to every presidential candidate who raised at least $5,000 in each of twenty states, from small donations only. After qualifying for matching funds, candidates would continue to receive them (matched at $250 or less per person) until they garnered less than ten percent in two primaries in a row. The nominees of each of the major parties would be given a set amount, on the condition that they not violate FECA-set spending ceilings. Each of the two main political parties would receive a set amount to conduct their conventions (Maisel 1991, p. 187).

Whether the FECA amendments of 1974 were meant to seriously address the issue of corruption in presidential politics or to enable the Democrats to keep pace with Republican party fundraising, the amendments were described to the American people as a step toward making American elections free, fair and without the distorting influence of big money. However, what actually happened after the passage of the 1974 and 1979 amendments to the FECA produced consequences that continue to thwart the intent of reformers.

Consequence Number One: The Rise of Direct Mail

After the FECA amendments, there remained only a few legal ways of raising the money that politicians need to reach the voters. It no longer becomes effective to fund presidential campaigns with PAC donations, since PACs can contribute only $10,000 each, and there is a limited number of PACs that give even that to campaigns. For example, in 1988 PACs contributed only 1.4 percent of total funding (Alexander and Bauer 1991, p. 25). So how did candidates solve their fund-raising problems? PACs were not enough, and individual contributions in legal amounts would have to be more numerous than ever before to make up for the vacuum created when large donations were declared illegal. Yet reformers did not take into account that most Americans will not donate money to political causes.

An anecdote from former Florida State Senator Louis de la Parte illustrates this problem that has frustrated American politicians for as long as there have been elections: "You can put 1,000 average voters in a room and say, `How many of you have ever contributed to a campaign, any campaign?' and not one of them will have contributed. Then you ought to be able to ask them, `Then where in hell do you think the money came from?'" (Broder 1976, p. 315). According to the National Election Survey the number of people reporting having contributed to campaigns is dismally low; from 1952 to 1988, the number of political givers fluctuated between four and thirteen percent of respondents (Alexander and Bauer 1991, p. 5). Even giving one dollar to the presidential election campaign fund check-off is too much for most taxpayers; so few contribute even this paltry sum that the fund may run out of money by 1996 (*The New York Times*, 7/9/91, editorial).

Here is a paradox in American political participation: if people do not want their politics bought and paid for by the wealthy few, why is it that few Americans do the one thing that could keep political fundraising from turning to the elite? It could be that people do not give money to politicians because they distrust politics; and they distrust politics because it seems to be tainted by special interests. Campaigns needed to find ways to get large numbers of people to part with their money to fund American political campaigns after 1974. The new fundraising technique used to do this difficult job is the direct mail solicitation letter. It has been called by Larry Sabato "The Poison Pen of Politics" (Sabato 1981, p.220).

If one is suddenly constrained from fundraising with big money givers, one has to find hundreds of thousands of small givers to make up the difference. Literally the only way politicians had of pursuing these millions of small givers was through the newly created industry of direct mail fundraising. And the only ways to get people to mail in their checks were to use emotional appeal and the most extreme kind of public discourse.

New computer technology allowed entrepreneurs to write, address, and mail thousands of targeted pieces every day. Software allowed these letters to be customized, inserting the solicitee's name in conspicuous places to create the illusion of a letter written just for him or her. This new industry began when Richard Viguerie, fresh from the 1964 defeat of Barry Goldwater, took with him the list of Goldwater contributors and rented and office above a Washington drugstore in 1965. Says a former employee, "Richard practically invented direct mail" (Shaw 1981).

Richard Viguerie was different from the others who were using new campaign techniques to sell candidates to voters. Viguerie's technique for soliciting funds through the mail succeeded because it was hot; the more shrill and extreme the letter, the higher the response rate. And it did not matter that this approach would seem too extreme to some recipients; direct mail could return great profits with response rates of less than ten percent. Old campaign techniques aim for the great bulge of voters in the ideological middle who would be turned off by extreme attacks and appeals. This new technique succeeded by milking a small number of people who would respond regularly only to the most extreme copy.

This entirely new way of raising political money combined what one reporter in 1981 termed "hype, hysteria, and a sometimes cynical assessment of the conservative marketplace" (Shaw 1981) to fund what became known as the New Right. An example of this can be found in a typical Viguerie letter from the early 1980s: "Your tax dollars are being used to pay for grade school courses that teach our children that CANNIBALISM, WIFE-SWAPPING, and the MURDER OF INFANTS and the ELDERLY are acceptable behavior" (emphasis in original; Shaw 1981). Political consultant David Keene described direct mail in this way: "You've got to be shrill. You've got to tell people that something awful is going to happen. Then you have got to tell them that it WILL happen to them unless they do something. And what they've got to do is give money" (Shaw 1981).

To match the example of right-wing hype, here is a sample of left-wing mail using emotional appeal to raise money: "Dear Friend: I am writing to you from Hiroshima. Here, 40 years ago, the nuclear arms race began .... earlier this morning, at Ground Zero, I was overwhelmed by the enormity of what happened here ... " (Waldman 1986). The letter goes on to say that having come "face to face" with the realities of nuclear war, Markey now believes "more firmly than ever that we must either reverse this insane arms race, or likely in this generation see the end of life as we know it" (Waldman 1986). The letter was printed on what looked to be the official stationery of the Nippon Hotel in Hiroshima. But the letter was printed in Washington, and of course was not written by Markey at all (Waldman 1986).

Direct mail now has become an important component of every presidential campaign, helping to raise money in those small, legal amounts. Although this is "clean money" in the sense that it does not represent special interests, these small donors are giving the money it takes to fuel presidential campaigns, especially in the pre-nomination stage. The interjection of extremist charges and escalation of anger targeted at "the Eastern Liberal Establishment" or "Those right-wing activists that make nuclear war more likely" may contribute to the radicalization of campaign messages. Rather than focus on complex problems or issues that require reasoned debate, campaign discourse may be coming down to the lowest common denominator of direct mail fundraising.

It is considered political suicide to send out confusing campaign messages. If someone contributes because Candidate X says liberals are lower than baby-killers, there may be some pressure created for Candidate X to say in other forms of campaign discourse what has already been said in direct mail. Since direct mail consists not of a single mailing, but a series of follow-up mailings, there is some rationale for giving the direct mail audience a reinforcement of previous messages, both in ads and in speeches, in hopes of keeping those response rates high.

There are no firm figures available to chart the growth in political direct mail or the number of solicitation letters that are delivered to voters in any given campaign. However, it has been documented that the Republican National Committee went from a contributors' list of some 34,000 in the 1970s to 870,000 contributors in 1980, with twenty-six dollars as the average contribution (Sabato 1981, p.224). Although both political parties use direct mail to raise funds, the Republicans began earlier than the Democrats and have led the way in this innovation.

Consequence Number Two: The Weakening of Political Parties

The American electorate has been abandoning traditional party loyalties for at least the last forty years. When the 1974 FECA amendments took away functions normally performed by the political parties in presidential elections, chiefly fundraising, and gave these functions to the federal government, this was obviously not going to help parties rebuild themselves as viable institutions in our political life.

Why should the strength of local political parties be of concern to the authors of campaign finance reform? Parties are necessary to the mission of a democracy, which is to translate the people's desires into public policy. The only instrument that exists to aggregate the desires of a group and communicate those desires effectively into legislation is the political party. Without such an instrument, individual political desires become isolated bits of the political landscape, unfocused and uncoordinated. Parties are considered by many political scientists to be essential to democratic governance. This view is summarized by legendary political scientist E.E. Schattschneider, who wrote in 1942 that "modern democracy is unthinkable save in terms of parties. As a matter of fact, the condition of parties is the best possible evidence for the nature of a regime" (Schattschneider 1942, p. 1).

When FECA was amended in 1974 to grant public financing of presidential campaigns, congressional debate did not include discussions of the effects this would have on the already declining political parties. Yet the amendments were soon seen as "an innovation of portentous significance ... Because the funds went to the candidates, not the party organizations, the dependence of candidates on parties was all but ended" (McCormick 1982, p. 231). Austin Ranney writing in *The Decline of American Political Parties* reported that "The party organizations simply are not actors in presidential politics" (Wattenburg 1984, p. 16). Because of stringent new reporting requirements of FECA, local party groups were actively discouraged from spending money in behalf of their party's nominee for President. Richard Cheney, who ran Gerald Ford's 1976 campaign, said some time shortly after the election: "I firmly believe that the effect of the campaign finance laws in this area has been to discourage grass-roots political activity, to discourage participation, and to place a premium on strategies that are easily controlled and reported" (Polsby 1983, p. 79).

Congress was asked in 1979 to try to undo the damage it had done to the nation's political parties. Allowed under the 1974 amendments to spend only $1,000 to aid their party's presidential nominee, state parties felt themselves becoming irrelevant to the process. So, in the name of reinvigorating local, grassroots politicking, the Congress amended FECA once more. The 1979 amendments were written in an effort to bring moribund local political parties back to life. What they did instead was to pave the way for big money donations to re-enter American presidential campaigns.

Consequence Number Three: Soft Money

In order to provide political parties with an avenue of participation in the presidential campaign at the state level, Congress created a category of political spending tailored for their needs. Parties were now given the ability to legally raise and spend unlimited amounts of money for activities termed "party-building." These activities, such as voter registration and get-out-the-vote drives, would obviously also help federal candidates, including each party's presidential nominee. This unregulated money was dubbed "soft money" to distinguish it from funds that had to be disclosed, limited, and regulated by the FEC.

Almost immediately, the definition of soft money became clouded in a welter of byzantine regulations. For example, the FEC's attempt to construe soft money as somehow clearly separable from the strict ceilings for presidential nominees in the 1974 amendments is enough to confuse anyone. A prominent campaign finance expert demonstrates just a portion of the complexity of soft money in the following:

> Soft money, given to state parties, is supposed to be used to support non-federal activities, or to fund state and local portions of political activities carried out in a particular state in so-called 'mixed activities' (where both federal and local candidates will receive a benefit, such as registration drives). Hard money is supposed to pay for the 'federal' portion of mixed activities ... But soft money CAN end up financing portions of a political activity attributable to federal races, if the state party allocates too high a portion of the cost of a mixed activity to a non-federal race .... The FEC had no clear guidelines [in 1988] .... the ambiguities in its regulation create a system ripe for abuse" ("Money and Politics: Soft Money, 1988" p. 11).

In 1907, corporations were barred from giving donations to presidential candidates. In 1947, federal law prohibited labor unions from using dues money to give directly to federal candidates. In 1974, individuals were strictly limited to $1,000 per candidate per race. All these measures were to some extent invalidated by the 1979 FECA amendments, which created a backdoor mechanism for just these kinds of contributions to aid federal campaigns.

In the first election (1980) in which soft money became a legal loophole for big givers, corporations, and unions, $19 million was spent in soft money alone. By 1988, soft money had swelled to $122 million (Alexander 1990). The reason donations to federal campaigns had been restricted in the 1974 amendments was to prevent the influence peddling of the Nixon years from recurring. Along with big donations come at least the appearance of big influence, negating the democratic ideal of one person, one vote. Soft money heralded the return of both political parties going after those who could contribute the most money. Would this skew American politics in favor of those who could write the big checks?

In 1984, while the Republican party was having little trouble raising $4.7 million from individuals donating at least $10,000 apiece, Mondale's soft-money fundraising was not going nearly as well (Alexander 1987, p. 335). Chair of Mondale's Victory Fund major gifts program, Stuart Moldaw, attempted to raise $4 million in contributions of $10,000 or more and failed by a little less than $500,000 to meet this goal. Moldaw blamed a particular policy difference as the reason for this soft-money gap: "You see a guy for $50,000, $100,000, he's upset [by Mondale's pledge to raise taxes on the wealthy]. It's him that Mondale's talking about" (Alexander 1987, p. 364).

The Mondale defeat gave the Democrats a chance to look for ways to change their party. One way they changed was to stop alienating potential big donors. Changing a pattern that goes back for decades in American politics, in 1988 the Democrats raised more soft money out of big contributors than the Republicans raised. Under the talented leadership of super-fundraiser Robert A. Farmer, the Dukakis campaign through soft money was able to amass $68 million dollars outside the federal limits. The Republicans were able to raise somewhat less, $54 million (Huston 1988). After the election, at a conference on campaign finance reform, Bush's deputy finance chair called for a new restriction on soft money, prohibiting donations over $50,000 per person. Bob Farmer saw nothing at all the matter with even the largest of individual donations, urging only that such givers be disclosed just as other donors are disclosed to the FEC (Huston 1988).

Possible Effects of Soft Money:
A Change in Discourse and Political Activity?

Thomas Byrne Edsall has noticed the irony in the way the Democrats in particular raise money:

> The Democratic party, which has traditionally claimed to represent the working man and woman, depends substantially more than the Republican party on the contributions of special-interest groups, corporations, and on the large donations of rich individuals .... much of it raised in soft money (Edsall 1989, p. 215).

In 1986, twenty-eight percent of the Democratic National Committee's funds came from soft money, compared to less than five percent of a much larger Republican National Committee budget (Edsall 1989). Two Furman University political scientists, John C. Green and James L. Guth, found in a survey of campaign contributors that "more than half the Democratic donors earned more than $100,000 a year, and it was only 43 percent for the Republicans ... The Democrats tend to draw pretty much from national level bigwigs, while the Republicans, in their direct mail campaigns, reached right down into Main Street across the country" (Edsall 1989).

A spokesman for the Democratic National Committee commented that there is no way "to square our financial base with our political base" (Edsall 1989). While the Republican party is openly pro-business, the Democratic party receives little money from the people its modern platforms have vowed to represent. The appearance of undue influence for wealthy contributors remains. These are exactly the complaints of past reformers; the worry that money influences policy is as old as Andrew Jackson and as recent as the last election.

More money was spent on the 1992 presidential election than on any previous presidential election in part because of the larger sums of soft money raised by the major-party candidates. During the general election phase of the 1992 race each of the major-party candidates had public funding in the amount of $65.5 million ($55.2 million paid directly to the candidates' campaigns and $10.3 million to the Democratic and Republican national committees). In addition, between April 1 and December 31 of 1992 the parties spent $24.4 million of soft money for Clinton and $18.7 million for Bush. (according to a personal communication from Herbert Alexander). On top of this spending by the major-party candidates, Ross Perot spent roughly $64 million, thereby helping to make the 1992 election the most costly presidential election thus far in American history.

More soft money was raised and spent in 1992 than in any previous presidential year. After three elections in which both parties experimented with soft money, 1992 showed just what the parties could do at full throttle. Already by the 1988 campaign, the presidential race had ceased to be publicly funded in any meaningful sense of the term. Political textbooks such as Dye and Zeigler's *The Irony of Democracy* inform students that "since, in 1988, public money accounted for less than one-third of the true cost of the presidential elections, one can hardly regard these elections as publicly financed" (Dye and Zeigler 1989, p. 190).

There is nothing inherently wrong with individuals desiring to contribute to their favorite candidates and parties. The reason that corporations and unions had been barred from doing so is the same reason strict limits were placed on individual and PAC giving in 1974. Where money enters politics, there is always the possibility of quid pro quo arrangements: bribery of public officials. If money buys more than just a chance to help a candidate, but also ends up helping your own company or union's wallet, then money has ceased to be a contribution and has become a kind of bribe.

During the 1991 Senate Ethics Committee hearings on the so-called Keating Five, senators were accused of being bought by the soft money contributions of Charles Keating, who described their relationship as emphatically not entailing any quid pro quo arrangement (Alexander and Bauer 1991, p. 80). Yet meetings were arranged with federal regulators at lightning speed for the Washington bureaucracy by senators who made Mr. Keating's problems a high-priority item on their daily schedules. The Ethics Committee eventually let everyone off with a slap on the wrist, except for Senator Alan Cranston of California, who had earlier announced his retirement due to health problems. The Committee never defined the line that is crossed when and if a campaign contribution becomes a bribe.

One of the few specifics in Bush's 1988 and 1992 presidential campaigns was a promise to implement a cut in the capital gains tax. Economists are divided concerning the wisdom of such a cut when the deficit remains an unsolved problem of enormous magnitude. Whether this tax cut would be good for the nation as a whole, it would certainly be good for those in the finance, oil, and real estate sectors, and "these interests are all well-represented on Team 100" (*All the President's Donors*, p. 25). It is possible that a government policy that favors big business might also be a policy beneficial to the nation as a whole; but as long as big business supplies so much cash to presidential candidates, how can the appearance of quid pro quo be avoided?

Several examples of what appear to be quid pro quo deals emerge in a Common Cause investigation of campaign financing. One is in the area of oil companies that have been trying for years to gain rights for off-shore drilling in the waters off the coasts of Florida and California. Environmentalists have been successful so far in keeping these companies from their goal. Oil companies and executives involved in oil companies gave a total of $1.7 million to Team 100. President Bush appointed Manuel Lujan, a vocal proponent of off-shore drilling, to be his Secretary of the Interior. The son-in-law of Team 100 donor Robert Holt, an oilman from Midland, Texas, long identified as a major Bush fundraiser, was "appointed to head an Interior Department Office that controls oil and gas leases on the Outer continental Shelf" (*All the President's Donors*, p. 25).

Another large group of Team 100 donors included the top names in high-risk financial transactions, such as leveraged buy-outs and junk bond financing. Michael Milliken, who was convicted for his role in junk-bond fraud, was a member of Team 100. What would this sector of the business community want from Bush? "Status quo," Columbia University economics professor Louis Lowenstein says. "What they have in the U.S. is almost no rules on how the game gets played, and they want to keep it that way" (*All the President's Donors*, p. 25).

Possibilities for Future Reform: Making Money Less Important in Presidential Campaigns

The FEC issued new soft money regulations on May 3, 1990. These rules required only disclosure of donors giving $200 or more to any soft money activity. According to *Campaign Practices Reports*, "The new regulations and forms, which several FEC commissioners admitted were complex and potentially confusing, will apply various allocation formulas for calculating how much soft money activity is to be governed by federal limits, depending on the type of committee and the type of cost involved" (Campaign Practices Reports 1990, p. 6).

Fred Wertheimer, president of Common Cause, was critical of the FEC response and called on Congress to pass legislation to take soft money out of presidential campaigns. Wertheimier was quoted as saying that "Reporting huge soft money contributions instead of shutting them down is tantamount to repealing the campaign contribution limits that were enacted precisely because disclosure is not enough to prevent corporate, labor union, and large individual contributions from having a corrupting impact on the White House and Congress" (Campaign Practices Reports 1990, p. 6).

It is difficult to show what our politics would be like if all possible influence of big money were removed from presidential campaigns. There has been, after all, only one presidential campaign where big money was completely forbidden: in the 1976 Ford-Carter race. One can speculate that perhaps the social issues favored by the working-class religious members of the New Right coalition would come to the fore and the Republican party might shift its emphasis away from items such as capital gains and toward a more conservative definite action strategy against abortion and for school prayer. Both parties perhaps could see a shift in their emphasis, from policies that work to the advantage of big contributors, to policies that benefit the greater number of each party's constituent base.

We are the only Western nation without free broadcast time for candidates, and one of few without direct subsidies for political parties. This reflects our heritage as a nation of rugged individualists, without campaigns as a reflection of the entrepreneurial culture. But just as we once were a nation where laissez-faire economics reigned supreme, we have been moving away from laissez-faire politics, too. With this caveat in mind, it is useful to compare our elections briefly with those in Great Britain and Germany. Much of the money used in elections in Britain and Germany comes as subsidies to the political parties from the government. Unlike American presidential elections, which are so expensive that soft money is needed to supplement government funding, European elections are relatively quick and cheap.

Elections in Great Britain

Britain is a parliamentary democracy, which means there is no direct national election for a president. Whichever political party has the largest number of representatives elected to the House of Commons will form the government, electing a prime minister from the ranks of the ruling party in Commons. Individual candidates for Commons are limited by law to spending about $10,000, depending on the size of the district. British campaigns last only about three weeks to a month.

The two major parties are Labour, identified strongly with trade unionism, and the Conservatives, identified strongly with business. Spending is not limited on the national level, and the Conservative party enjoys a fundraising edge over the Labour party. The British parties are membership parties, which means that voters who identify with a party pay dues to support the party. In the 1987 elections, the Conservative party spent nearly $16 million, while Labour spent more than $7 million. However, the real essential in modern political communication, television time, is distributed to the parties in a manner that negates much of the fundraising advantage of the Conservatives.

The way in which broadcast time is distributed offers modest exposure of political persuasion to the public, as opposed to the repetitive nature of American thirty and sixty second spots. Neither parties nor individual candidates are permitted to buy any television time for special programs, or even ads. Instead, free broadcast time is allotted to the major parties and these programs are carried by both the government owned BBC and the commercially operated ITV. The total time provided for all the parties in 1987 was only about two and one-half hours. Labour, the Conservatives, and the Alliance each had five broadcasts of ten minutes each, the Green party offered enough candidates to earn a single broadcast.

British campaigns consist of speeches, debates, posters, mailings, and door-to-door canvassing, in contrast to American campaigns where huge television costs insure a great amount of time and effort will be spent raising money to pay for thirty and sixty second ads. British political persuasion is done on a more face-to-face basis.

Germany

Most of the money in German politics is given by the government directly to the major political parties. Combined with membership dues, this leaves most German political parties dependent on donations for only a small amount of their monetary needs. For example, the two major political parties, the SPD and the CDU, get about a third of their income from public subsidies, while raising half (or more in the case of the SPD) from membership dues and loans. The Political Parties Act of 1967 uses a formula to determine how much government subsidy will be granted each party, depending on the number of votes the party garnered in the previous election. Even parties that received as little as a half percent of the vote receive some subsidy.

The German system is one that nurtures strong political parties through direct subsidy. The American campaign finance laws seem strange to German political scientist Arthur Gunlicks, who wrote in 1988:

> It is ironic that while the German party elites have turned to even more generous forms of public financing and tax expenditures for party contributions, the U.S. Congress has not only refused to provide any public financing for Senate and House races; in the 1986 tax law it has eliminated the—by German standards very modest—tax credit and deduction for political party contributions (Gunlicks 1988, p. 39).

The differences between German and American campaign finance can

be summed up in a German word *Chancenausgleich,* which means "equaliza-
tion of chances." The German constitution mandates that "equal access for
parties to the political system must be provided" (Von Reden 1984, p. 910).
Germany has a turnout rate of 90 percent, as opposed to the recent American
turnout rate of 50.1 percent in 1988 and 54 percent in 1992. What would the
American political system look like if it were governed by *"Chancenausgleich?"*

Conclusions Based on the European Experience

Clearly, the expense of buying broadcast time has been one of the factors
influencing the need for campaigns to raise millions of dollars more than
they are allocated through the current system of public financing. Noted
campaign finance expert Larry Sabato has written that in the 1980 presidential election, Ronald Reagan spent about half of his $29.4 million in public
grants on media advertising, and President Carter used more than two-
thirds of his allotment for the same purpose. In 1984, President Reagan used
about 63% of his $40.4 million grant on time buys and commercial produc-
tion, while Mondale devoted 46% of his public funding to the media"
(Sabato 1989, p. 27). In the 1988 race, both Bush and Dukakis spent "nearly
50% of the public grants they received on media" (Alexander and Bauer
1991, p. 35). As long as television and other media costs are paid for by the
campaigns, the need for money will continue to grow.

Soft money fulfills a need, and if soft money is outlawed there must be
some other means of fulfilling the needs of presidential candidates to
communicate with the American people. The current system, much of
which is the result of reforms passed in 1974 and 1979, allows for lengthy
campaigns that are biased toward the best fundraisers and provides the
wealthy an avenue of influence that undermines elections as representing
"the will of the people" in the idealized type of American elections reformers have always pursued.

A panel of seventeen former campaign finance chairs, experts on
campaign finance, and fundraisers gathered together by the Citizen's
Research Foundation to recommend changes in the FECA, and they wrote
in their position statement: "A strong consensus favors encouraging broadcasters to provide presidential candidates in both the pre and post nomination phases of the presidential selection process more free time" (Sabato
1989, p. 27). (For the complete recommendations of this group see Alexander
and Bauer 1991.)

Proposals to grant free broadcast time to candidates predate the days of
television. Alf Landon's 1936 running mate, Frank Knox, thought that too
much campaign money was being spent on radio. He suggested "mandatory allocation of free airtime to both parties before each presidential
election" (Alexander and Bauer 1991, Appendix). The Twentieth Century
Fund's commission on Campaign Costs and the Electronic Era was pub-

lished in 1967. Among its recommendations were these:

> that the federal government provide significant candidates in general
> election campaigns for President and Vice President of the United States
> with basic campaign broadcasting access to the American voting public,
> within the context of programs that will promote rational political discus-
> sion and that will be presented in prime evening time simultaneously over
> every broadcast and cable television facility in the United States (Sabato
> 1989, p. 27).

A Harvard Institute of Politics study group concluded in 1978 that
broadcasters ought to provide steeply discounted airtime, with stations
permitted to write off the revenue loss on their taxes (Sabato 1989, p. 28). The
most recent proposal for free air time has come from political scientist Larry
Sabato, who argues that "the public, not the stations, own the airwaves" and
that broadcasting is "among the most lucrative enterprises in America" and
can therefore afford to give free time without being compensated for it by
the federal treasury (Sabato 1989, p. 30). (For a complete description of
Sabato's plan, see his Chapter 3, *The Free Media Solution.*)

Conclusions

Even after decades of reform, there is still the pervasive perception
among American voters and nonvoters that our politics caters to the
interests of the wealthy few. A recent study prepared for the Kettering
Foundation drew these conclusions: "People believe two forces have corrupted democracy. The first is that lobbyists have replaced representatives
as the primary political actors. The other force, seen as more pernicious, is
that campaign contributions seem to determine political outcomes more
than voting. No accusation cuts deeper because when money and privilege
replace votes, the social contract underlying the political system is abro-
gated" ("Citizens and Politics..." 1991, p. v). These complaints appear
strikingly similar to those voiced in 1832, 1878, 1914, and 1974. Current
reforms are not enough to restore public confidence in American presidential elections; the tensions between freedom and equality remain.

The United States could adopt some of the aspects of European elections: the strict allocation of free broadcast time to the parties and complete
government financing of presidential elections, without soft money loopholes. Perhaps these measures might serve as a modest beginning in a
restoration of the linkage between people and government that has been
ruptured by mass cynicism and anger directed at the entire political process.

Since the 1970s, campaign finance scandals have included Watergate,

Abscam, Koreagate, the Keating Five, and the resignation from the House of Representatives by Speaker Jim Wright. The head of the House Banking Committee, Ferdinand St. Germain, has been forced to resign as well. These have added to public cynicism about politics. The irony is that the reforms of the 1970s have, while halting some practices, encouraged new ways of mixing big money and politics and new methods of fundraising that cannot succeed without using hype and emotional appeal.

What does this say about American self image as we head toward the twenty-first century? We have been through an era where wealth was celebrated as the apex of the American dream; where a character in a popular Oliver Stone film epitomizes the excess of 1980s materialism by stating that "greed is good." Our popular music celebrated "the material girl," Madonna, at the same time that ghetto youths were murdering each other not just over the traditional turf fights, but to attain the status symbols of a culture of wealth: gold chains, gold teeth, $100 sneakers.

Yet, another part of American culture has not disappeared. We are the heirs of the Revolution as well as the heirs of laissez-faire. Our presidential campaigns reflect this tension, as we strive to rid our politics of what *The New York Times* (10/12/88, editorial) calls "sewer money." The egalitarian and the individualist struggle for control of our politics and the reform impulse remains, one can only hope, as strong as ever.

PART FIVE

Presidential Campaigning and American Self Images: Agenda for Tomorrow's Research

14

Presidential Campaign Politics at the Crossroads

Arthur H. Miller and Bruce E. Gronbeck

Are Campaigns Irrelevant?

It has become fashionable among some political scientists to argue that presidential campaigns are irrelevant to election outcomes (e.g., see Frankovic 1985; Rosenstone 1985; Markus 1988). These authors suggest that elections are won and lost because of conditions (generally economic) that are in place long before the campaign ever begins. According to these writers economic conditions accurately predict the outcome of elections, and thus candidate images, policy stands, negative ads, campaign strategies, and media coverage of events all have minimal if any effect on the eventual outcome of elections.

Let us assume for the moment that these writers are correct and that macroeconomic factors such as unemployment, inflation, and change in income do determine election outcomes. On the surface this would suggest that Bill Clinton won in 1992 because he followed the dictates of James Carville's campaign sign "The economy—Stupid!" and focused his campaign message on the economy. But, this is not what the mathematical models predicted. On the contrary, the models generally predicted a Bush reelection victory (see Lewis-Beck & Rice 1992).

After all, George Bush was right: economic conditions, objectively speaking, were not as bad in 1992 as Clinton argued. Between 1988 and 1992 the American economy had certainly faltered. Economic growth (change in GDP) had slowed from 3.9% in 1988 to 2.1% in 1992, and unemployment had risen from 5.4% to 7.3%. Nevertheless, inflation had fallen from 4.1% to 2.9%, interest rates remained low, and according to the U.S. Department of Commerce the nation's per capita income increased 3.9% in 1992 after increasing only 2.4% in 1991; thus, technically speaking, the country was recovering from the 1991 recession. Yet, it was virtually impossible, as both the mathematical modelers and the Bush administration learned, to predict the outcome of the 1992 election from these objective economic indicators. Likewise, it was not possible to predict the campaign appearance of H. Ross Perot from traditional measures of economic conditions.

Even if the macroeconomic models were accurate in predicting election outcomes (who wins or loses), there would be good reasons to conclude that this is not all there is to know or learn from presidential election campaigns. Such an approach is far too limited in at least three important ways: in the model of human behavior that is conveyed by the approach, in the suggestion that the importance and meaning of campaigns and elections are based solely on objective facts and economic conditions, and in the restricted social significance attributed to elections. We address these concerns below. The discussion proceeds by first considering voters as more than calculating, economic maximizers. Next we turn to an examination of how the candidates, media and voters all contribute to constructing the meaning of campaigns and elections, and in the process reveal a great deal about American self images. In the final sections of the chapter we ask what is learned about American political culture more generally from examining campaign images, what reforms might produce a campaign process that is closer to democratic ideals, and what new agenda for tomorrow's research is suggested by all these considerations.

Voters as More Than Economic Maximizers

Macroeconomic models of election outcomes convey an image of voters as economic maximizers, rationally reacting to changing macroeconomic trends. The individual is seen as carefully sifting any available information regarding past and future economic benefits and the ideological positions of the candidates prior to making a reasoned electoral choice (Downs 1957; Popkin 1991). Social psychologists have challenged this image of the voter, finding it too reactionary and overly demanding of individual information processing capabilities (Herstein 1981; as well as Chapter 10 in this volume).

As we have argued throughout this book, voters do not merely react to economic conditions, the persuasive power of the media, or the messages created by campaign managers. Rather, they are actively involved in constructing the meaning attributed to these messages and conditions. There is no reality in the external social world separate from human perception of it. People actively construct social reality, including the meaning and significance of macroeconomic indicators, and then respond to these constructed realities. Certainly the meaning given to the objective indicators by the candidates, the press, and the voters depends on context;

for example, the unemployment rate could be objectively the same in a period when the U.S. is facing little foreign competition or when it is facing increased competition, but we interpret it differently in each case because of the context within which it occurs.

The important point theoretically is that voters do more than simply react to stimuli. They do more than calculate the net economic return if one candidate rather than the other is elected. The model of theoretical maximization has two shortcomings: it assumes that economic indicators have a materiality separable from the human beings who create and interpret them, and that economic meaning-making is an essentially rational enterprise detachable from the more emotional vagaries of life. The first problem is the result of the modernist revolution abetted by John Locke's *An Inquiry into Human Understanding* (1690), which effectively separated the knower from the known in a radical way, while the second is a difficulty capitalism has wrestled with through most of this century: the temptation to assume that the economic governs the other spheres, institutions, and group identities of citizens. Both problems get in the way of understanding large-scale American elections.

Throughout this book we have assumed a theoretical orientation deriving from critical and cultural theories of human action. We have argued that citizens are actively engaged in the creation of meanings in their daily lives, and that they bring those meanings—interpretations, attitudes, valuations, wishes, ideologies, mythic accounts of birth and death—to the raw data of their experiences. Social reality is what we call those raw data as they are shaped and valued through individual and collective interpretive processes.

Because social reality is created collaboratively, meaning-making is very much a dynamic, interactive process. Consider presidential elections: the candidate, along with parties and interest groups promoting particular electoral outcomes, produce messages encoded in symbols expected to evoke meaningful responses from the public. The media augment or detract from the significance of those messages through framing (putting campaign events in varied interpretive contexts), highlighting (positively or negatively valuing particular events or issues), and attributing responsibility (giving credit or blame to individuals for particular event outcomes). The public then heightens, levels, sharpens, suppresses, or in other ways modifies all of these meanings, finally filtering them through their own hopes, fears, and self conceptions. As Edelman (1988, p. 37) points out, "we know that political leaders must follow their followers, that conformity to widely held ideology is typically the key to success in winning and retaining high office ... History and theory suggest that followers create leaders rather than the converse." That is because those followers are the final arbiters in democratically based electoral systems.

Creating the Meaning of Presidential Campaigns

A principal goal of this book has been to capture the essence of these constitutive and constructive processes as they are evidenced in American presidential campaigns. We wanted to learn not only how the meaning of elections is constructed, but also what this process of construction tells us about America itself. In Part II we presented an intensive analysis of three sources of candidate messages and images: candidate film biographies, campaign ads, and the texts of campaign speeches. These chapters not only described the social content of candidate messages but provided deeper insights into American political culture, particularly as exemplified in the definition of American values through designated enemies or excluded groups (Chapters 2 and 3). In addition, Gronbeck's (Chapter 4) analysis of negative ads provides insight into the distinction between issues and characters, helping us better understand what might otherwise be seen as inconsistent public behavior—when voters cast their ballots for the candidate with whom they least agree on the issues. Such an outcome could occur if the campaign messages focused largely on character assassination, or, as others have argued, emphasized style over substance (Miller & Borrelli 1992). Under these circumstances it would be inaccurate to conclude that the meaning of the election outcome was a policy mandate, arrived at through a reasoned dialogue between the candidates and voters. But, the candidates should not be singled out as the culprits in this deviation from democratic ideals without first considering the possibility that the media and the voters themselves may have played a contributing role.

In the so-called postmodern, electronic age of politics, campaign managers and spin masters have developed the art of news coverage manipulation. The interaction between political leaders or candidates and the media has become akin to a giant chess game in which each side vies for control (Ansolobehere, Behr & Iyengar 1993). Part III of this volume investigates these candidate-media interactions, as well as drawing out the implications that these interactions have for the ability of citizens to make reasoned electoral choices. Candidates and their consultants have developed intricate strategies, such as the issue-of-the-day strategy discussed in Chapter 5, for controlling or evading the media to their advantage. Likewise, through the use of paid advertising, the candidates largely bypass the monitoring function of the press. Candidates with enough money to purchase large segments of advertising, such as Ross Perot did in 1992, can ignore the press completely. Moreover, the ability of the candidates to go on popular talk shows in 1992 allowed them to escape the careful scrutiny of professional journalists. As David Birdsell points out in Chapter 7, this made it possible for Ross Perot to keep alive unsubstantiated charges of GOP dirty tricks even after they had been called into question by 60 Minutes.

Despite these claims and incidents that suggest media totally vulnerable to manipulation by the candidates, considerable evidence suggests more independent effects attributable to the media per se. For example, as Covington, Kroeger and Richardson conclude in Chapter 5, even if candidate strategies might influence straight news stories, they often fail to affect the press's ability to independently interpret the substance and merits of the candidate's remarks in editorials and news analyses. The media also have begun to devise counter-strategies for enhancing their ability to independently monitor the candidates. In 1992, the major networks, many newspapers, and the National Public Radio network offered so-called truth analyses of candidate commercials, aimed at holding candidates accountable for claims and statements. While this was an important step in the direction of returning the press to its former watch-dog role, it was limited because the critiques were only of individual ads, rarely repeated, and with no mechanism for directly confronting any candidate with charges of inaccurate or misleading statements. The truth stories, however, did contribute to a political atmosphere in which truth-telling was valued—a significant effect on the political culture.

Other evidence also suggests that the media influence the meaning of campaign messages in ways that go well beyond these deliberate counter-strategies. For example, in Chapter 6 David Woodard argues that the heavy emphasis of media coverage devoted to primary elections rather than the general election distorts the image of American politics. Because primary coverage emphasizes the horserace aspects of elections rather than policy issues, and because it focuses on conflict among candidates of the same party, election coverage largely gives heightened meaning to institutionalized intra-party disarray, while understating substantive inter-party differences. Another example of direct media impact on the meaning of campaign messages can be found in the 1992 primary incident involving Genniffer Flowers. The media, including the major television networks and most prestigious newspapers, took their lead from a tabloid and gave top-billing to Flower's unsubstantiated allegations that she had an extended, extramarital affair with Bill Clinton. Although the media reported that there was no evidence to support the charges, this first large-scale questioning of Clinton's moral character gave increased relevance to the criticisms that Bush repeatedly raised about Clinton's character during the remainder of the campaign. Media coverage of campaign events alone may not result in shifting support from one candidate to another, but it definitely contributes to defining the social and political context within which campaigns occur, and it crafts coherent meaning for campaign events through emphasis and the juxtaposition of various news stories.

Voters, however, do not simply respond to the mediated campaign messages like a passive audience. On the contrary, as Boynton and Lodge

(Chapter 10) point out, the voter actively interacts with the messages, constructing candidate images and developing issue preferences out of the meaning that they bring to the messages. Citizens come to campaigns with their own general preference for what the government should be doing and what type of leader should represent them. The campaigns, interest groups, and media provide specific information about the various candidates, the past performance of the government, and the difficulties currently confronting the country. From all this information the voter constructs evaluations and images of the candidate they select as best able to govern. The understanding that voters bring to the campaign messages reflects their past socialization, social values and political ideology, as well as their assessment of current economic conditions. Because of unique life experiences, each voter has the potential for understanding campaign messages in a way different from every other voter, thereby resulting in a cacophony of voices rather than a convergent choice. Yet, in the end this is not what happens. Eventually the public does converge on a dominant choice reflecting common appraisals.

This convergence of evaluations and choice occurs partly because of the institutional arrangements of a two-party system. Out of all the state primaries, conventions, and caucuses, two candidates are eventually selected, thus narrowing the choice in the general election. The convergence on a major candidate is not, however, totally dictated by the institutional arrangements. After all, a third party or independent candidate has been on the ballot and received more than 1% of the vote in 13 of the 24 presidential elections between 1900 and 1992, although in only 5 of those elections did the candidate receive more than 5% of the vote. Institutional constraints aside, majority support for a candidate occurs largely because the winning candidate successfully devised a set of messages aimed at evoking or representing the shared fears and hopes of the electorate. This is not to say that the policy proposals of winning candidates always fully match the preferences of a majority of voters. Consider, for example, the declining turnout rates between 1960 and 1988, the growing percentage of citizens who perceive no difference between the parties (Wattenberg 1984), and the sizable vote for Ross Perot in 1992 (the 19% he garnered was the second highest for an independent candidate since 1900, surpassed only by the 27% won by Theodore Roosevelt in 1912). These examples indicate that at certain times a significant proportion of the public fails to find a satisfactory image of America personified by either major party candidate. Nevertheless, even during these historical periods of fragmentation most voters converge on the choice of a single candidate even if that choice is aimed at throwing the rascals out, or is the lesser of two or more evils. The media contributes to this convergence by framing the messages in ways that enhance a commonality of understanding. In addition, the fact that most citizens pay relatively little attention to politics leads to a decision-making process that tends to produce a candidate choice based on a relatively small number of commonly shared criteria.

The process of voter decision making generally involves numerous cognitive shortcuts that give more emphasis to candidate character, assessments of past performance, and perceived connections between candidates and particular groups or interests than to a detailed understanding of policy platforms. In Chapter 11, for example, Miller discussed the powerful impact on the electoral choice that can occur when voters perceive too close an association between a candidate and negatively evaluated social groups. In 1984 the visible labor union support for Mondale and the active efforts by feminists to get a woman vice presidential candidate on the Democratic ticket led Ronald Reagan to label the Democrats as the party of special interests. This criticism represented more than mere campaign hyperbole, as it reflected a shift in how the public viewed the two parties. Historically the Republican party had been thought of as the party of special interests—meaning "wealthy and powerful people." By 1984, however, the public had indeed come to perceive the Democrats as catering to special interests—meaning unions, liberal activist groups (such as feminists, gays and militant blacks), and people on welfare (Miller, Wlezien & Hildreth 1991). Reagan did not create these public sentiments, but he skillfully exploited them to his electoral advantage, and in the process reinforced these beliefs. Similarly, the revolving door and Willie Horton ads of 1988 aroused racial fears and prejudice that influenced public evaluations of Bush and Dukakis. Likewise, in 1992 the perception that Bush had become too closely aligned with pro-lifers, religious fundamentalists, and the far right hurt him among middle of the road voters, despite the fact that ultra-conservative groups felt that he was not conservative enough. In each of these cases the perception of a connection between a candidate and a social group provided a cognitive shortcut that influenced the vote decision.

Public judgments of candidate character also act as a cognitive shortcut for electoral decision making. As Morreale (Chapter 2) and Gronbeck (Chapter 4) demonstrate, candidate messages frequently emphasize character over policy details. Such messages are emotionally powerful and cognitively less demanding than consideration of alternative policy positions. For the public, candidate character is a multidimensional construct that incorporates not only issues of moral integrity, but also concerns about leadership ability and compassion for others (Kinder 1986; Miller, Wattenberg & Malanchuk 1986). In 1992, the Republican campaign strategy was to emphasize public concerns about Clinton's integrity because on questions of morality Bush was evaluated more positively relative to Clinton. According to data from the National Election Study (NES) conducted by the University of Michigan, 51% of voters perceived Bush as the more honest and trustworthy candidate, whereas only 15% saw Clinton as relatively more moral than Bush. However, with growing deficits and increasing global economic competition high on the public agenda of fears in 1992, voters were more attentive to messages dealing with strong leadership and concern for others than to attacks on moral character.

During the 1988 presidential campaign Bush had used his tough stand on crime and drugs to convey an image of a strong leader and thereby shed the label "wimp" that had developed during his vice presidency under Ronald Reagan. The involvement of the U.S. in the Persian Gulf War not only provided a huge boost to the Bush approval ratings, but further solidified his new image as a strong leader. But, after the Gulf War ended and domestic issues surged to the top of the public agenda, vacillation and indecisiveness became the hallmarks of the Bush administration. Breaking the "no new taxes" pledge was more than a statement of trustworthiness; it suggested that Bush would not stand up for his convictions. The image of Bill Clinton as a strong leader, on the other hand, increased as the primary and general election wore on. Every time Clinton "came back" after some charge or event that was sure to have knocked any other candidate from the race, he gained in stature as a strong leader. The net result was that by the time of the general election Clinton was perceived as the relatively stronger leader by 36% of the voters while 31% saw Bush as the stronger leader (33% saw no difference).

Even more important for the overall assessment of candidate character were public judgments regarding which candidate was more caring and compassionate. Already in 1988 Bush had considerable difficulty convincing the public that he cared about the condition of the average voter. Because of his patrician background and aloofness, 50% of voters saw him as lacking empathy. Although this was not a critical factor in the 1988 election outcome, it was in 1992. The hesitancy of the Bush administration to take an active, aggressive approach toward correcting the faltering economy, Bush's early opposition to extending unemployment benefits, and his inability in the second presidential debate to give a sincere and convincing answer to the question of how the recession had affected him personally all contributed to the public's perception that he was uncaring. By the time of the election only 34% of the voters saw him as a caring individual.

Both the Clinton and Perot campaigns tried to capitalize on this weakness in the Bush character by stressing symbols conveying the message that they, by comparison, really did care about ordinary people. Despite his wealth, Ross Perot—because of his down-home language and wit, as well as his knack for taking his message to the people on popular talk shows—was able to make voters feel that he cared about their concerns. Through numerous campaign activities Clinton was also able to convey his compassion for others. Clinton campaign ads, for example, frequently depicted him reaching out to people or talking to people in town hall meetings, news clips often showed him hugging supporters, and he became widely known for frequenting fast food restaurants just like the average voter. Moreover, the decision that the Democrats made to campaign around the country by bus during the period following the Democratic convention was a stroke of campaigning brilliance because it cemented the perception that the Democrats cared about the plight of the average voter and small-town America. In the end, relative to Bush, twice as many voters (53%) saw Clinton as the compassionate candidate (21% saw Bush as more caring while 26% saw no difference.)

By emphasizing attacks on Clinton's integrity, the Bush campaign was ignoring the major finding of Harold Zullow's chapter, namely that Americans vote for the candidate with the most optimistic image of the future. By spending all of his time tearing down his opponent, Bush failed to articulate his own vision for America; he never offered a compelling picture of what he would do or how he would do it. Lacking a message that provided an affirmative meaning to his campaign, George Bush not only lost in 1992, but he was abandoned by a larger percentage of Republicans, his natural constituency, than any other Republican candidate in the previous 40 years (see Miller 1993 for a more extensive discussion of the historical comparisons).

In short, the meaning of elections is not found in merely examining the outcome of elections, or even in successfully predicting the outcome. Rather, it is found in the dynamic process of symbol generation that arises out of the constructive interactions among candidates, media, and voters. Examining elections from the perspective of any one of these actors in the political realm is worthwhile, but taking them together adds deeper insight into the meaning of campaigns and elections. Presidential elections offer an opportunity for Americans to reconfirm every four years what they stand for as a collectivity and community. Through the social construction of issues, candidate character, and media portrayals, presidential campaigns reflect the political psyche and culture of American society, the values that are shared in common, as well as the schisms that divide the country into multiple interests. By contemplating the interaction among candidates, the media, and voters, we attain a broader understanding of American self images and political culture, we realize that deviations from democratic ideals are the shared responsibility of all three actors, and we gain insights into a new agenda for tomorrow's research.

Campaigns, Self Images, and Political Culture

The images of candidates, citizens, and society that are constructed

during campaigns reflect the beliefs, expectations, behaviors, and democratic ideals that characterize American political culture. The public opinion
polls that measure citizen attitudes and assessments of candidates certainly
provide clues to interpreting that political culture. Yet public opinion polls
cannot fully capture the political culture of a society. Likewise, the images
of American society created and articulated by candidates, or framed and
emphasized by the media, reflect the dominant themes of American political culture, although not the totality of that culture. But, we may ask, what
is the picture of American culture that is conveyed by the images generated
in recent presidential campaigns by all three actors taken together? In
general, it is an image that incorporates many contradictions between what
ought to be and what is.

Political messages are not only explicitly articulated but also are
communicated indirectly, in the act of communicating itself. In choosing to
say x to audience y rather than audience z, at time 1 rather than time 2, in
context A rather than context B, message makers convey an indirect or
secondary message by communicating in one set of circumstances rather
than another. So, in 1992 George Bush said his progress in creating the New
World Order and the economy ought to be the primary campaign issues, yet
in campaigning primarily on the personal attributes of his opponents (even
calling Clinton and Gore "bozos") rather than issue differences, his actions
suggested that he believed the electorate would find the characterological
issues more compelling than his policy record. The same was true of Bush's
handling of crime and racial issues in 1988, which seemingly depended for
its effectiveness on prejudiced voters and a society divided by racial
hatreds. In announcing his 1988 presidential ambitions in a park in the
Rockies, Gary Hart communicated a very different leadership style and
issue priorities than did John Glenn in 1984, when he announced from the
stage of John Glenn High School in his home town. Very different mythic
profiles flowed from those choices. In appearing on MTV so he could rock
the vote and on Arsenio Hall so he could blow his sax in good company, Bill
Clinton's actions made a much louder statement than anything he said on
the programs. His middle-of-the-road, comparatively conservative economic programs were counterbalanced by appearances among liberal
constituencies where he often articulated liberal social programs on abortion, women's rights, Supreme Court appointments, and affirmative action.

In other words, how candidates communicate is as important as what
they say; both words and actions become messages. Furthermore, because
words are explicit while actions are only implicitly communicative messages, candidates are able to offer contradictory messages without actually
contradicting themselves, to "speak" the unspoken. In such ways, the
electorate finds itself sitting betwixt and between: betwixt and between
Reagan's promises to cut and improve defense at the same time, Dukakis's

praises for both business tax breaks and higher taxes on corporations, and Clinton's views on "growing the economy" even while asking the wealthy to bear the brunt of tax increases.

All of this contrariness is complicated once these candidate messages move into the political environment. So, voters say they want candidates to be strong leaders even while they are distrustful of politicians and regularly say they would prefer to curtail rather than extend the powers of government. Voters say they want politicians to deal with substantive issues, creating an imperative for candidates and the media to deal with substance. The appeal of Perot's thirty-minute TV infomercials even gave some credence to the image of voters as rational decision makers just waiting for indepth discussion. But, Perot's success with the longer formats probably was due as much to his folksiness as his message, and perhaps his one- and two-minute ads were more powerful than his thirty-minute specials. Additionally, many voters show little interest in politics (voter turnout increased in 1992, yes, but only four percentage points to 55%), they find policy discussions boring, and they respond more readily to negative ads, symbolic gestures, and attacks on character than detailed policy white papers. The tension between policy and characterological issues is as taut as ever in America, as it likewise is between positions most candidates take on the difficult issues. "Image politics" is thus not so much non-substantive as multi-substantive, with voters forced to pick out bits and pieces of candidate statements and actions and to mold the bits into a kind of conceptual whole that becomes an important—in some cases determinative—aspect of voting behavior.

Images of society are also created by voters. The public revels in the conception of America as an extended community, a melting pot of diverse interests, yet citizens respond actively to exclusionary appeals subtly aimed at evoking race and gender stereotypes, as well as homophobic and xenophobic fears. Everyone worries in common about the decline of American economic prowess, but individually they are unwilling to sacrifice for the whole. The ethos of rugged individualism remains from the historic heritage of taming the west, yet the public is aghast when high risk, unchecked, selfish individualism produces huge costs for everyone, such as in the Savings & Loan scandals of the 1980s. Equal opportunity is seen by all as a virtue, but at times even the wealthiest, most powerful segments of society feel that they deserve more influence and that those in poverty or on welfare have more influence in society than they justly deserve.

In short, the images that we have of American political culture from recent elections is one characterized by high ideals and disappointing behavior. Candidates who are expected to maintain high standards of moral integrity, bringing dignity and respect to the office of president, frequently resort to name calling, fear arousal, and enemy-baiting to win an election.

A press that is expected to be an independent, principled, investigatory watchdog of democratic ideals turns out to be highly manipulated by government officials and candidates who largely determine the tone and content of news reporting. The press is more likely to air the sensational story than serious proposals, and given more to delivering the audience to advertisers than delivering accurate, informative messages to viewers. Citizen-voters are expected to be interested in and informed about political issues, but in fact have selective memories that are more attentive to sensationalized allegations than factual policy proposals and more susceptible to the influence of visual cues than verbal messages.

American self images, thus, are anchored in a series of counterpoised conceptions of candidates, society, the press and the press's role, and individual voters themselves—their understanding of their lots in life, their roles in the system, and their levels of hope and fear. From the millions of words and billions of electronic visual frames that sweep over an electorate every four years, visions of candidates, the press, and the country as an abstracted whole are sculpted. These are our self images, our views of where we came from, where we are as a collectivity today, and where we ought to be heading tomorrow. Those visions are seldom those of any single politician, journalist, or citizen. They never are perfectly in focus because consensus in a country of 265 million cannot be engineered. Even though they are a bit faded and blurry, however, such visions or self images are an essential by-product of presidential electioneering. For some little time after elections, they guide the executive and legislative branches' actions (or should) and become the lenses or frames through which a citizenry assesses the actions of the governors.

Attaining Democratic Ideals: An Impossible Dream?

Critics of American democracy find it very easy to condemn the press, indict politicians, or blame voters for the political problems, dysfunctional behavior, and deviations from democratic ideals mentioned above. Yet when the actions of these separate actors are considered together, it is evident that all three share responsibility for the so-called "governing crisis" in America. Nevertheless, all three actors frequently rationalize their own actions by blaming the others. Candidates argue that they emphasize style and character rather than policies because the media will not cover serious issue debates, and the public will abandon them if their proposals are realistic and call for public sacrifice. Reporters say they cover the horse race and candidate personalities because otherwise the audience would be bored. Voters, however, feel alienated from politics because candidates are not interested in their problems or what they really think, and believe that the politicians will say or do anything to get reelected and that they never fulfill their campaign promises, so why bother to participate. Recognizing this complex interaction, however, is a constructive first step in the direction of evaluating various proposals that have been made for reforming the system. Clearly all three actors must be more responsible if these problems are to be addressed successfully. It is up to candidates to raise the level of discourse, to promote overarching goals, and to devise equitable policies to attain them. It is up to the media to force the candidates to deal with the tough issues, to be honest when criticizing their opponents and reasonable when making promises about policies. It is up to the public to pay attention to substantive concerns, to participate, and to vote on issue differences. But what reforms will facilitate attaining these honorable aims?

Certainly reforms involving only one of these political actors are bound to fail or have limited effects. For example, some critics have suggested that the number one reform needed to deal with the "governing crisis" is to shift from a majority voting system to a proportional voting system for selecting congressional representatives (Bennett 1992). This suggestion is based on the assumption that such an institutional change will prompt candidates, the media, and voters to return to an "idea-based" politics. While there is some evidence that multiparty, parliamentary systems are more responsive to citizen grievances than are two party systems (Miller & Listhaug 1990), there is little evidence that proportionate voting systems produce a higher level of political discourse or better problem solving skills. In short, this suggested reform appears unrealistic.

Another set of reforms that also promise only limited effects involve suggested changes in the presidential primary system. These reforms arise from criticisms of primary elections as too expensive, involving too many primaries, and spread out over too long a period of time. Suggested reforms include holding a national primary, a small number of regional primaries, or restricting the time frame. Several new problems, however, arise from these suggestions. For example, candidates who could raise money early in the primary process, or any candidate who came from the region with the earliest primary, would be advantaged. Such changes would also give even more emphasis to television campaigning. Moreover, these suggestions focus too narrowly on primaries and candidates as the culprits for deviations from democratic ideals. Likewise, the call for fewer primaries, or a return to party conventions, ignores the historical reason for increasing the number of primaries during the 1970s; namely, as a remedy for a politics that was controlled by a few party bosses from the private confines of smoke filled rooms.

Reforms aimed at improving the electoral system by regulating political advertising or increasing voter registration also have certain limitations. Freedom of speech issues aside, proposals for regulating political ads because they are thought to be highly manipulative (see Chapter 8 by Rucinski for a discussion of how people perceive the impact of ads) fail to understand the power of symbols. Technically speaking, neither the revolving door or Willie Horton ads of 1988 could be labeled objectively racist. Yet, because of the symbols used in the ads it was quite evident that they were meant to evoke racial stereotypes and fears. Trying to regulate subtle cues symbolically generated by campaign ads would result in creating a bottomless legal morass. Some critics have suggested that legal problems connected with voter fraud likewise will be the only result from relaxed voter registration practices such as allowing citizens to register for voting when they obtain their drivers license. More likely, such reforms will produce a one-time increase in turnout, but they will not reverse the trend of declining turnout, nor will they produce more responsive candidates or more diligent journalists.

The types of reforms that will prove most effective are those that will increase competition among candidates and promote the watchdog role of the media. As Monica Bauer argues in Chapter 13, many of these reforms would involve changing the structure of financing campaigns. Those candidates who get more money obviously have greater access to the means of sending their message to the voter. The ability of a candidate to get his or her message to the voters does not necessarily guarantee that the message will be enthusiastically received, but if a candidate is unable, the inability to put the message before the public guarantees failure. The quality of the candidates we elect and the future of democracy should rest ideally on the content of the campaign message, not the volume or frequency. If a sound democracy depends on an unrestricted consideration of alternative views, then those factors that deter an open dialogue must be addressed in any attempt to reform the system. Campaign financing is clearly one of those factors.

No one would disagree with the argument that in many respects the ability of a candidate to raise money is a symbol of success and appeal. The issue, therefore, is not to restrict the competition for funding, but to assure that the sources of those funds represent a broad spectrum of society. Loopholes in campaign finance legislation have allowed lobbyists and big monied interests to dominate the financing of campaigns. Those loopholes need to be closed, and reforms that give political parties increased control over campaign financing ought to be considered. In this age of partisan dealignment, incentives are needed to return parties to their historical role of aggregating political interests—not only among the electorate but in Congress as well.

It takes more than good ideas for a president to govern effectively. The public has an image of the presidency as the most powerful political office in the country if not in the world. This image makes it difficult for the public to understand why the president is unable to fulfill campaign pledges. Yet, any president can only succeed if Congress is willing to work with him. During periods when party attachment and loyalty have declined it is very difficult for a president to accomplish his proposed legislative goals. Reforms that only focus on the presidency or presidential campaigns, therefore, are bound to have a limited effect. Out of frustration with gridlock and ineffective government, some states have initiated term limits for legislators, thus hoping to improve the quality of representation. There is some evidence indicating that the quality of representation (measured as the fit between constituency preferences and the positions taken by representatives on roll calls) does improve with election turnover (see Stone 1980). Nevertheless, while having new members in Congress may produce better representation of district interests, it does not necessarily increase loyalty to the president's program. Giving the national political parties more control over congressional campaign funding, however, might produce more congressional party loyalty and improve the effectiveness of government policy making.

Some critics argue that the two-party system itself is the basis of political problems in the United States. They suggest that the development of a third party would be the best way to reinvigorate the U.S. political system. These critics point to the rise in turnout that occurred in 1992, as well as the 19% vote for Perot, as evidence that a significant segment of Americans is alienated from the two-party system. We agree that political alienation is widespread, and that there is a good deal of disenchantment with both major political parties. An independent or third party candidate thus improves the functioning of democracy by giving voice to the otherwise unrepresented sentiments. But, pragmatically speaking, having an independent candidate elected president would be a disaster if the goal is effective government. In the case of Perot, he did not form a third political party with a slate of congressional candidates who, if elected, could pass his programs; rather he ran as a sole individual. Even if Perot had been elected, there would have been little incentive for Democrats or Republicans in Congress to support any of his policies. After all, there would be no third-party candidate waiting to defeat these uncooperative members if they failed to support the president's proposals.

However, independent candidates do serve to send a message to the two parties, and thereby have an impact on the political system. Both Clinton and Bush modified their positions and appeals somewhat in 1992 so as to attract potential Perot supporters. Independent candidates play an ongoing role in the reformation of the two-party system. They force the two parties to deal with issues that they might otherwise ignore, they act as an indicator of voter discontent, and they reaffirm the image of America as a place that is open to the exchange of alternative views.

Reforms directed at the media's role in campaigns that would seem most beneficial to meeting democratic ideals are those that would similarly promote increased expression of alternative views. For example, during the 1992 primaries the networks carried a number of debates among the early Democratic contenders. Debates also have become more commonplace during the general election, although the politics surrounding the debate schedule and format have frequently threatened to overwhelm the relevance of the debates themselves. The media had tried to eliminate the politics over the 1992 debates by specifying the format and number of debates prior to the start of the campaign, but the candidates were unwilling to abide by these guidelines. Further institutionalization of the debates are necessary to eliminate this unfortunate squabbling. For better or worse, the 1992 campaign also witnessed new debate formats that reduced the role of media correspondents in the debates. In particular, the second presidential debate involved a town meeting format with the candidates sitting on bar stools taking questions from the audience. In theory, this format served the purpose of making citizens feel that they were a part of the campaign process. This may have been true, but the format was far from neutral; it clearly advantaged Clinton. It gave him an opportunity to symbolically demonstrate responsiveness to people by allowing him to move from his bar stool and step into the audience when answering certain questions.

The candidate monitoring function of the media was also bypassed in 1992 when the candidates took to appearing more frequently on entertainment talk shows than before enquiring news correspondents for interviews. Again, this provides a more direct line of communication with a variety of audiences, but it eliminates the possibility for journalists to ask probing questions. To offset this evasion of the hard question, the serious correspondents and journalists will need to use more creative methods for critiquing the public statements candidates make by comparing those messages with voter preferences, calling on interest groups to comment on them, comparing them with the congressional agenda, or determining the accuracy of statements based on facts or factually based assumptions. These critiques, however, need to be cumulative, compare the candidates, and be relevant to voter concerns, or otherwise the public will be right to ignore them.

It is curious how the stipulation of reforms generally focuses on changing candidates and the media. Rarely does one read about reforming the public. Given our tripartite view of politics, it would be hypocritical to endorse systemic reforms aimed at changing the role of politicians and the media in the campaign process while ignoring the electorate. Yet what does it mean to aim reforms at the electorate? We certainly are not advocating social engineering. Systemic changes aimed at encouraging involvement and participation, such as universal registration, were mentioned earlier. These reforms fit with the goal of striving toward the image of an ideal democratic citizen, but history suggests that they will have limited impact.

After all, participation in U.S. elections during the modern era peaked in 1960 at 64%. Registration has become increasingly easy and widespread since 1960, but with no corresponding long-term rise in overall election participation rates.

Long ago we might have placed our hope for increasing civic involvement with the extension of higher education, but even this has proven disappointing. The public is far better educated in 1992 than it was in 1960; in 1960 only 22% had at least some college or professional training beyond high school, in 1992 that figure had risen to 47%. Yet the public today is no more interested in politics than it was 30 years ago. According to data from the NES, in 1960, when a sample of adults were asked to what extent they generally followed what was going on in government and public affairs, 22% responded "most of the time," 41% said "some of the time," and 37% said "only now and then" or "hardly at all." The corresponding figures obtained by the 1992 NES were 26% "most of the time," 42% "some of the time" and 32% "only now and then." The 1992 results are very similar to those obtained in 1960, and remember the 1992 data reflect a short-term boost in interest due to Ross Perot. Perhaps the obvious conclusion suggested by these data is that if the system needs reforming, then those reforms aimed at increasing the accountability and responsiveness of politicians and the media will be the most effective. As for the electorate, we can only wait until tomorrow to determine if the current indications of a growing citizen revolt (such as the support for Perot and the increasing call for term limits) will lead to demands that politicians rise above divisive, exclusionary politics to promote principled policy proposals, as well as insisting that the media provides accurate, substantively relevant coverage of presidential campaigns.

Tomorrow's Agenda

Every election provides a new agenda for tomorrow. Those who are elected turn to constructing a mandate and then strive to fulfill it. Those defeated in the election turn to reconstructing their party while deconstructing the actions, messages, and decisions that brought them defeat. Election scholars and political pundits set about sifting through the myriad speeches, surveys, broadcasts, and precinct returns searching for clues that offer a deeper understanding of social and human development.

Each iteration through the electoral process provides some new insights and some new answers, but invariably it also suggests unanswered questions that should be addressed in the examination of tomorrow's elections. This volume is no exception to that rule. Numerous questions deserve more attention in the future than they were given here. For example, the ways in which declining partisanship has altered the campaign process and the implications of this for American self images deserve extended analysis. The extent to which negative campaign ads undermine citizen respect for political authorities or government in general, as well as one's sense of citizen pride, also warrants further attention. Another topic deserving additional research is whether or not the use of political ads, or messages, that play upon divisions among social groups leave people feeling more comfortable with their stereotypes and prejudices, or in other ways enhance social polarization. Likewise, there is still a great deal to be learned about how individual judgments of moral virtue or right and wrong are influenced by the morality of candidates, or how personal feelings of political efficacy are affected by the success or failure of the president's legislative programs. All of these questions about the relationship between self images and presidential campaign politics remain to be answered by tomorrow's research. Based on the experience of this volume we conclude that this future research will be most fruitful if it utilizes an approach that simultaneously examines elections from the perspective of candidates, media and citizen-voters.

Every election also leaves a future agenda for society as a whole. Presidential campaigns offer all Americans an opportunity to create the image of the government and political community they want, as well as the types of leaders they prefer to represent them. If, in the process of electing and governing, they fall short of those ideal images, they find it easier to reject these particular leaders, or current circumstances, as exceptions, rather than rejecting the goals and the ideal images. Hence, every four years they return to reaffirm what they are striving for, and to determine once again how close they have come.

About the Book

This volume explores a central political paradox: why American scholars, journalists, and citizens periodically question the viability of their presidential electoral system and yet believe that presidential elections are our best hope for tomorrow. The book argues that the key to understanding this paradox lies in the concept of "self image," exploring relationships between campaign activities and political culture. After presenting an introduction to the history of presidential campaigning and a theory of political image, the book arranges essays in three parts: images centered on candidates, mass media, and the public. A final essay assesses explanations of the contrasts between the 1988 and 1992 elections and suggests tomorrow's research agenda.

About the Editors and
the Contributors

Arthur H. Miller is Professor of Political Science and Director of the Iowa Social Science Institute at the University of Iowa. He specializes in studies of public opinion and electoral behavior, both in America and comparatively.

Bruce E. Gronbeck is Professor of Communication Studies, the University of Iowa, Iowa City. He is a specialist in rhetorical studies, with particular interests in politics, media, and cultural studies.

Monica Bauer is Adjunct Professor of Political Science at Quinsigamond College in Worchester, MA, and the co-author of *Financing the 1988 Elections* (1990, Westview Press).

David Birdsell is Associate Professor of Speech at Baruch College of the City University of New York. He studies rhetoric and argumentation.

G. R. Boynton is Professor of Political Science at the University of Iowa. He specializes in political communication, with special interest in congressional committee and electoral decision making.

Cary R. Covington is Associate Professor of Political Science, the University of Iowa, Iowa City. His research focuses on the presidency, emphasizing both the electoral and governance aspects of the institution.

Kent R. Kroeger is a Ph.D. candidate at the University of Iowa.

Ronald Lee is Associate Professor of Communication Studies at the University of Nebraska-Lincoln. He is a specialist in rhetorical studies, with particular interests in contemporary American public address, political discourse, and public argumentation.

Milton Lodge is Professor of Political Science, State University of New York at Stony Brook. His general interest is in political psychology, with a particular interest in political cognition.

Daniel M. Merkle is a Ph.D. student in the Department of Communication Studies at Northwestern University. His research interests include mass communication effects, public opinion, and survey methodology.

Peter V. Miller is Associate Professor of Communication Studies and Journalism and Director of the Institute for Modern Communication at Northwestern University. He specializes in studies of public opinion and media measurement.

Joanne Morreale is Associate Professor of Communication Studies,

Northeastern University, Boston, MA. Her research interests are in televisual communication and politics.

Glenn Richardson is an instructor in the Department of Political Science and Philosophy at Weber State University in Ogden, UT. He is a specialist in political communication with particular interests in the media, campaigns, and the presidency.

Dianne Rucinski is Assistant Professor of Communication Studies at the University of Iowa. She is a specialist in media and politics with particular interest in the formation and political use of public opinion.

J. David Woodard is an Associate Professor of Political Science at Clemson University, Clemson, SC. He is interested in media research and Southern politics.

Harold. M. Zullow is a Research Psychologist at the New York State Psychiatric Institute, Columbia University, New York City. He is a specialist in political and economic psychology, with emphasis on the relationship between politics, the economy, and mental health in the U.S.

Bibliography

Abelson, R.P. (1968). Simulation of social behavior. In G. Lindzey & E. Aronson (Eds.), *The handbook of social psychology Volume 2: Research Methods* (2nd ed.) (pp. 274-356). Reading, MA: Addision-Wesley Publishing Company.

Abramson, L.Y., Seligman, M.E.P., & Teasdale, J.D. (1978). Learned helplessness in humans: Critique and reformulation. *Journal of Abnormal Psychology* 37: 49-74.

Abramson, P.R. (1983). *Political attitudes in America: Formation and change.* San Francisco: W.H. Freeman and Company.

Abramson, P.R., & Aldrich, J.H. (1982). The decline of electoral participation in America. *The American Political Science Review* 76: 502-521.

Abramson, P.R., Aldrich, J.H., Paolino, P., & Rhode, D.W. (1992). 'Sophisticated' voting in the 1988 presidential primaries. *The American Political Science Review* 86: 55-69.

Abramson, P.R., Aldrich, J.H., & Rohde, D.W. (1982). *Change and continuity in the 1980 elections.* Washington, DC: Congressional Quarterly Press.

_____ . (1990). *Change and continuity in the 1988 elections.* Washington, DC: Congressional Quarterly Press.

Adams, F.G., & Klein, L.R. (1972). Anticipation variables in macro-econometric models. In B. Strumpel, J.N. Morgan, & E. Zahn (Eds.), *Human behavior in economic affairs: Essays in honor of George Katona* (pp. 289-319). San Francisco: Jossey-Bass, Inc.

Adams, W.C. (1984). Media coverage of Campaign '84: A preliminary report. *Public Opinion* 7: 9-13.

Adams, W.C., & Schreibman, F. (Eds.). (1978). *Television network news: Issues in content research.* Washington, DC: George Washington University Press.

Ailes, R. (Executive Producer). (1988). *Bush campaign film.* [Film on videotape]. Available from Political Commercial Archives, University of Oklahoma, Norman, OK.

Aldrich, J.H., Gant, M.M., & Simon, D.M. (1978). *To the victor belong the spoils: Momentum in the 1976 nomination campaigns.* Unpublished manuscript. Cited in H.B. Asher (1992), *Presidential elections and American politics* (p. 261) (5th ed.). Pacific Grove, CA: Brooks/Cole Publishing Company.

Aldrich, J.H., & Simon, D.M. (1986). Turnout in American national elections. In S.L. Long (Ed), *Research in micropolitics Volume 1: Voting Behavior.* Greenwich, CT: JAI Press.

Alexander, H.E. (1971). *Financing the 1968 election.* Lexington, MA: Heath Lexington Books.

_____ . (Ed.). (1976). *Campaign money: Reform and reality in the United States.* New York: The Free Press.

_____ . (1987). *Financing the 1984 election.* New York: The Free Press.

Alexander, H.E., & Bauer, M. (1991) *Financing the 1988 election.* Boulder, CO: Westview Press.

Allport, F.H. (1940). Polls and the science of public opinion. *Public Opinion Quarterly* 4: 249-257.

Altschuler, B.E. (1982). *Keeping a finger on the public pulse: Private polling and presidential elections.* Westport, CT: Greenwood Press.

Anderson, B., Spiro, R., & Montague, J. (Eds.). (1977). *Schooling and the acquisition of knowledge.* Hillsdale, NJ: Lawrence Erlbaum Associates.

Anderson, J.A. (Ed.). (1991). *Communication yearbook 14.* Newbury Park, CA: Sage Publications.

Anderson, J.R. (1983). *The architecture of cognition.* Cambridge: Harvard University Press.

Anderson, N., & Hubert, S. (1963). Effects of concomitant recall on order effects in personality impression formation. *Journal of Verbal Learning and Verbal Behavior* 2: 379-391.

Anderson, N.H. (1989). Functional memory and on-line attribution. In J.N. Bassili (Ed.), *On-line cognition in person perception* (pp. 175-220). Hillsdale, NJ: Lawrence Erlbaum Associates.

Anderson, J.A. (Ed.) *Communication yearbook 14*. Newbury Park, CA: Sage Publications.

Apple, R.W., Jr. (1976 February 25). Ideology the key factor. *The New York Times*, 1+.

_____. (1992 January 21). Debate is mere tuneup on democrat's journey. *The New York Times*, A-19.

_____. (1992 March 2). Candidates go on attack, mostly gently, in three debates. *The New York Times*, A-12.

Aristotle. (1932). *The rhetoric of Aristotle*. (L. Cooper, Trans.). New York: Appleton-Century-Croft.

_____. (1954). *Rhetoric: Poetics*. (W.R. Roberts & I. Bywater, Trans.). New York: The Modern Library.

Arterton, F.C. (1984). *Media politics: The news strategies of presidential campaigns*. Lexington, MA: Lexington Books.

_____. (1987). *Teledemocracy*. Newbury Park, CA: Sage Publications.

Asher, H.B. (1992). *Presidential elections and American politics* (5th ed.). Pacific Grove, CA: Brooks/Cole Publishing Company.

Atkin, C. (1969). The impact of political poll results on candidate and issue preferences. *Journalism Quarterly* 46: 515-521.

Atkinson, R., Herrnstein, R., Lindzey, G., & Luce, R.D. (Eds.). (1983). *Stevens' handbook of experimental psychology*. New York: John Wiley & Sons.

_____. (1988). *Stevens' handbook of experimental psychology Volume 2: Learning and cognition*. New York: John Wiley & Sons.

Auer, J.J. (1962). The counterfeit debates. In S. Kraus (Ed.), *The great debates: Background, perspective, effects* (pp. 142-150). Bloomington: Indiana University Press.

Babbitt, B. (1988). The democratic workplace. In R.E. Levin (Ed.), *Democratic blueprints: 40 national leaders chart America's future* (pp. 3-12). New York: Hippocrene Books.

Baker, R.K. (1991 December 17). Simply put, the democrats lack guts. *Los Angeles Times*, B-7.

_____. (1992 January 22). Watch the republicans for the main event. *Los Angeles Times*, B-7.

Bartels, L.M. (1985). Expectations and preferences in presidential nominating campaigns. *The American Political Science Review* 79: 804-815.

Bartels, L.M., & Broh, C.A. (1989). The polls—A review: The 1988 presidential primaries. *The Public Opinion Quarterly* 53: 563-589.

Basil, M., Schooler, C., & Reeves, B. (1991). Positive and negative political advertising: Effectiveness of ads and perceptions of candidates. In F. Biocca (Ed.), *Television and political advertising Volume 1: Psychological processes* (pp. 245-262). Hillsdale, NJ: Lawrence Erlbaum Associates.

Bassili, J.N. (Ed.). (1989). *On-line cognition in person perception*. Hillsdale, NJ: Lawrence Erlbaum Associates.

Becker, S.L., & Lower, E.W. (1979). Broadcasting in presidential campaigns. In S. Kraus (Ed.), *The great debates: Carter vs. Ford, 1976* (pp. 22-55). Bloomington: Indiana University Press.

Behr, R.L., & Iyengar, S. (1983). Television news, real-world cues, and changes in the public agenda. *The Public Opinion Quarterly* 49: 38-57.

Belmore, S. (1987). Determinants of attention during impression formation. *Journal of Experimental Psychology: Learning, Memory and Cognition* 13: 480-489.

Beniger, J. (1976). Winning the presidential nomination: National polls and state primary election. *The Public Opinion Quarterly* 40: 22-38.

Bennett, W.L., & Edelman, M.J. (1985). Toward a new political narrative. *Journal of Communication* 35: 156-171.

Bennett, W.L. (1977). The ritualistic and pragmatic bases of political campaign discourse. *Quarterly Journal of Speech* 63: 219-238.

_____ . (1988). *News: The politics of illusion* (2nd ed.). New York: Longman.

_____ . (1992) *The governing crisis: Media, money and marketing in American elections.* New York: St. Martin's Press.

Berelson, B.R., Lazarsfeld, P.F., & McPhee, W.N. (1954). *Voting: A study of opinion formation in a presidential campaign.* Chicago, IL: University of Chicago Press.

Biocca, F. (Ed.). (1991). *Television and political advertising Volume 1: Psychological processes.* Hillsdale, NJ: Lawrence Erlbaum Associates.

_____ . (Ed.). (1991). *Television and political advertising Volume 2: Signs, codes, and images.* Hillsdale, NJ: Lawrence Erlbaum Associates.

Bitzer, L. (1968). The rhetorical situation. *Philosophy and Rhetoric* 1: 1-14.

Bitzer, L., & Reuter, T. (1980). *Carter vs. Ford: The counterfeit debates of 1976.* Madison: University of Wisconsin Press.

Black, C.M., & Oliphant, T. (1989). *All by myself: The unmaking of a presidential campaign.* Chester, CT: The Globe Pequot Press.

Black, E. (1973). Electing time. *Quarterly Journal of Speech* 59: 125-129.

Black, G. (1991 October 7). TV tinkering won't plumb Bush mystique. *Los Angeles Times*, B-5.

Black, G.S., & Black, B.D. (1993). "Perot wins!" The election that could have been. *The Public Perspective* 4: 15-16.

Bloom, M. (1973). *Public relations and presidential campaigns: A crisis in democracy.* New York: Thomas Y. Crowell.

Bloor, D. (1982). Durkheim and Mauss revisited: Classification and the sociology of knowledge. *Studies in History and Philosophy of Science* 13: 267-297.

_____ . (1983). *Wittgenstein: A social theory of knowledge.* New York: Columbia University Press.

Blumenthal, S. (1990). *Pledging allegiance: The last campaign of the Cold War.* New York: HarperCollins.

Bobo, L. (1983). Whites' opposition to busing: Symbolic racism or realistic group conflict? *Journal of Personality and Social Psychology* 45: 1196-1210.

Bode, C. (1968). *The American lyceum: Town meeting of the mind.* Carbondale: Southern Illinois University Press.

Boggs, C. (1983). The new populism and the limits of structural reforms. *Theory and Society* 12: 343-363.

Boller, P.F., Jr. (1985). *Presidential campaigns.* New York: Oxford University Press.

Boynton, G.R. (1990). Our conversations about governing. Paper presented at the 1990 meeting of the American Political Science Association.

Boyte, H.C. (1978). Building the Democratic movement: Prospects for a Socialist renaissance. *Socialist Review* 8: 17-41.

_____ . (1980). *The backyard revolution: Understanding the new citizen movement.* Philadelphia: Temple University Press.

_____ . (1986). Beyond politics as usual. In H.C. Boyte & F. Riessman (Eds.), *The new populism: The politics of empowerment* (pp. 3-15). Philadelphia: Temple University Press.

Boyte, H.C. & Riessman, F. (Eds.). (1986). *The new populism: The politics of empowerment.* Philadelphia: Temple University Press.

Brady, H.E., & Johnston, R. (1987). What's the primary message: Horse race or journalism? In G.R. Orren & N.W. Polsby (Eds.), *Media and momentum: The New Hampshire primary and nomination politics.* Chatham, NJ: Chatham House.

Brady, H.E. and Sniderman, P.M. (1985). Attitude attribution: A group basis for political reasoning. *American Political Review* 79, 1061-78.

Brewer, M.B. (1979). In-group bias in the minimal intergroup situation: A cognitive motivational analysis. *Psychological Bulletin* 86: 307-324.

Brock, B.L. (1969). 1968 Democratic campaign: A political upheaval. *Quarterly Journal of Speech* 55: 26-35.

Broder, D.S. (1975). The presidency and the press. In C.W. Dunn (Ed.), *The future of the American presidency* (pp. 255-268). Morristown, NJ: General Learning Press.

_____ . (1976). Assessing campaign reform: Lessons for the future. In H.E. Alexander (Ed.), *Campaign money: Reform and reality in the United States* (pp. 307-321). New York: The Free Press.

_____ . (1990 January 14). Five ways to put some sanity back in elections. *The Washington Post*, B-1+.

_____ . (1991 June 5). Why politics is alienating voters. *Des Moines Register*, 6A.

Broh, C.A. (1983). Polls, pols, and parties. *The Journal of Politics* 45: 732-744.

Brokaw, T. (1987). Networks should sponsor debates. In J.L. Swerdlow (Ed.), *Presidential debates: 1988 and beyond.* (pp. 73-76). Washington, D.C.: Congressional Quarterly Press.

Brown Brothers (Producers). (1923). *Master of emergencies.* [Film on videotape]. Available from Herbert Hoover Presidential Library, West Branch, IA.

Brown, C.A. (1982). A false consensus bias in 1980 presidential preferences. *Journal of Social Psychology* 118: 137-138.

Brown, R.H. (1987). *Society as text: Essays on rhetoric, reason, and reality.* Chicago, IL: University of Chicago Press.

Brown, W.B. (1960). *The people's choice: The presidential image in the campaign biography.* Baton Rouge: Louisiana State University Press.

Burke, E. (1780-1963). Speech to the sheriffs of Bristol. In C.A. Goodrich (Ed.), *Select British eloquence* (pp. 292-310). Indianapolis: Bobbs-Merrill Company.

_____ . (1774-1960). Speech to the electors of Bristol. In The Member for Barchester (Ed.), *British orations from Ethelbert to Churchill* (pp. 67-73). (revised ed.). New York: E.P. Dutton.

Burke, K. (1955). *A grammar of motives.* New York: George Braziller.

_____ . (1969). *A grammar of motives* (revised ed.). Berkeley: University of California Press.

Burns, J.M. (1978). *Leadership.* New York: Harper & Row.

Burt, R. (1980a August 28). Disclosure of radar-evading plane assailed at house panel's hearing. *The New York Times*, A-16.

_____ . (1980b September 7). Administration tightening system of keeping national secrets secret. *The New York Times*, A-1+.

Campbell, A., Converse, P.E., Miller, W.E. & Stokes, D.E. (1960). *The American voter.* Chicago, IL: University of Chicago Press.

Campbell, D.T. (1963). From description to experimentation: Interpreting trends as quasi-experiments. In C.W. Harris (Ed.), *Problems in measuring change* (pp. 212-242). Madison: University of Wisconsin Press.

_____ . (1958). On the possibility of experimenting with the 'bandwagon' effect. *International Journal of Opinion and Attitude Research* 5: 251-260.

Cantril, A.H. (1980). *Polling on the issues: A report from the Kettering Foundation.* Cabin John, MD: Seven Locks Press.

Cantril, A.H. & Cantril, S.D. (1991). *The opinion connection: Polling, politics, and the press.* Washington, DC: Congressional Quarterly Press.

Carmines, E.G. & Stimson, J.A. (1989). *Issue evolution: Race and the transformation of American politics.* Princeton, NJ: Princeton University Press.

Carroll, J. (1978). The effect of imagining an event on expectations for the event: An interpretation in terms of the availability heuristic. *Journal of Experimental and Social Psychology* 14: 88-96.

Carson, S. (1952 November 15). 'Ike and Mike': Television and the election. *Nation*, 449-450.

Carter, J. (1976 August 15). Democratic national convention: Acceptance speech. *Vital Speeches of the Day*, 642-644.

_____ . (1977). *A government as good as its people.* New York: Simon & Schuster.

_____ . (1982). Remarks accepting the presidential nomination at the 1980 Democratic national convention. *Public Papers of the Presidents of the United States: Jimmy Carter* 1980-1981 (pp. 1532-1540). Washington, DC: United States Government Printing Office.

Ceaser, J.W. (1984). *American government: Origins, institutions, and public policy.* New York:

McGraw-Hill.

Ceci, S.J., & Kain, E.L. (1982). Jumping on the bandwagon with the underdog: The impact of attitude polls on polling behavior. *The Public Opinion Quarterly* 46: 228-242.

Chagall, D. (1981). *The new kingmakers*. New York: Harcourt Brace Jovanovich.

Citizens and politics: A view from main street America. (1991). Dayton, OH: The Kettering Foundation.

Clancy, M., & Robinson, M.J. (1985). General election coverage: Part I. In M.J. Robinson & A. Ranney (Eds.), *The mass media in Campaign '84: Articles from Public Opinion magazine* (pp. 27-33). Washington, DC: American Enterprise Institute for Public Policy Research.

Cloutier, E., Nadeau, R., & Guay, J. (1989). Bandwagoning and underdogging on North-American Free Trade: A quasi-experimental panel study of opinion movement. *International Journal of Public Opinion Research* 1: 206-220.

Cohen, J., Mutz, D., Price, V., & Gunther, A. (1988). Perceived impact of defamation: An experiment on third-person effects. *The Public Opinion Quarterly* 52: 161-173.

Combs, J.E. & Mansfield, R.W. (Eds.). (1976). *Drama in life: The uses of communication in society.* New York: Hastings House.

Comstock, G. (1978). *Television and human behavior.* New York: Columbia University Press.

Congressional Quarterly (1972, 12 August). Weekly report. Republicans: Well organized, well financed in 1972, pp. 1984-87.

Conover, P. Johnston. (1984). The influence of group identification on political perception and evaluation. *Journal of Politics* 46: 760-785.

Conover, P., & Feldman, S. (1989). Candidate perception in an ambiguous world: Campaigns, cues, and inference processes. *American Journal of Political Science* 33: 912-940.

Cook, R. (1988 July 16). Dukakis shows potential for broad fall appeal. *Congressional Quarterly Weekly Report*, 1949-1951.

Cook, S.W., & Welch, A.C. (1940). Methods of measuring the practical effect of polls of public opinion. *Journal of Applied Psychology* 24: 441-454.

Coyne, J.C., & Gotlib, I. (1983). The role of cognition in depression: A critical appraisal. *Psychological Bulletin* 94: 472-505.

Cragan, J.F., & Cutbirth, C.W. (1984). A revisionist perspective on political ad hominem argument: A case study. *Central States Speech Journal* 35: 228-237.

Crane, M. (1982). Perceptions of public opinion. Unpublished doctoral dissertation, The University of Michigan.

Crespi, I. (1988). *Pre-election polling: Sources of accuracy and error.* New York: Russell Sage Foundation.

Crewe, I. (1982). 'Improving, but could do better': The media and the polls in the 1979 general election. In R.M. Worcester & M. Harrop (Eds.), *Political communications: The general election campaign of 1979.* (pp. 115-125) Boston: George Allen & Unwin.

Cronin, T.E. (Ed.). (1982). *Rethinking the presidency.* Boston: Little, Brown and Company.

Crotty, W. (Ed.). (1991). *Political science: Looking to the future Volume 3.* Evanston, IL: Northwestern University Press.

Czitrom, D.J. (1982). *Media and the American mind: From Morse to McLuhan.* Chapel Hill: University of North Carolina Press.

Dallek, R. (1984). *Ronald Reagan: The politics of symbolism.* Cambridge: Harvard University Press.

Davis, R. (1992). *The press and American politics: The new mediator.* New York: Longman.

Davison, W.P. (1983). The third-person effect in communication. *The Public Opinion Quarterly* 47: 1-15.

De Rochemont, L. (Producer). (1948). *The Dewey story* [Film on videotape]. Available for viewing at Schuck Collection, Kennedy Presidential Library, Boston, MA.

Deardourff, J. (1990 December 14). Interview with John Deardourff, Political Consultant, Bailey-Deardourff Associates, Falls Church, VA.

Debates '92: The PBS format. (1992 February 8). *The Washington Post*, A-20.

DeBono, K.G. (1987). Investigating the social-adjustive and value-expressive functions of attitudes: Implications for persuasion processes. *Journal of Personality and Social Psychology* 52: 279-287.

DeMaio, T.J. (1984). Social desirability and survey measurement: A review. In C.F. Turner & E. Martin (Eds.), *Surveying subjective phenomena Volume 2* (pp. 257-282). New York: Russell Sage Foundation.

Demers, D.P. (1987). Use of polls in reporting changes slightly since 1978. *Journalism Quarterly* 64: 839-842.

Dennis, J. (1987). Groups and political behavior: Legitimation, deprivation, and competing values. *Political Behavior* 9: 323-372.

DeNove, R. (Producer). (1960). *The new frontier* [Film on videotape]. Available from Kennedy Presidential Library, Boston, MA.

Denton, R.E., Jr. (1982). *The symbolic dimensions of the American presidency.* Prospect Heights, IL: Waveland Press.

_____ . (1988). *The primetime presidency of Ronald Reagan: The era of the television presidency.* New York: Praeger.

_____ . (1991). Primetime politics: The ethics of teledemocracy. In R.E. Denton, Jr. (Ed.), *Ethical dimensions of political communication* (pp. 91-114). New York: Praeger.

_____ . (Ed.). (1991). *Ethical dimensions of political communication.* New York: Praeger.

Descutner, D., Burnier, D., Mickunas, A., & Letteri, R. (1991). Bad signs and cryptic codes in a postmodern world: A semiotic analysis of the Dukakis advertising. In F. Biocca (Ed.), *Television and political advertising Volume 2: Signs, codes, and images,* (pp. 93-114). Hillsdale, NJ: Lawrence Erlbaum Associates.

DeVries, W & Tarrance, L., Jr. (1972). *The ticket splitter: A new force in American politics.* Grand Rapids, MI: William B. Eerdmans Publishing Company.

Diamond, E., & Bates, S. (1984). *The spot: The rise of political advertising on television.* Cambridge, MA: MIT Press.

Diamond, E., & Friery, K. (1987). Media coverage of presidential debates. In J.L. Swerdlow (Ed.), *Presidential debates: 1988 and beyond* . Washington, DC: Congressional Quarterly Press.

Digging past political pearls. (1991 December 17). *The New York Times,* A-20.

Dionne, E.J., Jr. (1988 January 4). Stump speeches. *The New York Times,* 12.

_____ . (1991). *Why Americans hate politics.* New York: Simon & Schuster.

Dizney, H.F., & Roskens, R.W. (1962). An investigation of the bandwagon effects in a college straw election. *Journal of Educational Sociology* 35: 108-14.

Dovidio, J., & Gaertner, S.L. (Eds.). (1986). *Prejudice, discrimination and racism.* New York: Academic Press.

Downs, A. (1957). *An economic theory of democracy.* New York: Harper & Row.

Drew, D.G., & Weaver, D. (1991). Voter learning in the 1988 presidential election: Did the debates and the media matter? *Journalism Quarterly* 68: 27-37.

Drucker, S.J., & Platt Hunold, J. (1987). The debating game. *Critical Studies in Mass Communication* 4: 202-206.

Duncan, D. (1991). *Grass roots: One year in the life of the New Hampshire presidential primary.* New York: Viking.

Dunn, C.W. (Ed.). (1975). *The future of the American presidency.* Morristown, NJ: General Learning Press.

Dusenberry, P. (1990 December 13). Interview with Phil Dusenberry, Vice President, BBD&O, New York.

_____ . (Producer). (1984). *A new beginning* [Film on videotape]. Available from Republican National Committee, Washington, DC.

Dye, T.R., & Zeigler, H. (1975). *The irony of democracy: An uncommon introduction to American politics* (3rd edition). North Scituate, MA: Duxbury Press.

_____ . (1989). *American politics in the media age* (3rd ed.). Pacific Grove, CA: Brooks/Cole Publishing Co.

Dyer, M.G. (1983). *In-depth understanding; A computer model of integrated processing for narrative comprehension*. Cambridge, MA: MIT Press.

Edelman, M. (1964). *The symbolic uses of politics*. Urbana: University of Illinois Press.

_____ . (1971). *Politics as symbolic action: Mass arousal and quiescence*. New York: Academic Press.

_____ . (1977). *Political language: Words that succeed and policies that fail*. New York: Academic Press.

_____ . (1988). *Constructing the political spectacle*. Chicago, IL: University of Chicago Press.

Editors of Time. (1988). *The winning of the White House 1988*. New York: Time, Inc.

Edsall, T.B. (1989). *Power and money: Writing about politics, 1971-1987*. New York: W.W. Norton.

Edsall, T.B. & Edsall, M.D. (1991). When the official subject is presidential politics, taxes, welfare, crime, rights, or values ... the real subject is race. *The Atlantic Monthly* 267: 53-86.

_____ . (1992). *Chain reaction*. New York: W.W. Norton.

Ehrenhalt, A. (1987 May 9). Gary Hart: Downfall of a rootless candidate. *Congressional Quarterly Weekly Report*, 955.

Elbert, D. (1984 October 14). Iowa poll discloses gains by Democrats. *Des Moines Register*, 1A+.

Election Special. (1988 November 21). *Newsweek*.

Epstein, E.J. (1974). *News from nowhere: Television and the news*. New York: Random House.

Erickson, P.D. (1985). *Reagan speaks: The making of an American myth*. New York: New York University Press.

Ervin, Sam J., Jr. (1974). Foreward. In F.C. Mosher et al. (Eds.), *Watergate: Implication for responsible government*. New York: Basic Books.

Evans, R., & Novak, R. (1966). *Lyndon Johnson: The exercise of power*. New York: Signet Books.

Evans, S.M., & Boyte, H.C. (1986). *Free spaces: The sources of Democratic change in America*. New York: Harper & Row.

Face off: A conversation with the presidents' pollsters Patrick Caddell and Richard Wirthlin. (1981). *Public Opinion*, 3: 2-12, 63-64.

Fair, R.C. (1988). The effect of economic events on votes for presidents: 1984 update. *Political Behavior* 10: 168-179.

Fallows, J. (1984). The presidency and the press. In M. Nelson (Ed.), *The presidency and the political system* (pp. 264-281). Washington, DC: Congressional Quarterly Press.

Farley, J.A. (1938). *Behind the ballots: A personal history of a politician*. New York: Harcourt, Brace and Company.

FCC v. Pacifica Foundation 438 U.S. 726.

Feldman, S., and Conover, P. (1991). Explaining explanations of changing economic conditions. In H. Norpoth, M.S. Lewis-Beck and J.D. Lafay (Ed.), *Economics and politics: The calculus of support* (pp. 185-206). Ann Arbor: University of Michigan Press.

Fielding, R. (1972). *The American newsreel: 1911-1967*. Norman: University of Oklahoma Press.

Fields, J.M., & Schuman, H. (1976). Public beliefs about beliefs of the public. *Public Opinion Quarterly* 40: 431-445.

Fiorina, M.P. (1981). *Retrospective voting in American national elections*. New Haven, CT: Yale University Press.

Fisher, W. (1973). Reaffirmation and subversion of the American dream. *Quarterly Journal of Speech* 59: 160-167.

_____ . (1987). *Human communication as narration: Toward a philosophy of reason, value, and action*. Columbia: University of South Carolina Press.

Fiske, S. (1980). Attention and weight in person perception: The impact of negative and extreme behavior. *The Journal of Personality and Social Psychology* 38: 889-906.

Fiske, S., & Taylor, S.E. (1984). *Social cognition*. New York: Random House.

Fleser, A.F. (1966). Coolidge's delivery: Everybody liked it. *Southern States Communication Journal* 32: 98-104.

Fouhy, E. (1992 December 12). Comments at the election debriefing Annenberg School for Communication.

Fox, W. (Producer). (1916). *The life of Calvin Coolidge* [Film on videotape]. Available from The

National Archives, Washington, DC

Frank, R. (1988 April 17). 1948: Live ... from Philadelphia ... it's the national conventions. *The New York Times Magazine*, 62-65.

Frandovic, K. (1981). Keeping the voter's limits in mind: A cognitive process analysis of decision making in voting. *Journal of Personality and Social Psychology* 40, 843-61.

Frye, N. (1958). *Anatomy of criticism: Four essays*. Princeton, NJ: Princeton University Press.

Gallup, G. (1972). *The sophisticated poll watcher's guide*. Princeton, NJ Princeton Opinion Press.

Gallup, G., & Rae, S.F. (1940a). Is there a bandwagon vote? *Public Opinion Quarterly* 4: 244-249.

——————— . (1940b). *The pulse of democracy*. New York: Simon & Schuster.

Gans, H.J., Glaser, N., Gusfield, J.R., & Jencks, C. (Eds.). (1979). *On the making of Americans: Essays in honor of David Riesman*. Philadelphia: University of Pennsylvania Press.

Gardner, J.W. (1976). Foreword. In H.E. Alexander, (Ed.), *Campaign money: Reform and reality in the States* (pp. v-x). New York: The Free Press.

Garramone, G.M. (1984). Voter responses to negative political ads. *Journalism Quarterly* 61: 250-259.

——————— . (1985). Effects of negative political advertising: The roles of sponsor and rebuttal. *Journal of Broadcasting & Electronic Media* 29: 147-159.

Germond, J.W., & Witcover, J. (1981). *Blue smoke and mirrors: How Reagan won and why Carter lost the election of 1980*. New York: Viking Press.

Gibb, C.A. (1969). Leadership. In G. Lindzey & E. Aronson (Eds.), *Handbook of social psychology Volume 4: Group psychology and phenomenon of interaction* (2nd ed.) (pp. 205-282). Reading, MA: Addison-Wesley.

Gilbert, R.E. (1972). *Television and presidential politics*. North Quincy, MA: Christopher Publishing House.

Goldman, P., & Mathews, T. (1988). *The quest for the presidency: The 1988 campaign*. New York: Simon & Schuster.

Goldwin, R.A. & Schambra, W.A. (Eds.). (1987). *How federal is the Constitution?* Washington, DC: American Enterprise Institute for Public Policy Research.

Gollin, A.E. (1987). Polling and the news media. *Public Opinion Quarterly* 51: S86-S93.

Graber, D. (Ed.). (1982) *The president and the public*. Philadelphia: Institute for the Study of Human Issues.

——————— . (1986). Mass media and political images in elections. In S.L. Long (Ed.), *Research in micropolitics Volume 1: Voting Behavior* (pp. 127-160). Greenwich, CT: JAI Press.

——————— .(1987). Kind pictures and harsh words: How television presents the candidates. In K. Lehman Schlozman (Ed.), *Elections in America* (pp. 115-142). Boston: George Allen & Unwin.

——————— . (1988). *Processing the news: How people tame the information tide*. (2nd ed.). White Plains, NY: Longman.

——————— . (1991). Media and politics. In W. Crotty (Ed.), *Political science: Looking to the future Volume 3* (pp. 91-124). Evanston, IL: Northwestern University Press.

Grady, S. (1989 November 4). Mud-slingers dirtying themselves. *Des Moines Register*, 6-A.

Granberg, D., & Brent, E. (1983). When prophecy bends: The preference-expectation link in U.S. presidential elections, 1952-1980. *Journal of Personality and Social Psychology* 45: 477-491.

Granberg, D., & Nanneman, T. (1986). Attitude change in an electoral context as a function of expectations not being fulfilled. *Political Psychology* 7: 753-765.

Greenstein, F.I. (1990). Proximate and remote antecedents of political choice. *Psychological Inquiry* 1: 62-63.

Grimes, W. (1992 July 17). Film tribute to Clinton focuses on simple values. *The New York Times*, A-11.

Gronbeck, B.E. (1978). The functions of presidential campaigning. *Communication Monographs* 45: 268-280.

——————— . (1984). Functional and dramaturgical theories of presidential campaigning. *Presidential Studies Quarterly* 15: 386-399.

_____ . (1985). The presidential campaign dramas of 1984. *Presidential Studies Quarterly* 14: 386-393.

_____ . (1986). Ronald Reagan's enactment of the presidency in his 1981 inaugural address. In H.W. Simons & A.A. Aghazarian (Eds.), *Form, genre, and the study of political discourse* (pp. 226-245). Columbia: University of South Carolina Press.

_____ . (1989). Mythic portraiture in the 1988 Iowa presidential caucus bio-ads. *The American Behavioral Scientist* 32: 351-364.

_____ . (Ed.). (1989). *Spheres of argument: Proceedings of the sixth SCA/AFA conference on argumentation*. Annandale, VA: Speech Communication Association.

_____ . (1990). Electric rhetoric: The changing forms of American political discourse. *Vichiana* (pp. 141-161) (3rd series, 1st year). Napoli: Loffredo Editore.

Guggenheim, C. (Producer). (1972). *The McGovern story* [Film on videotape]. Available from Nixon Presidential Materials, division of The National Archives, Alexandria, VA.

_____ . (1990 October 16). Interview with Charles Guggenheim, film producer, Guggenheim Productions, Washington, DC.

Gunderson, R.G. (1940). The calamity howlers. *Quarterly Journal of Speech* 26: 401-411.

Gunlicks, A.B. (1988). Campaign and party finance in the West German 'Party State.' *The Review of Politics* 50: 30-48.

Gunther, A. (1991). What we think others think: Cause and consequence in the third-person effect. *Communication Research* 18: 355-372.

Hadley, A.T. (1976). *The invisible primary*. Englewood Cliffs, NJ: Prentice Hall.

Hall, R.G., Varca, P.E., & Fisher, T.D. (1986). The effect of reference groups, opinion polls, and attitude polarization on attitude formation and change. *Political Psychology* 7: 309-321.

Hallin, D. (1990). Sound bite news: Television coverage of elections, 1968-1988. Washington, DC: Woodrow Wilson International Center for Scholars.

Hallin, D. (January/February 1991). Whose campaign is it anyway? *Columbia Journalism Review*, 43+.

Hamill, R., Lodge, M., & Blake, F. (1985). The breadth, depth, and utility of partisan, class and ideological schemes. *American Journal of Political Science* 29: 850-870.

Harris, C.W. (Ed.). (1963). *Problems in measuring change* . Madison: University of Wisconsin Press.

Harris, L. (1984 October 11). Voters getting tired of campaign commercials. *The Harris Poll*. New York: Louis Harris and Associates.

_____ . (1988a October 23). Last chance for Dukakis: Defend himself and blast Bush's campaign tactics. *The Harris Poll*. New York: Louis Harris and Associates.

_____ . (1988b November 1). Dukakis cuts Bush lead to 7 points, Bush furlough ad backfiring. *The Harris Poll*. New York: Louis Harris and Associates.

Hart's final flourish. (1984 June 9). *The Economist*, 22-24.

Hart's run. (1984 March 3). *The Economist*, 11-12.

Harwood, R. (1991). *Citizens and politics: A view from main street America*. Prepared for the Kettering Foundation by the Harwood Group. Dayton, OH: The Kettering Foundation.

Hastie, R., & Park, B. (1986). The relationship between memory and judgment depends on whether the judgment task is memory-based or on-line. *Psychological Review* 93: 258-268.

Hastings, E.H., & Hastings, P.K. (Eds.). (1984). *Index to International Public Opinion, 1982-1983*. New York: Greenwood Press

_____ . (1985). *Index to International Public Opinion, 1983-1984*. New York: Greenwood Press.

_____ . (1987). *Index to International Public Opinion, 1985-1986*. New York: Greenwood Press.

_____ . (1990). *Index to International Public Opinion, 1988-1989*. New York: Greenwood Press.

Havick, J. (1991). *American democracy in transition*. New York: West Publishing Co.

Hayes, S.P. (1936). The predictive ability of voters. *Journal of Social Psychology* 7: 183-191.

Heale, M.J. (1982). *The presidential quest: Candidates and images in American political culture, 1787-1852*. New York: Longman.

Heider, F. (1958). *The psychology of interpersonal relations*. New York: John Wiley & Sons.

Hellweg, S.A., Pfau, M., & Brydon, S. (1992). *Televised presidential debates: Advocacy in contemporary America*. New York: Praeger.

Herbst, S. (1993). *Numbered voices: How opinion polling has shaped American politics*. Chicago, IL: University of Chicago Press.

Hersey, M.R. (1991). Congressional elections. In S.L. Maisel (Ed.), *Political parties & elections in the United States: An encyclopedia Volume 1*. New York: Garland Publishing.

Herstein, J.A. (1981). Keeping the voter's limits in mind: A cognitive process analysis of decision making in voting. *Journal of Personality and Social Psychology* 40: 843-861.

Hertsgaard, M. (1988). *On bended knee: The press and the Reagan presidency*. New York: Ferrar, Strauss, Giroux.

Hesse, M. (1974). *The structure of scientific inference*. Berkeley: University of California Press.

Hibbs, D.A., Jr. (1973). *Mass political violence: A cross-national causal analysis*. New York: John Wiley & Sons.

Hickman, H. (1991). Public polls and election participants. In P.J. Lavrakas & J.K. Holley (Eds.), *Polling and presidential election coverage* (pp. 100-133). Newbury Park, CA: Sage Publications.

Hirt, E.R., Zillman, D., Erickson, G.A., & Kennedy, C. (1992). Costs and benefits of allegiances: Changes in self-ascribed competencies after team victory versus defeat. *Journal of Personality and Social Psychology* 63: 724-738.

Hofstadter, R. (1963). *Anti-intellectualism in American life*. New York: Vintage.

Hollander, E.P. (1985). Leadership and power. In G. Lindzey & E. Aronson (Eds.), *Handbook of social psychology Volume 2: Special fields and applications* (3rd ed.) (pp. 485-538). New York: Random House.

Holley, J.K. (1991). The press and political polling. In P.J. Lavrakas & J.K. Holley (Eds.), *Polling and presidential election coverage* (pp. 215-237). Newbury Park, CA: Sage Publications.

Honomichl, J.J. (1984). *Marketing/research people: Their behind-the-scenes stories*. Chicago, IL: Crain Books.

Hughes, M. (1982). The fruits of cultivation analysis: A reexamination of some effects of television watching. *The Public Opinion Quarterly* 44: 287-302

Hunter, R.E. (1992 July 22). Perot's legacy: Pitting TV against itself. *The Christain Science Monitor*, 19.

Institute for Propaganda Analysis. (1937). How to detect propaganda. *Propaganda Analysis* 1: 1-4.

_____ . (1940). Polls, propaganda, and democracy. *Propaganda Analysis* 4: 1-8.

Ionescu, G., & Gellner, E. (Eds.). (1969). *Populism: Its meaning and national characteristics*. New York: The Macmillan Company.

Iyengar, S. & Kinder, D. (1987). *News that matters: Television and American opinion*. Chicago, IL: University of Chicago Press.

Jackson, J.L. (1987). *Straight from the heart*. Philadelphia: Fortress Press.

Jackson, L.A., & Sullivan, L. (1987). The ingroup favorability bias in the minimal group situation. *Journal of Social Psychology* 127: 461-472.

Jameson, F. (1988). Postmodernism and consumer society. In E. Ann Kaplan (Ed.), *Postmodernism and its discontents: Theories, practices* (pp. 13-29). New York: Verso.

Jamieson, K.H. (1984). *Packaging the presidency: A history and criticism of presidential campaign advertising*. New York: Oxford University Press.

_____ . (1988). *Eloquence in an electronic age: The transformation of political speechmaking*. New York: Oxford University Press.

_____ . (1992). *Dirty politics: Deception, distraction, and democracy*. New York: Oxford University Press.

Jamieson, K H., & Birdsell, D.S. (1988). *Presidential debates: The challenge of creating an informed electorate*. New York: Oxford University Press.

Jaros, D., & Mason, G.L. (1969). Party voice and support for demagogues: An experimental examination. *American Political Science Review* 63: 100-110.

Jennings, M. Kent. (1992). Ideological thinking among mass publics and political elites. *Public Opinion Quarterly* 56: 419-441.

Johnson-Cartee, K.S., & Copeland, G.A. (1991). *Negative political advertising: Coming of age.* Hillsdale, NJ: Lawrence Erlbaum Associates.

Kagay, M.R. (1992). Variability without fault: Why even well-designed polls can disagree. In T.E. Mann & G.R. Orren (Eds.), *Media polls in American politics* (pp. 95-124). Washington, DC: The Brookings Institution.

Kalb, M. (1992 July 3). From sound bite to a meal. *The New York Times*, A-25.

_____ . (1991 December 26). Campaign coverage: What price virtue? *The New York Times*, A-25.

Kammer, D. (1983). Depression, attributional style, and failure generalization. *Cognitive Therapy and Research* 4: 383-395.

_____ . (1984). Attributional style processing differences in depressed and nondepressed individuals. *Motivation and Emotion* 8: 211-220.

Kaplan, E. Ann. (Ed.). (1988). *Postmodernism and its discontents: Theories, practices.* New York: Verson.

Kaplowitz, S.A., Fink, E.L., D'Alessio, D., & Armstrong, G.B. (1983). Anonymity, strength of attitude, and the influence of public opinion polls. *Human Communication Research* 10: 5-25.

Kaster, S., & Zukin, C. (1982). New romances and old horses: The public's image of presidential candidates. In D. Graber (Ed.), *The president and the public* (pp. 39-82). Philadelphia: Institute for the Study of Human Issues.

Katona, G. (1960). *The powerful consumer: Psychological studies of the American economy.* New York: McGraw-Hill.

_____ . (1980). *Essays on behavioral economics.* Ann Arbor, MI: Institute for Social Research.

Katz, D. & Cantril, H. (1937). Public opinion polls. *Social Psychology Quarterly [Sociometry]* 1: 155-179.

Katz, G. (1988 October 27). Memories made of campaign negatives. *USA Today*, 6-A+.

Katz, J. (1991 June 27). Say goodnight, Dan ... *Rolling Stone*, 81-84.

Katz, P.A., & Taylor, D.A. (Eds.). (1986). *Eliminating racism: Profiles in controversy.* New York: Plenum Press.

Kavanagh, D. (1981). Do opinion polls influence elections? *Parliamentarian* 62: 199-203.

Keenan, K. (1986). Polls in network newscasts in 1984 presidential race. *Journalism Quarterly* 63: 616-618.

Kellerman, B. (1984). *The political presidency: Practices of leadership.* New York: Oxford University Press.

Kelley, S., Jr. (1956). *Professional public relations and political power.* Baltimore: John Hopkins University Press.

_____ . (1983). *Interpreting elections.* Princeton, NJ: Princeton University Press.

Kennedy, J.F. (1960 August 1). The Democratic national convention: Acceptance address. *Vital Speeches of the Day*, 610-612.

_____ . (1962 July 15). The myth and reality in our national economy. *Vital Speeches of the Day*, 578-581.

Kennedy, R.F. (1967). *To seek a newer world.* New York: Bantam.

_____ . (1968a March 21). *Address at values symposium at Vanderbilt University.* Available from the J. F. Kennedy Presidential Library, Boston, MA.

_____ . (1968b May 31). *Remarks at Commonwealth Club luncheon in San Francisco.* Available from the J.F. Kennedy Presidential Library, Boston, MA.

_____ . (1968c May 3). *Remarks in Crawfordsville, IN.* Available from the J.F. Kennedy Presidential Library, Boston, MA.

_____ . (1968d May 21). *Remarks at press gang luncheon in San Francisco.* Available from the J.F. Kennedy Presidential Library, Boston, MA.

Keplinger, H.M., & Donsbach, W. (1987). The influence of camera perspectives on the perception of a politician by supporters, opponents, and neutral voters. In D.L. Paletz, (Ed.), *Political communication research: Approaches, studies, assessments* (pp. 62-72). Norwood, NJ: Ablex.

Kern, M. (1989). *30-second politics: Political advertising in the eighties.* New York: Praegar.

Kertzer, D.I. (1988). *Ritual, politics, and power.* New Haven, CT: Yale University Press.

Kessel, J.H. (1980). *Presidential campaign politics: Coalition strategies and citizen responses.* Chicago, IL: Dorsey Press.

Kiewet, R.D. (1983). *Macroeconomics and micropolitics: The electoral effects of economic issues.* Chicago, IL: University of Chicago Press.

Kimberly, H. S. (1923). *Upbuilding with prosperity* [Film on videotape]. Available from Herbert Hoover Presidential Library, West Branch, Iowa.

Kinder, D.R. (1986). Presidential character revisited. In R.R. Lau & D.O. Sears (Eds.), *Political cognition: The 19th annual Carnegie symposium on cognition* (pp. 233-256). Hinsdale, NJ: Lawrence Erlbaum Associates.

Kinder, D.R., & Kiewet, R.D. (1981). Sociotropic politics: The American case. *British Journal of Political Science* 11: 129-161.

Kinder, D.R., & Sears, D.O. (1981). Prejudice and politics: Symbolic racism versus racial threats to the good life. *Journal of Personality and Social Psychology* 40: 414-431.

Kitman, M. (1992 January 26). Another debate (yawn). *Newsday*, 19.

Klapper, J.T. (1960). *The effects of mass communication.* Glencoe, IL: The Free Press.

_____ . (1964). Bandwagon: A review of the literature. Unpublished manuscript. Columbia Broadcasting System: Office of Social Research.

Kohut, A. (1986). Rating the polls: The views of media elites and the general public. *The Public Opinion Quarterly* 50: 1-10.

Kraus, S. (Ed.). (1962). *The great debates: Background, perspective, effects.* Bloomington: Univeristy of Indiana Press.

_____ . (Ed.). (1979). *The great debates: Carter vs. Ford, 1976.* Bloomington: Indiana University Press.

Kuhl, J. (1981). Motivational and functional helplessness: The moderating effect of state versus action orientation. *Journal of Personality and Social Psychology* 40: 155-170.

_____ . (1984). Volitional aspects of achievement motivation and learned helplessness: Toward a comprehensive theory of action control. In B.A. Maher & W.B. Maher (Eds.), *Progress in experimental personality research* (pp. 99-171). Orlando, FL: Academic Press.

Kurcz, I., Shgar, G.W., & Danks, J.H. (Eds.). (1986). *Knowledge and language.* New York: Elsevier Science Publishers.

Ladd, E.C. & Benson, J. (1992). The growth of news polls in American politics. In T.E. Mann & G.R. Orren (Eds.), *Media polls in American politics* (pp. 19-31). Washington, DC: The Brookings Institution.

Lang, A. (1991). Emotion, formal features, and memory for televised political advertisements. In F. Biocca (Ed.), *Television and political advertising Volume 1: Psychological processes* (pp. 221-243). Hillsdale, NJ: Lawrence Erlbaum Associates.

Lasorsa, D. (1989). Real and perceived effects of "Amerika." *Journalism Quarterly* 66: 373-378, 529.

Lau, R. (1983). Preliminary report on social identification, reference groups, and political behavior: The importance of social, political and psychological contexts. Paper presented at the annual meeting of the American Political Science Association, Chicago, IL.

_____ . (1986). Political schemata, candidate evaluations, and voting behavior. In R.R. Lau and D.O. Sears (Eds.), *Political cognition: The 19th Annual Carnegie symposium on cognition* (pp. 95-126). Hillsdale, NJ: Lawrence Erlbaum Associates.

_____ . (1989). Individual and contextual influences on group identification. *Social Psychology Quarterly* 52: 220-231.

Lau, R.R., & Sears, D.O. (Eds.). (1986). *Political cognition: The 19th annual Carnegie symposium on cognition.* Hillsdale, NJ: Lawrence Erlbaum Associates.

Lavrakas, P.J. (1990). An experimental study of underdog and bandwagon effects in the 1988 U.S. presidential campaign: Implications for future elections. Paper presented the annual meeting of the International Communication Association, Dublin, Ireland.

Lavrakas, P.J., & Holley, J.K. (Eds.). (1991). *Polling and presidential election coverage*. Newbury Park, CA: Sage Publications.

Lavrakas, P.J., Holley, J.K., & Miller, P.V. (1991). Public reactions to polling news during the 1988 presidential election campaign. In P.J. Lavrakas & J.K. Holley (Eds.), *Polling and presidential election coverage* (pp. 151-183). Newbury Park, CA: Sage Publications.

Lazarsfeld, P.F. (1972). Mutual effects of statistical variables. In P.F. Lazarsfeld, A.K. Pasanella & M. Rosenberg (Eds.), *Continuities in the language of social research* (pp. 388-398). New York: The Free Press.

Lazarsfeld, P.F., Berelson, B., & Gaudet, H. (1968). *The people's choice: How the voter makes up his mind in a presidential campaign* (3rd ed). New York: Columbia University Press.

Lazarsfeld, P.F., Pasanella, A.K., & Rosenberg, M. (Eds.). (1972). *Continuities in the language of social research*. New York: The Free Press.

Lee, R. (1986). The new populist campaign for economic democracy: A rhetorical exploration. *Quarterly Journal of Speech* 72: 274-289.

Lemert, J.B. (1986). Picking the winners: Politician vs. voter predictions of controversial ballot measures. *Public Opinion Quarterly* 50: 208-221.

Lerner, M. (1957). *America as a civilization: Life and thought in the United States today*. New York: Simon & Schuster.

Levin, R.E. (Ed.). (1988). *Democratic blueprints: 40 national leaders chart America's future*. New York: Hippocrene Books

Levy, M.R. (1984). Polling and presidential election. *The Annals of the American Academy of Political and Social Science* 472: 85-96.

Lewis, A. (1976 April 12). Ice on a hot stove. *The New York Times*, 29.

Lewis, G.F. (1940). The congressmen look at the polls. *The Public Opinion Quarterly* 4: 229-231.

Lewis, I.A. (1991). Media polls, the 'Los Angeles Times' poll and the 1988 presidential election. In P.J. Lavrakas & J.K. Holley (Eds.), *Polling and presidential election coverage* (pp. 57-82). Newbury Park, CA: Sage Publications.

Lewis-Beck, M., & Rice, T.W. (1992). *Forecasting elections*. Washington, DC: Congressional Quarterly Press.

Lewis-Beck, M.S., & Skalaban, A. (1989). Citizen forecasting: Can voters see into the future? *British Journal of Political Science* 19: 146-153.

Lichtner, R.L. (1987). *Media monitor*. Washington, DC: George Washington University.

Lindzey, G., & Aronson, E. (Eds.). (1968). *The handbook of social psychology Volume 2: Research methods* (2nd ed.). Reading, MA: Addision-Wesley Publishing Company.

_____ . (1969). *Handbook of social psychology Volume 4: Group psychology and phenomenon of interaction* (2nd ed.). Reading, MA: Addison-Wesley.

Lodge, M., McGraw, K., & Stroh, P. (1989). An impression-driven model of candidate evaluation. *American Political Science Review* 87: 399-419.

Lomas, C.W. (1955). Dennis Kearney: Case study in demagoguery. *Quarterly Journal of Speech* 41: 234-242.

Long, S.L. (Ed.). (1986). *Research in micropolitics Volume 1: Voting behavior*. Greenwich, CT: JAI Press.

_____ . (Ed.). (1981). *Handbook of political behavior Volume 4*. New York: Plenum Press.

Lowi, T.J. (1979). *The end of liberalism: The second republic of the United States* (2nd ed). New York: Norton.

Luthanen, R., & Crocker, J. (1992). A collective self-esteem scale: Self-evaluation of one's social identity. *Personality and Social Psychology Bulletin* 18: 302-318.

Luntz, F. (1988). *Candidates, consultants and campaigns: The style and substance of American electioneering*. New York: Basil Blackwell.

MacDougall, M. (1977). *We almost made it*. New York: Crown Publishers.

MacDougall, M. (Producer). (1976). *Ford election-eve campaign film* [Film on videotape]. Available from Gerald Ford Presidential Library, Ann Arbor, MI.

MacIntyre, A. (1981). *After virtue: A study in moral theory*. Notre Dame, IN: University of Notre Dame Press.

Maclean, M. (1989). *Narrative as performance: The Baudelairean experiment*. New York: Routledge.

Madsen, A. (1991). Partisan commentary and the first 1988 presidential debate. *Argumentation and Advocacy* 27: 100-113.

Maher, B.A., & Maher, W.B. (Eds.). (1984). *Progress in experimental personality research*. New York: Academic Press.

Maisel, S.L. (Ed.). (1991). *Political parties & elections in the United States: An encyclopedia Volume 1*. New York: Garland Publishing.

Mann, T.E., & Orren, G.R. (Eds.). (1992). *Media polls in American politics*. Washington, DC: The Brookings Institution.

Markus, G.B. (1988). The impact of personal and national economic conditions on the presidential vote: A pooled cross-sectional analysis. *American Journal of Political Science* 32: 137-154.

Marsh, C. (1984a). Back on the bandwagon: The effect of opinion polls on public opinion. *British Journal of Political Science* 15: 51-74.

_____ . (1984b). Do polls affect what people think? In C.F. Turner & E. Martin (Eds.), *Surveying subjective phenomena Volume 2*. New York: Russell Sage Foundation.

Marsh, C., & O'Brien, J. (1989). Opinion bandwagons in attitudes towards the common market. *Journal of the Market Research Society* 31: 295-305.

Martin, J.L. (1984) The genealogy of public opinion polling. *The Annals of the American Academy of Political and Social Science* 472: 12-23.

Maslow, A.H. (1954). *Motivation and personality*. New York: Harper & Brothers.

Masters, R.D. (1990). Candidate rhetoric, political leadership, and electoral success: The broader context of 'pessimistic rumination.' *Psychological Inquiry* 1: 65-68.

Mattelart, M. & Mattelart, A. (1990). *The carnival of images: Brazilian television fiction* (D. Buxton, Trans.). New York: Bergin & Garvey.

Matthews, D.R., & Prothro, J.W. (1966). *Negroes and the new southern politics*. New York: Harcourt, Brace & World.

Mauss, A. (1971). On being strangled by the stars and stripes: The new left, the old left, and the natural history of American radical movements. *Journal of Social Issues* 27: 183-202.

McAllister, I., & Studlar, D.T. (1991). Bandwagon, underdog, or projection? Opinion polls and electoral choice in Britain, 1979-1987. *The Journal of Politics* 53: 720-741.

McAvoy, J. (1988). A new spin on 'spin doctors'. *Public Relations Journal* 44: 12-13.

McBride, F.W. (1991). Media use of pre-election polls. In P.J. Lavrakas & J.K. Holley (Eds.), *Polling and presidential election coverage* (pp. 184-199). Newbury Park, CA: Sage Publications.

McCarthy, E.J. (1969). *The year of the people*. Garden City, NJ: Doubleday.

McCloskey, H., & Brill, A. (1983). *Dimensions of tolerance: What Americans believe about civil liberties*. New York: Russell Sage Foundation.

McCloskey, H., & Zaller, J. (1984). *The American ethos: Public attitudes toward capitalism and democracy*. Cambridge, MA: Harvard University Press.

McCombs, M.E. (1981). The agenda-setting approach. In D.D. Nimmo & K.R. Sanders (Eds.), *Handbook of political communication* (pp. 121-140). Beverly Hills, CA: Sage Publications.

McConahay, J.B. (1986). Modern racism, ambivalence, and the modern racism scale. In J. Dovidio and S.L. Gaertner (Eds.), *Prejudice, discrimination, and racism* (pp. 91-125). Orlando, FL: Academic Press.

McCormick, R.P. (1982). *The presidential game: The origins of American presidential politics*. New York: Oxford University Press.

McDowell, G.L. (1987). Federalism and civic virtue: The Antifederalists and the Constitution. In R.A. Goldwin & W.A. Schambra (Eds.), *How federal is the Constitution?* (pp. 122-44). Washington, DC: American Enterprise Institute for Public Policy Research.

McGee, M.C. (1975). In search of 'the people': A rhetorical alternative. *Quarterly Journal of Speech* 61: 235-249.

McGinniss, J. (1969). *The selling of the president, 1968.* New York: Trident Books.

_____ . (1970). *The selling of the president, 1968* (2nd ed.). New York: Pocket Books.

McGraw, K., Lodge, M., & Stroh, P. (1990). On-line processing in candidate evaluation: The effect of salience, order and sophistication. *Political Behavior* 12: 41-58

McWilliams, W.C. (1989). The meaning of the election. In G.M. Pomper et al. (Eds.), *The election of 1988: Reports and interpretations* (pp. 177-206). Chatham, NJ: Chatham House.

Melder, K. (1992). *Hail to the candidate: Presidential campaigning from banners to broadcasts.* Washington, DC: Smithsonian Institution Press.

Mendelsohn, H., & Crespi, I. (1970). *Polls, television and the new politics.* Scranton, NJ: Chandler Publishing Company.

Merelman, R.M. (1976). The dramaturgy of politics. In J.E. Combs & R.W. Mansfield (Eds.), *Drama in life: The uses of communication in society* (pp. 285-301). New York: Hastings House.

Merkle, D.M. (1991a). The effects of opinion poll results on public opinion: A review and synthesis of bandwagon and underdog research. Paper presented at the 41st annual conference of the International Communication Association, Chicago, IL.

_____ . (1991b). The impact of prior beliefs and disclosure of methods on perceptions of poll data quality and methodological discounting. Paper presented at the annual conference of the Association for Education in Journalism and Mass Communication, Boston, MA.

_____ . (1992). Biased formation of judgments about opinion poll accuracy: The roll of prior attitudes. Paper presented at the annual conference of the International Communication Association, Miami, FL.

_____ . (1993). Ph.D. research, Northwestern University, Evanston, IL.

Merritt, S. (1984). Negative political advertising: Some empirical findings. *Journal of Advertising* 13: 27-38.

Merten, K. (1985). Some silence on the spiral of silence. In K. Sanders, L.L. Kaid, and D. Nimmo (pp. 31-42).

Messaris, P., Eckman, B., and Gumpert, G. (1979). Editing structure in the televised versions of the 1976 presidential debates. *Journal of Broadcasting* 23, 359-63.

Miller, A.H., & Borrelli, S.A. (1991). Confidence in government during the 1980s. *American Politics Quarterly* 19: 147-173.

Miller, A.H., Hildreth, A., Leyden, K. & Wlezien, C. (1988). Judging by the company candidates keep: What's a democrat to do? *Public Opinion* 11: 14-16.

Miller, A.H. & Listhaug, O. (1990). Political parties and confidence in government: A comparison of Norway, Sweden and the United States. *British Journal of Political Science* 29: 357-386.

Miller, A.H., & Somma, M. (1988). Candidate viability and the dynamics of the Iowa caucus campaign. Presented at a meeting of the Western Political Science Association, San Francisco, CA.

Miller, A.H., & Wattenberg, M.P. (1985). Throwing the rascals out: Policy and performance evaluations of presidential candidates, 1952-1980. *The American Political Science Review* 79: 359-372.

Miller, A.H., Wattenberg, M.P., & Malanchuk, O. (1986). Schematic assessments of presidential candidates. *The American Political Science Review* 80: 521-540.

Miller, A.H. & Wlezien, C. (1993). The social group dynamics of partisan evaluations. *Electoral Studies* 12: 5-22.

Miller, A.H., Wlezien, C., & Hildreth, A. (1991). A reference group theory of partisan coalitions. *Journal of Politics* 53: 1134-1149.

Miller, G. (1956). The magical number seven, plus or minus two: Some limits on our capacity for processing information. *Psychological Review* 63: 81-97.

Mondale, W.F. (1992 February 26). Primaries are no test of character. *The New York Times*, A-21.

_____ . (1984 August 15). Acceptance speech. *Vital Speeches of the Day*, 642-644.

Monroe, K.R. (1984). *Presidential popularity and the economy.* New York: Praeger.

Moore, D.W. (1992). *The superpollsters: How they measure and manipulate public opinion in America.* New York: Four Walls Eight Windows.

Morello, J.T. (1991). Who won? A critical examination of newspaper editorials evaluating nationally televised presidential debates. *Argumentation and Advocacy* 27: 114-127.

_____ . (1988). Argument and visual structuring in the 1984 Mondale-Reagan debates: The medium's influence on the perception of clash. *Western Journal of Speech Communication* 52: 277-290.

Morreale, J. (1990). *A new beginning: A textual frame analysis of the political campaign film.* New York: State University of New York Press.

Moscovici, S. (1991). Silent majorities and loud minorities. In J.A. Anderson (pp. 298-308).

Mosher, F.C. et al. (1974). *Watergate: Implications for responsible government.* New York: Basic Books.

Mueller, J. (1988). Trends in political tolerance. *Public Opinion Quarterly* 52: 1-25.

Mullen, B. et al. (1985). The false consensus effect: A meta-analysis of 115 hypothesis tests. *Journal of Experimental Social Psychology* 21: 262-283.

Murray, H.A. (1938). *Explorations in personality: A clinical study of fifty men of college age.* New York: Oxford University Press.

Mutz, D.C. (1989). The influence of perception of media influence: Third person effects and the public expression of opinions. *International Journal of Public Opinion Research* 1: 1-23.

Mutz, D.C. (1990). Impersonal influence: Effects of representations of public opinion on political attitudes. Paper presented to the annual conference of The Midwest Political Science Association, Chicago, IL.

Napolitan, J. (Executive Producer). (1968). *What manner of man?* [Film on videotape]. Available from Minnesota Historical Society, St. Paul, MN.

_____ . (1990 October 14). Interview with Joe Napolitan, Political Consultant, Napolitan Associates, Springfield, MA.

Navazio, R. (1977). An experimental approach to bandwagon research. *Public Opinion Quarterly* 41: 217-225.

Nederhof, A.J. (1985). Methods of coping with social desirability bias: A review. *European Journal of Social Psychology* 15: 263-280.

Nelson, M. (Ed.). (1984). *The presidency and the political system.* Washington, DC: Congressional Quarterly Press.

Neuman, R. (1986). *The paradox of mass politics: Knowledge an opinion in the American electorate.* Cambridge, MA: Harvard University Press.

Neustadt, R. (1980). *Presidential power: The politics of leadership from FDR to Carter.* New York: John Wiley & Sons.

New U.S. plane said to foil radar. (1980 August 21). *The New York Times*, A-1+.

Newell, A., & Simon, H. (1972). *Human problem solving.* Englewood Cliffs, NJ: Prentice-Hall.

Newfield, J. (1969). *Robert Kennedy: A memoir.* New York: E.P. Dutton & Company.

Newhagen, J.E., & Reeves, B. (1991). Emotion and memory responses for negative political advertising: A study of television commercials used in the 1988 presidential election. In F. Biocca (Ed.), *Television and political advertising Volume 1: Psychological processes* (pp. 197-220). Hillsdale, NJ: Lawrence Erlbaum Associates.

Newman, L.S., & Uleman, J.S. (1989). Spontaneous trait inference. In J.S. Uleman & J.A. Bargh (Eds.), *Unintended thought* (pp. 155-188). New York: The Guilford Press.

New York Times (1936, November 13). Straw ballots. p. 22.

Nie, N.V., Verba, S., & Petrocik, J.R. (1976). *The changing American voter.* Cambridge, MA: Harvard University Press.

Nimmo, D. (1981). Mass communication and politics. In S.L. Long (Ed.), *The Handbook of political behavior Volume 4* (pp. 241-288). New York: Plenum Press.

_____ . (1992). Socio-political myths as the enactment of voters' fantasies. Paper presented to the Speech Communication Association, Chicago, IL.

Nimmo, D., & Combs, J.E. (1980). *Subliminal politics: Myths & mythmakers in America.* Englewood

Cliffs, NJ: Prentice-Hall.

_____ . (1983). *Mediated political realities*. New York: Longman.

_____ . (1990). *Mediated political realities*. (2nd ed.). New York: Longman.

Nimmo, D.D., & Sanders, K.R. (Eds.). (1981). *Handbook of political communication*. Beverly Hills, CA: Sage Publications.

Nimmo, D.D., & Savage, R.L. (1976). *Candidates and their images: Concepts, methods, and findings*. Pacific Palisades, CA: Goodyear Publishing Company.

Nisbett, R.E., & Wilson, T.D. (1977). Telling more than we can know: Verbal reports on mental processes. *Psychological Review* 84: 231-259.

Noelle-Neumann, E. (1974). The spiral of silence: A theory of public opinion. *Journal of Communication* 24: 43-51.

_____ . (1977). Turbulences in the climate of opinion: Methodological applications of the spiral of silence theory. *Public Opinion Quarterly* 41: 143-158.

_____ . (1979). Public opinion and the classical tradition. *Public Opinion Quarterly* 43: 143-156.

_____ . (1984). *The spiral of silence: Public opinion, our social skin*. Chicago, IL: University of Chicago Press.

_____ . (1985). Spiral of silence: A response. In K. Sanders, L.L. Kaid, and K. Nimmo (pp. 66-94).

_____ . (1989). The public as prophet: Findings from continuous survey research and their importance for early diagnosis of economic growth. *International Journal of Public Opinion Research* 1: 136-150.

_____ . (1991). The theory of public opinion: The concept of the spiral of silence. In J. A. Anderson (pp. 256-87).

Norpoth, H., Lewis-Beck, M.S., & Lafay, J.D. (Eds.). (1991). *Economics and politics: The calculus of support* (pp. 185-206). Ann Arbor: University of Michigan Press.

Nunnally, J.C. (1967). *Psychometric theory*. New York: McGraw-Hill.

O'Shaughnessy, N.J. (1990). *The phenomenon of political marketing*. New York: St. Martin's Press.

Opinion Research Service. (1989). *American public opinion index, Volume 2: 1988*. Boston, MA.

Orren, G.R., & Polsby, N.W. (Eds). (1987). *Media and momentum: The New Hampshire primary and nomination politics*. Chatham, NJ: Chatham House.

Osborn, M. (1986). Rhetorical depiction. In H.W. Simons & A.A. Aghazarian (Eds.), *Form, genre, and the study of political discourse* (pp. 79-108). Columbia: University of South Carolina Press.

Our generation has a duel with destiny. (n.d.). Washington, DC: Cranston for President.

Oxford English Dictionary [OED].

Page, B.I., Shapiro, R.Y., & Dempsey, G.R. (1987). What moves public opinion? *American Political Science Review* 81: 23-43.

Paletz, D.L. (Ed.). (1987). *Political communication research: Approaches, studies, assessments*. Norwood, NJ: Ablex.

Paletz, D.L., & Elson, M. (1976). Television coverage of presidential conventions: Now you see it, now you don't. *Political Science Quarterly* 91: 109-131.

Parenti, M. (1986). *Inventing reality: The politics of the mass media*. New York: St. Martin's Press.

_____ . (1993). *Inventing reality: The politics of the mass media*. (2nd ed.). New York: St. Martin's Press.

Park, B. (1989). Trait attributes as on-line organizers in person impressions. In J.N. Bassili (Ed.), *On-line cognition in person perception* (pp. 39-60). Hillsdale, NJ: Lawrence Erlbaum Associates.

Patterson, T.J. (1980). *The mass media election: How Americans choose their president*. New York: Praeger.

Patterson, T., & Davis, R. (1985). The media campaign: struggle for the agenda. In M. Nelson (Ed.), *The elections of 1984* (pp. 111-127). Washington, DC: Congressional Quarterly Press.

Patterson, T.E. & McClure, R.D. (1976). *The unseeing eye: The myth of television power in national politics.* New York: Putnam's.

Payne, D. (Producer). (1988). *Dukakis convention film* [Film on videotape]. Available from Public Affairs Video Archives, Purdue University, West Lafayette, IN.

_____ . (1990 March 20). Interview with Dan Payne, Political Consultant, Payne & Associates, Boston, MA.

Payne, J. (1982). Contingent decision behavior. *Psychological Bulletin* 92: 382-402.

Payne, J.G. (1989). A videotaped collection of primary and general election advertisements from Campaign '88. Available from Emerson College, Boston, MA.

Payne, J.G., & Baukus, R.A. (1985). *Trend analysis of the 1984 GOP senatorial spot.* Presented at the McElroy symposia "Current Trends in Broadcasting Advertising," University of Northern Iowa.

_____ . (1985). A videotaped collection of senatorial race advertisements from Campaign '84. Available from Emerson College, Boston, MA.

Perloff, R.M. (1989). Ego-involvement and the third-person effect of televised news coverage. *Communication Research* 16: 236-262.

Peterson, C. (1992). Explanatory style. In C.P. Smith (Ed.), *Thematic content analysis for motivation and personality research* (pp. 376-382). New York: Cambridge University Press.

Peterson, C. & Seligman, M.E.P. (1984). Causal explanations as a risk factor for depression: Theory and evidence. *Psychological Review* 91: 347-374.

Pfau, M., & Burgoon, M. (1989). The efficacy of issue and character attack message strategies in political campaign communication. *Communication Reports* 2: 53-61.

Pierce, W.M. (1940). Climbing on the bandwagon. *Public Opinion Quarterly* 4: 241-243.

Pincoffs, E.L. (1986). *Quandaries and virtues: Against reductivism in ethics.* Lawrence: University Press of Kansas.

Piven, F.F., & Cloward, R.A. (1988). *Why Americans don't vote.* New York: Pantheon Books.

Polkowska, A., Kurcz, I., & Danks, J.H. (1986). Verification of an interactive model of text comprehension: linguistic information, text difficulty, and language (Polish and English). In I. Kurcz, G.W. Shugar & J.H. Danks (Eds.), *Knowledge and language* (pp. 237-258). New York: Elsevier Science Publishers.

Polsby, N.W. (1983). *Consequences of party reform.* New York: Oxford University Press.

Pomper, G.M. et al. (Eds.). (1989). *The election of 1988: Reports and interpretations.* Chatham, NJ: Chatham House.

Popkin, S.L. (1991). *The reasoning voter.* Chicago, IL: University of Chicago Press.

Powell, L. (1989). Analyzing misinformation: Perceptions of congressional candidates' ideologies. *American Journal of Political Science* 33: 272-293.

Pratkanis, A.R. (1989). The cognitive representation of attitudes. In A.R. Pratkanis, S.J. Breckler, & A.G. Greenwald (Eds.), *Attitude structure and function* (pp. 71-98). Hillsdale, NJ: Lawrence Erlbaum Associates.

Pratkanis, A.R., Breckler, S.J., & Greenwald, A.G. (Eds.). (1989). *Attitude structure and function.* Hillsdale, NJ: Lawrence Erlbaum Associates.

Price, V., & Allen, S. (1990). Opinion spirals, silent and otherwise: Applying small-group research to public opinion phenomena. *Communication Research* 17: 369-392.

Pryor, A. (Producer). (1952). *Election-eve report to Ike* [Film on videotape]. Available from Dwight D. Eisenhower Presidential Library, Abilene, KS.

Rafshoon, G. (Producer). (1976). *Jimmy who?* [Film on videotape]. Available from Consolidated Productions, Washington, DC

_____ . (Producer). (1980). *This man, this office* [Film on videotape]. Available from Consolidated Productions, Washington, DC

Raines, H. (1980a August 17). Reagan denies plan to answer Carter. *The New York Times*, 1+.

_____ . (1980b August 19). Reagan calls arms race essential to avoid a Surrender or Defeat. *The New York Times*, A-1.

_____ . (1980c August 24). Reagan campaign runs into unexpected obstacles. *The New York Times*, 28.

_____ . (1980d August 25). Reporter's notebook: To-do in China. *The New York Times*, A-18.

Ranney, A. (1983). *Channels of power: The impact of television on American politics*. New York: Basic Books.

Rasinski, K.A., & Tourangeau, R. (1991). Psychological aspects of judgments about the economy. *Political Psychology* 12: 27-40.

Ratzan, S.C. (1989) The real agenda setters: Pollsters in the 1988 presidential campaign. *American Behavioral Scientist* 32: 451-463.

Rauch, B. (Ed.). (1957). *The Roosevelt reader: Selected speeches, messages, press conferences, and letters of Franklin D. Roosevelt*. New York: Holt, Rinehart & Winston.

Redding, J. (1958). *Inside the democratic party*. New York: Bobbs-Merrill.

Rholes, W.S. (1989). Action control as a vulnerability factor in depressed mood. *Cognitive Therapy and Research* 13: 263-274.

Rippey, J.N. (1980). Use of polls as a reporting tool. *Journalism Quarterly* 57: 642-646,721.

Robertson, N. (1964 October 21). GOP depicts moral decay. *The New York Times*, 35.

Robinson, C.E. (1937). Recent developments in the strawpoll field—Part II. *Public Opinion Quarterly* 1: 42-52.

Robinson, M.J. (1985). The media campaign '84: Part II Wingless, toothless, and hopeless. *Public Opinion* 8: 43-48.

_____ . (1987). News media myths and realities: What the network news didn't do in the 1984 general campaign. In K. Lehman Schlozman (Ed.), *Elections in America* (pp. 143-170). Boston: George Allen & Unwin.

_____ . (1988). Can values save George Bush? *Public Opinion* 11: 11-13, 59-60.

Robinson, M.J., & Ranney, A. (Eds.). (1985). *The mass media in campaign '84*. Washington, DC: American Enterprise Institute for Public Policy Research.

Robinson, M.J., & Sheehan, M.A. (1983). *Over the wire and on TV: CBS and UPI in campaign '80*. New York: Russell Sage Foundation.

Rogish, S. (1991 April 17). Interview with Sir Rogish, Advertising Director, 1988 Bush campaign, Washington, DC.

Roll, C.W., & Cantril, A.H. (1972). *Polls: Their use and misuse in politics*. New York: Basic Books.

Roosevelt, F.D. (1933/1965). First inaugural address. In *Inaugural addresses of the Presidents of the United States* (pp. 235-239). Washington, DC: United States Government Printing Office.

Roper, B.W. (1986). Evaluating polls with poll data. *The Public Opinion Quarterly* 50: 10-16.

Rosenstiel, T. (1990). Policing political ads. *Los Angeles Times*, A1+.

Rosenstone, S.J. (1983). *Forecasting presidential elections*. New Haven, CT: Yale University Press.

_____ . (1985). Why Reagan won. *Brookings Review* 3: 25-32.

Rossen, C. (1991 March 13). Interview with Clay Rossen, Project Coordinator for 1988 Bush campaign film.

Rucinski, D., & Salmon, C.T. (1990). The 'other' as the vulnerable voter: A study of third-person effect in the 1988 U.S. presidential election. *International Journal of Public Opinion Research* 2: 346-368.

Rumelhart, D.E., & Norman, D.A. (1988). Representation in memory. In R. Atkinson, R. Herrnstein, G. Lindzey & R.D. Luce (Eds.), *Stevens' handbook of experimental psychology Volume 2: Learning and cognition* (pp. 511-587). New York: John Wiley & Sons.

Rumelhart, D., and Ortny, A. (1977). The representation of knowledge in memory. In B. Anderson, R. Spiro, and J. Montague (Ed.), *Schooling and the acquisition of knowledge*. Hillsdale, NJ: Lawrence Erlbaum Associates.

Runyon, J., Verdini, J., & Runyon, S. (1971). *Source book of American presidential campaign and election statistics, 1948-1968*. New York: Ungar.

Sabato, L.J. (1981). *The rise of political consultants: New ways of winning elections*. New York: Basic Books.

_____ . (1989). *Paying for elections: The campaign finance thicket*. New York: Priority Press.

Sabato, L. (1985). *Pac power*. New York: W.W. Norton.

_____ . (1989). *Paying for the elections: The campaign finance thicket*. New York: Priority Press

Publications.

Sale, K. (1973). *SDS*. New York: Random House.

Salmon, C.T., and Kline, F.G. (1985). The spiral of silence ten years later: An examination and evaluation. In K. Sanders, L.L. Kaid, and D. Nimmo (pp. 3-30).

Sanders, K., Kaid, L.L., and Nimmo, D. (Eds.). (1985). *Political communication yearbook 1984*. Carbondlae: Southern Illinois University Press.

Santayana, G. (1920/1956). *Character and opinion in the United States*. Garden City, NJ: Doubleday.

Schaeffer, S.D. (1981). A multivariate explanation of decreasing turnout in presidential elections, 1960-1976. *American Journal of Political Science* 25: 68-95.

Schambra, W.A. (1982). The roots of the American public philosophy. *The Public Interest* 67: 36-48.

Schambra, W.A. (1985). Progressive liberalism and American 'community.' *The Public Interest* 80: 31-48.

Schank, R.C. (1982). *Dynamic memory: A theory of reminding and learning in computers and people*. New York: Cambridge University Press.

Schelsky, H. (1974). The new strategy of revolution: The 'long march' through the institutions. *Modern Age* 18: 345-355.

Scherer, H. (1991). Personal opinions and the perception of public opinion: conformity or projection? A test of two alternative models. Paper presented at the 42nd annual conference of the International Communication Association, Chicago, IL.

Schieffer, B., & Gates, G.P. (1989). *The acting president*. New York: E.P. Dutton.

Schlozman, K. Lehman. (Ed.). (1987). *Elections in America* . Boston: George Allen & Unwin.

Schlozman, K. Lehman, & Tierney, J.T. (1986). *Organized interests and American democracy*. New York: Harper & Row.

Schmeisser, P. (1988 April 17). Taking stock: Is America in decline? *The New York Times Magazine*, 24-96.

Schram, M. (1977). *Running for president 1976: The Carter campaign*. New York: Stein & Day.

Schweitzer, D.R., & Elden, J.M. (1971). New left as right: Convergent themes of political discontent. *Journal of Social Issues* 27: 141-166.

Sears, D.O. (1988). Symbolic racism. In P.A. Katz & D.A. Taylor (Eds.), *Eliminating racism: Profiles in controversy* (pp. 53-84). New York: Plenum Press.

Sears, D.O., Lau, R.R., Tyler, T.R., & Allen, H.M., Jr. (1980). Self-interest versus symbolic politics in policy attitudes and presidential voting. *American Political Science Review* 74: 670-684.

Sears, D.O., Huddy, L., & Schaffer, L.G. (1986). A schematic variant of symbolic politics theory, as applied to racial and gender equality. In R.R. Lau and D.O. Sears (Eds.), *Political cognition: The 19th annual Carnegie Symposium on Cognition* (pp. 159-202). Hillsdale, NJ: Laurence Erlbaum Associates.

Sennett, R. (1979). What Tocqueville feared. In H.J. Gans, N. Glaser, J.R. Gusfield & C. Jencks (Eds.), *On the making of Americans: Essays in honor of David Riesman*. Philadelphia: University of Pennsylvania Press.

Shaw, D.L. & McCombs, M.E. (1977). *The emergence of American political issues: The agenda-setting functions of the press*. St. Paul, MN: West Publishing Company.

Shapiro, H.T. (1972). The index of consumer sentiment and economic forecasting—A reappraisal. In B. Strumpel, J.N. Morgan, & E. Zahn (Eds.), *Human behavior in economic affairs: Essays in honor of George Katona* (pp. 433-451). San Francisco: Jossey-Bass, Inc.

Shapiro, R.Y., & Conforto, B.M. (1980). Presidential performance, the economy, and the public's evaluation of economic conditions. *Journal of Politics* 42: 49-67.

Sherif, M. et al. (1961). *Intergroup conflict and cooperation: The Robber's Cove experiment*. Norman: University of Oklahoma Press.

Sherman, S.J. et al. (1985). Imagining can heighten or lower the perceived likelihood of contracting a disease: The mediating effect of ease of imagery. *Personality and Social Psychology Bulletin* 11: 118-127.

Shields-West, E. (1992). *The world almanac of presidential campaigns*. (J. MacNelly, Illus.). New

York: World Almanac.

Shils, E.A. (1956). *The torment of secrecy: The background and consequences of American security policies.* London: Heinemann.

Sigelman, L., & Bullock, D. (1991). Candidates, issues, horse races and hoopla: Presidential campaign coverage, 1888-1988. *American Politics Quarterly* 19: 5-32.

Sigelman, L., & Knight, K. (1983). Why does presidential popularity decline? A test of the expectation/disillusion theory. *Public Opinion Quarterly* 47: 310-324.

_____ . (1985). Expectation/disillusion and presidential popularity: The Reagan experience. *Public Opinion Quarterly* 49: 209-213.

Silverman, K. (1983). *The subject of semiotics.* New York: Oxford University Press.

Simon, H.A. (1957). *Models of man.* New York: John Wiley & Sons.

_____ . (1979) *Models of thought.* New Haven, CT: Yale University Press.

_____ . (1979). How big is a chunk? In H.A. Simon (Ed.), *Models of thought* (pp. 50-61). New Haven, CT: Yale University Press.

Simon, R. (1990). *Road show: In America, anyone can become pesident, it's one of the risks we take.* New York: Farrar, Straus, Giroux.

Simons, H.W., & Aghazarian, A.A. (Eds.). (1986). *Form, genre, and the study of political discourse.* Columbia: University of South Carolina Press.

Simons, H.W., Chesebro, J.W., & Orr, C.J. (1973). A movement perspective on the 1972 presidential election. *Quarterly Journal of Speech* 59: 168-179.

Simonton, D.K. (1985). Intelligence and personal influence in groups: Four nonlinear models. *Psychological Review* 92: 532-547.

_____ . (1986). *Why presidents succeed: A political psychology of leadership.* New Haven, CT: Yale University Press.

_____ . (1990). Some optimistic thoughts on the pessimistic rumination thesis. *Psychological Inquiry,* 1: 73-75.

Smith, C.P. (Ed.). (1992). *Thematic content analysis for motivation and personality research.* New York: Cambridge University Press.

Smith, H. (1980 September 7). Reagan's packagers worry over loose ends. *The New York Times,* E-2.

Smith, H. (1988). *The power game: How Washington works.* New York: Random House.

Smith, P. (1963). *John Adams II: 1784-1928.* Westport, CT: Greenwood Press.

Smith, R.W. (1959). Comedy at St. Louis: A footnote to nineteenth century political oratory. *Southern Speech Communication Journal* 25: 122-133.

Smith, T. (1980 September 3). Carter assails Reagan remark about the Klan as an insult to the South. *The New York Times,* B-8.

Smoller, F.T. (1990). *The six o'clock presidency: A theory of presidential press relations in the age of television.* New York: Praeger.

Sniderman, P.M., Piazza, T., Tetlock, P.E., & Kendrick, A. (1991). The new racism. *American Journal of Political Science* 35: 423-447.

Sniderman, P.M., & Tetlock, P.E. (1986). Symbolic racism: Problems of political motive attribution. *Journal of Social Issues* 42: 129-150.

Solo, P. (1988). *From protest to policy: Beyond the freeze to common security.* Cambridge, MA: Ballinger Publishing Company.

Special issue. (1992 November/December). *Newsweek.*

Stahl, L. (1992 December 12). Comments at the election debriefing, Annenberg School for Communication, Temple University, Philadelphia, PA.

Stempel III, G.H., & Windhauser, J.W. (1991). *The media in the 1984 and 1988 presidential campaigns.* New York: Greenwood Press.

Stevenson, A. (1952 August 15). I accept your nomination and your program. *Vital Speeches of the Day,* 645-646.

_____ . (1956 September 1). The democratic national convention: Acceptance address. *Vital Speeches of the Day,* 679-681.

Stewart, C.J. (1975). Voter perceptions of mudslingling in political communication. *Central States Speech Journal* 26: 279-286.

Stone, W.J. (1980). The dynamics of constituency electoral control in the House. *American Politics Quarterly* 8: 399-424.

Strumpel, B., Morgan, J.N., & Zahn, E. (Eds.). (1972). *Human behavior in economic affairs: Essays in honor of George Katona*. San Francisco: Jossey-Bass, Inc.

Sullivan, J.L., & Marcus, G.E. (1988). A note on 'trends in political tolerance.' *Public Opinion Quarterly* 52: 26-32.

Surveys of consumers. (1992). Historical data. Ann Arbor, MI: Institute for Social Research.

Sussman, B. (1985 June 10). Do pre-election polls influence people to switch their votes? *Washington Post*, 37.

Swanson, D.L. (1972). The new politics meets the old rhetoric: New directions in campaign research. *Quarterly Journal of Speech* 58: 31-40.

Swerdlow, J.L. (Ed.). (1987). *Presidential debates: 1988 and beyond.* Washington, DC: Congressional Quarterly Press.

Tajfel, H. (1972). Some developments in European social psychology. *European Journal of Social Psychology* 2: 307-322.

_____. (1978). The structure of our views about society. In H. Tajfel and C. Fraser.

_____. (1981). *Human groups and social categories.* Cambridge, MA: Cambridge University Press.

Tajfel, H., Flament, C., Billig, M.G., & Bundy, R.F. (1971). Social categorization and intergroup behavior. *European Journal of Social Psychology* 1: 149-178.

Tajfel, H., and Fraser, C. (Eds.). (1978). *Introduction to social psychology.* Harmondsworth, Eng: Penguin Press.

Tarrance, V.L., Jr. (1982). *Negative campaigns and negative votes: The 1980 elections.* Washington, DC: Free Congress Research & Education Foundation.

Taylor, P. (1988). The election nobody liked: A reporter's reflections. *Washington Post*, C-2.

Tetlock, P.E. (1981). Pre- to post-election shifts in presidential rhetoric: Impression management or cognitive adjustment? *Journal of Personality and Social Psychology* 41: 207-212.

Text of Senator Kennedy's speech on presidency at National Press Club luncheon. (1960 January 15). *The New York Times*, 14.

Texts of Kefauver, Harriman and Stevenson talks at Chicago dinner. (1955 November 20). *The New York Times*, 66.

Tharp, M. (1980 August 20). China rift follows Bush on Japan visit. *The New York Times*, B-9.

The Kennedy statement. (1960 January 3). *The New York Times*, 44.

The state of the debates. (1992 March 7). *The New York Times*, 24.

Thomsen, A. (1941). Psychological projection and the election: A simple class experiment. *Journal of Psychology* 11: 115-117.

Tiemens, R.K. (1978). Televisions portrayal of the 1976 presidential debates: An analysis of visual content. *Communication Monographs* 45: 362-370.

_____. (1989). The visual context of argument: An analysis of the September 25, 1988 presidential debate. In B. Gronbeck, (Ed.), *Spheres of argument: Proceedings of the sixth SCA/AFA conference on argumentation* (pp. 140-146). Annandale, VA: Speech Communication Association.

Tiemens R.K., Hellweg, S.A., Kipper, P., & Phillips, S.L. (1985). An integrative verbal and visual analysis of the Carter-Reagan debate. *Communication Quarterly* 33: 34-42.

Toner, R. (1987 April 14). Hart, stressing ideals, formally enters the 1988 race. *The New York Times*, A-16.

Tonnies, F. (1887/1988). *Community and society.* New Brunswick, NJ: Transaction.

Transcript of 2d TV debate between Bush, Clinton and Perot. (1992 October 16). *The New York Times*, A-11.

Transcript of Senator Johnson's news conference on his presidential candidacy. (1960 July 6). *The New York Times*, 18.

Traugott, M.W. (1991). Public attitudes about news organizations, campaign coverage, and polls. In P.J. Lavrakas & J.K. Holley (Eds.), *Polling and presidential election coverage* (pp. 134-150). Newbury Park, CA: Sage Publications.

Trent, J.S., & Friedenberg, R.V. (1983). *Political campaign communication: Principles and practices.* New York: Praeger.

_____ . (1991). *Political campaign communication: principles and practices* (2nd ed.). New York: Praeger.

Tufte, E.R. (1978). *Political control of the economy.* Princeton, NJ: Princeton University Press.

Tune in, turn on, vote. (1992 June 26). *Chicago Tribune,* 22.

Turner, F.J. (1893). *The significance of the frontier in American history.* Chicago, IL: Annual Report of the American Historical Association.

Turner, R.L. (1991 December 17). Rookies light up the Democrat's TV debate. *The Boston Globe,* 23.

Turner, C.F., & Martin, E. (Eds.). (1984). *Surveying subjective phenomena Volume 2.* New York: Russell Sage Foundation.

Tyson, J.L., & Kaplowitz, S.A. (1977). Attitude conformity and anonymity. *Public Opinion Quarterly* 41: 226-234.

Uleman, J.S., & Bargh, J.A. (Eds.). (1989). *Unintended thought.* New York: The Guilford Press.

van Dijk, T.A. (1988). *News as discourse.* Hillsdale, NJ: Lawrence Erlbaum Associates.

Viguerie, R.A. (1980). *The new right: We're ready to lead.* Falls Church, VA: The Viguerie Company.

Wagner, U., Lampen, L., & Syllwassachy, J. (1986). In-group inferiority, social identity, and out-group devaluation in a modified minimal group study. *British Journal of Social Psychology* 25: 15-23.

Waldman, S. (1986). The Hiroshima hustle: Yet another way to fleece campaign contributors. *The Washington Monthly* 18: 35-40.

Walker, J. (1983). The origins and maintenance of interest groups in America. *American Political Science Review* 77: 390-406.

Walton, R. (1991 February 27). Interview with Russ Walton, Publicity Director, 1964 Goldwater-Miller Committee, Keene, NH.

Walton, R.J. (1976). *Henry Wallace, Harry Truman, and the Cold War.* New York: Viking.

Wattenberg, M.P. (1984). *The decline of American political parties.* Cambridge, MA: Harvard University Press.

Wayne, S.J. (1982). Great expectations: What people want from presidents. In T.E. Cronin (Ed.), *Rethinking the presidency* (pp. 185-199). Boston: Little, Brown and Company.

Weaver, D.H., Graber, D.A., McCombs, M.E., & Eyal, C.H. (1981). *Media agenda-setting in a presidential election: Issues, images, and interest.* New York: Praeger.

Weiss, C.H. (1974). What America's leaders read. *Public Opinion Quarterly* 38: 1-22.

West, D.M. (1983). Press coverage in the 1980 presidential campaign. *Social Science Quarterly* 64: 624-633.

_____ . (1991). Another look at negative ads. *Political Communication Report* 2: 1, 6.

Westbrook, R. (1983). Politics as consumption. In R. Wightman Fox & T.J. Lears (Eds.), *The culture of consumption: Critical essays in American history, 1880-1980* (pp. 143-173). New York: Pantheon.

Wightman Fox, R. & Lears, T.J. (Eds.). (1983). *The Culture of consumption: Critical essays in American history, 1880-1980.* New York: Pantheon.

Whitaker, R.W. (Ed) (1982). *The new right papers.* New York: St. Martin's Press.

White, T.H. (1961). *The making of the president, 1960.* New York: Atheneum.

_____ . (1965) *The making of the president, 1964.* New York: Atheneum.

_____ . (1969) *The making of the president, 1968.* New York: Atheneum.

_____ . (1973) *The making of the president, 1972.* New York: Atheneum.

_____ . (1982). *America in search of itself: The making of the president 1956-1980.* New York: Harper & Row.

Wiles, P. (1969). A syndrome, not a doctrine: Some elementary theses on populism. In G. Ionescu & E. Gellner (Eds.), _Populism: Its meaning and national characteristics_ (pp. 166-179). New York: The Macmillan Company.

William, D. (1992 February 18). New Hampshire fizzle beckons Mario Cuomo. _The Atlanta Journal and Constitution_, 37.

Wills, G. (1970). _Nixon agonistes: The crisis of the self-made man._ New York: New American Library.

Wilson, C.N. (1982). Citizens or subjects. In R.W. Whitaker (Ed.), _The new right papers_ (pp. 106-127). New York: St. Martin's Press.

Winter, D.G. (1987). Leader appeal, leader performance, and the motive profiles of leaders and followers: A study of American presidents and elections. _Journal of Personality and Social Psychology_ 52: 196-202.

_____ . (1990). Leadership, presidential elections, and pessimistic rumination. _Psychological Inquiry_ 1: 77-79.

Winter, J.P., & Eyal, C.E. (1981). Agenda setting for the civil rights issue. _Public Opinion Quarterly_ 45: 376-383.

Wirthlin, R., Breglio, V., & Beal, R. (1981). Campaign chronicle. _Public Opinion_ 4: 43-49.

Witcover, J. (1970). _The resurrection of Richard Nixon._ New York: G.P. Putnam's Sons.

Wolfinger, R.E., & Rosenstone, S.J. (1980). _Who votes?_ New Haven, CT: Yale University Press.

Wolper, D. (Producer). (1991 January 28). Interview with David Wolper, Wolper Productions, Los Angeles, CA.

Woodward, G.C. (1983). Reagan as Roosevelt: The elasticity of psuedo populist appeals. _Central States Speech Journal_ 34: 44-58.

Worcester, R.M. & M. Harrop, M. (Eds.). (1982). _Political communications: The general election campaign of 1979._ Boston: George Allen & Unwin.

World almanac book of facts 1992. (1991). New York: World Almanac.

Wyckoff, G. (1968). _The image candidates: American politics in the age of television._ New York: The Macmillan Company.

Zullow, H.M. (1984). The interaction of rumination and explanatory style in depression. Unpublished master's thesis, University of Pennsylvania.

_____ . (1985). Manual for rating action styles. Unpublished manuscript, University of Pennsylvania.

_____ . (1988). The hopeful edge: A new tool for forecasting elections. _The Polling Report_ 4: 22, 4-6.

_____ . (1990). Presidential greatness and action-oriented rumination in the inaugural address. Paper presented at the 13th annual meeting of the International Society of Political Psychology, Washington, D.C., July 1990.

_____ . (1991). Pessimistic rumination in popular songs and newsmagazines predict economic recession via decreased consumer confidence and spending. _Journal of Economic Psychology_ 12: 501-526.

Zullow, H.M., Oettingen, G., Peterson, C., & Seligman, M.E.P. (1988). Pessimistic explanatory style in the historical record: CAVing LBJ, presidential candidates, and East versus West Berlin. _American Psychologist_ 43: 673-682.

Zullow, H.M., & Seligman, M.E.P. (1990a). Pessimistic rumination predicts defeat of presidential candidates, 1900 to 1984. _Psychological Inquiry_ 1: 52-61.

_____ . (1990b). Author's reply. _Psychological Inquiry_ 1: 80-85.

Index